To Elizabeth
with warm good
wishes

[illegible] & Dave

The Life and Times of J. Neville Keynes

J.N. Keynes 'The Beacon at the Old Registry'

The Life and Times of J. Neville Keynes

A Beacon in the Tempest

Phyllis Deane

Professor Emeritus of Economic History at the University of Cambridge, an Honorary Fellow of Newnham College and a Fellow of the British Academy, UK

Edward Elgar

Cheltenham, UK • Northampton, MA, USA

Published by
Edward Elgar Publishing Limited
Glensanda House
Montpellier Parade
Cheltenham
Glos GL50 1UA
UK

Edward Elgar Publishing, Inc.
136 West Street
Suite 202
Northampton
Massachusetts 01060
USA

A catalogue record for this book is available from the British Library

Library of Congress Cataloguing in Publication Data
Deane, Phyllis.
The life and times of J. Neville Keynes : a beacon in the tempest / Phyllis Deane.
p. cm.
Includes bibliographical references and index.
1. Keynes, John Neville, 1852–1949. 2. Economists—Great Britain—Biography. I. Title.

HB103.K47 D43 2001
330'092—dc21
[B]

2001023014

ISBN 1 84064 534 2

Typeset by Manton Typesetters, Louth, Lincolnshire, UK.
Printed and bound in Great Britain by MPG Books Ltd, Bodmin, Cornwall.

A Beacon in the Tempest

'It does not become a Cambridge man to claim too much for his university, nor am I much tempted to do so. But there is, I think, a certain type, rare, like all good things, which seems to be associated in some peculiar way with my alma mater ... It is a type unworldly without being saintly, unambitious without being inactive, warm-hearted without being sentimental. Through good report and ill such men work on, following the light of truth as they see it; able to be sceptical without being paralysed; content to know what is knowable and to reserve judgment on what is not. The world could never be driven by such men, for the springs of action lie deep in ignorance and in madness. But it is they who are the beacon in the tempest, and they are more, not less, needed now than ever before'.

Quoted by J. Maynard Keynes (*Essays in Biography*, p. 340) from Goldsworthy Lowes Dickinson's memoir of Frank Ramsey who died in 1930.

TO JOAN
Friend and Companion for Over Half a Century

Contents

Illustrations

Preface

My own interest in the life and times of John Neville Keynes was aroused almost twenty years ago when my researches in the history of economic thought attracted an invitation to write an introduction to an Italian translation of his classic text – *The Scope and Method of Political Economy* – first published in 1891. Setting the argument of that monograph in the personal, intellectual and historical context of the methodological debate to which it was designed to contribute led me to the long series of J.N. Keynes diaries preserved in the Cambridge University Library, as well as to much relevant (published and unpublished) correspondence that flowed between him and contemporary scholars. Unexpectedly, these sources uncovered a broader and more fascinating area of personal, social and academic history than was pertinent to my original brief. It was unexpected, because, although the name of J.N. Keynes, as founder of a famous Cambridge family, flits in and out of numerous biographies of his brilliant son, Maynard, and figures repeatedly (hence invisibly) in lists of examiners, lecturers or administrators, or in signatures attached to official university documents over more than four decades, neither his personality nor his function has attracted more than a glancing notice in print. This book represents an attempt to justify my conviction that his was a remarkable, if self-effacing, personality and that the story of his life and achievements opens up an unusually fruitful perspective from which to view social and academic developments in Cambridge during the late nineteenth and early twentieth centuries.

The result is not a biography in the sense of a creative reconstruction of the life of an historically famous character. It is focused on the life and times of John Neville Keynes, a Victorian graduate in Cambridge moral sciences when that honours course comprised four broad subjects – philosophy (moral and political), logic and political economy. He studied, matured, fell in love, raised a family and served the University of Cambridge first as a teacher of logic and political economy and then as an increasingly responsible administrator during the period when it was transformed from a loose federation of 15 religious communities into an integrated institution dedicated to scientific learning, education and research. His career as logician, economist and administrator lasted from 1876 (when he became Pembroke College's first nonconformist fellow) until 1925 when he retired as registrary (the university's top permanent administrator). The starting-point and the core source for this life story is a virtually continuous Diary – candidly recording his pleasures, griefs, problems, ambitions and achievements over the half-century ending in 1917, and providing an intimate commentary on the university developments in which he was personally closely involved. What gave the Diary a particularly illuminating perspective from which to view the academic revolution – which began in Cambridge early in the last quarter of the nineteenth century and continued through the first quarter of the twentieth century – was the moral integrity of the diarist as well as his central role in the actual sequence of change. The other main primary source, of course, has been the formidable series of annual *Cambridge University Reporter* volumes – with their detailed record of changes in, and debates on, the human, institutional and financial context within which the academic revolution gradually, and sometimes stormily, developed.

When 14-year-old Neville, the son of provincial middle-class parents, whose antecedents were commercial, rather than professional, entered a private nonconformist boarding school at Amersham in 1866, his prospects of becoming a Cambridge don were remote; but by the 1860s and 1870s, religious and class barriers to higher education in the two ancient English universities were collapsing under the combined weight of progressive academic opinion and parliamentary pressure. After 1856 – when the Cambridge University Act abolished the condition that the award of a degree (other than in divinity) required the candidate formally to declare his acceptance of the liturgy of the Anglican Church – nonconformists could at last qualify for a Cambridge degree. In 1871 the University Test Act abolished religious tests for senior, as well as junior, members of the colleges and university. So, when Neville Keynes was admitted to Pembroke College in 1872 – without the public school or family connections that had traditionally lubricated entry to Cambridge University – he was aware that he could, in principle, work his way to a life fellowship through a succession of competitive examinations. His first hurdle was the London University matriculation examination where he won a scholarship to University Hall, the Gordon Square hostel of University College, The second was a Cambridge college entrance examination. Three years residence at a London college that openly disavowed all denominational distinctions and tests and insisted on the sanctity of private judgement in matters of religion, offered young Neville a mind-broadening finishing school. It gave him access to a wider range of honours courses than were available at Cambridge (or Oxford), whilst providing the time and additional coaching to improve his performance in the two subjects sure to win high marks in Cambridge college entrance examinations – mathematics and classics.

In the event, Neville's academic ambitions wilted as soon as he occupied his rooms at Pembroke's small, exclusively male, Anglican community of bachelors, and realized that the only certain way to a life fellowship involved three years cramming mathematical bookwork under the tuition of hired coaches skilled in grooming their pupils for a first class result in the mathematical tripos. His Diary suggests that he would have abandoned Cambridge at the end of his first term, had he not instantly been scooped up into a lively nonconformist social network centring on a congregationalist grocer's family home located a few hundred yards along the road from Pembroke. It was there that he met two individuals who determined the direction of his future career. The first was James Ward, then a mature Trinity student of moral sciences, who encouraged him to switch (at the end of his first year) from mathematics to a less prestigious but intellectually more stimulating course of study – where a modern breed of dons (who included Henry Sidgwick, Alfred Marshall and John Venn) were obviating the need for coaches by personally teaching the undergraduates who audited their lectures. In the same nonconformist family home – after justifying his subject switch by topping the final list in the moral sciences tripos and being elected a fellow of Pembroke – Neville met and fell in love with Florence Brown, a young Newnhamite, marriage to whom involved resigning his Pembroke fellowship.

As it turned out, Neville Keynes's six years as a Pembroke fellow were dominated by central government pressure for university reform. The 1874 Report of the Royal Commission on Oxford and Cambridge had revealed that progress in standards of teaching and research at both universities was paralysed by the concentration of most of their disposable wealth in colleges whose exclusive and privileged governing bodies accepted no responsibility for promoting educational reform at university level. Accordingly, under the 1877 Universities of Oxford and Cambridge Act, statutory commissions were appointed at each to rewrite university and college statutes, with a view to introducing administrative and financial structures designed to divert from colleges to central bodies the funds needed to improve overall standards of teaching and scholarship and to finance the libraries, museums, scientific equipment and other facilities essential to a modern university. The effect of the statutes finally approved in 1882 was to cap college dividends, end the system of life fellowships (unless attached to the most senior college offices), create new openings for paid employment as university lecturers, readers or professors, and lay the foundations for an effective university bureaucracy. By the time the new statutes came into force in October 1882, Neville's marriage to Florence Brown, for whom he had built a substantial family home in central Cambridge, had determined his career options. Already a regular lecturer in both logic and political economy for the Moral Sciences Board and for Newnham College, he had taken an administrative post at the Local Examinations and Lectures Syndicate, which he was to serve at increasing levels of responsibility for almost 30 years. In 1884 he was among the first batch of Cambridge University lecturers ever appointed. He thus became one of the earliest examples in Cambridge of a new breed of professional academics – a university employee whose link with his college had dwindled to dining-rights and common-room privileges and whose teaching and/or organizational skills were at the disposal of faculty boards and other central bodies responsible for raising overall standards in education, learning and research.

For the rest of his 97-year life span Neville Keynes resided in the house where, within three years of their wedding, Florence bore their three children – Maynard, Margaret and Geoffrey – each of whom was destined to achieve national distinction. The problems and pleasures of giving birth to, rearing and educating these distinctive offspring, as well as of running a hospitable household in Victorian Cambridge, are fully spelt out in Neville's Diary. Less detailed, but none the less revealing, are the entries relating to his career as lecturer and examiner in logic and political economy and to the pair of classic textbooks inspired by the research that informed his teaching activities. Especially significant is the light shed by his perspective – as secretary (and would-be mediator) to the moral sciences faculty – on the often bitter conflicts between warring dons that led to the foundation of the modern Cambridge economics and politics tripos and to the exclusion of political economy from the moral sciences tripos, although not from the history tripos.

It was in his forties that Neville Keynes began to evolve into an administrator rather than a teacher (or writer) in moral science. In March 1892 the Syndicate for Local Lectures and Examinations (which he had served as one of two assistant secretaries for over a decade) formally appointed him its chief secretary for examinations. The crucial watershed in his career came early in the next academic year, when he reached 'cabinet rank' by being elected to the Council of the Senate, the university's supreme governing body. Four months later, having established his credentials for sound common sense and orderly thinking, he was invited by the Council – consisting of four heads of houses, four professors or readers and four other resident members of the Senate – to act as its secretary. This unpaid, but challenging, office was to place him at the centre of policy making in the university for the rest of his working life. It called for administrative talents of a kind that few academics cared to cultivate but which Keynes himself was genuinely concerned to develop: for example, a methodical approach to policy problems; a capacity to identify and assess the agenda, or the strategy, essential to effective executive action; an ability to draft unambiguous, concise and accurate minutes (or university notices) and to formulate lucid recommendations for validation by the Senate in congregation; and a genuine commitment to promote policies preferred by the Council majority even when he had himself voted in the minority.

The Council, chaired by the current vice-chancellor, generally met at least twice weekly each term and its members represented it on the many boards, syndicates or committees that managed university departments or faculties, or planned new projects and sought solutions to urgent policy problems. Its secretary's responsibilities included drawing up its meetings agenda (in agreement with the vice-chancellor), compiling, or drafting, associated papers for advance circulation to Council members, writing its minutes and drafting its reports or recommendations to be published in the *University Reporter* for discussion and ratification by the Senate in congregation. Because each vice-chancellor's term in office normally lasted no more than two years, successive vice-chancellors had to be initiated, and guided by, the secretary through the current policy problems confronting the Council over which they were to preside. The dedicated impartiality which ensured that, whenever his own term came up for renewal, he would be renominated for election to Council by both the 'liberal' and 'conservative' wings of the academic community, also put him under continual pressure to act as chairman – first of the Moral Sciences Board and later of the new Economics and Politics Board. As early as 1896, when he briefly contemplated applying for the relatively high-profile registrarship of the recently reformed London University, an anxious flurry of letters from present and past vice-chancellors persuaded him that he was an indispensable element in Cambridge's central bureaucracy. On becoming registrary in 1910 he was obliged to resign both his university lectureship and his Local Exams secretaryship. By remaining secretary to the Council, however, he continued to play a pivotal role in the slow, controversial and intellectually challenging process of academic reform that characterized the first 14 years of the twentieth century. More than a decade before the end of his 32 years of unbroken service on the university's governing body he had become its most experienced and well-informed member. Given the vision, idealism and intelligence of the leading academics then actively seeking to bring the University of Cambridge into the twentieth century, the extent of the reforms achieved by 1914 was extraordinarily limited. The prime obstacle was the need to submit each change to the approval of a Senate that included among its members an army of non-resident MAs who could readily be summoned to vote against any proposal conflicting with traditional prejudices – such as the admission of women to degrees, the abolition of compulsory Greek in the Previous examination or the admission of a Roman Catholic hostel to college status.

With the outbreak of war, the problem of modernizing Cambridge University's antiquated constitution lost its urgency and Neville Keynes was abruptly freed from the chore of drafting and redrafting Council reports that were fated to be rejected by the Senate's irresponsible non-residents. By October 1915, when the university's resident membership had shrunk by two-thirds, its most urgent policy problems revolved around protecting the interests of senior and junior personnel engaged in the war effort. It then became necessary to pass through the Senate and coordinate with the colleges a multiplicity of changes in statutes and regulations covering the special circumstances of those whose studies and jobs had been suspended for an uncertain duration. In all the practical and financial problems raised by such unanticipated external events, the registrary was the ultimate oracle. He became the beacon in that tempest as he had been in earlier more localized storms, provoked by conflicts within and between faculties and special interest groups. The end of the war called for another rapid redeployment of human, physical and financial resources at both central and college levels. In these circumstances, Neville Keynes was still the beacon to which the elderly academics who had steered the university through the past four and a half years looked to first, when focusing on peacetime goals. For recently demobilized men grappling with problems of teaching, examining and researching within the framework of a desperately impoverished university he was the familiar amiably accessible adviser at the Registry. Meanwhile, issues of radical reform which had preoccupied his working hours in the prewar decade were transformed by financial crisis in the aftermath of war. The need for substantial government aid was such that another Royal Commission on Oxford and Cambridge was inevitable. Appointed in 1920 it reported in 1924, and Cambridge's second revolution by Royal Commission began to be put into effect. When Neville Keynes retired at the end of 1925, it was in the knowledge that most – if not all – of the reforms at which he had aimed throughout his administrative career were being systematically embodied in the statutes and ordinances of the university and its colleges.

Researching and writing this book has taken an inordinate amount of time – in spite of the fact that I have by no means followed up all the sometimes voluminous Diary entries and that I have been able to draw – more often than my footnote references might suggest – on the dependable scholarship of historians published, for example, in such books as C.N.L. Brooke's *History of the University of Cambridge, 1870–1990* (1993) or in Rita McWilliams-Tullberg's *Women in Cambridge* (1975) – as well as on the exhaustively researched biographies of Maynard Keynes by R.F. Harrod, R. Skidelsky, and D.E. Moggridge or of Alfred Marshall by P. Groenewegen plus J.K. Whitaker's splendidly informative three volumes of Alfred Marshall's *Correspondence*. It would be superfluous to name all the friends and colleagues (including university librarians and staff) who have directly encouraged, advised and assisted me in this enterprise over the past years; they know I am grateful. I feel impelled, however, to mention those who have patiently read their way through drafts of the manuscript (in part or in whole, sometimes more than once) and whose comments, frank criticisms or corrections have substantially reduced the number of errors of fact, exposition, judgement or interpretation in the final version. Among them are the first and penultimate grandchildren of my subject – Polly Hill and Milo Keynes; Donald Winch; Don Moggridge; Mark Perlman; Geoffrey Harcourt; Daniel Merrill; and Jayne Ringrose. My debt to Milo Keynes has been further compounded by his kindness in finding me suitable photographs and (on behalf of the family) for allowing me to quote extensively from the diaries and letters of which they own the copyright. On the matter of copyright, I am grateful also to the Syndics of the Cambridge University Library for granting me access to and permission to quote from the material of which they are the custodians, and for the kind permission of the Chancellor, Masters and Scholars of the University of Cambridge for allowing me to use important extracts from the *Cambridge University Reporter*.

Finally it must be said that putting the manuscript in the hands of a specialist publisher, staffed by a remarkably helpful team of vigilant professional editors, has helped this grateful author to exclude a great many errors, omissions and obscurities from the printed text.

PHYLLIS DEANE
16 January 2001

I Origins

1 CARNATIONS, PICOTEES AND PINKS

John Neville Keynes was born in 1852, one of only two children in a middle-class Salisbury family, whose forebears had settled in the town in the middle of the eighteenth century. His grandfather, also a John Keynes (1782–1852), had owned and managed a successful brush factory during the first half of the nineteenth century, but his father, another John Keynes (1805–78) chose a more colourful career. Apprenticed to the family brushmaking trade in his early teens, Neville's father relieved the tedium of processing wood and hog bristles by growing and propagating garden flowers in his spare time. He was winning prizes at local flower shows when still in his twenties and before he had decided to create a business out of his hobby. By 1872 his national reputation as an innovative and successful floriculturalist was such that the leading English florists and horticulturalists came together, to celebrate his half century as a prizewinning exhibitor. So popular was he that his fellow gardeners hosted two banquets in his honour – one at the Crystal Palace (in August) and the other at a Fleet Street hotel (in November). At the well-publicized Crystal Palace event, John Keynes is reported to have told an appreciative audience of friends and business colleagues that, as a lad, 'riding on the stage-coach from Salisbury to Andover, he saw in the coat of a fellow-passenger sitting opposite to him, a bloom of Butt's Lord Rodney, a purple-flake carnation, of some note in that day'. It was this incident, Mr Keynes told his audience, that led him 'to take up the culture of Carnations, Picotees and Pinks'.[1]

Starting from these popular cottage-garden fancies, John Keynes began to propagate new flower varieties (in collaboration with florists and market gardeners), went on to specialize in a more upmarket product – dahlias – and eventually acquired extensive nurseries of his own in Castle Street. According to another of the long, eulogistic obituaries which appeared in gardeners' periodicals after his death in 1878:

> [H]e soon became a good man of business. He possessed the great advantage of having been well trained in business habits in a very lucrative brush-making

1. See the obituary of John Keynes in the *Gardeners' Chronicle*, for 23 February 1878, which quotes from a report of his speech at the Crystal Palace banquet.

> manufactory which he continued to manage for many years after he became a nursery man. Business for him was a source of great pleasure; he had great confidence in himself and … kept all his books, it is said, up to a short time before his death.[2]

Responding to changes of fashion in the market for new varieties of florists' flowers – a market which was to expand dramatically during the so-called Great Victorian Boom of the third quarter of the nineteenth century – John Keynes went on extending the range of his output, won fame as an early innovator of fine roses and kept his large glasshouses in profitable year-round operation by filling the seasonal gaps with grapevines grown in pots for sale to the trade. At the same time, he played an active and responsible part in the wider Salisbury community. He was elected as a Liberal to the Municipal Council, for example, took an active personal interest in the formation of the Salisbury British School and was generous with both time and money as superintendent of the local nonconformist chapel Sunday school.[3] In November 1876 he was elected mayor of Salisbury and, had his health not begun to fail in the summer of 1877, he might have yielded to popular pressure to serve a second year in that capacity.

It was in this lively and comfortable business environment that John Neville Keynes, known to his family and friends as Neville, was reared. Until he was 30 years old, the house that he thought of as home stood against the flourishing Castle Street Nurseries, with their shining glasshouses and brilliant beds of roses, dahlias, verbenas and carnations, among other summer blooms. Besides Neville's parents and two female live-in servants, the household accommodated his widowed grandmother (1776–1869), his Aunt Mary (1811–95) and his stepsister Fanny, almost 15 years his senior. John Keynes's first wife, Matilda, had died in the cholera epidemic of the late 1830s, leaving the widower in charge of a little daughter – Fanny. Fortunately for both of them, Aunt Mary, then in her late twenties and living with her parents, gladly stepped in to keep house for her brother and to mother his bereft toddler. Some years later, John Keynes took a second wife, Anna Neville (the daughter of a London businessman) and she bore him his only son. Thus the family unit into which Neville was born contained three generations: apart from his 30-year-old mother and his 47-year-old father, there was his widowed grandmother in her seventies, 14-year-old Fanny and 42-year-old Aunt Mary.

2. See 'The Late John Keynes of Salisbury' in *The Garden*, 4 May 1878, p. 417. John Maynard Keynes seems to have had doubts about his grandfather's bookkeeping skills. According to Geoffrey Keynes, *The Gates of Memory* (Oxford: Oxford University Press, 1981), p. 7: 'He made a great success of his floral nurseries, though my brother always believed that he never kept any accounts at all – I do not know what evidence he had of this'.
3. See *The Gardener's Magazine*, 23 February 1878, p. 91.

Fanny married Edward Purchase in 1861 and set up home with him in Kington (on the borders of Herefordshire and Shropshire) where he was in business as a grocer and where they produced seven children. Although a degree of tension prevailed between Fanny and her stepmother – a suppressed hostility which was to erupt sporadically (if temporarily) in later years – the evidence of the Diary consistently indicates a stable, loving, nonconformist household with regular churchgoing habits and a strong sense of family coherence. Even after Fanny became mistress of her own home, there was much coming and going between the two households. Aunt Mary, for example, regularly migrated to Kington to nurse Fanny through each of her seven pregnancies and stayed to look after the toddlers; and Fanny frequently brought her children on extended visits to Castle Street.

Neville was thus reared in a caring, middle-class, home that was open house to a constant stream of relatives and friends. If there were any money problems they never appear to have constrained his unpretentiously comfortable life style. As the only son of a highly respected nonconformist businessman, with a wide circle of supportive associates and family friends, Neville participated in a full social life and enjoyed access to a broad range of other hospitable households where he could develop pleasantly enduring personal relationships and get wise advice from influential advisers. The warmth of his feeling for family and friends shines out repeatedly from his Diary entries.

2 THE SCHOOLBOY DIARIST

The earliest of the JNK diaries now deposited in Cambridge University Library begins when Neville was a schoolboy in his twelfth year, then boarding at a small preparatory school in Poole, kept by members of the Dorset branch of the Keynes family. Two small, dog-eared, tersely-scribbled, paper-backed notebooks, contain the entries for 1864 and 1865. They suggest an unenthusiastic diarist, responding to the recommendation of some respected adult – Papa no doubt – with tantalizingly little comment or background information. They come alive only occasionally, mainly during the school holidays, though even then the brief references to family parties, walks, visits to friends, excursions to places of interest, and weekly sermons (morning and evening) at the Salisbury chapel, give the barest hint of the diarist's personality or feelings. What does show up prominently (as often in his later diaries) is Neville's preoccupation with all kinds of competitive games and his passion for keeping detailed records of their results. For he regularly noted his opponents' names, his wins and losses (and often his scores) in such varied activities as chess, backgammon, bagatelle, bridge, cricket, croquet and miscellaneous board games. The very first entry of all, for New Year's Day 1864, reads, for example:

> In the morning I beat Frank in a game of bagatelle and 1 game of bridge, he beat me in a game of bridge. W. Chubb came to tea. I beat him in a game of archery also in 3 games of chess and 2 games of steeplechase. He beat me in 2 games of chess and 2 games of steeplechase.[4]

The main holiday high-spot in the schoolboy's calendar was an annual excursion to London with his father, who visited the capital for several days each January – primarily to confer with horticulturalist friends and competitors, but also to buy book prizes for Salisbury's meritorious Sunday school pupils. Very occasionally Neville's references to the special delights of these trips – such as visits to the theatre or to the zoo, or watching skaters on the Serpentine – are lit by rare expressions of pleasure, for example, 'enjoyed myself very much'. In term-time, however, relatively few days seemed noteworthy and the entries are laboriously thin. For example, in 1864, after long lists of hourly lessons in the first week or so of term, the blanks predominate – interrupted only by such bald entries as 'I had a medal for Latin given me by Mr Gill', or 'letter from Mama', or 'I write home', or 'my cold is worse' or even 'nothing particular took place'. Indeed, in the 1865 diary, the pages from the beginning of the school winter term to mid-June (when holidays began) have been excised from the booklet – perhaps because they later seemed too boring, or too empty, to deserve preservation. No doubt, what then seemed to be the outstanding events in the boy's life were duly noted, and relatively laconic entries offer clues to his current life style. For example, on 12 August 1865 he recorded that his pet rabbit had given birth to five young ones; and the fact that the most welcome items in the next hamper from home were 'oats and peas for the rabbits and apples and pears for myself', suggests that the school encouraged its boarders to bring their pets when returning from holiday. The omissions are also intriguing. Particularly striking, in view of Neville's subsequent career and interests, is the fact that we find only two references in the scribbled early diaries to his having read a book. Both relate to 1864, one in October of that year, when a schoolfriend lent him Bulwer Lytton's *Pelham*, the other in December when he mentioned reading *The Legend of Montrose* by Walter Scott. On neither occasion did he comment on the novel in question, nor did he say what interested him in the *Boys' Journal*, of which he seems to have been a regular reader.

4. Frank Tiffin was the son of a Salisbury family who were close friends of the Keyneses. He remained Neville's closest Salisbury friend until the early 1880s, by which time he was a Lloyd's agent (with Neville one of his 'names') and had developed a drink problem which distanced him from his own family and friends.

Whether the reluctant schoolboy diarist continued to maintain his thin daily record of events during 1866 and 1867 is a matter for speculation. The next in the deposited series of JNK diaries begins in mid-1868 and ends in 1873. In contrast to the tatty little notebooks containing the scribbled 1864 and 1865 entries, we now have a superior hard-back quarto journal book into which has been transcribed in careful copybook handwriting (at least until 1873 when the flow is such as to suggest firsthand entries), brief notes that are presumably selected and edited extracts from some earlier record. For 1868 the list of entries begins on 8 June and takes up less than a full page. By then he was a boarder at Amersham Hall school, a private nonconformist institution near Reading, with a reputation for rigorous university-orientated standards. The longest entry is for 11 July (when the diarist was nearly 17 years old) reporting details of his end-year examination results at Amersham Hall, results which were best for mathematics (giving him second place in the class) and worst for Greek and French (in each of which he was ranked eighth). He remained, apparently, an attentive chapel-goer, certainly whilst in Salisbury. The first 1868 entry, for example, notes that Mr Short was invited to become the Brown Street chapel pastor,[5] and there recur later references to Mr Short's sermons, as well as (in late August) the information that the new pastor was giving Neville holiday coaching two or three times a week to improve his Greek. The entry for 23 September 1868, records his return to Amersham Hall, where he was to share a bedroom with six other boys, one of whom was Harry Bond.[6] Thereafter there seems to have been little of note to record for 1868 except (on 2 November) the onset of a 'rather bad cough', requiring the school doctor's attention, and (a few days later) there was an outbreak of scarlet fever spreading through the school. The fever epidemic presumably accounted for the fact that, on 14 November: 'Papa and Mama came to see me unexpectedly' and that school broke up earlier than usual that year, allowing Neville to go back to Salisbury on 5 December: 'returned home because of illness in the School. My cough has turned out to be croup'.

By 1869 Neville, now in his final year at Amersham Hall, was studying for the matriculation examination that would qualify him to enter London University. The neatly transcribed Diary for that year runs to 19 quarto pages and is more redolent of his fun-loving personality than of his intellectual interests. It begins in January with the usual round of family parties, enlivened by

5. John Keynes was Sunday school superintendent of the Brown Street Baptist chapel. The obituary printed in the *South Wiltshire Express* for 23 February 1878 and headed 'From the Wiltshire County Mirror' says of John Keynes: 'Though differing from them as to their distinctive rites, he for many years had been a communicant with the Baptist Church in this city and all his days was accustomed to attend the Baptist Chapel of which he had long been a most liberal supporter'.
6. Harry Bond, the son of a Cambridge grocer, was to become his contemporary as an undergraduate in London and Cambridge and they remained close friends in later years.

charades, dancing and (for example, on 5 January) 'games of various sorts during which I had the felicity of kissing Emily Williams', and on other occasions her sister Flossie. Both the Williams sisters returned his kisses with sufficient warmth to make the incidents memorable. The annual companionable trip to London with Father (no longer Papa) to buy Sunday school prizes and attend floricultural shows and events was again enlivened with theatres, concerts and social calls. By now the budding academic had his head in his books and was reading novels by Bulwer Lytton, Wilkie Collins, Alexandre Dumas, Charles Kingsley and Mrs Henry Wood among others. He was also anxiously recording his own and his friends' examination results. The entry for 21 April (during the Easter vacation) reads: 'My report came from Amersham Hall. Mr West [the headmaster] says "Conduct and diligence all that can be desired: quite safe for a good place at the Matriculation even if a large margin be left for marks lost through nervousness"'. Evidently young Neville had made the grade expected of Amersham Hall boys. He went on to win first prize in mathematics and second in classics (both subjects of prime importance to a would-be Cambridge man). Finally, he distinguished himself (and his school) in the University of London matriculation examination by winning the Gilchrist scholarship to University Hall, the Gordon Square hostel for students of University College.[7] He was frequently a martyr to toothache and to the bronchial infections that afflicted most school boarders of his era. A long entry for 4 July 1869, which began by transcribing the letter offering him the University College scholarship ends with the information:

> Mr Coates [the Salisbury GP] came to see me on account of the bad cough I had had for some time past. He sounded me all over and said I have a bronchial affection [sic] on the right side under the collar bone and the right lung is not so thick as the other. He prescribed several things and I must not be out in the evening.

Nevertheless, the summer holiday that fell between the last school term and his first term at University College was obviously a happy one, crammed with such social occasions as croquet parties, flower shows and picnics with his Salisbury contemporaries. Neville's flirtations with the Williams girls continued to merit frequent reference in the Diary. The evidence that he was then particularly smitten by Flossie brought him 'a decided cut from Emily' on 3 September. Among the other Salisbury families who were close friends of his parents were the Fawcetts, one of whose sons had married Polly

7. According to F.A. Keynes, *Gathering Up the Threads: A Study in Family Biography* (Cambridge: Heffer & Sons, 1950), p. 47: the Gilchrist scholarship was 'awarded annually for only fourteen years and eleven of these fourteen awards fell to pupils from Amersham Hall'.

Keynes (Neville's cousin):[8] the other son, Henry Fawcett, had been elected professor of political economy at Cambridge in 1863 and Liberal Member of Parliament for Brighton in 1865. Henry Fawcett (and his wife) were regular visitors to their family home in Salisbury during the vacations, and it was natural for young Neville to call on him for advice at the start of his own university career. The entry for 23 August reads: 'Called on Professor Fawcett. He advised to go for 2 years to London and then on to Cambridge'. Neville set out to follow this advice and the Diary entry for 5 October reads: 'To London and University Hall'.

8. Ibid., p. 48.

II The undergraduate experience

1 LONDON UNDERGRADUATE

When Neville entered the matriculation class at Amersham Hall and set his sights on an academic career, he was inspired by the example of the headmaster's undergraduate son, Alfred West, who was reading moral sciences at Trinity College Cambridge, having taken the route via London University. Founded in 1825 by the Benthamites, University College was designed to offer a broader and more utilitarian education than was available in either Oxford or Cambridge. For the son of a nonconformist businessman it had obvious attractions. From the start it was based on the principle of religious liberty and confined its teaching to secular subjects on the assumption that its students would acquire such religious instruction as they wanted either at some denominational residential hostel or at home. University Hall, Gordon Square, was the hall of residence set up in 1848 to provide them with the accommodation and social advantages of college residence, whilst openly disavowing all denominational distinctions and tests and insisting on the sanctity of private judgement in matters of religion.[1] It was in this self-consciously open-minded academic community that young Neville took up residence in October 1869. Its current principal, Edward Beesly, was a radical positivist professor of history in University College (as well as of Latin at Bedford College) and had acquired notoriety in the early 1860s as a defender of militant trade unions.[2]

By the late 1860s, University College had built up a strong reputation as a medical school and as a centre for the promotion of experimental science – even before it set up its own faculty of science in 1870. According to its historian, Hale Bellot:

> It had failed, where as a child of the utilitarians it should have succeeded, to become a great school of law and politics. Yet it remained an inspiriting place to

1. See H. Hale Bellot, *University College London 1826–1926* (London: University of London Press, 1929). The objectives are quoted on p. 300 from an inscription on the walls of University Hall which was founded 'to celebrate the passage of the Dissenters Chapel Bill' in 1844.
2. *Punch* derided him as 'Professor Beastly' for his advanced views on trade unions. See Hale Bellot (1929), p. 394. There was at one stage a move in the Council to remove him from his chair, but it says something for the prevailing ethos in the University of London that the move attracted little support and fell away.

> work in, and in the 'sixties and 'seventies was upon the threshold of great material success. That this was so, was because it held in honour one, preeminently, among the precepts of its founders. It kept an open mind. It continued to be ready to give welcome to branches of learning which had not yet become orthodox.[3]

Although London University was neither as academically prestigious, nor as rich in professional career openings for its alumni, as were the two ancient English universities,[4] University College (like its sister institution King's) offered a wider range of formal undergraduate courses than either Oxford or Cambridge. In effect it provided a kind of finishing school, as well as a mind-broadening experience, for a young middle-class nonconformist, without public school backing, who needed a college scholarship to put him on course for the good Cambridge honours degree[5] that might bring an academic career within his reach. At London he could study any of the traditional school arts or science subjects that interested him as well as strengthen his performance in the two areas that were most likely to win high marks in a Cambridge college entrance examination – mathematics and classics.

The three academic years that Neville spent at University College – 1869/70, 1870/71 and 1871/72 – are covered by selectively transcribed diaries. They were years in which he could take advantage of the extensive opportunities for instruction and recreation open to a London University undergraduate. He chose freely which courses he would take, and how hard he would work at each; he participated in a variety of social and cultural activities and he sampled the rich entertainment resources available in the metropolis. The entry for 17 March 1870, for example, records that he worked for eleven hours, escorted his mother through London on her way to Nottingham, played chess with an undergraduate friend and attended a University Hall debating society meeting where he 'voted in favour of ladies under certain conditions being eligible as members. The motion was lost'.[6] Sunday was always a rest day, but on Saturday 6 April he put in four hours work and still found time to go with his friend John Lord to watch

3. Hale Bellot (1929), p. 305.
4. Peter Allen, *The Cambridge Apostles* (Cambridge: Cambridge University Press, 1978), p. 200 quotes an anonymous pamphleteer writing in 1836, who enumerated the 'pecuniary enticements' which Oxford and Cambridge could offer to their members: 'the bait which Cambridge holds out, is about 330 livings, 17 headships of colleges, about 420 fellowships, many hundred scholarships and exhibitions, 15 masterships of schools, and the various University offices – a few of which have a large emolument attached to them'.
5. Henry Fawcett, for example, his ambitions focused originally on a career in law and politics, had gone to King's College, London, and taken classes in mathematics and classics for one year before he sat for the Peterhouse scholarship which enabled him to enter Cambridge in 1852. At the end of his first year, daunted by the competition for fellowships at Peterhouse, he migrated to Trinity Hall where he won his fellowship on the strength of being classed seventh wrangler in the 1856 tripos.
6. This was the year University College first admitted women to lectures.

Cambridge win the boat race.[7] On 1 June, after recording twelve hours work and taking tea with a friend he added: 'It seems to be the general opinion that I work too hard'. Evidently, such industry paid off, for on 24 June he noted with surprise that he got the first prize in everything he went in for, and on 29 June was able to rejoice that he had passed his end-of-year freshman examinations for the BA in the first division. By 12 July he ceased keeping an account of daily hours worked, though he continued to drive himself. On 17 November, for example, he reported 'working very hard now – almost too hard. I sit up late but I dont well see how I can make my work less. I have toothache a good deal, it makes me feel poorly'. Back in Salisbury, however, enjoying a December vacation among old friends, his spirits lifted again. He took his first lesson in skating on Christmas Eve and on New Year's Eve 1870 he 'skated a good deal hand in hand with Flossie' at Clarendon.

When Neville returned to University Hall in January 1871, he had forgotten his toothache and recovered his usual zest for life in the capital. The Diary reports frequent visits to theatres with friends, and sometimes with his father who visited London regularly on business. On 9 February he 'went with [Henry] Bond to see the Queen on her way to open Parliament. The people displayed hardly any enthusiasm'. On 24 February, after wryly noting, 'Beesly halled me for not getting up earlier in the morning', he offered the news that 'We [himself and seven others] have got up a Shakespeare Society in the Hall', adding 'Lord, Huxley and I are appointed a Committee to apportion parts etc.'. Thereafter the Diary contained regular references to the plays read at the weekly meetings of the Shakespeare Society, often with a full cast list spelt out. All of this suggests a somewhat relaxed approach to his formal studies, but it was at University College that he developed his distinctive capacity for unflagging concentration, which enabled him in later years to sustain long sequences of ten- to twelve-hour working days, whenever pressed by teaching or administrative problems. Although he had (temporarily as it turned out) stopped recording the daily stint of hours worked, there is a revealing entry for 18 March which reads: 'During the week I had a race with Lord to see who could do most work. I won by about 7 hours. Monday I did 12, Tuesday 11½, the other days not more than usual'. Similarly, on 1 April, instead of 'joining most of the men at the boat race' he gave priority to Beesly's history lecture. According to Florence, his widow, writing almost 80 years later: 'He has often said that

7. John Lord shared a dormitory with Neville at Amersham Hall school and was at University College with him for two years before graduating in 1870. He went up to Trinity (Cambridge) in 1871, achieved the highest distinction in the mathematical tripos (senior wrangler) and became a Fellow of Trinity in 1876. See Enid Porter, *Victorian Cambridge: Joseph Chater's Diaries* (London: Phillimore, 1975).

he never worked so hard at any other time in his life as during the three years he spent at University College'.[8]

It is hardly surprising that the Diary did not mention any of the women who began to attend undergraduate lectures at University College during Neville's first year, for in the early years of their experimental admission, elaborate precautions were taken to prevent the sexes from actually meeting. The women's lectures began on the half hour instead of on the hour, so that 'the men might be safely occupied at their coming and going, and the women were admitted by a side door to avoid the risks of crossing the quadrangle'.[9] At 18 he was, however, at the age to be romantically susceptible to charmers he met on vacation. His cousin Minnie Todd, for example, 'who is nice as well as pretty', spent Easter with the Keynes family in Salisbury and a week or so later he joined her at a Chapel service in London on Sunday 23 April. After Chapel, when walking with her in the garden, Minnie 'showed me in her Bible two flowers that I had given her while at Salisbury. She promised me a lock of her hair! and I duly received the precious token next morning'. Nevertheless, during a Swiss summer holiday with the Williams family and their two delectable daughters, Neville was again in thrall to Flossie. Back in Salisbury on 10 August, he 'walked about with Flossie for a considerable time. I enjoyed myself once more with her as if there were no Minnie Todd in existence'.

In October of his third year, Neville was successful as usual at the beginning of term college examinations. He was also elected president of the University Hall Chess Club and honorary secretary of the college Debating Society. Winter began early that year, and when skating on Regents Park Ornamental Water on 21 November, Neville was concussed by a fall – to the great alarm of both his skating companion Henry Bond and Beesly the principal, who put him to bed. According to the Diary he woke the next day with 'no remembrance of anything that had happened the preceding day'. Fortunately his mother, who was then staying with friends at Camberwell, was able to visit him daily that week. 'The doctor also came to see me every day. He forbad my going in for any examination before Xmas so I have been obliged to give up the Trinity Minors. I scarcely did any work for the remainder of the term.' On the other hand, he attended a succession of London theatres and continued to read his parts at the weekly Shakespeare Society

8. F.A. Keynes, *Gathering Up the Threads* (Cambridge: Heffer & Sons, 1950), p. 47.
9. See Hale Bellot (1929), p. 370. The women's classes at University College were organized by the London Ladies Educational Association and were the responsibility of the professors rather than the College, which simply licensed them to lecture to women on its premises. The separation of the sexes broke down quite soon. J.E. Cairnes, the professor of political economy, for example, rebelled against duplicating his lectures and admitted a mixed audience as early as 1871/72, while the Slade School began admitting mixed classes in 1872/73.

meetings. By the second week of December he was again merrily skating in Regents Park. Many of the Diary entries for his third year record visits to London theatres or to various college debating societies. The most hotly debated issue of the day among his contemporaries seems to have been the higher education of women, and his sympathy with the women's cause was always plain. For example, on 25 January he wrote:

> The Debating Society had to adjourn from the Reading Room to the Botanical Theatre in consequence of the number of men present. The whole evening was taken up with private business. I seconded Birchenough's motion interpreting our rules as admitting ladies. It was carried by 30 to 20.

A month later he went with his friend Arthur Spokes to St George's Hall to hear Henry Fawcett's wife Millicent lecture on the education of women.[10]

During their third year at University College, those of Neville's contemporaries who shared his ambition to win a scholarship to Cambridge were trying their luck at college entrance examinations. Having been prevented by the November skating accident from sitting for Trinity in December 1871, he went to Cambridge on 18 March to try for a scholarship at Trinity Hall:[11] 'I was very much troubled with headache and toothache during the examinations and the papers were not such as were calculated to suit me. I did worst in Trigonometry'. He was unsuccessful; Harding, his mathematics teacher at University College was 'surprised and rather angry' when he confessed what he had done at the examination. After this setback Neville brought his friend Agate with him to Salisbury for the Easter vacation. On the way (he wrote): 'I unburdened my soul to him. I had done so to Bond about 6 weeks previously'. The earlier confession must have taken place in mid-February, well before he sat (and failed) the Trinity Hall examination. Tantalizingly, he did not say what was bothering him on either occasion. Perhaps he had edited out of the fair copy (then characterizing the entries in the Diary right up to the end of 1872) a depressing cloud of doubt as to whether it was worth slogging away at mathematical bookwork in order to be sure of landing a college fellowship at the end of it all. That cloud surfaced in the Diary in summer 1872. Fortunately or unfortunately, however, there were other college entrance examinations still open to him and on 3 June he was in Cambridge again, trying for a Pembroke scholarship. 'Before I left, Mr Searle, the Tutor,

10. Neville had already met Millicent Fawcett socially in Salisbury, for she married Henry Fawcett in 1867. The Fawcetts' drawingroom in Cambridge was the location in 1869 for the momentous meeting to set up university lectures for women, leading on to the establishment by Henry Sidgwick of the hall of residence that was to evolve into Newnham College. After her husband's death, Millicent went on to make a name for herself as a leading suffragist.
11. Henry Fawcett was then a fellow of Trinity Hall.

told me I had done pretty well and asked me a few questions as to the previous course of my education, etc.'. This time he was brilliantly successful. A telegram from John Lord (who had matriculated at Trinity College earlier in 1872) brought the good news to Salisbury on 8 June that he had got the top maths scholarship of £60.

2 CAMBRIDGE UNDERGRADUATE

Founded in 1337, Pembroke was one of the oldest of the smaller colleges. Its dozen resident fellows had all taken the mathematical or classical tripos and four of them had taken (or were about to take) holy orders – thus formally establishing their clerical credentials, whilst opening up the possibility of a college living should they choose to marry, or feel the need for a larger basic income than was offered by the annual college dividend. Most of them were under 50 years old and in 1870 they had elected as Master John Power – 'a man who believed in progress'.[12] It seems unlikely that this traditionally Anglican college would have admitted its first nonconformist member, had it not been on the verge of a dramatic expansion in its undergraduate numbers and had Neville not won the top mathematical scholarship in its entrance examination. For the man in charge of undergraduate admissions was then Charles Searle, a former fellow who had been brought back from his Suffolk living in 1870 to accept the official position of tutor – a post which enabled the most charismatic senior member of the college to take the lead in determining its future character as an educational institution. When Searle became tutor the number of undergraduates at Pembroke was 44; by 1880 there were 122. Determined to strengthen the academic quality as well as the size of Pembroke's undergraduate population, Searle welcomed the clever, earnest young nonconformist among its undergraduate admissions; and Neville was as impressed as most of his contemporaries by his authoritative charm. Yet, within days of arriving at Pembroke, after lunching with Searle and choosing his rooms, Neville was plunged into 'a fit of despondency' during which he seriously contemplated dropping out of Cambridge altogether at the end of the 1872 October term. The mood of despair was at its peak when he was

12. The phrase is Christopher Brooke's, in *A History of the University of Cambridge, 1870–1990*, Vol. IV (Cambridge: Cambridge University Press, 1993), p. 66. I am indebted to Jayne Ringrose, honorary archivist of Pembroke College, for the information that by 1872 the Pembroke fellowship was by no means exclusively clerical, and that the preponderance of mathematicians did not preclude a diversity of individual careers – including several barristers, a wine merchant, a professor of astronomy (J.C. Adams) who had moved from St John's to avoid the obligation to take Holy Orders, the Cambridge Lucasian Professor of Physics and secretary to the Royal Society (G.G. Stokes), and the professor of civil engineering and applied mechanics at London University College (Moore).

visited in his rooms, on Thursday, 19 October by Mrs Bond, the mother of his close friend Henry, and wife to his father's friend, a leading Cambridge congregationalist grocer. She had come to invite Neville to family supper on his first Sunday evening in Cambridge. When she alerted his parents to his state of mind, both hastily took the train from Salisbury on 22 October to talk him out of abandoning his Cambridge career.

In effect, Neville's first term at Pembroke was characterized by an unexpected cultural shock. For an undergraduate who had sampled the varied à la carte menu offered to a London University student and was now more concerned to develop his academic potential than to acquire a ticket of entry to a comfortable professional position, the trouble with Cambridge in the 1870s was the suffocatingly restrictive character of its examination procedures. According to Rothblatt:

> Unlike Oxford, Cambridge ranked its honours men on a strict order of merit from the senior wrangler or senior classic don down. This intensified the competition for honours and made many believe that the tripos system of marking was a scrupulously objective method of selection.[13]

There was also a clearly identified order of merit in the academic prestige of the honours courses available. Conventional wisdom ranked mathematics above all other tripos options, with classics second and the two 'modern' triposes (natural and moral sciences) introduced at mid-century, a long way behind either. In these circumstances, it was to be expected that the mathematical tripos would attract the cream of the candidates for honours. According to Noel Annan, for example:

> The first ten Wranglers stood an excellent chance of a Fellowship even at Trinity and St John's; a man from a small college could hope for a Fellowship if he were placed among the Wranglers … a first or second Wrangler had a testimonial of ability that would open doors in London.[14]

Consequently, few of the minority of undergraduates reading for honours in the 1850s, 1860s and 1870s chose to take either the moral tripos or the natural science tripos. Indeed, hardly any of the potential high-flyers would have failed to opt for the mathematical tripos, whatever the ultimate career they had in mind. Henry Fawcett, for example, was whole-heartedly convinced by what his friend and biographer, Leslie Stephen called 'the official Cambridge theory' concerning the overall superiority of mathematics as a

13. Sheldon Rothblatt, *The Revolution of the Dons* (Cambridge: Cambridge University Press, 1968), p. 182.
14. Noel Annan, *Leslie Stephen: Godless Victorian* (London: Weidenfeld & Nicholson, 1984), p. 26.

training in mental gymnastics. He had himself chosen the mathematical tripos as the best foundation for a career in the law.

> A Senior Wrangler, as he would argue, might be absolutely ignorant of the law: but three years after his degree, he would be a far better lawyer than the man who had been crammed with legal knowledge in place of being trained in the use of his logical faculties.[15]

Even Henry Sidgwick, the leading defender of the moral sciences tripos, and one of its intellectual mainstays, conceded in October 1870 that it had a deserved reputation for demanding less intellectual effort than either of the long-established triposes. After remarking that there had been so far only one occasion when a college fellowship had been awarded 'for attainments in this subject alone', he wrote:

> The Moral Sciences Tripos is shut out from … [the colleges'] rewards by a wellknown 'vicious circle': the standard of a First-Class is low because the most able and industrious men do not devote themselves to the study; they do not devote themselves to the study because it is not rewarded; and it is not rewarded because the standard of the First-Class is low … and as long as it is undeniable that men not of transcendent genius obtain the highest (or all but the highest) places in the Tripos on less than a year's reading, they must be admitted to have a strong case.[16]

By the time Neville came up to Pembroke in October 1872, however, traditional assumptions concerning the hierarchy of the academic disciplines no longer went unchallenged in the ancient English universities. In Cambridge, for example, a new generation of dons (such as Henry Sidgwick and John Seeley) had begun to exert intellectual influence and authority. Fawcett, though still under 40, represented a previous, less progressive tradition and was defending an outdated set of attitudes. He was the unreconstructed product of the narrow Cambridge teaching and examination system that had prevailed in the 1850s. 'His own education', to quote Leslie Stephen again, 'had been limited: his tendency fell in with the general disposition of the society to which he belonged' (p. 93). The next generation of dons, on the other hand, were scholars actively developing new philosophical and scientific ideas, mistrustful of traditional dogma, and advocating radical reforms in university teaching, examination and admission systems. One significant consequence of the winds of change that were gathering force in Cambridge during the late 1860s and early 1870s was the abolition of the religious tests that had effectively excluded all serious

15. Leslie Stephen, *Life of Henry Fawcett* (London: Macmillan, 1885), p. 91.
16. *Cambridge University Reporter* (hereafter *CUR*), October 1870, p. 47. Sidgwick was writing a letter to the editor responding to certain criticisms of the moral sciences tripos that had recently been made by C.W. Ingleby.

dissenters from taking positions of responsibility in the university.[17] Less than a year before Neville sat the Pembroke entrance examination, the Universities Tests Act of 1871 had completed its passage through parliament and finally removed the statutory obligation on masters and fellows of colleges, and professors and readers of the university, to sign a declaration of conformity with the liturgy of the Church of England. Individual colleges could still insist that all their dons should publicly profess the Anglican faith, but the prevailing ethos was changing. As the number of new generation dons holding fellowships in the university increased, so did the community's respect for scholarship. Colleges which valued their academic reputation began to compete to attract to themselves the cream of the annual intake of potential first-class graduates, whatever their religious affiliations.[18]

Neville's first term at Cambridge was miserable. The Diary (still in the fair-copy style of the 1868-onwards series) is morosely uninformative about his work programme. He entered cheerfully enough into a new and invigorating sporting activity – rowing on the river Cam – but was oppressed and depressed by the advice of his valued mentors (particularly Searle and Fawcett) that he should resign himself to three years cramming with mathematical bookwork. His years at University College had extended his academic horizons and given him a taste for more open-ended and philosophical branches of knowledge. His modest talent for mathematics had won him a place at Pembroke, but he realized that he could expect no intellectual stimulation from reading it for honours. Far from being a challenge to a thoughtful student, the Cambridge mathematical tripos was – to quote Noel Annan again – simply 'a trial of memory and nerves'.[19] What was discouraging for Neville, whose sporting instincts were strong, was not the fierce competition involved, it was the prospect of three years hard labour in what seemed to be an intellectual blind alley.

The Diary for 1873 reverts to a more fluent handwriting style, which, taken in conjunction with fuller and more spontaneous entries, suggests that we are now reading a first-hand, unedited record. It begins, as usual, in Salisbury,

17. Unprincipled dissenters or agnostics had no hesitation in paying lip service to the Thirty-Nine Articles of the Church of England. By contrast, thoughtful Anglicans agonized over certain details of the Liturgy, so that some (such as Henry Sidgwick) resigned their fellowships, while others such as Leslie Stephen left Cambridge altogether to escape the false position in which they found themselves.
18. It took much longer for women than for dissenters to gain admission to Cambridge. But when the Cambridge Local Examinations Syndicate opened up to girls, its exams marking the transition from school to university, the campaign to offer women students lectures of university standard gathered strength in Cambridge (as in University College London). For it became clear that there were enough liberal dons willing to lecture to women (and informally mark their examination papers), to justify setting up the halls of residence that evolved into Girton and Newnham Colleges.
19. Annan (1984), p. 24.

where he was again fascinated by Flossie, revelling in her company but plagued by intermittent toothache. On 5 January, for example, after a reference to one of the seasonal parties at her parents' house, where he 'devoted nearly the entire evening to her', he added: 'She said that I was very changeable in my attitude towards her, being sometimes very cool and sometimes very friendly. In the night I was driven nearly mad by toothache which came on worse than usual'. At another party on 17 January, he 'had to powder her face for a charade and this necessitated her shutting her eyes. We were in the room together and I gave her a kiss. Afterwards she gave me some violets'. That vacation was overshadowed for Keynes, however, by more anxious issues. On 12 January, after reporting that he was reading *Ecce Homo*,[20] he added: 'I have written to Mr Searle to tell him that I mean to give up mathematics and read morals instead. I did not ask for his advice as I have quite made up my mind on the subject'. The following day the mental agony continued: 'I went for a walk with Prof. Fawcett. He strongly urges me to go on with mathematics. He told me that Miller of Peterhouse thinks I shd be at least among the first twenty wranglers. But this would not satisfy me'. The point was that although Neville had set his heart on getting a college fellowship, he had also developed an interest in the wider intellectual horizons that Cambridge was now opening up to keen young scholars. Fawcett, by contrast, had, at the outset of his university career, identified success in the mathematical tripos as the route to a lifetime college fellowship that would fund him while he read for the law and took the first steps in an unpaid political career.[21] When the two of them travelled back to Cambridge on 21 January, he again tried to persuade his young friend to accept the rational option. That night Neville reported: 'In the evening a very bad attack of the blues commenced. I am seriously doubtful whether I took the right step when I came to Cambridge'. The next day he gave way – provisionally:

> I called on Mr Searle. He was very kind and by dint of saying that he thought I should get a fellowship, his advice, added to what I know to be Father's wish, has

20. *Ecce Homo* by John Seeley (published anonymously in 1865) was a radical contribution to the theological debates of the 1860s and generated considerable interest and debate among modern academics. Sidgwick, for example, reviewed it in the *Westminster Review* (86), 1866, and remarked that it depicted Christ as a proto-Benthamite. By the time Neville was reading it, its anonymity had been blown, and his interest then may have been fired by the fact that Seeley was the Cambridge Regius Professor of History, driving the new tripos in history and a notorious critic of the competitive examination system there prevailing. See, for example, Seeley's 'Liberal Education in the Universities', in F.W. Farrar, *Essays on a Liberal Education London* (1867) where he concluded (p. 167) that 'The all-worshipped tripos produces in fact what might be called a universal suspension of the work of education'.
21. Fawcett had been elected a fellow of Trinity Hall immediately after being classified seventh wrangler in the mathematical tripos.

> at last prevailed on me to continue reading Mathematics till May. I do not myself consider the step to be a wise one and I cannot begin work with any 'go' but at any rate I please others.

Meanwhile he characteristically raised his spirits, by making a game of his work schedule and entering into a pact with Lord (a willing candidate for the mathematics tripos) 'to pay into a common fund a penny an hour for each hour less than eight we work each day'.[22] On the other hand, he was resolutely determined to abandon mathematics for moral sciences in his second year, whatever the career consequences predicted by his seniors. On 20 February, he speculated gloomily: 'I suppose that all chances of my getting a fellowship are at an end now that I have definitely decided on giving up Mathematics'.

During the next term Neville focused on two main objectives: (1) doing just enough mathematics to give a good account of himself in the college end-year examinations (popularly called the 'Mays'); and (2) reading for the first London BSc examination which he intended to sit in the early part of the summer vacation. He had told W.H. Besant his maths coach, on 3 February, that he wanted to confine himself 'chiefly to reading Mays subjects with him'. But he spent most of his working time cramming for the London BSc, which involved a raft of scientific subjects – chemistry, physics, mathematics, zoology and botany – for the last of which he hired (on 8 February) a coach appropriately named 'Mudd of the Botanical Gardens' who came to him three times a week and charged 50 shillings a term. Success in the London BSc would eventually, he hoped, weigh in his favour when competing for a Pembroke fellowship with graduates who had bowed to conventional wisdom and read mathematics or classics instead of morals. Before sitting for the Mays, however, Neville found it necessary to deal with the elementary hurdle which all candidates for a Cambridge degree had to surmount – the Previous examination, popularly known as 'Little-Go'. Preparing for that was the most tedious of tasks on which he admitted to 'a little work now and then'.[23] He wrote the examination at the end of the Lent term and his performance was

22. Later that week they persuaded two other friends to join their 'Working Club' and by the end of term the four of them had amassed a sufficient fund in 'fines' to pay for their celebratory dinner held in the evening of the second day of the Little-Go examinations. See the Diary for 27 March, which makes it clear it was Keynes who had kept his working day up to the target of eight hours daily more consistently than any of them.
23. The subjects of the Previous (alias Little-Go) were few and easy. They involved one of the Gospels in Greek, a Latin and a Greek classic, William Paley's *Evidences of Christianity* (1794), the first three books of Euclid and arithmetic. The examination was, however 'a thorn in the side of the candidate for honours, as it compelled him to keep up his schoolwork when he ought to have been devoting all his time to his tripos'. See D.A. Winstanley, *Later Victorian Cambridge* (Cambridge: Cambridge University Press, 1947), p. 144.

atypically mediocre. Given the amount of time he was giving to the university Chess Club – of which he had been elected secretary on 3 February,[24] that was not surprising. On 5 April he wrote irritably:

> I have only got a second class in my Little-Go. This I attribute to the haste in wh I did some of the papers in order to win my bet with Hamilton.[25] Of course I dont mind the second class in itself in the least, but people at Salisbury are annoying me by offering condolence. Dr Lush says I evidently have not recovered from my accident on the ice and that I ought not to be allowed to open another book for a year.

In fact it was not necessary to do more than pass Little-Go and his Cambridge friends and advisers were in general too contemptuous of it to regard his poor result as a serious matter. On 21 April, for example, he noted that Searle (who in March had been 'very grumpy' when he asked leave to cut down his workload in order to play in the university chess match against Oxford) was 'very jovial notwithstanding my 2nd class in Little-Go. It seems I was very nearly ploughed in Euclid!'.

The entries for the Easter term 1873 suggest a marked improvement in Neville's spirits – partly no doubt because he could see light at the end of the grim mathematical tunnel, but also because it was the merriest term in the Cambridge calendar. Although he still suffered intermittently from neuralgia, that had abated sufficiently by mid-May to let him enjoy to the full the company of his many friends on walks, or at croquet parties and on the river. He saw a good deal of the Bond family, whose hospitality he returned in some measure by hiring boats to take them and their guests to view the May races and providing lunch or supper for such parties in his college rooms. On Saturday 24 May he admitted having 'enjoyed the May races very much, but they have cut up my work fearfully'. In spite of this hectic social activity he managed to top the list of Pembroke freshmen in their May examinations – which he took wholly in maths apart from a Latin translation paper. The result established his reputation as a Pembroke high-flyer, guaranteed the renewal of his scholarship for two more years and effectively won him the right to choose his tripos. He still felt it necessary, however, to boost his chances in a future fellowship competition by averaging five hours daily working for the first part of the London BSc during June and July – with only

24. There are frequent references in the Diary to chess, for example, on 10 March: 'I am now to be put fifth in the list of players against Oxford, if the Little-Go does not prevent my playing altogether'. On 12 April he reported: 'One of my games is published in the *Illustrated London News*' and 'I won the chess tournament in Cambridge'.
25. The bets with Hamilton hinged on his spending less than one hour on each Little-Go paper. He won a shilling on the Paley paper and on Euclid; but the arithmetic took him nearly two hours.

a short walking holiday in Devon and Cornwall. After getting a disappointing second class in that examination, he went to the London Senate House in order to discover exactly where he had lost marks – only to learn that he 'had done brilliantly in the Maths papers'.

He could, however, now rejoice that he had finished the long grinding slog at mathematics, although – right up to the end of his first academic year – he was relentlessly pressured to reconsider his decision to switch to morals. Neville noted in the Diary some of his coaches' laudatory comments which Searle relayed to him; for example:

> Stephen had told him that I was best in his class. But this amused me most! Rust says that I might go out in Classics for I am 'accurate and well-taught.' Searle fears that Morals will not be sufficient to occupy my remaining time, and he suggests Law in addition.

Besant, his maths coach, took a similar line. The Diary reports their last meeting: 'He again said what a pity it was I was giving up Mathematics. He speaks contemptuously of Morals and thinks that I have too good powers of reasoning logically to be in my proper element as a logician'. Finally, on 30 June, Neville quoted from Fawcett's letter of congratulation on his Mays result: '"After your success in your college examination upon which I very sincerely congratulate you. I wd strongly urge you to reconsider your decision to give up reading mathematics"'. On which the diarist commented: 'I have replied that I cannot do so. It is a trouble to have to reject the advice of so many who take an interest in me'.

Neville Keynes never regretted his choice of tripos. Had he been persuaded to read for the mathematical or classical tripos, he would have had to rely for intellectual stimulus in his second and third years on a few hard-pressed, specialist coaches whose function was the intensive drilling of undergraduate minds to succeed in certain highly competitive written examinations. In contrast, as an honours man reading moral sciences, he was privileged to draw direct inspiration, encouragement and personal tuition from a group of new-generation scholars who included Henry Sidgwick, Alfred Marshall and John Venn. Before the end of the Easter term 1873 he had obtained practical advice from Venn (the logician and fellow of Caius) who, according to the Diary: 'promised to help me all he can in the way of giving me advice as to the course of my reading in the Moral Sciences'. So, armed with a list of challenging books, Neville went eagerly into residence in the Long Vacation term, and during August, worked six to eight hours daily (Sundays excepted) reading his way into his chosen tripos. He began with J.S. Mill's *Principles of Political Economy* (1848) (the basic text for the economics course), which he enjoyed 'immensely'. Better still, at 3 Brookside, where he and other nonconformist undergraduates enjoyed the Bond family's 'usual warm welcome',

Neville found a rewardingly stimulating walking companion in James Ward – the mature Trinity scholar in moral sciences with whom he could explore in depth the new ideas confronting him.[26] He even found time for his current hobby – working up chess problems for publication in newspapers and periodicals – an activity in which he had some success.

Neville had now embarked on a course of study that differed radically from all his previous experience at school or university. It was less rigorous in the specificity of its demands than any of the mathematical or classical or scientific subjects in which he had so far presented himself for examination. At the same time it was more challenging in its range and in the extent to which it called for original judgement and analytical thought (from both teachers and pupils), rather than technical expertise or mental gymnastics or detailed recall of bookwork. His task was to prepare himself for a written examination in late 1875 (over two years hence), when he would be required to address a sufficient number of questions posed in twelve three-hour papers set on four related, but distinct, branches of knowledge – (1) moral and political philosophy; (2) mental philosophy; (3) logic; and (4) political economy. To obtain the first-class result which was crucial to his prospects of a fellowship, he had to satisfy four or five examiners (one of whom might be from another university) of his superior knowledge and analytical ability in each of these broad fields.[27] In principle, the budding moralist had no need to hire coaches. For each branch of moral science he was supplied with a list of twelve to 20 books recommended by the Board of Studies for Moral Sciences, treatises which he was expected to read carefully and critically (if not exhaustively).[28] He could attend recommended sets of lectures in each branch, and – for each set he chose to audit – he could expect the lecturer concerned to provide appropriate question papers, his answers to which would be read and assessed in detail (for a fee of £1 per term), either by the lecturer himself or by a younger don deputizing for him.

It was a system which gave the candidate for honours full responsibility for planning his own work schedule and freedom to make direct personal contact

26. James Ward who was nine years older than JNK, had served briefly as a pastor at Emmanuel Church before competing successfully for a Trinity moral sciences scholarship in 1873.
27. Sidgwick's response to Ingleby's critique of the moral sciences tripos referred to in fn 16 above admitted that many past examiners in the tripos had been 'persons whose proficiency in the subject was quite uncertified' but insisted that by the 1870s this was not so: 'out of eight examiners appointed during the last 4 years there is not one who has not given evidence of his knowledge of the subject'. *CUR*, 2 November 1870, p. 68.
28. The members of the Moral Sciences Board in 1874 were: the Regius Professor of Law, the professors of modern history and political economy, Mr J. Venn (Caius), Mr Scott (Jesus), Mr J.B. Pearson (St John's), Professor A.C. Fraser (Edinburgh), Mr J.P. Taylor (Clare), Mr T.W. Levin (St Catharines), Mr J.R. Mozeley (King's), and Mr H. Sidgwick (Trinity). Fraser was an examiner for the 1874 tripos. No other board of studies in Cambridge at the time had an external examiner who was not a Cambridge graduate.

with the dons he found most rewarding as teachers. Neville could decide for himself each term, which of the recommended books to read, which of the lectures on offer he would attend and which of the dons might be expected to give him the most helpful advice on how to tackle questions of the kind that might appear in the final tripos examination. In the 1873 Michaelmas term Neville focused on two of the four moral sciences he was expected to master over the next two years, that is, on moral philosophy and logic. Accordingly, he sat at the feet of Sidgwick – lecturing on ancient ethics each weekday at 9 a.m. and of Venn – on inductive logic thrice weekly at 12 noon. During the next term he stayed with Sidgwick, now lecturing on modern ethics, and with Venn on mental philosophy (especially Descartes and Kant). In each case he was one of a small audience (generally less than ten men) most of whom took the opportunity to write answers to questions set by the lecturer and to have their replies criticized in front of the class. Moralist undergraduates thus became personally well acquainted with the dons who lectured and examined for the tripos.[29] It was not actually until the Saturday morning after his return to Cambridge for the Easter term 1874 that Neville Keynes introduced himself to Alfred Marshall.[30] The Diary for 18 April records that he 'called on Marshall of John's, lecturer in Pol. Econ. – found him in his tub'. This laconic entry nicely illustrates the informality of the relationship between the younger generation of dons and their students. It was the first of several such Saturday morning visits to Marshall, whose notice in the *University Reporter* of 21 April 1874 read: 'Mr Marshall will be in his room to answer questions arising out of either the private reading or the lectures to members of the advanced class on Mondays from 10 to 1 and to members of the elementary class on Saturdays from 9.30 to 11.30'.[31] During that term Neville attended three lecture courses: Marshall's on elementary political economy; Sidgwick's on Jeremy Bentham and political philosophy; and Venn's on formal logic (William Hamilton and H.L. Mansel). Before the end of term, however, he had abandoned Venn's lectures on Hamilton, because (according to the Diary) 'they were useless', and he began on 13 June to fill the gap by reading for himself Hamilton's and R. Whateley's texts on *Logic*.

29. Only nine men read for the 1875 moral sciences tripos. There had been eleven in 1874. The lectures announced by the Board for the academic year 1873/74 were mainly given by Sidgwick (on ethics and political philosophy), Marshall (on political economy), Venn (on logic) and Levin (on mental philosophy and logic). In addition, Professor Fawcett lectured thrice weekly on political economy during the Lent term; his lectures were designed not for honours men but for poll men who needed to attend a minimum number of professorial lectures to qualify for an ordinary degree.
30. Keynes had not attended Marshall's lectures on Mill's *Political Economy* during the first two terms of the academic year, presumably because he judged that he had spent enough time reading that book during the preceding Long Vacation term.
31. *CUR*, 21 April 1874, p. 336.

Neville's second academic year at Cambridge was an altogether happier experience than his first. Although he was no longer recording his daily tally of hours worked, his time was evidently fully occupied by a satisfyingly varied work and play programme. During the first term he cheerfully mopped up the 'Little-Go extras' which he had been allowed to skip the previous March (because they clashed with the university chess match), he participated in various university societies and sporting events and he continued to 'meddle with chess problems'. The first 1874 Diary entry, for example, boasted: 'a problem of mine is published in the *Westminster Papers* for this month'. Whilst staying at Salisbury over the Christmas vacation, he read Mill's *System of Logic* (1843) and wrote a review of Mill's *Autobiography* (1873) for a student magazine called *The Itinerant Omnibus* to which he had promised to contribute regularly. He also read and commented on a draft paper by Alfred West on 'Philosophy at Cambridge' which the latter asked him to look over before sending it to the *Westminster Review*.[32] Meanwhile the Salisbury social round was livelier than ever. 'I dont think', he wrote happily on 20 January, 'we have ever had so many dancing parties before at Xmas'.

Back at Cambridge in late January 1874 he continued to find time for such varied amusements as chess, rowing, fives and Shakespeare-reading groups. He ran with the Pembroke rattle at the March 'bumps' and did 'absolutely no work' during the last week of term when he was absorbed in the rowing races and associated social occasions. As president of the university Chess Club he led the Cambridge team to victory at the annual inter-university match organized by the City of London Chess Club on 27 March – and on the following day cheered the Cambridge oarsmen to victory over Oxford on the Thames. Easter 1874 was his last virtually work-free vacation. He still had until December 1875 before sitting the tripos examination, but he remained conscious of the need to increase his credit-rating by acquiring additional honours that might impress the Pembroke fellowship electors when his time came to compete with graduates from the mathematical or the classical tripos. So in the 1874 summer vacation, after a month's walking and riding holiday in Salisbury, he returned to Cambridge for the Long Vacation term to study for the second part of the London BSc. Determined to better his previous year's result, he got himself coached in geology and chemistry by a St John's don and settled down to a month of really hard cramming, leavened by socializing with old friends. His studious dedication did not go unnoticed. After one of his several walks with the blind Henry Fawcett (at Salisbury in September),

32. Alfred West had taken first class honours in the moral sciences tripos in 1869. He became an examiner for the tripos, and hence an ex-officio member of the Board, in 1875. He was to succeed his father as headmaster of Amersham Hall School in 1876 and was elected a fellow of University College London in 1897.

Neville noted that the latter 'still thinks I have some chance of a Fellowship at Pembroke'. This cheerful prognostication was confirmed on 23 October by Searle, who 'still talks as if I had some chance of a Fellowship provided I do well in Morals, both at Cambridge and London'.

Young Keynes was thus in high spirits when he went up to London for the BSc examination, which occupied him for most of the October term. His parents had taken lodgings in the Edgeware Road for the first phase of the examination, lasting four days – the evenings brightened for all of them by social visits and theatres with Neville's and their many London friends. The second phase, scheduled to begin two weeks later, was more important to his career prospects for two reasons: first because it was focused on two of the moral sciences he was reading for the tripos – logic and mental philosophy; and second because one of the London examiners was Venn of Caius, whose Cambridge lectures Neville had audited during the preceding academic year and whose opinions carried weight in Oxbridge. After the first phase his morale was raised by a postcard on 7 November from Spokes (also a candidate for the London BSc) saying 'that we had both passed in the first division'. Fawcett (then London University examiner in political economy) passed on the news to Searle and at his first interview with the latter Neville was again encouraged to hear that he had 'a very fair chance' of a Pembroke fellowship. He embarked on the second round of papers with renewed confidence. This time he stayed at the Inns of Court Hotel with Bond and Ingham who accompanied him at three more London shows. The final results were even better. On 21 November he recorded in the Diary: 'Telegram from Spokes. You have the scholarship. There is no one else in the first class'.

It was not until 23 November that Neville got back on stream with the tripos. The time spent on the London examinations had served its purpose without an appreciable gap in his Cambridge studies. He was able to attend H.S. Foxwell's last few psychology lectures that term, to borrow the latter's notes of the preceding lectures and to write 'a good many papers for Sidgwick'. Before the end of term he called on Venn (who had set and marked the inductive logic paper for the London BSc) to hear a detailed critique of his performance. Apparently the London examiners observed more discreet conventions than their Cambridge counterparts,[33] for on 5 December the Diary reported:

33. In contrast to Cambridge where, to judge from the evidence of the Diary, tripos examiners seem to have readily leaked the details of their marks and conflicting opinions to friends and colleagues. See, for example, the entry for 15 December 1874, quoting Henry Bond's letter announcing the results of that year's moral sciences tripos in which their friend James Ward was '*facile princeps* alone in his glory in the 1st class. Miss Bulley in the 2nd class. Miss Paley is either in the 1st or the 2nd class. Two examiners put her in the first, two in the second and neither seems disposed to give way'. On which Neville speculated sarcastically: 'I suppose Pearson and [P.] Gardner were the corking individuals who wanted to put her in the 2nd'.

> [Although Venn] was very agreeable … he did not give me much information as to how I did in the London examination. He said I was a long way above the next man and he hoped I shd do well in my Tripos. He had undermarked me on the Logic paper as he recognised some of his ideas.[34] He hoped they would give me a fellowship at Pembroke and he would speak to Prior on the subject.[35]

Accordingly when Neville returned to Salisbury for the 1874 Christmas vacation, he was happy in the belief that his success in the 2nd London BSc was good enough to lift his academic reputation at Cambridge and cheerfully determined to catch up with his reading for the tripos. As usual he did not get through as much as he had planned during the vacation, but he worked his way doggedly through Plato's *Republic*, Cicero's *De Officio*, Adam Smith's *Wealth of Nations* (1776) and Fawcett's *Manual of Political Economy* (1863), without missing any of the seasonal fun. New Year's Day, for example, found him skating with a merry party of young friends. The first Diary entry for 1875 painted a carefree picture of the occasion:

> On the ice we had first snow, then hail, then rain, with a high wind throughout. While it was snowing and hailing we had a fair game at hockey. When the rain came we retired to the waiting room at the station, but there was no train for an hour and a half. We danced Sir Roger, à la rustic, to keep ourselves warm and we rather scandalized the station master.

Meanwhile, his Cambridge mentors were again reviewing his prospects. The Diary for 25 January cites a 'Letter from Fawcett reporting':

> 'a very satisfactory interview with Searle. Of course he does not pledge himself for anything, but he plainly indicated to me that if you are Senior in the Moral Sciences Tripos both he, the Master, and others wd vote for you. I think they were pleased at your getting a scholarship at the London University, and if you could get the gold medal too, that would materially assist you.'

As it turned out, Neville found it as much as he could do in 1875 to cover the broad field of the tripos. He went to Sidgwick's thrice weekly lectures on metaphysics and to Marshall's twice weekly lectures on advanced political economy and wrote papers for each of them. On 6 March, he noted anxiously: 'I have not had time to read much. My time has been taken up by doing papers and keeping up with my lectures'. Accordingly, although Searle still urged him to go in for his London MA in June 1875, he was not ready for it. He did, however, accept the invitation to do a practice run at old Mr Fawcett's house in Salisbury, by writing the papers which Fawcett and Walter Bagehot had set that

34. Keynes had audited Venn's Cambridge lectures on inductive logic during the October term of 1873.
35. C.H. Prior was a senior fellow of Pembroke.

year. His answers were assessed for him by Fawcett. On 3 July, Neville wrote: 'I called on Prof. and Mrs Fawcett who were down for a day or two. They said I was a very long way first in the MA and DSc papers'. After that encouraging verdict Keynes went up to Cambridge for the Long again, but did not drive himself as hard as he had done the previous year. On 25 August, for example, he confessed having 'wasted most of the day at a couple of chess problems' and added, with evident satisfaction, 'there has been a good deal of breakfast giving and breakfast going this Long'. The Diary also referred to various companionable walks and rides with friends. At the end, on 27 August, he wrote: 'I have very much enjoyed this Long at Cambridge', and took the train to Kington, in Shropshire, to spend his 23rd birthday at the home of his married half-sister Fanny where his parents joined them. It was a relaxed few days during which he indulged himself by playing and winning – blindfold – a series of chess games against a succession of friends and relatives.

At his Finals, which ran from Monday 29 November to Saturday 4 December, Neville achieved his ambition of becoming senior moralist, that is, of topping the list of first-class candidates. The examiners were: H.S. Foxwell, a young lecturer at St John's, who had taken a first in the 1870 moral sciences tripos; W. Stanley Jevons, then professor of logic and philosophy at Owen's College, Manchester; Stephen Mansell, a fellow of Trinity; and Alfred West, the Amersham Hall headmaster's son, who had won a first in the 1869 tripos and had been Neville's friend and role model for seven years. Only eight candidates actually entered in 1875; one other finished in the first class, three in the second, two in the third and one man who failed to reach honours standard was judged to have reached the standard of an ordinary degree. Neville transcribed the letter he got from the 1874 senior moralist, James Ward (who was taken into the examiners' confidence) in his Diary for 13 December:

> 'It was agreed unanimously' Ward wrote 'that, as Marshall puts it, you have a very clear mind: for the rest the Logic and Economy people rate you the highest. Jevons said that you floored the Logic papers and that your answers were a pleasure to read. I shd fancy that you pleased him better in Logic than in Economy: he evidently doesn't believe much in Marshall and was amused by your curves. Foxwell praises your precision but says you shirk difficulties and lack originality in philosophy … All are agreed that Pembroke ought to give you a Fellowship and Marshall thinks you ought to lay yourself out for Economic History, a subject that wants treating thoroughly both for the Moral and the History man.'[36]

During the Christmas vacation Neville spent some days with Alfred West at Amersham Hall: 'where Alfred shewed me the marks I got for every question in his part of the Tripos'.

36. The new history tripos (inaugurated 1873) held its first examination in December 1875.

Keynes returned to Cambridge, as usual, at the beginning of the Lent term 1876 to take his degree and wait for his fellowship. He was warned that it might take some time before he was elected, but was allowed to keep his rooms in Pembroke: 'Searle told me that they wd give me one almost in so many words, but he said they were waiting to see what form the Cambridge University Bill wd take before electing any more Fellows'.[37] Meanwhile, the new graduate coached pupils in logic and political economy. He also 'accepted an offer from Sidgwick to lecture in Logic as deputy for Venn in the October term'. He now enjoyed the unusual luxury of having time to spare. He joined various university debating societies including the senior Chess Club. Prudently he kept open his London connections and career options. On the way back to Cambridge after Easter he stayed in London, entered at the Middle Temple, and ate his first three obligatory dinners as a potential barrister. The May term would have been equally leisured – with only three pupils to coach and his logic lectures to prepare for next October – had it not been for the fact that he chose to confront one more examination hurdle, that is, the London MA. So he averaged more than five hours work daily until 17 June, when he went to London to write the MA examinations and to dine again at the Middle Temple. The MA papers covered logic, philosophy and political economy and his examiners were Venn, T.S. Baynes, Fawcett and Bagehot. On 27 June a telegram arrived with the news that he had been awarded that year's gold medal.

Over the hot summer of 1876 Neville was in an uncertain and emotionally vulnerable state of mind, the uncertainty compounded by the fact that his academic career was in a restless limbo. His return to Salisbury was clouded by the illness of his father's sister Mary, who had been a second mother to Fanny and a much loved member of the Keynes household since Neville's birth. He arrived home on 26 June to find his parents still in Bath where his father was 'taking the waters' as a remedy for rheumatism. The Diary reports:

> I had hoped to find Aunt Mary well. But she did not seem at all well, the swelling in her neck having returned. Aunt Anne called and managing to get to speak alone with me, told me that Mr Coates feared cancer; but he dared not tell Aunt Mary because of her nervous temperament. I could not sleep much that night.

On 28 June, after meeting his parents at the station, he wrote: 'I told Mother what Mr Coates thought about Aunt Mary. We agreed not to tell Father [still in pain with rheumatic gout] till next morning'. On 29 June he continued the

37. Searle was referring to the Bill (then being discussed in parliament) which became the Oxford and Cambridge Act of 1877, and which set up statutory commissions (for each of the two ancient English universities) in order to rewrite the statutes of the universities and colleges.

story: 'Father was told about Aunt Mary but he did not seem to regard it as seriously as we did'. In the event, John Keynes's imperturbable reception of the doctor's pessimistic diagnosis was justified, for the following day's entry reads: 'Now Mr Coates says that after all the swelling may be due to a deep-seated abscess'; and on 30 June the doctor successfully lanced Aunt Mary's abscess under chloroform.

The other person who stirred Neville's emotions during that limbo summer was Flossie Williams, whose flirtatious company he had enjoyed on numerous Salisbury social occasions, and for whom his feelings were generally light-heartedly affectionate. They were to reach an agitated peak, however, on 3 July when the Diary reported a somewhat bizarre event:

> The Tiffins gave a picnic at Wardour.[38] We started at 9.30. About half past four Emily and Flossie went to sit down on what looked to be a low wall, but wh unsuspected by any of us was fourteen and a half feet down on the other side. I ran to sit with them, and Flossie swung round to prevent my doing so, thus slightly losing her balance. Immediately afterwards I must have pushed her in stopping my own run, and she fell on the other side. After seeing her fall I scarcely remember what I felt till I got round and saw her sitting where she had fallen, shaking all over, but immediately laughing and saying she was not hurt. Most providentially she had fallen on her feet. She was soon surrounded by friends, and helped to walk to the cottage close by. Besides being shaken, she appeared only to have cut her right knee rather badly, making her very stiff. In some respects, this accident seemed to upset me more than it did her. About 8.30 we started home. I sat next to Flossie trying to keep her as comfortable as possible.

Neville evidently described this drama in a letter to his level-headed friend Henry Bond, who, though a year his junior, was more experienced in romantic relationships. According to the Diary:

> Bond writes: – 'I dont wonder that the episode at the picnic made a considerable impression on you. I have no doubt that you will be as prudent as one can expect and will remember that if one is instrumental in pushing a young lady, whom one has always been fond of, more or less, down a precipice, it is next to impossible to avoid falling in love with her entirely, especially if she behaves like a brick and doesnt go into hysterics at once. These crises sometimes clear up the real state of one's feeling, but I fancy they now and then hang out false lights.' I wonder which it is. I am certainly thinking a good deal about Flossie just now, but I shall do nothing in a hurry.

Neville's anxiety was to recur in chapel on the following Sunday, when he saw Flossie so overcome by the heat that she 'had to go out nearly fainting'.

38. The Tiffins were family friends of the Keynes as were the Williamses, whose two daughters, Flossie and Emily, figured frequently in the Salisbury social events which Neville attended during his holidays from school and university.

As for Flossie, she was obviously intrigued by Neville's repeated calls at her home to enquire about her health. A few days later, the Diary reported that she had returned his call and 'stayed to tea and afterwards we sat in the garden chatting. She was very anxious to know about the tenure of Fellowships'.

Meanwhile, during that torrid July, Keynes managed to do a little every day towards preparing his lectures in logic. He noted with pleasure that he was to lecture to women next term, as well as to Venn's young men at Caius. The women's lectures were organized by Sidgwick, from whom there came on 29 July (when Neville was visiting his sister's family at Kington), a typically helpful letter from which he quoted in the Diary:

> 'You will find enclosed the list of books and chapters selected for the women's logic course. I conceive that the best way of dividing the subject is to take Whately, and Mill i and ii, in the Michaelmas term, the rest of Mill in the Lent term (with parts of [W.] Thomson and [A.] Bain as they may suggest themselves) and in the May term to give some general view of Logic, its relation to other sciences, different schools of logicians, etc. with something more from Thomson and Bain according to your taste. At least that is how I shd work it out'.

Fortified by this advice Neville went to Lyme Regis to stay with another Salisbury friend, Herbert Lush, whose family had taken a house there for the summer. Lucy Fawcett (Henry's sister) was also a guest of the Lush family on that occasion and the young people swam, rode horses, walked and read together. When it rained they played billiards, though Neville was not an enthusiastic performer. On 4 August, for example, he grumbled to the Diary: 'I am sorry to say that billiards tries my temper a good deal'. Then suddenly, the interminable wait was over and the Pembroke fellows finally decided to elect a new fellow. On 9 August, the Diary reported the arrival of 'a letter from Searle saying that I shall probably be elected to a Fellowship tomorrow and it will be as well to hold myself in readiness to go to Cambridge at once, if sent for'. The telegram confirming his election arrived the next day and he sped joyously to London by a late train. At noon on 11 August, Keynes went through the formal ceremony of admission to the Pembroke fellowship and reported with relief: 'I was told that I had been elected unanimously and almost without discussion'. Within a very few days he and Spokes, his London friend, were travelling on a long continental holiday. It was over two months before he referred again in the Diary to the girl who had so preoccupied him during July 1876. The entry for 13 October, after Neville had returned to Cambridge for the 1876/77 academic year, suggests that Flossie's romantic aura had quite vanished. It reads briskly: 'I have opened an account at the Bank. Flossie Williams talks about the Buckells in a very objectionable way, shewing by no means an amiable spirit. She often annoys me very much'. Now 24 years old, and a senior member of his Cambridge college, he was loftily detached from earlier boyish fancies.

III College fellow in a changing university

1 BACHELOR DON'S FIRST YEAR

When Keynes was elected a fellow of Pembroke in August 1876 he became a privileged senior member of a small well-endowed community of scholars comprising twelve fellows and a Master. He thus acquired modestly distinguished professional status, a share in the college dividend (then amounting to between £380 and £400 annually) and valuable rights of residence at one of the two traditionally prestigious English universities. This provided instant access to a congenial life style. It allowed him to eat well, to enjoy spacious comfort in rooms serviced by college staff, and to entertain friends and colleagues in socially agreeable surroundings. At the same time, Pembroke's claims on his time were minimal. Normally he could expect to be summoned to, at most, one or two meetings a term.[1] Apart from that he was absolutely free to decide for himself where to live, how to spend his time and how to supplement his college income from other sources. In short, Neville was ostensibly launched on a career the aims and details of which he could specify (and alter) as external opportunities arose for him.

His ambitions were then firmly focused on becoming a university teacher – a role which had been idealized for him by the modern generation of dons who had directly inspired him over the past three years. With this objective in view he could expect to add to a basic college income (assured for life so long as he did not marry) supplemented by regular fees from coaching, lecturing to, or examining for any English college or university and by publishing scholarly books or articles. In principle, he was equipped to teach any of the broad range of subjects covered in the moral sciences tripos. In practice, his strength and interests lay mainly in logic and political economy. He was happy to teach either or both. Marshall, his principal economics teacher, had already identified the 1875 Senior Moralist as a promising convert to the new analytical approach that he was himself promoting; he was therefore eager to persuade him to specialize in economic history – so as to be able to teach candidates for the new

1. In the special circumstances of the years 1878/81 – when the Statutory Commission set up by the Oxford and Cambridge Act of 1877 was negotiating a radical revision of the statutes of the university and its colleges – Keynes (as all Cambridge dons) found himself obliged to attend an unprecedentedly large number of extraordinary meetings of his college's governing body.

historical tripos as well as the moral sciences tripos.[2] This, however, was one of Marshall's empire-building fantasies. When Keynes won his fellowship, the Board of Studies in Moral Sciences had – in Sidgwick, Foxwell and Marshall himself – a more than sufficient supply of reputable scholars able and willing to teach economics to the small number of men then reading it. At the same time, the lectures on political economy for women students were competently provided by Newnham's first resident lecturer – Mary Paley.[3] As for the History Board, it was hardly likely to invite a recently graduated moralist to lecture on economic history when it had on its list a Trinity fellow (V.J. Stanton, 20th wrangler in 1870) who had already devised the kind of elementary course on political economy plus economic history, that met its requirements. Clearly, even if Neville had been attracted by the idea of specializing in economic history – and the Diary offers no evidence that he ever was – there was little prospect of his being invited by the History Board to teach in that area. As far as the Moral Sciences Board was concerned, its urgent teaching needs were in logic, where John Venn needed a deputy and where a steady stream of male and female students chose to read it, either for the tripos or for the Senior Local examinations.

During his first term as a fellow of Pembroke, Keynes undertook a conscientiously limited teaching programme, involving twice weekly lectures in logic to women students (organized by Sidgwick), a similar course to honours men (at Venn's request), and various ad hoc sessions of personal tuition (in either logic or political economy) with undergraduate men or Girton women reading for the tripos.[4] He embarked on this programme with total earnestness. For example, on 17 October, he reported in the Diary:

> I met my women's class for the first time. Six came. I was nervous and did not lecture, but merely set them a paper. They seemed disappointed. I have refused several private pupils; and I have refused to lecture on Descartes at Girton.

2. See the Diary of 13 December 1875 which transcribes Ward's letter summarizing what Marshall and the tripos examiners then thought of Keynes (cited above, p. 27).
3. Mary Paley, who wrote the moral sciences tripos in 1874, was informally graded in the second class (see above, p. 25). She became Newnham's first resident lecturer and left to marry Alfred Marshall in the summer of 1877.
4. It was not until 1881 that women were entitled to enter tripos examinations; but in the 1870s some tripos examiners were willing to let them enter informally. See, for example, M. Agnes Hamilton, *Newnham: An Informal Biography* (London: Faber & Faber, 1930), p. 110: 'Their getting the papers at all was a personal favour of the examiners themselves: the papers therefore had to be collected from them and returned to them after they were written; invigilation had to be provided; the examiners if well disposed, had then to be persuaded to place the women, again informally, in a class'. The classics examiners obstinately refused to class any of the women candidates whose papers they marked before 1881, with the result that neither Jane Ellen Harrison, who wrote the classics tripos in 1879, nor Margaret Merrifield in 1880 (both of whom went on to distinguished academic careers) were classed.

Fear of overloading his beginner's capacity for effective teaching evidently prompted his refusal to lecture to Girtonians on philosophy, for he willingly trudged the two miles to (and from) Girton in order to give his relatively industrious female pupils individual instruction on political economy.

Examining was a part of the university teacher's function which most of the modern generation of Cambridge dons took seriously, and one way of testing the quality of new fellows was to involve them in a college scholarship exam. Keynes was encouraged therefore by Sidgwick's invitation, on 22 November 1876, to set the logic paper for the next Trinity scholarship examination in March. On the other hand, he was reluctant, when W.H. Besant called on him a few days later, to discuss the primer on political economy that he had rashly agreed to write in the euphoric aftermath of his election to the Pembroke fellowship. 'I shd rather like to get out of it altogether', he confided to the Diary on 28 November. The fact was that the effort of preparing two new (and different) lecture courses on logic – a labour which entailed setting, reading and discussing, face to face, written papers submitted by each member of his classes – had proved unexpectedly time-consuming. Fortunately, before the end of his first term as a fellow, he was provided with an unassailable reason for backing out of the commitment to Besant. At the annual tripos dinner party which Marshall (that year's chairman of examiners) gave to the members of the moral sciences faculty on 2 December, Neville learned that Mary Paley (now Marshall's fiancée) was already writing a political economy textbook for students attending the university extension lectures.

The invitation to Marshall's dinner party – marking the last day of the 1876 tripos examination – represented Keynes's formal induction into the moral sciences faculty. Earlier that Saturday, after the last batch of scripts had been bundled up for distribution to the examiners (Marshall, Sidgwick, T.W. Levin, and West), Neville had treated to a celebratory lunch, in his rooms at Pembroke, the three (out of eight) examinees whom he had personally taught. A week later he was to hear how well his pupils had done. J. Jacob, already identified by Keynes in his Diary as 'the best man I had coming to my lectures', was nominated that year's Senior Moralist, and the other two (J.S. Nicholson and F. Ryland) were bracketed second in the first class. It was a heartening result for the new don. On the day after the tripos results were announced, Neville walked the departing external examiner – Alfred West – to Cambridge station, on his way back home to Amersham Hall. Whilst walking he listened to a riveting blow-by-blow account of the examiners' deliberations and views on the performance of the individual candidates.

As his workload mounted during the 1877 Lent term, Neville withdrew from the debating societies he had joined the previous year. He now lectured at Caius to an expanded intercollegiate group of logic honours men – encouraged no doubt by the success of his finalists in the 1876 tripos – as well as to his Newnham class, where he was fortified by Lucy Fawcett's report (relayed to him by her brother Henry) that the women greatly appreciated being taught logic by the handsome young Mr Keynes. He also coached a variety of pupils, including an eccentric Girtonian (with 'shocking' handwriting) who was 'far gone in transcendentalism'. Meanwhile the senior members of the faculty were increasingly making use of him. On 18 February, for example, Marshall paid Keynes the compliment of inviting him to read part of the manuscript of a projected new book on foreign trade. Determined, as ever, to keep his interest in political economy alive, Marshall also pressured him to enter for the Cobden prize essay competition.[5] The Diary entry for 5 March reports: 'Marshall is affording me considerable assistance in writing for the Cobden prize'. However, Marshall was not always his latest disciple's favourite mentor. The entry goes on to record: 'a very pleasant dinner party at Mrs Sidgwick's. I always find a talk with Sidgwick intellectually bracing and I go back to work after it with renewed energy'. A couple of weeks later Neville again dined with the Sidgwicks, this time as a prelude to the final meeting of examiners in the Trinity and St John's scholarship examination in which he had taken responsibility for the logic paper. Among the other dinner guests on this occasion were Marshall and Helen Gladstone (the Liberal prime minister's daughter), soon to become one of his Newnhamite students.

Drafting the Cobden essay became Neville's main preoccupation during the Easter term of 1877. This first attempt to write a sustained thesis proved a disappointing, if instructive, experience. To begin with he was uninspired both by the set topic – 'the effect of machinery on wages' – and by the cast of examiners. T.E. Cliffe Leslie, the external adjudicator, was an Irish historical economist of international repute who seemed to Neville to represent a totally alien tradition of thought to the abstract deductive Ricardian/Marshallian orthodoxy with which the 1875 Senior Moralist had so recently been indoctrinated.[6] The other two examiners were Henry Fawcett (a friend for whom Neville had a genuine affection but who was not a distinguished economist), and the vice-chancellor's representative, Samuel Phear (a theologian and Master of Emmanuel). In this group of three the external examiner was

5. The prize – worth £20 for 'an essay on some subject connected with Political Economy' – was funded by a committee of the Cobden Club. The regulations had been formulated by an eight-man syndicate (including Marshall and Sidgwick) set up by the University in early 1876. See *CUR*, 29 February 1876, p. 265. This was the first year of its operation.
6. See G. Koot, *English Historical Economics 1870–1926* (Cambridge: Cambridge University Press, 1987), pp. 42–9, for an informed discussion of Cliffe Leslie's critical approach to Ricardian deductive political economy and for his 'especially low opinion of economics at Cambridge'. JNK was probably right to fear the external examiner's bias for Koot quotes (p. 46) a later letter from Cliffe Leslie rejoicing at Nicholson's election to the Edinburgh chair of political economy and commenting 'Nicholson is on my side'.

obviously destined to dominate. 'The chief part of what I have already written is in direct opposition to Cliffe Leslie' Neville groaned to the Diary when he learned who were to be that year's adjudicators, but he resisted Marshall's worldly advice to delete all the passages that might offend Cliffe Leslie. At the end of his labours on the Cobden essay, young Keynes was ill-served by the man he hired to produce the final clean copy: 'My copyist causes me a good deal of annoyance', he lamented on 20 June, 'He seems to have given his wife some of the work to do. Her writing is not good and some of her mistakes are atrocious'. He could obviously have produced a better final version himself, had he not feared that he might miss the deadline. 'I had a great rush to get my essay finished in time. It is too long, 365 pages', he wrote on 23 June after handing in the final version.

By then Keynes had realistically abandoned all hope of winning the prize. As early as 15 June he had identified his ex-pupil and friend as the likely winner. On 8 July, after noting with regretful surprise: 'Nicholson has managed to miss the gold medal at the London MA', he added 'He has shown me a summary of his Cobden Essay and I feel sure he will get the prize'. As indeed he did.[7] Two months later, during a Sunday afternoon walk from Salisbury to Clearbury, Neville learned from Fawcett the inner story of the London MA examination. The Diary for 9 September records:

> I asked how it was that Nicholson had missed the gold medal at the last London MA examination. Fawcett replied that no one of the examiners felt justified in recommending him for it ... He only got 70 on 150 in Fawcett's paper. Fawcett spoke very strongly against Nicholson's style, just as he spoke against Ward's. I am growing more and more doubtful how far he is a competent examiner for men who have advanced beyond a certain stage in Political Economy; he does not properly appreciate wider views than his own nor the theoretical intricacies in which such a man as Marshall delights. He told me my style was far better the year I was examined informally, than it was when I got the medal.

This was the first explicit reference in the Diary to Neville's professional assessment of his old friend and mentor, the blind fellow of Trinity Hall, who had held the Cambridge chair of political economy since 1863 and the appointment of examiner in the subject at the University of London for almost as long. Henry Fawcett belonged to an earlier generation of Cambridge dons and was wholly detached from the revolution in economic ideas that gathered momentum in the 1870s. Like Keynes he came from provincial middle-class

7. Nicholson's successful essay was published the following year and almost certainly supported his elevation to the Edinburgh chair. In the preface to the 2nd (1892) edition of his *Effect of Machinery on Wages* he acknowledged that he had written his Cobden essay while 'deeply impressed with the value of the historical method as exemplified in England by Thorold Rogers and Cliffe Leslie'.

origins. His father was a politically active Salisbury lawyer who electioneered for the Liberals, his mother a solicitor's daughter. When young Henry went up to Cambridge in 1852 his heart was set on a political career. He aimed at a college fellowship because it would give him income and time to read for the law – a profession that could support him until he found a parliamentary seat, as well as when he was returned as an unpaid Liberal MP. Starting as he did from a good school record in mathematics, he chose that tripos as his safest route through the rigid system of competitive examinations which characterized Cambridge in the mid-nineteenth century. By 1856, when Fawcett had achieved the status of seventh wrangler and won his Trinity Hall fellowship (bringing with it an assured income of £250 a year), he had already learned to speak effectively on political issues at Cambridge Union debates and had entered Lincoln's Inn with the object of being called to the Bar. He was then reading himself into his parliamentary role – basing his political philosophy and economics on a simplistic interpretation of J.S. Mill's doctrines and building up his knowledge of practical policy issues from newspapers and reports of parliamentary debates. His further education was suddenly interrupted, however, by a tragic shooting accident which blinded him in 1858. By then he had had a limited undergraduate training in mathematics but had hardly begun to acquire a basis of knowledge in the law. In any case, he saw no future for a blind barrister and, in June 1860, he abandoned his legal studies.

It was symptomatic of the academic standing of political economy in Cambridge University in the 1860s that it was more realistic for a blind wrangler to aspire to the only chair in economics than to cram for a sequence of law exams. At a stage when most Cambridge dons with academic ambitions would have been extending their intellectual horizons and filling the yawning gaps in their examination-dominated undergraduate education, Henry Fawcett found himself obliged to depend on others reading to him, and on dictating rather than writing out his arguments. Partly from sheer force of circumstances then, and partly because of his practical policy-orientated interest in economics, he went on to develop his understanding of the subject within exceedingly narrow confines. He relied almost exclusively on Mill's *Principles of Political Economy* for the sketchy theoretical framework of his economic analysis as well as for his grasp of David Ricardo's *Principles of Political Economy and Taxation* (1817) or Thomas Malthus's *Essay on the Principle of Population* (1798). He accepted Mill's *System of Logic* as definitive on scientific method and was totally convinced by Mill's writings on political philosophy. Although his blindness severely restricted the range of his access to contemporary economic writing and new ideas, it did not prevent him from actively participating in economic debate at the annual meetings of the British Association for the Advancement of Science. So, in 1860, when

Alexander Macmillan – who had already accepted several of Fawcett's lively politico-economic articles for *Macmillan's Magazine* – encouraged him to write an introduction to political economy, designed to provide the general reader with a down-to-earth exposition of Mill's *Principles*, he took the advice with enthusiasm. At that time, the incumbent professor of political economy at Cambridge was George Pryme (himself an MP from 1833–41) who had set abysmal standards of academic performance since his appointment to the chair in 1828 and who was now beginning to decline in health. Fawcett was shrewd enough to recognize that writing a textbook that could be intelligible to poll men would enhance his prospects of being elected to the chair when it became vacant. In the event, Fawcett's *Manual of Political Economy* had just been published when Pryme at last resigned, and the initial reviews were favourable. He was well known and personally popular among the Cambridge resident fellows who constituted a large part of the electoral roll for the professorship. Moreover, as an articulate and regular member of the London Political Economy Club since 1861, he could cite an impressive list of friendly referees, such as J.S. Mill, Thorold Rogers, Cliffe Leslie, W. Newmarch and W.T. Thornton.

It was fortunate for Fawcett that he was pursuing his academic ambitions in Cambridge rather than Oxford and that his chance to compete for the chair arose in the 1860s rather than the 1870s. In contrast to Oxford, where divisive theological controversies dominated the academic scene, Cambridge of the 1850s and the early 1860s was characterized by a respect for hearty common sense and by a religious tolerance that was close to indifference. Fawcett faithfully reflected the prevailing ethos. At the same time the methodological divisions that were to erode the orthodox classical consensus in the 1870s and 1880s had not yet ruffled the image of a solidly grounded science of political economy, created by Smith, extended by Malthus and Ricardo and authenticated by Mill. This was a comfortable ambiance for an economist whose authority was founded on Mill's *Principles*. The professorship gave Fawcett (then in his late twenties) a respectable platform from which to speak publicly on economic questions and an assured income (along with his fellowship) of about £550 a year in return for 18 weekly lectures to poll men, that is, to a conscript audience of ordinary degree candidates.[8] It was an ideal launch-pad for a parliamentary career and after several unsuccessful election attempts Fawcett was returned as MP for Brighton in 1865 – at the General Election which put J.S. Mill into parliament as member for Westminster. Except for a brief interruption in 1874, when he was defeated for Brighton in

8. Until 1876 the majority of Cambridge undergraduates were reading for an ordinary (rather than an honours degree). These so-called 'poll men' were obliged to sit through a minimum number of professorial lectures in order to qualify.

February and elected for Hackney in April, Fawcett remained a member of the House until he died in 1884. It is unlikely, however, that any of the honours men reading political economy for the moral sciences tripos would have attended Fawcett's lectures, though Neville had taken the time to read the professor's *Manual* in January 1875.

It was thus not surprising that the 1875 Senior Moralist, a convert to Alfred Marshall's deductive style of economic analysis, was unimpressed by the Cambridge professor's competence to examine postgraduate political economists – either for the London MA or the Cobden essay. Nevertheless, on a September afternoon walk with his old friend (before the Cobden award had been decided), Keynes listened with interest to Fawcett's characteristically uninhibited account of the examiners' struggles to agree on which of eight anonymously submitted essays (each identified by an obscure motto) deserved to win the prize. According to the Diary:

> Fawcett told me in all probability the Cobden Prize would not now be awarded, as the examiners could not agree in their verdict, and also because the regulations seemed to require that the same essay must be best both in matter and in literary style in order to gain the prize. Cliffe Leslie and Phear thought Nicholson's essay (I made it out to be his) best in matter, Fawcett an essay bearing the motto 'Deus ex machina'. My essay was nowhere. I was not surprised and scarcely disappointed. I still think a good essay could have been made out of the materials, but I see more and more clearly that the arrangement was quite sufficient to down it; the essay moreover was far too long, there were too many quotations and the materials were not sufficiently assimilated and welded into one whole; they were put together too mechanically. This failure may prove a very valuable lesson to me in any future work I may attempt.

Before then, Neville had derived some slight comfort from a typically barbed piece of Marshallian flattery. According to the Diary for 10 July: 'Whatever the result of the Cobden Prize I have the satisfaction of knowing that Marshall thinks me the best political economist he has recently had to teach though my style is inferior'.[9] However, the context for the flattery ensured that it would be received with due reserve. Marshall had called,

9. The reference to Keynes's 'style' was the pot calling the kettle black! See the letter dated 14 April from Macmillan to Marshall, telling him what their reader had thought of the manuscript of his projected book on foreign trade: 'as regards the style, his judgement is that though fairly clear it wants vividness and the reader is not carried along. Perhaps the word that might convey best what he means might be that it is rather too meditative, as if you were thinking your own thoughts without fully bearing in mind the audience … I would suggest reading bits of it aloud to a friend and seeing where and in what way he found it hard to understand'. The original of this masterpiece of tactful criticism is in the Marshall Library Papers 2: 37. It is quoted at length in J.K. Whitaker, *The Early Economic Writings of Alfred Marshall, 1867–1890*, Vol. I (London: Macmillan, 1975), p. 60.

bringing more chapters of his projected first book for Keynes to 'look over',[10] and brandishing copies of the testimonials supporting his own application for the post of principal and chair of political economy at Bristol. Marshall's impending marriage to Mary Paley was then driving him to seek alternative employment. He could have remained a lecturer at St John's, but its statutes (as of most Cambridge colleges) insisted on celibacy as a condition of fellowship;[11] and the stipend of a college lecturer was about £100 less than that of a fellow.[12] Nor did it carry such valuable board and lodging entitlements. Given Marshall's lean private means, and his marriage plans, the prospect of losing his fellowship had such serious financial implications that he actually toyed briefly with the absurd notion of applying for the ritual university post of Esquire Bedell, which fell vacant in April 1877. At that point he asked Keynes to canvass in support of his candidacy. Perhaps Mary Paley talked him out of it. At any rate, Neville wrote with some amusement in the Diary of 25 April: 'Marshall decided after all not to become a candidate for the Esquire Bedellship. He said "The more I look at the poker the less I like it"'.[13]

Excluding his abortive attempt to win the Cobden prize, Neville's first academic year as a Pembroke fellow was both rewarding and relaxed. He had leisure to enjoy the varied social events that made Cambridge such a pleasant domicile for an outgoing young man with a wide circle of friends and no money problems. He continued to participate in some of the university and college societies which he had joined as an undergraduate – for example, the Chess Club, the Whist Club and the Shakespeare-reading group. As a resident senior member of one of 18 male collegiate communities, he enjoyed a succession of invitations to feasts at which Cambridge dons entertained, or were entertained by, their counterparts. At Christ's, for example, where he was guest of a school friend, he admired the 'fine show of plate in their Combination Room'. At St John's he was proud to be Marshall's guest in his first term and Foxwell's later in the year. Whenever the weather was clement he took long walks in the vicinity of Cambridge with old and new companions – most often with blind Professor Fawcett or young Harry Bond. He

10. Marshall never completed the book on foreign trade on the grounds that 'it will never make a comfortable book in its present shape'. See the letter quoted by Whitaker (1975), p. 62.
11. Not all: and the changes in college statutes were introduced piecemeal. See Christopher Brooke, *A History of the University of Cambridge, 1870–1990* (Cambridge: Cambridge University Press, 1993), Vol. 4, p. 254: 'By 1886 the fellows of Caius had been allowed to marry for twenty six years'.
12. See Whitaker (1975), p. 19, fn 46.
13. The Esquire Bedell is the functionary who carries the mace, heads honorary degree processions and generally officiates at Cambridge degree ceremonies. It is hard to visualize Alfred Marshall competently performing this essentially ritual function.

remained in close touch with his London and Salisbury friends. On regular trips to 'keep terms' at the Middle Temple, for example, he usually stayed with Ingham, a London undergraduate contemporary, who joined him in visits to theatres. In mid-November 1876 he spent two nights in Salisbury to attend the meeting of the City Council at which his father was elected mayor and to help host the celebration lunch which each new mayor gave to councillors and their relatives. Meanwhile Cambridge offered Neville not only the comforts and companionship of collegiate life, but also a continuously warm welcome at the Bonds' hospitable family home on Brookside – only a short step from Pembroke.

In the unreformed decade of the 1870s, dons and undergraduates for whom the December tripos examinations represented the climax of their working year, could relax when the day of judgement lay half a year or more away – a prospect rendered more distant by an intervening summer vacation.[14] The Easter term was then the merriest in the academic year. The poll men faced examinations towards the end of May, but they were unlikely to let these relatively easy tests spoil their enjoyment of the concerts, bumps, balls, garden parties and other festive occasions that filled the Easter term. Dons found even serious honours men undemanding at this time of year, although many of the women continued to call for individual teaching and advice. On 3 May, for example, Neville wrote: 'I play tennis every day when I have not to go to Girton'. He then had two women taking lessons from him in the more distant women's college. One was the diligent Miss Constance Jones, whom he had already coached for over a year, and to whom he was still sending question papers for assessment in July. Half a century later, when Dr Keynes retired as university registrary, she was Mistress of Girton, and his speech recalled publicly: 'the trepidation with which I gave instruction to this lady, accompanied by the click of the knitting needles of Miss Bernard, then Mistress of the College, who in conformity with the conventions of those days, thought it unsuitable to leave us tête à tête'.[15] Another Girtonian who was still coming to him in May 1877 was the 'transcendental Miss Borchardt' who had, he considered, 'an exalted opinion of herself'. Worse still, she expressed highly unconventional views. 'She is a decidedly advanced thinker' he commented on 4 May, and added with uneasily sexist disapproval: 'There is something

14. But see Brooke (1993), p. 298: 'In 1880 the university, hell-bent on educational reform, suddenly moved the main season of exams from January to May, sending May Week flying as they came. But not to a great distance, for May Week has been in June ever since'.

15. The speech, reprinted in full in F.A. Keynes, *Gathering Up the Threads* (Cambridge: Heffer & Sons, 1950) pp. 109–14, was made in Pembroke College Hall on the occasion of the presentation to the university of Sir Gerald Kelly's portrait of him. Constance Jones became Mistress of Girton in 1903.

repulsive to me in an avowed infidelity in a girl, though I dare say the feeling cannot be justified'.[16]

Castle Street was still home to Neville during his first academic year as a Cambridge don and he returned there each vacation; but his sense of belonging to the Salisbury social community was fast weakening. The seasonal junketings that had dominated earlier entries in his Diary during Christmas vacations attracted little notice now. The Williams girls had fallen into prosaic perspective; of an evening spent at Moorland House (their family home) he wrote merely: 'I like Bessie's singing very much. Flossie's singing is painful to listen to'. Such familial evenings occupied less of his time than ever before. Indeed, Neville spent the evening of Christmas Day 1876 playing billiards at a club he had joined, rather that at his own or some other family home. The high spot of that vacation was a visit from Alfred West with whom he spent a dismally wet day at Stonehenge, resuming their absorbing discussion (begun four weeks previously in Cambridge) of the 1876 tripos results. On the way back to Pembroke in January 1877, Keynes broke his journey to spend a couple of days with Ingham in London – where he kept another Middle Temple term and enjoyed Ellen Terry's 'delightful' performance at the Court Theatre.

Nor did the Easter vacation in Salisbury prove at all memorable. Neville spent longer there than he might otherwise have done 'to keep Aunt Mary company' while his parents were holidaying in Scotland. The Diary records that on one occasion Ernest, Emily and Edith Williams came to Castle Street to make up a set at lawn tennis with him; and that a few days later he took tea and supper at Moorland House where he played billiards with the head of the house and whist with younger members of the family. Letters from Cambridge increasingly held more interest for him than local encounters and social events. For the first part of the summer vacation Neville brought Henry Bond, then working for the 1877 historical tripos, back to Castle Street with him. The Diary for 27 July described how they spent their days:

> After breakfast I do a little work at Marshall's book – get on slowly at this, however – writing is very much inferior to print in giving one a connected view of a book and one much sooner gets tired of reading it. Marshall's style of composition is base, or rather he has no style. About 12 Frank [Tiffin] comes and we go to

16. Neville never warmed to Miss Borchardt, though he admired her pluck and worked hard teaching her. Their last coaching session was on 23 November when he wrote: 'My last time with Miss Borchardt and I was not sorry for it'. She wrote the 1877 moral science papers and was put in the second class. After getting this news from the examiners at Sidgwick's dinner party, Neville went at once to her Cambridge lodgings to tell her personally: 'She was very excited indeed when I went in and did not seem absolutely satisfied with the result, altho she had asked me only a fortnight before whether I did not think she had better scratch altogether. Sidgwick seemed to think, and I agreed with him, that she had got her deserts'.

> the club to play billiards. Bond works all the morning for his Historical Tripos. After dinner, billiards or books. In the evening lawn tennis finishing up with going on the river. … Ernest Williams … sometimes joins us. This evening at Moorland House. On our way home I astonished them by climbing a lamp post.

In August, Keynes joined Ingham and they started out together on a long walking holiday in Scotland.

2 DONS DIVIDED BY UNIVERSITY REFORM

After being distinguished as Senior Moralist in the December 1875 tripos, Keynes had to wait in limbo for almost eight months before Pembroke elected him a fellow. He already knew – as did the rest of the Cambridge academic community – that a major reform in the financial relationship between the university and its constituent colleges was imminent. What was quite uncertain, however, was: how revolutionary the inevitable constitutional changes would be, when they could be expected to take effect and what might be the implications for the financial situation of individual colleges and their fellows.

The process of change had been triggered in January 1872 when William Gladstone appointed the second of two Royal Commissions on Oxford and Cambridge. The prime minister was then responding to urgent lobbying from a minority of Oxbridge dons, who were passionately concerned to improve standards of teaching and scholarship in the two ancient universities. Their efforts were frustrated, however, by the fact that the disposable wealth of both universities was largely controlled by their independent colleges, most of whose governing bodies had absolutely no interest in funding projects of education or research at the university level. Gladstone's Commission was asked simply to 'inquire into the property and incomes, belonging to, administered or enjoyed by the Universities of Oxford and Cambridge and the colleges and halls therein … and also to report on the uses to which such property and incomes are applied'.[17] When its report finally appeared in 1874, it lit the fuse of an explosive controversy that raged inside and outside the two universities under investigation. For it revealed that, in both, a substantial proportion of university resources was going to elected fellows whose life-time rights to a share in their college's annual dividend were unattached to any useful function – academic or otherwise. They were not even required to reside in or teach for their college – though, on election, most of them would have had to pay lip-service to the doctrine of the established church.

17. D.A. Winstanley, *Later Victorian Cambridge* (Cambridge: Cambridge University Press, 1946), p. 246.

Henry Sidgwick, one of the leading advocates of academic reform in Cambridge, spelt out the consequences of this situation in an article published in the April 1876 *Contemporary Review*. He wrote with informed passion:

> This University has for years been struggling and starving in the most pitiable manner, unable to provide decently for the most indispensable functions, while what are commonly talked and thought of as 'her rich endowments' have been distributed among thriving schoolmasters, school inspectors, rising journalists, barristers full of briefs, and barristers who never work for briefs. Many most important branches of study are not represented at all within the limits of the University; several more are inadequately and precariously represented by college lecturers only. The Professorships that do exist, outside the sacred and fruitful precincts of theology are supported by incomes varying in amount from a third to a fifth of the salary of a county court judge. The utmost economy is unable to provide Cambridge with a sufficiency even of the ugliest buildings required for scientific teaching and research in the present stage of the progress of knowledge.'[18]

He then quoted statistics collected by a fellow and tutor of Jesus who showed that, of more than 300 fellows elected to Cambridge colleges from 1857–68 inclusive, only about a quarter 'have adopted an academic career; most of these are now resident in Cambridge, either as holding college offices or as private tutors, while a few others have obtained professorships elsewhere'.[19] All of them, however, whether resident in or out of Cambridge, whether in paid employment or not, were entitled to a full share in the annual distribution of their college's dividend.

Moreover, according to Sidgwick, Cambridge's problem was not merely that university reform was effectively paralysed by the severely limited fraction of its total resources at the disposal of its central bodies. He went on to lament the fact that the pursuit of knowledge for its own sake was being smothered by the system of prize fellowships. Competition between colleges to attract the cleverest among each year's crop of new graduates, and competition between ambitious undergraduates to win the life-time income that came with a fellowship, was destroying the true spirit of scholarship. He insisted that 'the University should be, as it were, a shrine in which the noble ardour of disinterested curiosity is kept ever burning and communicated in each generation of students to all who are in any degree capable of receiving it'[20] and he stressed:

> [H]ow difficult it is to resist the strong perpetual pressure exercised on the minds of teachers and pupils alike, by this fatal possession of large pecuniary prizes for

18. H. Sidgwick, 'Idle Fellowships', *The Contemporary Review*, April 1876, p. 679.
19. Ibid., p. 685.
20. Ibid., p. 688.

> successful study as tested by examinations. It is almost inevitable that the pursuit of knowledge should gradually be turned into a training for an intellectual wrestling match … . Examination, instead of being merely the means of testing the thoroughness with which a subject has been taught and learned, becomes the end to which teaching and research are directed.

Thus the student's chief aim had become 'not so much to know truth as to be able to write it out rapidly in fragments of a certain size'. In these circumstances a talented young man who

> very likely would prefer on other grounds to enter for one of the new Triposes … is led to choose one of the older lines of study because he rightly thinks he is more sure of obtaining a Fellowship by distinction in these; and he is more sure of this because that College rightly thinks that the competition in these older lines is more keen, and that there is consequently more security that the men who attain distinction in them will be men of real ability.[21]

Keynes had undoubtedly read this article in the *Contemporary Review*, and he was certainly familiar with Sidgwick's views, which had encouraged his own brave decision to escape from mathematics to morals at the end of his first undergraduate year.

By the time the Royal Commission had completed its report, Gladstone had been succeeded as prime minister by Benjamin Disraeli, so that it fell to the latter's conservative administration to design the legislation required to solve the problems presented by two undeservedly prestigious English universities. The Universities of Oxford and Cambridge Act, which became law in August 1877, was designed to channel an increasing share of substantial collegiate funds in directions which could improve standards of learning, teaching and research in both universities, and also finance the libraries, museums, scientific equipment and other relevant facilities essential to a modern institution of higher education. Statutory commissions were appointed in each centre to rewrite university and college statutes and to set up appropriate administrative structures. The Cambridge University Commission was chaired by Sir Alexander Cockburn (then Lord Chief Justice) and the secretaryship was shared between G.W.F. Browne (then secretary of the Local Examinations and Lectures Syndicate), and Henry Davidson (a lawyer who was a fellow and former bursar of Trinity Hall). The commissioners, all of whom were Cambridge graduates, included four senior wranglers, one Senior Classic and a parliamentary representative: among them were two current professors – J.B. Lightfoot (a theologian) and G.G. Stokes (a mathematician); a former college head – Philpott, currently Bishop of Worcester; and Lord Rayleigh, a former fellow of Trinity (until his marriage in 1871), later to

21. Ibid., p. 689.

become Cavendish Professor of Experimental Physics. The fourth senior wrangler was G.W. Hemming, who acquired the reputation of being prejudiced against the colleges.[22] Together they constituted an undeniably distinguished body of formidably self-confident individuals.

The Act gave the colleges until the end of 1878 to redraft their own statutes for approval by the commissioners. Each college had the right to appoint three of its fellows to be ad hoc commissioners when its new statutes were finally approved or imposed; but it was carefully stipulated that college commissioners should never constitute a majority at any meeting of the Commission. Whilst the separate Cambridge colleges wrestled bad-temperedly with the task of revision, the commissioners themselves spent the interval discussing and coordinating appropriate general objectives and solutions with their Oxford counterparts. According to Browne: 'The most pressing of the questions were of a financial nature' and he listed six examples:

> (1) What did they think the University ought to provide 'in the interests of education, religion, learning and research'; (2) what did that imply in terms of additional university revenues and sources; (3) where should the revenues come from; (4) how should the college contribution be raised; (5) should all colleges contribute in proportion to their prospective revenues; (6) should it be uniform each year

and so on.[23] The statutory commissioners gradually developed a joint view of what main kinds of constitutional change needed to be made. According to Christopher Brooke:

> [they] set their faces to limit tenure to six years; and also by ending the rule of celibacy and the insistence on orders, to make teaching fellowships more attractive to a wider variety of belief or disbelief, seeking to make a lifelong profession of university teaching.[24]

The modern generation of dons, who were totally committed to education, learning and/or research, cooperated readily enough with the statutory commissioners; they shared their broad objectives, though they might differ on the details of the statutes designed to secure those aims. On the other hand, many of the older dons resented – on principle – any government intervention in college statutes. Dr G.E. Corrie, for example, Master of Jesus 1849–85, was one of the older generation of theologians. He responded to the commissioners' questionnaire by announcing: 'the present chief want of the University is exemption from the disturbing power of Royal and Parliamentary Commis-

22. D.A. Winstanley, *Later Victorian Cambridge* (1947), p. 307.
23. G.W.F. Browne, *The Recollections of a Bishop* (London: Smith & Elder, 1915), p. 168.
24. Brooke (1993), pp. 88–9.

sioners'.[25] Most heads of houses realized that some reduction in the financial and constitutional freedom of colleges was now inevitable. They focused on minimizing change in directions they found particularly objectionable. When the long series of agonizing meetings to revise the statutes was over, Dr E. Perowne (Master of Corpus Christi), who as vice-chancellor had been at the heart of the bitterest battles, wrote to Browne, secretary to the Commission, thanking him personally for all he had done

> to reduce to a minimum what has been terribly painful to some, difficult to many, troublesome to all. ... I am not satisfied – God forbid I should be! – with the doings of the Commissioners. My heart is very very sad, well-nigh broken. But I try to see in this alleviation of the trial of which I write, a token for good, which I humbly and gratefully acknowledge.[26]

During the years 1878–81 when the Cambridge statutory commissioners were trying to reconcile 17 independent college governing bodies to the reforms necessary to implement the intentions of the 1877 Act, Keynes's position in the political spectrum was not in doubt. As a young nonconformist moralist, deeply impressed by Henry Sidgwick and strongly motivated to becoming a professional university lecturer, he was on the side of the reformers. As a fellow of Pembroke his position was more complex, for changes in the conditions of tenure of college fellows would certainly affect his income and might well force him out of his fellowship. So he continued to keep options open at the Middle Temple, and in early January sat for the Bar examination in Roman Law, for which he had crammed so conscientiously during his Christmas vacation in Salisbury. 'The examination was conducted in the most extraordinarily casual way' he wrote in the Diary for 5 January: 'When I first saw the paper I thought of retiring immediately but finding that I could translate the passages of Latin that were given us, I plucked up more courage. I had my viva voce from Dr Waraker and did not enjoy it'. Being no doubt a more experienced examinee than most of the other candidates, he passed the test, and went on to eat more of the obligatory dinners at the Middle Temple before returning to Cambridge at the end of January.

The Pembroke fellowship embarked on the agony of root-and-branch revision of college statutes at a series of extraordinary Saturday meetings in the Lent term of 1878. When the meetings started, Neville was distracted by the

25. A. Gray and F. Brittain, *History of Jesus College Cambridge* (London: Heinemann, 1960), p. 168.
26. Browne (1915), p. 225. What had grieved Perowne above all else was his failure to shake the commissioners in their determination to leave open the possibility that the Corpus fellowship might one day elect as their Master 'any person irrespective of his religious beliefs and professions, so that the Mastership may be held by an avowed atheist'. See Winstanley (1947), p. 257, where Perowne's protest is quoted together with the information that he was not the only head of house who had protested on these grounds.

fact that his father was terminally ill in Salisbury. The first took place on Saturday 16 February. According to the Diary:

> I stayed at Cambridge till this evening to attend our college meeting for the revision of Statutes. But no vote was taken and I might just as well have been away. We talked chiefly of married fellows. The Master says that the present introduction of women into the University is a very serious evil; their influence is pernicious; their society and the parties that are given to and for them are demoralising for those who wish to study; they have a preponderance that they ought not to have and members of the University have been unable to find room at Prof. [S.] Colvin's lectures because they are so crowded with Ladies. Searle says that the Master is suffering under the preponderance of women personally, and it is this that makes him so bitter!

In the end the college meeting and after-dinner discussion went on so long that he spent the night in London (having missed the rail connection to Salisbury) – only to learn, when he arrived home on Sunday that his father had died the previous day. His family had not telegraphed him because 'they wished me on no account to miss the college meeting on Saturday'.

In view of his father's condition, Keynes had already arranged for colleagues to take over his teaching for the rest of the Lent term, so that he could stay with his mother in Salisbury. He returned weekly for the Saturday meetings, missing only the one that fell in the week of his father's funeral. On 2 March he noted with satisfaction that there had been no voting at the missed meeting: 'as my vote is now of the utmost importance'. Then, and in the entries for each of the following Saturdays, he listed the issues that were brought to a vote. Occasionally he commented on the result or on remarks that seemed to him significant; for example, on 16 March:

> We were principally concerned with determining the conditions of life fellowship. The Master will not vote on any questions concerned directly or indirectly with our decision on the matrimonial question. Searle says that the tutorship is not worth more than £500 a year.

On 23 March he noted: 'We decided that the Governing Body shd in future as heretofore be the Master and all the Fellows: and also that there should be four clerical fellows'. By then the Pembroke fellows were suffering from severe statute fatigue and at the last college meeting of the Lent term they turned their attention instead to current building projects: 'We decided not to pull down the first court and not to employ Waterhouse any more'. There was only one college meeting in the Easter term and that ended, according to the Diary, 'without any important results being arrived at. We decided amongst other things that we shd pray and sing a hymn before proceeding to the election of a Master'.

They were left with a number of highly contentious issues to be resolved. These were dealt with during the Whitsuntide break in a daily sequence of heated meetings beginning on 10 June. On the first day they considered a matter of personal concern to Neville who, on the death of his father, had become a man of property. The Diary reported: '*The principal votes on Monday were that there should be a property limitation* [on fellows' entitlement to stipends] … This is not to include savings, but only what comes by way of gift or inheritance'. The amount agreed was £600 and Keynes was in the minority who voted for a higher limit. On that day tempers flared painfully: '[G.] Henderson was very rude to [T.H.] Orpen and also to Searle. The latter got very excited, said that Henderson's remarks were offensive and if they were repeated he should leave the meeting'. On 11 June the majority carried the following propositions: (1) that an optional profession of faith on admission should be introduced into statutes. On this the Master's vote was decisive and Keynes was predictably in the minority; (2) that it should be possible for some university officials to become permanent fellows; and (3) that £300 should be the limiting stipend attached to a fellowship. After summarizing the results in the Diary Neville commented irritably: 'Under the influence of Searle and [C.H.] Prior, Orpen is becoming a satisfactorily orthodox voter; and in his votes I think he looks after his own interests. I have little to hope from Searle. He speaks very contemptuously of college readers this afternoon'. On 12 June the Master's stipend was fixed at £1200 by a slim majority, five in favour, three against and three abstentions; Keynes voted against (this time with Orpen and Searle) on the grounds that it had already been decided that the Master should normally also be principal tutor. They also decided that 'at least two of the defined college officers (exclusive of the Master) should reside in college during term'. Finally two matrimonial issues, on both of which Neville abstained, were carried: (1) 'That the Principal Tutor shd be unmarried (unless the Master)' … and (2) '*We decided (in spite of opposition) that no fellow should be allowed to bring his wife and family to reside in college thereby precluding the possibility of houses being built in college for married fellows*'. The following day an exhausted governing body reverted once more to building matters on which they could agree without friction. According to the Diary: 'We decided to employ Mr Gilbert Scott junior to put the first court in order and to build an entirely new set of rooms on the Tennis Court'.

It had been a gruelling experience for the small community of Pembroke fellows and they did not reassemble as a governing body until the afternoon of 25 October 1878, when a complete draft of the revised statutes was tabled. By then, Neville's struggle to decide whether he was in love with Fanny Hoyle (a flamboyant Newnhamite reading for the moral sciences tripos), largely crowded out of the Diary almost two days of meetings ending on

Saturday 26 October. He did, however, note with satisfaction: 'We abolished the Property Disqualification Clause'. The revised statutes were formally approved for despatch to the commissioners on 10 December. For the rest of the 1878/79 academic year, college affairs rarely merited more than a glancing reference in the Diary, although the frequency with which Searle's name recurs leaves no doubt that his personality and influence exercised as strong an impression on Keynes as a fellow as they had when he was an undergraduate. On 14 May, for example, he noted anxiously: 'Young Ward tells me that Searle the tutor has practically been refusing men at Pembroke because they are dissenters. I hope this is not true'. However, on 25 May he wrote: 'Bump supper in the Hall. ... Searle presided and was an extraordinary success. He made 3 or 4 of the best after dinner speeches I have ever heard ... and all the men went away more convinced than ever that he is the best tutor in the University'. A week later he reported: 'I have been talking with Searle about lecturing next year and he treated me quite differently from what I expected. He promised to let me have a lecture room at any rate; and perhaps he will recognise me as a lecturer with a nominal stipend'. On 10 October 1879, moreover, Keynes was elected to the college office of bursar which put him in charge of the kitchen and buttery accounts. During the 1879 summer vacation he had moved into the rooms vacated by Orpen, which were more spacious and comfortable than his own. Accordingly, at the beginning of the academic year 1879/80, he wrote cheerfully:

> My front room will look better when it has some books and pictures in it. At present ... it is in danger of looking too much like an upholsterer's showroom. We have 40 freshmen so that we are on the way to being one of the largest colleges after Trinity and John's.

Orpen's rooms brought with them a new bedmaker who was to cherish the young don devotedly. 'Mrs Prime quite answers to her name', he wrote approvingly on 17 October, 'I believe she is in every respect the best bedmaker in the University'.

All this seemed to augur a stronger attachment to his college on the part of the young nonconformist. Circumstances had changed, however, in ways that were eventually to detach Keynes from Pembroke. As the fellows reluctantly argued through the statute revisions, they were forced to confront ideological and political differences which had barely surfaced in the past, but which had exploded into unforgettably angry scenes in 1878 when their privileged life style was threatened. In the aftermath, Neville himself rarely referred in the Diary to the further arguments provoked, in most college combination rooms, by the schemes then being ventilated by the commissioners who had to coordinate the changes at college and university level. However, on 20 November 1879, when it was suggested that Pembroke should accept into its fellowship a professor elected under the auspices of the Board of Moral Sciences, their solitary moralist declared his hand and found himself in the minority. According to the Diary: 'The University Commissioners propose to attach a professorship of Mental Philosophy and Logic to Pembroke. Searle, [W.] Burnside, Prior and [R.A.] Neil are very violent on the subject and we had a rather heated discussion in the Combination Room'.[27] Clearly Keynes's position in the divisive debates about reform of the relationship between the university and its colleges hinged more on his commitment to a university teaching faculty than on his loyalty to a traditional Anglican college.

It was the first college meeting of the 1880/81 academic year that brought home to Neville the fact that he was unlikely to retain his fellowship for more than two years. Under the old statutes he could have retained his fellowship for life, so long as he remained celibate; but he had already announced his engagement to Florence Brown in the summer of 1880. Under the new statutes (designed to come into force in 1882) the tenure of a college fellowship was to be limited to six years – except in the case of certain college officers of whom the treasurer was one and the bursar was not. As bursar he had rescued the buttery and kitchen accounts from the sorry mess in which the previous incumbent had left them and had reason to expect that he would get the treasurer's job when it became vacant in a year's time. His hopes were dashed on 11 October. After reporting that the meeting had re-elected him bursar, Keynes added ruefully:

> According to what was I think a cut and dried scheme between Searle and Prior, Burnside was appointed assistant treasurer; and I am afraid that destroys my chances of ever becoming treasurer. I was quite surprised to find that Burnside was willing to take office at all. And what is annoying is that I believe he will not hold it for long, but just long enough to keep me out of it.

Personally popular though he was, Pembroke's nonconformist moralist had failed to slot into any of the alliances that formed among its fellows during the in-fighting over the statutes and the subsequent reforms. Consequently the fact that he was obviously the most competent of them all to serve as treasurer was not enough to ensure that he would eventually be elected to the only post (apart from senior tutor) that could guarantee him a life fellowship.

Neville thus urgently needed to identify the alternative sources of income he would need to set up home for Florence and himself when his fellowship lapsed in 1882. His colleagues in the moral sciences faculty were already concerned for him. On 7 October, for example, he wrote:

27. Similar debates were raging in other college combination rooms. See the Diary for 26 November 1877: 'Everybody is talking now of the scheme proposed by the University Commissioners and most of the criticisms are adverse'.

> Sidgwick wants to know what I propose doing when I am married. He points out quite truly that I cannot have much chance of a readership for some time to come. If one is offered in Logic Venn would get it, if in Political Economy Marshall. I told him, however, that if I could get work to bring in say £200 a year I shd be satisfied, at any rate for the present. This ought not to be difficult. As Venn remarks Cambridge is a good place for a man who will be content with 'pickings' having a private income to fall back upon. Both Sidgwick and Venn think my prospects wd be improved if I were to 'write a book'; and the latter thinks that a textbook of Logic such as I was proposing to write is very much wanted.

Keynes himself was increasingly attracted by the prospect of an administrative appointment in Cambridge. So, when William Cunningham, then assistant secretary to the Local Examinations Syndicate, announced his intention of resigning the post, Neville expressed an interest in applying for it. His mentors advised so strongly against that he hesitated. For example, on 21 February 1881: 'Sidgwick called to advise me not to go for the assistant secretaryship, implying that I was worth something better'. The next day: 'Searle also advised me not to go for the assistant secretaryship: and I have made up my mind not to do so. Yet I am sorry. I think I could do a secretary's work well and that it is the only work for which I am really fitted'. The following day, however, he decided to revert to his own best judgement when: 'Cunningham called to advise me to be a candidate for the assistant secretaryship, saying that from what he hears he thinks I have a very good chance of getting it. So I shall after all send in my name to the VC'. This he did. Immediately after the syndicate meeting on 5 March 1881, G.W.F. Browne sent him a note saying that the 'Syndicate has elected you to the Assistant Secretaryship – an appointment very agreeable to me'. Neville was to learn a few days later from Cunningham, who gave him an account of the syndicate meeting, that Sidgwick spoke strongly in his favour and that the Pembroke member on the syndicate praised his business capacity.

Before he landed the university post, however, a potentially more interesting possibility had presented itself. In November 1880, W.S. Jevons resigned the London chair of political economy at University College. At first Keynes hesitated to pursue the matter because Foxwell, who had several years more experience than himself, announced an intention to stand. In the event Neville decided to seek support (and testimonials) from his seniors – partly because Foxwell assured his pupil and friend that he was happy to 'run in competition with him', but mainly because he was emboldened by the advice he got – from Sidgwick in particular – and by the unexpectedly warm testimonials he collected. According to the Diary for 16 November 1881: 'Sidgwick writes "I wish you success and will certainly give you a testimonial. I do not personally know any man in whose hands I wd rather see the work, Marshall being out of the question"'. About Marshall's testimonial, Neville wrote on 9 February: 'Marshall has sent me a wonderful testimonial so much too good that I am ashamed to use it'. He must have known that both Marshall and Sidgwick were also providing testimonials for Foxwell. What he could not have known was that Marshall's recommendation for Foxwell was more glowing and convincing than the one he found flattering to himself.[28] In any case Neville decided to withdraw from the contest as soon as he knew that he had got the assistant secretaryship at the Locals Syndicate.

Although he wrote on 9 March:' I shall be sorry not to go in for my contest for the University College Professorship – partly because I shall not now be able to use my testimonials!', he seems to have settled for the less adventurous option without any sense of disappointment – either then or later. The fact was that in 1881 the London chair was neither financially nor professionally attractive to a 29-year-old academic, on the brink of radical changes opening up in his own university and endowed with sufficient private resources to build a new house for the bride he expected to wed within a very few months. The secretaryship promised an annual stipend of £100 (which was actually raised to £250 in May 1883). Jevons himself thought of his London chair as 'almost an honorary one'. Foxwell (being single) could combine it with a John's fellowship and the London Newmarch lectureship, and could continue to enjoy college board and lodging privileges for most of the year; even in full term he did not normally have to spend more than three days a week in London.

Meanwhile, there had been a crucial change at Pembroke. On 24 November 1880, the day that they buried their previous Master, John Power, the Pembroke fellows unanimously elected Searle to succeed him – the unseemly haste (according to the Diary) 'being necessitated by the Statutes'. Since Searle retained the post of senior tutor he now held a position of unprecedented power in the government of the college. Henceforth the Diary provided recurrent evidence of Neville's uneasiness at the direction in which the college was being taken. For example, on 6 April, he worried:

> I am sometimes doubtful whether we did not do the wrong thing in electing Searle to the Mastership. I fear jobbery. In a recent sermon in chapel he said – 'You may think that what we most care for is your intellectual welfare, And if you, coming up not members of the Church of England, influenced by our example and our lives, are induced to join our Communion, our delight will know no bounds!'.

There was still a possibility – after Keynes was elected college praelector in October 1881, as well as bursar – that the Pembroke governing body would

28. Marshall was then at University College Bristol. His testimonials for Keynes and Foxwell are both printed in J.K. Whitaker, *The Correspondence of Alfred Marshall, Economist*, Vol. I (Cambridge: Cambridge University Press, 1996), pp. 132–3.

declare him a 'half-timer' as the holder of two minor college posts. In that case he could have held his fellowship for longer than six years; however, such an interpretation of the statutes would have depended on the goodwill of the Master (among other clerics on the governing body), and was hardly likely to be exercised in favour of their sole nonconformist.

At last, on 10 May 1882, the ideological rift – based on a mixture of religious and political differences – between Keynes and Searle developed into an absurd public quarrel. According to the Diary:

> Before hall I had a serious row with the Master. I told him I was entering a bottle of champagne I had given on Monday; it was to have been in honour of Forster who I understood was returning to Ireland – but as this rumour was not correct I gave it in honour of Gladstone.[29]
>
> 'You will not do that'.
>
> 'Yes.'
>
> 'It is an affront to the combination room. Do not enter it.'
>
> 'You were not present when it was given and have no voice in the matter.'
>
> 'I shd have spat the wine out of my mouth – Do you put that man on a pinnacle of glory *now*? now that he is responsible for these murders?'
>
> 'I am pained and disgusted to hear you talk like that.'
>
> 'You put yourself in opposition to all in the combination room. You will not make an entry in the fine book.'
>
> 'I am doing so.'
>
> We hardly spoke during dinner. Fortunately Burnside came in and maintained the conversation. Directly after dinner the Master left. I told Burnside what had happened and he entirely sympathised with me. I hope some time elapses before I meet the Master again.'

Following this ill-tempered exchange, Keynes and Searle studiously avoided each other's company for several weeks. The Master was again gratuitously unpleasant in June, when Keynes was embarrassed before the vice-chancellor and registrary by a trivial error which he, as praelector, had committed when putting up Pembroke's degree candidates.[30] Peace was not restored until late

29. It was unusual for the amicable relationship between Searle and Keynes to be disturbed by the political gulf between the former's unswerving Tory principles and the latter's openly liberal stance on most issues. In May 1881, however, opinions on Irish Home Rule policy were suddenly inflamed by a notorious terrorist incident in Dublin. W.E. Forster had resigned as Irish Secretary on 2 May (the day that Gladstone decided to release the Irish nationalist leader Charles Parnell from prison). The Tory opponents of Home Rule were even further outraged after the new chief Secretary Lord Charles Cavendish and his under-secretary Thomas Burke, were assassinated on 6 May in Phoenix Park.
30. Keynes had signed a Supplicat for a Pembroke BA which entered incorrect initials and it was sent back to the college by an officious clerk stamped 'false supplication', the penalty for which was loss of vote and of power of acting, as praelector for two years. 'The Master made the most of it' Neville complained to the Diary. He apologized personally to the registrary and the vice-chancellor for his error, thus putting the matter right without further ado.

July, when Keynes's intention to put himself under the new statutes (thus finally relinquishing his fellowship) had appeared on the agenda for the college meeting due to take place in mid-August. On 25 July the Diary reported: 'The Master called on me today and was most affable. He thinks it entirely reasonable that I should keep my rooms until Christmas' – on the understanding of course that Keynes would continue to perform the duties of praelector and bursar till then. Two days later, the Master handed over a peace offering in the form of a fine wedding present, described in the Diary as: 'a stationery case and candlesticks made out of the old oak of the college and nicely carved with the college arms – a very appropriate and acceptable present'. On 12 August the Diary reported:

> I put myself under the new statutes and so ceased to be a fellow. Farewell dinner in hall with Prior and Neil. I gave a bottle of champagne. '*Eheu moriturus salutavit*' Farewell tennis and Napoleon with Neil. I think it is perhaps rather a good sign that cards are beginning to bore me.

Neville was married to Florence Brown three days later.

Thereafter Keynes continued to have the dining rights attached to membership of the combination room, though he seldom exercised these rights more than four or five times in a year, and even then only on special occasions such as feasts or guest nights. From time to time he did 'odd jobs' for the college, such as annually auditing the mission accounts. The ill-feeling between Keynes and the Master seems to have dispersed once the former ceased to be resident in college. For example, in 1892, when Keynes was a candidate for election to the Council of the Senate, the Diary reported on 2 November: 'The Master says he will vote for me next Monday although he does not approve of my principles'. Neville himself was not a man to harbour grudges and in 1902, when Searle was seriously ill with asthma, the Diary entry for 2 May demonstrated a genuine affection for an old friend:

> Call at Pembroke Lodge to see the Master. I could not understand what he said but Mrs Searle was able to interpret. It was very sad to see him so ill and apparently suffering, but the grasp of his hand was wonderfully firm. I owe a great deal to him.

Florence Keynes (early 1880s)

J.N. Keynes (early 1880s)

IV Bachelor don at large

1 THE BOND FAMILY AT 3 BROOKSIDE

Neville was almost 24 when he was elected to a fellowship at Pembroke and he remained a double oddity in the college for being both a dissenter and a moralist. It is interesting to note that he made only one close friend at Pembroke – R.A. Neil, a young Senior Classic also elected in the summer vacation of 1876. Nor did he teach any of the Pembroke undergraduates, for he alone among them had been maverick enough to read moral sciences in the 1870s or early 1880s. Fortunately for Neville, the nonconformist connection admitted him to a more open and attractive meeting place for young people. That was 3 Brookside – a Cambridge shopkeeper's family home – roughly half a mile from Pembroke College. The head of the household was William Bond, a friend of Neville's father, and a leading member of the Cambridge congregationalist community. His only son Henry was a contemporary and close companion of Neville's at Amersham Hall and at London's University Hall who had matriculated at Cambridge a few months later than Neville, after entering Trinity Hall in March 1873. There were two daughters at home – Annie, who was five years older than their brother's friend, and Minnie, who was four years younger. The whole family regularly attended congregational chapel and constantly invited visiting preachers or student worshippers currently resident in colleges or lodging hostels, to Sunday tea or supper at their home in Brookside. Neville was introduced to this mixed-gender social circle five days after moving into his undergraduate rooms. As we have seen, it was Harry's mother herself who had first alerted Neville's parents to the fact that their son was so deeply depressed by his first few days in Pembroke College, that he contemplated dropping out of Cambridge altogether after Christmas; but when John and Anna Keynes arrived to talk him out of such a precipitate retreat he had already enjoyed the first of many happy Sunday suppers with the varied company at 3 Brookside and was extending his social horizons beyond the narrowly limited male community at Pembroke.

Among the earliest and most durable of the friendships that Neville made at Brookside was with James Ward, then a 30-year-old non-collegiate student studying for the Trinity scholarship examination. Ward had already been through a chequered educational experience. The eldest son of a northern businessman (gifted with more enterprise than judgement), he had been snatched from a Rugby preparatory school at the age of 13 (after one of his father's spectacular business failures) and then articled to a firm of Liverpool architects. While there he decided to train for the congregationalist ministry and in 1864 gained admission to Birmingham Spring Hill College where he successfully completed the arts and theological course as well as the London BA and BSc examinations. He then won a scholarship which enabled him to travel to Germany to further his studies in theology and philosophy. Meanwhile the leaders of the Cambridge congregationalist community – of which William Bond was a prominent member – were seeking a new pastor and were seriously considering this highly recommended Spring Hill graduate. They had expressed an interest in him before he went to Berlin in the summer of 1869, but it was not until he returned that he accepted an invitation to preach to them for the month of January 1871. He was at once warmly welcomed at Brookside.

Ward's letters home described William Bond as 'a fine specimen of earnest, honest, manly Christian tradesman', with whom he could work 'splendidly'.[1] In the event, Ward ministered to the congregationalists for just over a year, without actually being ordained. That year saw the climax of the personal crisis of faith that drove him to resign his mission. According to his daughter's account, published in 1927: 'Mr Bond had hoped that a broadminded and intellectual ministry would bring the chapel more into touch with the life of the University: he had reckoned without the more militant section of Nonconformity'.[2] He had also reckoned without James Ward's blistering honesty and failure to conciliate the members of his congregation who revered sectarian dogma and feared heresy. Writing in despair to his sister Lucy, Ward described himself as 'a minister among strangers and not perhaps strangers merely, but suspecters too in many cases. I do not care either for death or life. What I prize is truth'.[3] In these circumstances, he found a haven of peace in the university library and inspiration in the thoughtful, open-minded rationalism of modern Cambridge dons – such as Henry Sidgwick – who shared his passion for truth and intolerance of dogma.

In March 1872 Ward resigned his ministry, to the evident distress of most of his congregation; there were only six dissentients to their plea that he should remain. The majority hoped that after he had been ordained he would lead them to the new chapel they planned to erect in Trumpington Street. For

1. For Ward's life story and extracts from his correspondence, see the memoir by Olwen Ward Campbell introducing James Ward, *Essays in Philosophy* (Cambridge: Cambridge University Press, 1927).
2. Ibid., p. 40.
3. Ibid., p. 43.

his part he worried lest his broad church views might inhibit potential donors to the building appeal. Moreover, he had fallen in love with philosophy and needed intellectual space and scholarly guidance to recover his moral purpose. Over half a century later, in May 1924, after refusing an invitation to attend the Jubilee of the opening of Emmanuel Congregational Church, James Ward – then Cambridge's professor of mental philosophy and logic – looked back on the year when he ministered to Cambridge congregationalists as 'the darkest and the saddest of a long and eventful life', adding that 'the fine building in Trumpington Street … is a monument to two men, Henry Allen and William Bond, but it is the tombstone of a buried life for me'.[4]

It was characteristic of William Bond, that although bitterly disappointed by Ward's resignation; he provided funds to support him in Cambridge until such time as he could win the Trinity scholarship he craved. Bond offered the money as a gift and it was gratefully accepted by Ward as a loan. That was the situation on 25 January 1873 when Neville wrote in his Diary: 'I went up to the Bond's in the evening to meet Mr Ward. I think I shall like him'. Their friendship was cemented over the next few years in the course of long, earnestly argumentative, walks in the flat Cambridge countryside. On 25 April, the Diary rejoiced in the good news that: 'James Ward has got the Moral Sciences scholarship at Trinity'.[5] It was an impressive achievement; the Trinity scholarship examination was the most fiercely competitive in the whole university. Within months Ward had resolved his religious crisis. In a letter from Trinity College he wrote, in July 1873: 'The doubting phase is pretty well passed over for me now. I reject the whole system of Christian dogma from beginning to end and rationalize the history. Yet I see more clearly than ever that Christianity can do more for the world than it ever has done before'.[6] Neville was greatly captivated by James Ward's judgement, personal philosophy and example. Undoubtedly his friendship with this mature scholar then reading for the moral sciences tripos significantly stiffened his determination to resist the advice of his hitherto most respected mentors, and to make the switch from mathematics to morals in the summer of 1873.

James Ward was, of course, the kind of intellectual heavyweight that Neville might expect to meet in university or college circles, although it was easier to make and maintain a companionable relationship in the ambiance of a family home. A more remarkable consequence of Neville's connection with the Bond family lay in the impact it had on his social life and long-term emotional development. For it introduced him to a group of nonconformists

4. Ibid., p. 52.
5. The first Trinity scholarship in moral sciences open to all comers had been awarded in the previous year, 1872. It went jointly to William Cunningham and F.W. Maitland, both of whom went on to distinguish themselves as economic historians.
6. Quoted by Campbell (1927), p. 52.

of his own generation with whom he could actively enjoy social and sporting events, exchange intimate confidences and develop easy friendships. Most important of all for a shy, yet outgoing young man who was highly susceptible to the charms of the opposite sex, it helped him to relax in the company of some of the intelligent and adventurous young women then taking advantage of the new, tightly constrained, educational facilities offered to females by the University of Cambridge.

When Neville matriculated in 1872, women students were an exotic species in Cambridge. Two embryo women's colleges which had appeared on the scene during the previous year, provided institutional bases for women who wished to be taught and examined by the slowly growing number of Cambridge dons willing to extend their educational services to the female sex. The first five Newnham students were accommodated in a house rented and furnished by Henry Sidgwick in central Cambridge. Also in 1871, Girton – originally established at Hitchin, 20 miles from Cambridge – moved its 15 students to the adjacent village from which it took its name, about two miles from the town centre. In addition, a number of young women (living in small lodging hostels such as Norwich House) were being coached for the Cambridge Local examinations, success in which could provide budding governesses or school teachers[7] with a certificate of competence. In the 1870s, women students were invariably taught separately from male undergraduates, who had little prospect of meeting any of them socially outside a respectable private household. No Cambridge college (least of all Pembroke) would allow its junior members to invite any of these 'nasty forward minxes'[8] to talk or take tea in their rooms unchaperoned. Nor indeed would either of the two women's colleges permit its charges to accept invitations to a private party or household – unless assured that they would be continuously chaperoned by women of appropriate age and status.

In these circumstances, Neville was particularly fortunate in becoming a welcome regular guest at 3 Brookside, where – after chapel, or a Sunday walk, or a game of croquet with Henry Bond – he could expect to meet not only Henry's sisters, but also many of their women friends, including a succession of Newnhamites. At the end of the 1873 summer term (and annu-

7. The Cambridge Local examinations had been extended to girls in 1865. During the 1870s the Higher Local served Newnham and Girton as proxy for a scholarship examination, that is, the two women's colleges awarded scholarships to girls who achieved first class results. When the university gave women students formal permission to write tripos papers and to be examined by the relevant examiners (though without the right to proceed to a degree) the Higher Local became the qualifying hurdle for women tripos candidates – instead of the Previous or Little-Go examination which was the prerequisite for male candidates.
8. Adam Sedgwick, quoted by Rita McWilliams-Tullberg, *Women at Cambridge* (London: Victor Gollancz, 1975), p. 35.

ally for some years thereafter) he partially repaid the Bonds' hospitality, by hiring a boat to take their family and friends to the May races and giving them lunch in his Pembroke rooms. In the middle of his final year as an undergraduate he noted contentedly in the Diary that he was spending nearly every Sunday evening with the Bonds. He called on them more often still during the Long Vacation terms, when he stayed up to study (for example, to prepare for his switch to moral sciences in August 1873 or to cram for his tripos finals in the summer of 1875), for Brookside had become a second home to which he went whenever he wanted to relax in congenial company. In January 1876, when he came up to take his BA degree, his parents, John and Anna Keynes stayed at 3 Brookside to attend the ceremony. Later that year William and Anne Bond paid a return visit to the Keyneses in Castle Street, Salisbury, where their son had been a frequent guest during holidays from school or university over the last decade.

Young Bond (he is not familiarly referred to in the Diary as Harry until 1877) was Neville's natural confidant on romantic encounters. Although he was a year younger, he was plainly more self-confident and extrovert in his approach to members of the opposite sex. Neville admired his easy capacity to engage them in amusing conversation. Naturally in that limbo summer of 1876 – when the new graduate was waiting in Salisbury for Pembroke to decide on its fellowship elections, and when his own boyish flirtation with Flossie Williams filled the vacuum by developing into a bizarre, if short-lived, obsession – Neville wrote at length to Henry in Cambridge. The Diary quoted Bond's level-headed response, warning his vulnerable friend not to be taken in by 'false lights'.[9] The advice was timely and Neville added cautiously: 'I am certainly thinking a good deal about Flossie just now, but I shall do nothing in a hurry'. What finally cooled his superficial ardour and restored his emotional equilibrium was the news of his fellowship election, which instantly focused his attention on more urgent matters, such as his teaching programme for the following year. Subsequent references to Flossie in the Diary suggest that he would certainly have avoided a serious commitment to her. On the other hand, during his first year as a bachelor don, there were numerous Diary entries which indicate that, although he was still fancy-free, Neville had marriage on his ultimate agenda. For example, in April 1877, while he was at Salisbury on vacation, he reported in the Diary a letter from Miss Bond (not referred to as Annie until 1878) carrying the news of an engagement between John Cox and Caroline Bulley, frequent guests at 3 Brookside.[10] 'I am glad', wrote Neville, adding 'Miss Bond seems to have

9. See above, pp. 29–31.
10. Caroline Bulley had been a Newnham student and both she and John Cox, a Trinity graduate, were regularly guests of the Bonds.

assisted to some extent in bringing about the match and she offers to assist me in a similar way if ever the occasion arises'. Annie's offer to matchmake was apparently made, and received, jokingly. For Neville had not, as yet, developed a romantic interest in any of the young women he had met at Brookside. That did not prevent him, however, from taking pleasure in his friends' engagements or from enjoying Harry's endless fund of stories. For example, after a Sunday walk with Harry, he wrote on 21 October: 'Bond has been telling me more about his Platonic attachments. There was the girl at Schandau who, bye the bye, seems to have lost her heart to him; then there was little Annie at Richmond; and now it is a nursemaid at Hunstanton'. As usual the Sunday walk with Harry was followed by an evening at Brookside, and the Diary continued: 'We had a particularly animated talk about women and women's suffrage. I was in a minority of only one'. Apparently Harry did not then advocate women's suffrage.

Another of Harry's numerous conquests, Fanny Hoyle, had joined Neville's elementary logic course for women in October. A week later, after a Sunday walk with James Ward, Neville wrote: 'We called at Brookside. Miss Hoyle was there. It is the first time I have spoken to her this term, although she is one of the best in the class'. At one point he was to rank her third out of the 13 women in his class. But it was her provocative behaviour rather than her intellect that made her conspicuous, for he added: 'Of course she is my favourite pupil although she seems more or less to despise my lectures. I often see her shaking her head as if to say, now he is talking more foolishly than usual'. No doubt he confided these thoughts to Harry, for a week later he wrote: 'Bond tells me that Miss Hoyle says my lectures are not popular enough; they find them very difficult to follow'. This remark caused Neville real concern. He was a conscientious teacher who worked hard to present his material intelligibly and lucidly. So, when he next met Fanny, at another of the Bonds' evening parties, he took advantage of the fact that Harry was busily charming Daisy Duncan to encourage his pupil to enlarge on her criticisms directly: 'Miss Hoyle thinks that the papers I set are too long; at any rate they take a long time to answer', he wrote in the Diary, adding 'She seems very bored with her work in Logic and I suppose also with my lectures. At any rate she does not bore me'.

There was as yet no hint in the Diary that Neville had any interest in Fanny Hoyle, apart from that of a teacher for a bright, if wayward, pupil. On 30 November she enlivened Neville's end-of-term interviews; he wrote: 'I called at Newnham and saw most of my pupils separately. Miss Hoyle tells me that I rate her too highly; she imagines herself to have a peculiar power of imposing on examiners, chiefly as I understand, by the use of long words'. After a Brookside evening at which she prattled with her usual flippancy Neville reported:

> Miss Hoyle complains that they cannot sometimes get the point of my lectures, because I have a habit of hiding myself behind the desk at the critical moment. I explained that this was my nervousness. When I told her she underrated her own ability she said that she was in reality extremely conceited.

On Sunday 9 December, after another Brookside tea he wrote: 'Harry and I walked back to Newnham with her. It was against rules and Miss Bond was rather alarmed, but she herself did not mind.[11] She has borrowed my analysis of Adam Smith rather reluctantly'. As the men returned to Brookside, Harry repeated Fanny's confidences to him about her unhappy home life: 'Her people are of the narrowest sect of Wesleyans and look upon her as a child of the devil'. Neville saw her, briefly, the next day, when she called to thank the Bonds for their abundant hospitality over the past term.

2 THE DEATH OF JOHN KEYNES

On his 25th birthday, Neville had opened a new volume of his Diary whilst holidaying with Ingham in Scotland. The book thus began on 31 August 1877 with a self-conscious announcement:

> My 25th birthday: a fitting occasion for the commencement of a new volume of my Journal which I intend to make more of a Commonplace book than hitherto. A third of my life is over; even if I live to be as old as 75 wh is more than I can expect! If the rest of my life is as happy as my first 25 years I shall have very much to be thankful for: but the 'cares of life' are in the future and I must experience greater trials than I have yet done. I have not yet lost any of those dearest to me and I have had no serious illnesses since I can remember.

The premonition in the tail of this statement was probably associated with certain early indications of a breakdown in his father's health. Even before his son's 25th birthday, John Keynes's normally sunny disposition and unflappably impartial response to trivial family frictions was wilting. It was then that he began to worry about the details of his last will and testament. An entry in the Diary for 16 July 1877, for example, reflected Neville's puzzled response to his father's uncharacteristic over-reaction to a recurrence of an ancient tension between his sister and her stepmother:

> Father talks of leaving me £10,000 more than he does Fanny. Mrs Carter[12] thinks he is fully justified in this; but I do not and I shall try to get him to alter it. He

11. The rules, of course, required a suitable female chaperon to be present.
12. Mrs Carter, a friend of Anna Keynes, lived at Little Totham Hall in Essex and was a frequent house guest in Castle Street.

> sometimes speaks very harshly of Fanny. I have no doubt she has often behaved badly to Mother and done much to alienate his affection.

Although John Keynes must have known as well as anyone that Fanny's quick temper faded almost as fast as it flared, it does not seem to have been easy to persuade him that he should make a more equitable distribution between his two children. Indeed, Neville's efforts to make the point provoked an unprecedented rift between father and son. On 30 September, for example, Fanny's husband, Edward Purchase, then spending Sunday with his Salisbury in-laws, expressed surprise to Neville, 'at Father's greatly increased irritability towards me'.

With hindsight John Keynes's unusually irascible behaviour towards his nearest and dearest can be explained in terms of the anxiety of a responsible head of family grappling with an inadequately diagnosed, possibly terminal, illness. This possibility had apparently not occurred to Neville in September 1877; for although he was sufficiently concerned about his father's health to hope that he would resist popular pressure to serve for a second year as mayor of Salisbury, Neville did not hesitate to accompany Edward home to Kington. There he spent a carefree week with his sister's family – well away from the Castle Street tensions – before returning to Cambridge on 8 October. Nor, at the end of that term, did he return home to Salisbury as promptly as usual. Instead he spent ten days with his mother's friends, the Carters of Little Totham Hall, Essex, and another two or three days with maternal relatives at Forest Hill. When at last he did arrive home on 22 December he was shocked to find his father's health and temper deteriorating markedly. On New Year's Day 1878 he noted sadly: 'Father is not at all what he used to be. He is very depressed and irritable, especially with the servants'. However, he added with satisfaction that John Keynes had at last been induced:

> to alter his will to Fanny's advantage. In his old will he left £5000 to her, £10,000 to Mother to be equally divided between us at her death and the residue to me. Now he leaves £5000 to me, £12,000 to Mother to be equally divided between us at her death, furniture, plate, pictures etc. to Mother absolutely, the residue to be divided equally between us. Perhaps even this is too favourable to me but I had considerable difficulty in inducing Father to go so far.

As Neville conceded, however, one reason for his father's determination to leave the lion's share of his assets to his second wife and her issue, was that her contribution to the family business had been substantial. By contrast, the Keynes side of the family seems to have been relatively impecunious. Aunt Mary was semi-dependent on them, for example, and 'a good deal may ultimately be lost through Uncle William of Nottingham and his loss would probably fall on me'.

John Keynes was now going downhill rapidly. On 15 January Neville wrote: 'Mother and I are getting very anxious about Father's health, he seems to be wasting away almost to a shadow'. In desperation they sought medical advice from a London consultant. According to the Diary, the latter diagnosed

> an internal tumour, but he must not on any account know of this himself; this did not alarm us as much as it wd otherwise have done because of the addition that altho' a cure could not be effected, considerable good might be done and that Father might live for years and perhaps die of some other complaint.

On the other hand, the effect of this injunction to secrecy was to drive a miserable wedge between the dying man and his family. When back at Pembroke, on 2 February, Neville copied into his Diary the first of what was to be a daily sequence of letters from his mother: '"Your Father seemed too poorly to go to Dr Jones [the London consultant] again yesterday so I got his consent for me to call on Mr Coates"', that is, the Salisbury GP who came the same day. He followed his London colleague's line by insisting that the patient must be kept in ignorance of their diagnosis. This was even after the GP had been forced to admit, under the patient's persistent questioning, that his condition was serious. '"When you write"', wrote Anna Keynes to her son, '"put in a little note wh I can manage for him not to see. He is writing a letter or two now, but generally sits quietly all day. He is in no pain whatsoever and Mr Coates says he will not suffer"'. The following day the patient apparently turned the interrogation on to his deeply distressed wife, for she wrote:

> 'Your dear Father cannot understand why Mr Coates shd call it a dangerous case; but poor dear he little thinks what the complaint is. We are obliged to be cheerful before him, but it is a difficult thing. I have told Fanny [who probably wrote more often to her father than to her stepmother] that he is suffering from an affection of the stomach. I shall write to you very often but dont expect I shall ever be able to say that he is much better.'

The next day, Tuesday, she wrote:

> 'The doctors give your dear Father no medicine and wish him to take as much milk and beef tea as possible. He got up about 1 o clock today and at the same time yesterday. He is mercifully in no pain. … It seems a month since you left. … Your dear Father is sitting writing at his desk now. It seems very nice to see him there. He is very patient.'

Fearing the worst, Anna had asked both Fanny and Neville to come home at the weekend of Saturday 9 February. According to the Diary:

> I reached home at seven o clock in the evening and found Father even worse than I had expected from Mother's letters. Almost his first words were (with an effort of cheerfulness) 'Well, how do you think I am looking? Do I look worse than when you left home?' What could I say? I mumbled something about his looking pretty well. He is very patient; and this evening we seemed drawn together in closer bonds of sympathy than for a long time past; but he is unaware that there is no hope. It is terrible to see him wasting away; for Mother especially. Fanny came from Kington the same evening. He told us how he had left everything in his will and he said Fanny ought to be thankful she ever had a stepbrother. Indeed I do not think she is now in the slightest degree jealous of me; I believe she loves me quite as much as if I were her brother by the same mother and I entertain a kindred affection towards her and her children. When he had finished Father said 'But you neither of you want me to die do you?' He must have exerted himself very much to say all that he did say, and he did not pass a very good night afterwards.

On the Sunday morning the doctor came on his daily visit and assured Neville that he need not hesitate to return to his duties in Cambridge next day. Neville wrote in his Diary for Sunday 10 February: 'Father still talks as if he should get better; it is all very painful and sad. I told somebody not long ago that nothing wd make me cry; but now the tears flow altho' I try to control myself as much as I possibly can'.

During the following week Neville planned, with Sidgwick's permission, to delegate the rest of his teaching that term to J.S. Nicholson. On Friday, he wrote: 'I must be with Father to the end wh cannot be far off'. In the event he was devastated to arrive too late. He had stayed late on the Saturday evening at Pembroke to the end of the first of a series of college meetings scheduled that year for the massive revision of statutes, missed the last rail connection to Salisbury and spent the night in London. His brother-in-law Edward, who met him on Sunday at Salisbury station with a hired carriage, broke the news with insensitive clumsiness:

> As soon as we had got into the fly he told me that I had not come a moment too soon, that Father appeared to be getting unconscious, and so on, and then just as we reached the house that he was dead. I got into the dining room and spoke to Mother, Aunt Mary and Fanny, but I had to struggle to prevent myself from going off into a faint … it was a great shock and I found that I was quite unprepared.

His father had died at ten to five on the Sunday morning.

Neville was shattered by his first involvement in the death of a close member of family and he poured out his grief at great length in the Diary:

> My regret was very keen that I had not stayed with him during the week and that I had not said a last goodbye to him. … They tell me that he said remarkably little during the week and bid goodbye to no one. He did not at any time express a desire to see me, but said he was glad I was back at my work and I must on no account miss the college meeting. … He sent an affecting message to the Sunday

> School children a day or two before his death. A still greater source of regret to me now is the want of sympathy and confidence between us wh seemed to increase rather than to decrease of late years. Perhaps this was inevitable but I am sure we felt more towards each other than either of us expressed. I know that he must have gone through much suffering recently – and alone. I wd give anything to have been able to take part of this burden from him. … I read prayers before we went to bed, and was able to add something of my own to the written word.

The funeral took place in the afternoon of 22 February at Salisbury cemetery and was a public occasion, as befitted a recent mayor. According to the *Salisbury and Winchester Journal*, which printed a full account on the following day, the cortège was met at the gates of the cemetery by

> the Mayor and several members of the Corporation, the deacons of Brown Street Chapel and the male and female teachers of the Baptist Sunday School who followed in procession. The funeral service was performed by the Reverend George Short and a large number of the inhabitants of Salisbury were present.

Most of the shops of the town were closed for part of the day. For Neville it was both a painful ordeal and a turning point – the day he inherited the role in which his father had been a tower of strength to family and friends for as long as he could remember. In accordance with custom, none of the female members of the family attended the service.[13] In the evening: 'Stephen Hill read the will to Fanny, Edward and me. … He told them whilst I was away, the influence I had had in its making and Fanny spoke very kindly to me about it afterward'.

Neville's grief at his father's death was deepened and protracted by recollections of the unnecessary estrangement that had overshadowed their relationship during the previous eight months or so. There are recurrent references in later Diary entries to his own inability either to bridge the unaccustomed rift or to cope with the pain of bereavement. He now confronted the problem of responding constructively as well as supportively to his mother's loss, for he added: 'Mother is still painfully depressed. She wants to leave Salisbury'. In spite of having many friends and relatives with whom she could exchange confidences and visits, the widow – now in her late fifties – clung so desperately to her only son that he felt guilty whenever he left her side. The resident servants in Castle Street were also shattered by their master's death. Two days before the funeral Neville wrote: 'Both our

13. The chief mourners were John Neville Keynes; Edward Purchase and his two eldest sons, Keynes and John; the Reverend J. Keynes of Wimbourne, J. Blake and Sam Bartlett – cousins of John Keynes; Dr Todd, a relative of Anna Keynes; Mr Short and Mr Clarkson – both nonconformist ministers; Mr W. Fawcett (Henry Fawcett's father); Mr Dodds, a nurseryman formerly a partner of John Keynes; and Mr Wyatt, foreman in the Castle Street Nurseries.

servants were taken ill and had to go home'; and it was some weeks before they could settle down to the new regime in Castle Street. As late as 12 April, for example, the Diary reports: ' Back to Salisbury [after a night in London]. Our servants are a great trouble to Mother'. At the same time, Neville found himself taking his father's place in the Salisbury household, not only as his mother's chief support and confidant, but also as adviser on business matters to other members of family and friends who had learned to depend on John Keynes's authoritative and kind wisdom.

After the Cambridge term ended on 24 June 1878, Neville returned at once to Salisbury and took his mother to Kington where they stayed for a happy couple of weeks with the Purchase family; but when he left her there in order to spend a few days visiting various Amersham Hall and London friends, the friction between mother and stepdaughter flared again. Returning to Salisbury on 10 July, he heard his mother's version of the quarrel and wrote: 'I was surprised and very sorry to find Fanny had been making herself anything but agreeable to mother. I am sometimes very much afraid of what her freaks of temper may bring about'. When Edward Purchase came to Salisbury later that week to help Neville draw up the final settlement of John Keynes's will and business interests,[14] he did his best to soothe frayed family feelings and Neville noted: 'He regrets that Fanny spoke to Mother as she did but he says that no one knows how much he has to put up with himself'. In the long run, however, Neville's unstinted affection for Fanny was only rarely diluted by her propensity to snap at his mother – as well as her own husband and children – though never (judging from the evidence in the Diary) at her half-brother. From the very beginning he took pride and pleasure in watching his nephews and nieces grow up, sharing in their games and hobbies, trying to extend their social horizons and actively concerning himself with their educational progress and general welfare.

As it happened, John Keynes's death brought Neville even closer to his sister and her family, On 10 October, for example, the Diary quoted the following passage from one of Fanny's letters: '"Dearest Father said, not many days before his death 'Neville will always love you and your children Fanny' and so it is, you are very good and kind to us all"'. Meanwhile, in the same evenhanded spirit in which Neville had persuaded his father to alter his will, he had treated Edward as an equal in arranging the disposal of the nursery business. At one point the brothers-in-law had contemplated the possibility of a three-way partnership between themselves and John Wyatt (then acting manager of the firm). However, neither the don nor the grocer had the time, or the inclination or, more importantly, the practical expertise to

14. That is, to make out the residuary account under the will and to work out the terms of the agreement over management of the Castle Street Nurseries from the following Christmas.

oversee the operation of such a highly specialized enterprise, and they seem to have abandoned the idea rapidly. So when cousin Joseph Keynes (a brother of the Rev. John Keynes of Wimborne) proposed himself as a joint partner with Neville and Edward, their minds were already made up and they 'saw at once that it would not do'. That was on 1 July 1878. By then Neville was actively negotiating the sale of the business to his father's old friend Charles Williams (also a Salisbury nurseryman); and on 12 July it was agreed that the latter should take over the nursery at Christmas. 'The returns have been falling off lately', noted Neville in the Diary, 'and on this account we reduced our demand from £1000 to £500' – that was presumably for the goodwill of the business. At the end of the year the stock was independently valued by representatives of themselves and Charles Williams and the handover was completed early in 1879.

Taking all debits and credits into account, it would appear that the proceeds of the sale of the nursery fell short of the beneficiaries' expectations. However, Neville ensured that John Wyatt was fully rewarded for his long and faithful service to the family. The Diary quotes Wyatt's letter, received in early 1879: '"For your very handsome present I beg to return to you and Mr Purchase my very sincere thanks. I shall at all times be most happy to render you any assistance and hope for many years to have opportunities of obliging you and your dear Mother."'[15] The nursery business was not all that was involved in John Keynes's estate. For Fanny and Edward, with seven children of school age and under to rear and educate, their substantial legacy must have represented a timely windfall. By 22 June 1880, when Edward came down to Salisbury for the day, to go over the outstanding accounts for the last time, he was feeling sufficiently affluent to contemplate active participation in the Stock Exchange. According to the Diary: 'He suggested our going into a stockjobbing partnership, borrowing money for the purpose from the Wilts and Dorset Bank. But I declined, at any rate for the present'. Neville himself was an informed but instinctively cautious investor, who had already made some modestly successful bargains on his own account, and had always been ready to share his knowledge and experience of the market with his brother-in-law. He was well aware of Edward's eager interest in the potential gains obtainable through Stock Exchange transactions but was the last person to encourage his brother-in-law's more speculative propensities.

15. John Wyatt continued to manage the Castle Street Nurseries under the new management and bought the business in 1894.

3 THE BONDS AND FANNY HOYLE

Except when commuting to Pembroke to attend the weekly meetings on college statutes, Neville spent most of the Lent term in Salisbury with his mother. To please her he slipped back into the familiar social circle. He paid frequent visits to Moorland House, played billiards with Mr Williams, chatted with Emily, sparred with Flossie, and flirted somewhat sheepishly with Edith, the youngest of the sisters who was still at school. On 7 March, for example, he wrote: 'Edith was very charming. I think of her more than I ought'; and again on 15 March: 'Billiards at Moorland House. Edith marked for us. ... We have got into the habit of squeezing each other's hands at saying goodbye, wh is childish'. On his Saturday visits to Cambridge Neville occasionally spent the night with the Bonds, whom he found in turmoil because Harry's interest in Daisy Duncan had become an infatuation. 'Bond seems to be head over heels in love with Miss Duncan', he wrote on 2 March adding 'He and his father do not always hit it off together'.

Easter came late that year and Neville did not go back into residence at Pembroke until 29 April, for one of the shortest May terms on record. By then he was conspiratorially involved in Harry's pursuit of Daisy Duncan. On 1 April the Diary reported:

> Bond is very much in earnest with respect to Miss Duncan. He is afraid that she will not have sufficient funds to stay up at Cambridge for another year, so we have arranged that £60 shall be sent to her anonymously. I am to try to get Emily Williams to write her a letter.

Emily was drawn into the plot on Good Friday, and on 29 April Neville posted Harry's letter (in Emily's handwriting) on his way through London to Cambridge. Harry was conveniently on holiday in Germany until 3 May. For the rest of that short and merry term, Neville's Diary was dominated by the Harry Bond/Daisy Duncan affair.

By Friday 17 May, the anonymous letter plot had provoked a letter to *The Times* which reached Harry by first post on 20 May. He found this message: 'Sixty pounds. M.D. cannot possibly accept. Please send address to wh. it can be returned'. Miss Margaret Duncan (Daisy) did not go to the races that afternoon, but she did join the large supper party given by the Bonds in the evening. It was then, according to the Diary, that: 'Bond showed her the address on the envelope that had been sent to him from the *Times*. She said that she knew the handwriting but could not imagine what the person in question might have to write to him about'. Two days later, Neville wrote: 'Bond received an anonymous letter abusing him for having written anonymously to Miss Duncan. He then wrote to her in his own name telling her that he loved her and that that must be his excuse for acting as he had done'. Her reply came next day and Neville summarized it in the Diary:

> She was at any rate utterly indifferent to anyone else, and she had never been indifferent to him since she knew him; but she was too young and they did not know enough of each other; they had better not see each other again. He replied that she must at any rate see him once more.

When Neville returned from a night in London two days later a radiant Bond was awaiting him on Cambridge station. According to the Diary: 'He had had another letter from Miss Duncan saying that he had misunderstood her first; and that he might call and see her at Norwich House Saturday evening at 7' – that very evening. Evidently the chaperon system was less strictly applied in relation to outstudents than to the students resident at Newnham Hall under the watchful eye of Miss Clough.

The following morning Harry came to Sunday breakfast with Neville to report progress. According to the Diary:

> He had actually stayed at Norwich House two hours last night, under what circumstances it is needless to add. Towards the end of the time Madame Roache herself came into the room where they were, to light the gas. Harry politely lighted it for her and bowed her out. She was so overpowered with astonishment at his audacity that she went without saying a word. When Bond told his own people they were immensely astonished and not at first particularly pleased. They thought it too sudden, that they did not know enough of each other and above all they were horror struck at Norwich House being made the scene of operations. Harry wrote a very nice note to Madame Roache however and she appears quite reconciled.

Neville, who rejoiced with Harry at the successful outcome of his courtship, endeavoured to persuade Annie and Minnie that no harm had been done by their brother's unconventional tactics. But the sisters – whose full social lives hinged crucially on the reputation of their home as a properly chaperoned venue for Cambridge's nonconformist students – were as anxious as their mother to preserve the family from the slightest breath of scandal. In time, however, when those in charge at Norwich House appeared unperturbed by the circumstances of the engagement, and since Daisy was obviously as much in love with Harry as he was with her, the females in his family opened their arms to his prospective bride.

Mr Bond, on the other hand, was becoming increasingly restive with the endless stream of uninhibited youngsters taking advantage of the family's hospitality and threatening to corrupt his daughters or encourage his son's cavalier behaviour. A yawning generation gap separated him from his children. On 17 July, for example, when Neville and his mother were on holiday with the Bonds at Grasmere, the Diary reported that Mr Bond approved of Minnie's plans to go to Brighton High School as a music teacher:

> because it will remove her from the sceptical influence of Edith Pinsent and also from Ernest Rogers who loafs about Brookside too much to please him … [and] is not likely to settle down into a good working husband. I have since heard from Mother that Mr Bond and Harry did not part on very good terms. Mr Bond said that Harry was growing insufferable in his conceit. … Mr Bond also speaks slightingly of Daisy Duncan; he told my Mother that he did not think the engagement would come to anything as Harry was so changeable.

As it turned out, that proved an accurate prediction; for the Bonds, who had been so shocked by the way the engagement to Daisy had been brought about, were destined to be appalled, a year later, by the manner in which Harry unilaterally ended it.

Neville passed the 1878 Easter term in a relatively relaxed frame of mind. He knew that he would have to stay up for at least an extra week at the end of term, to endure further college meetings needed to complete Pembroke's revision of statutes; but his father's will had not only assured him a modest independent income, it provided comfortably for his mother throughout her lifetime and freed his sister's family from money problems for the foreseeable future. The change in his financial situation was soon the subject of rumour in Cambridge colleges. On 3 June, he confided to the Diary, with wry amusement:

> Bond was dining at Trinity Hall last night and my name arose as a subject of discussion. Fawcett informed the company that I had recently come into a good deal of money; probably as much as £10,000.[16] He suggested to Bond that I might choose a parliamentary career; but Haskyns at once remarked that I had not enough 'go' and others considered me too diffident.

The inheritance was not a fortune; it did mean, however, that the financial implications of the projected alterations in the terms of fellowships had become appreciably less significant for Keynes's personal career options and prospects.

Meanwhile, in the hope of rescuing his mother from the black misery of bereavement, Neville had arranged to take her on holiday to the Lake District in July and had persuaded the Bond family to join them there – excluding, of course, Harry, still at odds with his father and still cherishing every moment spent alone with Daisy. With his holiday arrangements satisfactorily settled, Neville disposed of the relatively minor teaching commitments of the short

16. According to R. Skidelsky, *John Maynard Keynes: I: Hopes Betrayed, 1883–1920* (London: Macmillan, 1983), p. 19. John Keynes left assets worth over £40,000 of which Neville's share came to £17,000 and his Mother's £12,000 plus the Salisbury house.

May term. The last of his elementary logic courses ended on 8 June; and after seeing his women pupils individually at Newnham he commented in the Diary: 'I think all the girls will do well in their examination and Miss Hoyle and Miss Marshall ought to do particularly well. I am satisfied with the year's work so far as these lectures are concerned'.[17] He did not expect to see any of them again until October, and then only if they elected to read moral sciences and to attend his lectures again. Miss Marshall had already announced her intention to read for the history tripos, and he learned of Miss Hoyle's firm intention to read for the moral sciences tripos, when they met at the Brookside end-of-term party on 13 June. However, he had by no means heard the last of Miss Hoyle that summer. On 3 July she surprised him with a letter on the subject of Harry's engagement. It was not obvious to Neville why she chose to write to him, but in essence what she said was that she had seen a good deal of Miss Duncan since the end of term and that she was 'getting satisfied both that she is as good as Harry deserves and that she is what he wants'. It may be that she was moved to write to Harry's closest friend in these terms – ostensibly approving of the engagement – after hearing from Daisy how helpful he had been in bringing it about. Daisy had already written to thank Neville for his assistance in the matter and had pleased him by saying that she liked him best of Harry's friends. Alternatively she may have been stimulated to write to the diffident young lecturer by the distinctive glamour he had acquired as a result of the rumours then current in Cambridge concerning his recent legacy. In any case, Neville responded briefly to her unexpected communication and on 13 July he got a second letter about Harry and Daisy. Upon which he commented in amusement: 'Miss H. sounds in love with Harry herself'.

Two days later, Neville took his mother from Salisbury to Grasmere on the first lap of a holiday to which he (and she) had been looking forward since Easter. They were in relatively good spirits. On the long train journey he began to read Charlotte Bronte's *Villette*, a novel in which he had struggled to get interested, on first reading some years previously. He now 'read it with avidity'. The next day, after rowing his mother around Grasmere in the morning, and climbing Wansfell Pike in the afternoon, Neville hurried to Ambleside to meet the coach bringing the Bonds. The weather was gloriously sunny for the whole of the following week – too hot for the energetic hill climbing to which he had so eagerly looked forward, but ideal for gentle rowing expeditions, or lake steamer excursions, or the scenic drive from Ambleside to Patterdale, where the group planned to spend the second week of their holiday. On their way to Patterdale they began by taking a steamer the length of Windermere (and back), before boarding a carriage at Bowness to drive through the Kirkstone Pass. It

17. The examinations for which the two Newnhamites were entered were the Senior Local examinations, scheduled for late June.

was on the other side of the Pass, in the middle of the afternoon, that they found Miss Hoyle waiting for them. Neville was amazed and pleased to meet her there, and to learn that she proposed to join them in the 'most delightful lodgings' they had sought out (and reserved only four days ago) on an exploratory day-trip from Grasmere. Whether the Bond family were surprised the Diary does not reveal, but evidently either Annie or Minnie (probably the former) had informed Fanny Hoyle about the timing and route of their move to Patterdale, if not the exact address they had in view. For, when reporting the 'very pleasant walk' he had with her alone in the garden of their new lodgings, Neville noted, with surprise: 'She said that she had been a good deal disturbed by the fear that we should miss each other altogether'.

Freed at last from the chaperoning rules expressly designed to inhibit the formation of relationships between Cambridge dons and their women pupils, Miss Hoyle did her extravagant best to attract and hold the attention of the unattached young bachelor. Instead of staying two or three days as she had originally proposed, she stayed seven. She might well have spent even longer with the party had they not already arranged to join Harry Aves and his sister in Keswick at the end of the week. Meanwhile the entries in the Diary – expanded to two or three times their usual length – bear witness to the success of her efforts to dazzle Neville. She talked incessantly, acting out a kaleidoscope of moods.

Most of the time, of course, she was showing off to Annie and Minnie as well as to Neville, but there were occasions when he and she could talk freely and inconspicuously together, while walking, or hill climbing, or merely waiting for the other members of the party to assemble for a joint expedition. Neville was alternately surprised, amused and intrigued by Fanny Hoyle's performance. For him it was an unusually exciting experience to be continuously and deliberately targeted by a woman of imagination and intelligence, whose volatile moods and behaviour were so unpredictable. On their first full day in Patterdale, for example, the Diary reported happily:

> Annie, Minnie, Miss Hoyle and I went for a little row on Ullswater. … We were all lively and in good spirits. … I think I am beginning to understand Miss Hoyle rather better, but I wish I understood her yet more because I like her so much. It is still difficult to tell how far she speaks in earnest, but I am perhaps getting over the feeling that she is always making fun of me.

The following day when the whole party joined a steamer excursion on Ullswater: 'Annie, Miss Hoyle and I got out at Howtown to call on Mr and Mrs Marshall Bulley who have taken a cottage there for a few weeks'.[18] It

18. Mrs Bulley a former Newnham student, Anne Armitage, had married a brother of the three Bulley sisters also Newnhamites.

was an idyllic spot which inspired the ebullient Newnhamite to announce that she wanted to have her honeymoon there. This fantasy seems to have left Keynes speechless for the Diary goes on: 'She has got it into her head that I am not enjoying myself now because I dont talk much or if I do it seems to be with an effort. She is wrong'. The next day, since the weather remained brilliant, Neville hired a pony and a guide to take the three girls up Helvellyn, where they could enjoy a magnificently clear view in all directions. The Diary, however, focused more on Miss Hoyle's enigmatic utterances and dramatic behaviour rather than on the landscape.

Neville's failure to understand 'Miss Hoyle' (as he still referred to her in the Diary) was a recurrent topic of conversation whenever they were alone together for any length of time. For example, on 27 July they loitered in the garden while the rest of the group were assembling for a boat trip and the Diary reported their brief conversation at some length – including a passage to the effect that: 'On my saying how glad I should be if I could really understand her, she replied that she was simple enough to understand if one only had the key. Harry Bond she thought had it'. Their last full day at Patterdale was a Sunday. After church and lunch the younger members of the group sat in a field talking, reading or writing letters and after tea set off to climb Place Fell. This expedition presented an opportunity for the longest private conversation they had ever had; for only Neville and Fanny reached the top and they kept the others waiting more than an hour. As a result Neville fancied that he was beginning to understand her, although his account of their dialogue does not indicate a meeting of minds – for example:

> We compared religious experiences and beliefs. They are not so very different, but I think she gives free play to sceptical tendencies, I have generally done my best to restrain them, though not with very great success. I told her that I was glad she had stayed because it had enabled me to overcome a growing feeling that she was beginning to dislike and despise me. She said that she had always liked me because she felt that we had much in common. She had promised to give me a written apology for sundry remarks she had made.

The 'apology' (duly copied into the Diary) was an incoherent note – pushed under his bedroom door – which read: '"Sunday. 5.30. Dear Mr Keynes, I hereby retract every word and epithet"', and ended: '"I now consider retraction unnecessary, because a better understanding has been arrived at, which I hope will go on to be a better one still: *please*. Quite seriously, and without joking, yours, F.E. Hoyle"'. Reading this letter seems to have encouraged Neville to fill one and a half pages of the Diary with romantic extracts from his current bedside reading – Tennyson's *Princess*.

On 29 July the whole party took the steamer to Penrith. According to the Diary: 'Minnie and I walked with Miss Hoyle to the station where we had to say farewell to her. … We talked a good deal about Harry and Miss Duncan'. Mr and Mrs Bond returned home two days later. It had not been the kind of holiday that they would choose to repeat since William Bond turned out to be nervous of water trips and his wife to dislike long drives in hilly country. On the other hand, Neville confided to his Diary that the holiday had been a success beyond his expectations and that there had been remarkably little friction between members sharing in it. Presumably Anna Keynes had been happy with the holiday since her son was particularly sensitive to his mother's feelings. As for Annie and Minnie, both of whom stayed for the whole of the strenuous Keswick week with the Aves pair, they told Neville that they had 'never before enjoyed a trip as much as this one'. Meanwhile, Miss Hoyle had launched the first in a veritable bombardment of letters. It arrived in Keswick the day after she left Penrith. Significantly it was a letter to Annie, the matchmaker, who – as no doubt, was expected of her – read Neville selected extracts from the letter whilst they were scrambling down Skiddaw with Minnie, Harry Aves, a guide and a pony. Two days later Neville admitted getting 'a good deal of pleasure' from a letter to himself in which Miss Hoyle, complained bitterly 'how miserable she was at home. She said she was in actual tears when she began to write. She said she would go to hell with anybody she cared for'. The Diary elaborated exhaustively on his talks with Annie, who clearly relished her role as confidante to both Fanny and Neville but, as later events were to demonstrate, she was not as frank with either of them as she should have been.

Back in Salisbury, on 8 August, Neville was delighted by the arrival of two letters from Brookside. One was from Minnie containing the results of the Senior Local examinations for Fanny Hoyle and Daisy Duncan. The Diary records with satisfaction that Miss Hoyle had topped the lists of firsts in Group D for both logic and political economy, and that Miss Duncan had passed in Group A with three stars, on which Neville gleefully commented 'a score off Harry who had had to scratch his examination'.[19] The other letter, from Annie, contained the following cryptic message: '"Just remember once and for all that if there is anything at any time that I could do for you I am ready to do it. I know that having Harry and other friends you dont want much else, but a woman may sometimes be useful where a man can't"'. Miss Hoyle's own letter about her results arrived two days later. According to the Diary:

> She has been offered the Group D scholarship, but I dont understand whether she has yet definitely accepted it. She says, – I shall write to you as often as I think you care to hear (and perhaps oftener owing to my infirmity) because I always liked you and felt as if we might be friends: and also because (you will have to

19. The examination which Bond had scratched was the Whewell, a postgraduate competition.

hear it) I feel as if I shd not get tired of you as is the remote possibility in the case of most people I know.

By this time Neville had other matters on his mind and did not take time to answer until a week later when he wrote to say that he would be touring in Switzerland for some weeks, and to give her an address for further correspondence. Consequently his reply did not reach her in time to forestall her furious postcard, provoking an angry response of which he instantly repented and followed with an apology within the day. Fanny's answer, a characteristic mixture of contrition and spite, reached him the day before he left for Switzerland and Neville was either too bemused or to busy to reply. During his eventful Swiss tour, accompanied first by Alfred West, then by Arthur Spokes and finally by John Lord (exiled at a Davos clinic with consumption), Neville's Diary offered no evidence that his thoughts had reverted to the young woman whose flamboyant display had so fascinated him in the last fortnight of July.[20] True, at Chamonix, on 1 September it reported the arrival of 'a jolly letter from Miss Hoyle' in which she 'writes warmly in defence of Walt Whitman'. Answering this letter was again crowded out of his holiday programme, however, until September 14, by which time he was at Davos with Lord – to whom he had confided the story of his Lakeland experience with the dazzling Miss Hoyle. Eleven days later she re-entered his Diary when he found another two letters from her awaiting him on his return to Salisbury.[21]

Neville's voluminous Diary entries in the summer of 1878 suggest that for most of the two months between 29 July (when Neville and Minnie left Miss Hoyle at Penrith station) and the end of September, his histrionic pupil barely entered his thoughts – except when a letter from (or about) her brought her sharply to notice. This is hardly surprising. Their asexual holiday romance had lasted just a week, during which their private conversations were limited to few snatched occasions, and were hard to recall rationally. Given Neville's passion for reducing his thoughts to order and clarity, his memories of her must have acquired a somewhat tenuous quality – unless stirred into consciousness by another letter. Back in Salisbury, however, what was becoming an 'affair by correspondence' developed a strange momentum. Of her two letters awaiting him there, 'one perhaps the most charming I have ever received' stimulated an instant reply. She reacted fulsomely and begged him not to begin his letters with the formal 'Dear Miss Hoyle'. On the day that letter arrived the Diary listed some puzzled questions:

20. The Swiss holiday was full of excitement and adventure and generated lengthy lyrical entries in the Diary.
21. When Neville returned from his holiday to find Miss Hoyle's two letters (to which he replied instantly) his mother had asked 'whatever we can have to write to each other about so much'.

> Is she afraid that I imagine that she cares for me more than as a mere friend? Does she? I am afraid to think so, much as I want to. … Shall I go on caring for her as I do now? I would tell her that I love her if I were sure of myself and surer that I could make her happy. But she will find me so dull and stupid when she knows me better.

Not for the first time in his life, Neville wrote for advice to Harry whom he believed to be happily engaged to Daisy.

This time Bond was oddly disturbed by Neville's revelation of the problematic relationship that he was developing with Fanny Hoyle. Far from offering the sympathetic understanding and clearheaded realism that Neville expected, he merely injected unexpected uncertainties into the situation. On 1 October the Diary quoted Harry's surprising response:

> 'The concluding remarks of your letter gave me some uneasiness. You are sensible of an attraction other than that of the lecturer towards Miss Hoyle; there is another attraction at home; they are so totally different that it is quite clear that a man who ought to think seriously of one might not of the other. Which will suit you, you know best and you shd, as soon as you know even enough of both, better make up your mind and not drift. I do not know anything about your pretty little friend in Salisbury, but I do know Fanny Hoyle better than most people do and I like her very much indeed. I should be a good deal surprised I must confess if she is the girl to suit you, but I dont wonder at all at your being attracted'.

Neville reacted irritably in the Diary:

> I have been thinking about Fanny Hoyle and Edith. I have not seen Edith since Easter, but it cannot be anything more than her face that attracts me. It is at least more than this that I care for Fanny Hoyle. If it is true that she is never at home with Harry he may perhaps not know her so well after all.

The last sentence referred obliquely to Fanny's latest letter which arrived that day, informing him that Harry Bond had called on her at home in Manchester – probably soon after getting Neville's letter requesting his advice – that she had felt 'awkward' and also that (in her words): '"I am right glad he has gone. Now I can breathe"'.

It was at last obvious that there had been more to the relationship between Harry and Fanny than Neville had supposed. But since neither had chosen to enlighten him he was obliged to wait until he returned to Cambridge in mid-October and could talk to Harry. Meanwhile Fanny maintained the provocative flow of petulant postcards or incoherently emotional letters. At the same time – in an effort to fathom what she felt about him, as well as to clarify his own feelings for her – he copied into the Diary large chunks of her sometimes opaque, often irrational, outbursts of sententious rhetoric. After answering a letter from which he quoted at length on 5 October, for example, he confessed: 'I could not help writing today faintly hinting how much she is in my thoughts and in what way I regard her. Most men would have said more but I am cold, cautious, calculating'. Then he quoted from her letter:

> 'I think you might have called me Fanny in this last letter to complete the cure of my wounded feelings. I wish I had a nicer name to be called by. You may tell Mrs Keynes if you like that the reason of all these letters is pure friendship, we have made friends suddenly and may stop some day as suddenly.[22] … I am a very changeable person too. Some day *I* can tell *you* – several strange stories relating to that'.

Upon which the diarist reflected with evident bewilderment: 'She goes on to prophesy several unpleasant things'.

Back at Pembroke during the weekend before term began, Neville called at Brookside on Saturday 12 October. The usual throng of visitors left little opportunity for private conversation and he had only the briefest of exchanges with Harry. According to the Diary: 'He regards me as a man sitting on a barrel of gunpowder, without seriously knowing it, and hopes to heaven that it will come to nothing between us. Carrie Bulley he says was as much surprised to hear what we had drifted into as he was himself. What can it mean?' The answer came the next day when, after a breakfast party in Pembroke, he and Harry took a familiar morning stroll out of Cambridge towards Madingley. The Diary entry for 13 October runs to four pages from which the following is a greatly abridged extract:

> Stated in the briefest terms this is what he told me. Although he never responded except in the way of the calmest friendship, she was all through last year, and betrayed herself as being, passionately in love with him. During this spring while he was himself in love with Daisy, she was writing him letters day after day, sometimes more than one a day. She was up at Brookside every day to see him and poured forth complaints and upbraidings because he tried to avoid her as much as he could in a quiet way. At last he decided that it must be put a stop to and told her so. He says that she behaved remarkably well considering the occasion, but she wrote him a long letter which was bad to read – it was evidence of such intensity of feeling. Then she meets me at Patterdale and solaces herself for her disappointment with me – anyone else would have done as well – might have done better; for she is not likely for long to find all she wants in such a creature as I am. … Harry hinted too at her having run away and committed herself rather sadly before she came to Cambridge; he seemed to imply that he might tell me more … if he chose. … Harry has talked the whole thing over with Caroline Bulley … [who] is doubtful whether her health and strength are such that she ought to marry even if all other difficulties were cleared away. But what would I care for this? What would I care for all the past if I did not fear the future in another aspect? I cannot wonder at her preferring Harry to me if he returned her

22. See footnote 21.

> love, but he cannot and I can. … In a foolish moment I told Harry what she had asked me – namely not to talk much with him about her. It seems she does not want me to know that I was only a dernier resort. He thought her disingenuous and I was wild that I had told him. What am I to do? I am not a man to be hurried along by my feelings contrary to reason, but I cannot give her up without a word. … Harry came back with me to lunch; we sat in silence for the most part. … Then we went up to Brookside together where I had told her I so much looked forward to meeting her there this afternoon. So I did, but now I felt afraid. Yet when we did meet I seemed to forget altogether what Harry had been telling me. I could hardly drag myself away in time for our hall

– to which he had invited dinner guests.

It took some time for Neville to digest the full implications of what he had been told. When he cross-questioned Harry again, the following day, during another walk, he learned that Annie had been well aware of the intensity of Fanny's feelings for her brother. No doubt it was Annie's compassion for Fanny's wounded feelings – immediately following the announcement of Harry's engagement to Daisy – that had prompted her to engineer the joint holiday at Patterdale. For Neville the most disturbing implication of these revelations was not simply that Fanny's startling focus on himself was associated with her disappointment at Harry's engagement to Daisy. It was that even Harry had not been her first passion. A day later, after leafing through some of her innumerable letters, which had alternately charmed, puzzled, intrigued and infuriated him, he wrote:

> I find that she says in an old letter: 'I have always thought that I should never get married because if anyone were such a miserable fool as to fall in love with me … I should go off to Italy with someone else.' This doesnt sound like mere banter now.

Meanwhile, apparently oblivious to the change in Neville's attitude to her when they met at Brookside that Sunday afternoon – for the first time since they had parted at Patterdale station ten weeks previously – Fanny continued her barrage of letters. One of these included a relatively demure request for advice on her lecture programme. When that letter reached him, Neville – who had as usual discussed with Sidgwick the class list for the course on advanced logic which he was to give Newnham students that term – was relieved to be able to pass on to her the Master's advice that 'Fanny Hoyle had better not attend'. Whereupon Fanny went directly to Sidgwick to justify her serious interest in logic, and on 16 October the Diary reported:

> Postcard from Sidgwick: 'Miss Hoyle is going to your lectures, – she is very anxious to do Advanced Logic' … In the afternoon I got a letter from Fanny Hoyle herself '… you arent kind: you ought to let me come to your Logic. I hate them all but I want to come to it. … I can see this term is going to be very miserable

> instead of very happy. … My respect and awe and despair at your position in this University is rising to boiling point. … Miss Clough gave me much advice on Saturday on the subject of the Bonds: I had the most terrifying talk that I ever had from her. I wish you had been there. … *Why* did you think I ought not to take Logic?'

The indignant outburst went on at length as usual.

Thus Neville gave his first advanced logic lecture of the term to an audience of three women – of whom Fanny Hoyle was one. He was still sentimentally vulnerable – to the extent of worrying anxiously about her 'slight cough and her hereditary tendency to consumption'.[23] On the other hand, he stayed away from Sunday tea at the Bonds', knowing that she would be there. After the evening service at Emmanuel Chapel, he accompanied the visiting preacher back to Brookside, where they encountered Fanny coming disconsolately away. Touched by the sight of her, he could not resist penning an affectionate note – which gave fresh impetus to their fraught correspondence. After another agitated exchange of letters he quoted at length in the Diary from one of hers begging him to '"come to Brookside when I am there and when we can have quiet talks. This writing is folly"'. Torn by conflicting emotions, Neville told Harry of his intention to go to Brookside the next Sunday afternoon, only to be derided for being 'like a silly moth fluttering round a candle; he cannot understand the fascination'. Eventually Neville relieved a particularly boring college meeting (called to confirm Pembroke's revised statutes) by writing to Fanny to say that he would be at tea with the Bonds the following afternoon and hoped to see her there. Brookside had now been alerted, however. He confided to the Diary:

> Only Mr and Mrs Bond were at home and the former went out while we were there; I am afraid we prevented Mrs Bond from having a sleep wh wd have done her good. It was not a very satisfactory interview. I had another long talk about her with Harry in the evening. He speaks sometimes as if he had not yet told all.

Enraged by their closely supervised encounter, Fanny scribbled an unusually spiteful letter on which Neville confided to the Diary: 'She is right. She can never care for me as much as she once cared for Harry Bond; even now I am not sure that she does not still care for him more'.

For Neville, if not for Fanny Hoyle, their relationship seems to have lost its emotional drive towards the end of October, when the Diary began to expand on other events in the life of a sociable bachelor. On 30 October, for example, he was delighted to be one of only three young dons invited to a breakfast party at the Sidgwicks' to meet their house guests – Mr, Mrs and Miss

23. Fanny Hoyle lived until 1947 when she was probably in her late eighties. However, the Bonds and Bulleys seem to have believed in her 'hereditary tendency to consumption'.

Gladstone.[24] Neville, still a staunch liberal, was confirmed in his current admiration of the Prime Minister and 'exceedingly pleased' to find him so uncondescending and affable. By then Fanny's hysterical screeds had persuaded him that there was no future for either of them in a closer relationship. So, back in college after the Sidgwicks' breakfast party, he sat down to write a deliberately gentle reply to the furious outburst that had reached him two days previously: 'I said that I could never again look upon her as a mere acquaintance and I begged that we might at least continue to be true friends to each other'. Unable to accept the finality implicit in this affectionate letter, Fanny's response pleaded and flattered desperately. On 31 October he wrote again telling her:

> I loved her, but I also told her the miserable certainty that I feel we are utterly unsuited to each other. I said that I was not going any more to think of her as a wife, but only as a dear sister; and I asked her if she could learn to care for me as a brother. I was very excited and dont remember exactly what I wrote.

When Neville called on Bond that evening, after dining with the Fawcetts, and brought him up to date with their correspondence, the latter was 'surprised and troubled' at the tenderness with which Neville had displayed his affection for Fanny in a letter which was intended to end their mutual misunderstandings. There were indeed further exchanges and even another meeting at Brookside. What finally killed any prospect of adapting their relationship to a friendly conclusion, however, was Fanny's reckless tongue. Late in the evening of 3 November, after dining with the Venns, Neville went to Brookside in response to an agitated message from Harry:

> He told me that Miss Harland had told Annie that it was all over Newnham that I was engaged to Miss Hoyle. He begged that if we were engaged it shd not be made definitive till the vacation. Then I had a talk with Annie. She spoke quite as strongly as Harry about the unsuitableness of Fanny and me for each other and I felt very much crushed by what she said.

The threat of scandal was decisive. According to the Diary for 5 November:

> I could not understand the cause of the rumour at Newnham that Fanny and I were engaged to each other but I felt that no ground must be given for its continuance, especially considering the relation of pupil and lecturer in wh we stand towards each other. I wrote a damnably rough letter to her saying positively that we must be strangers once again. I felt a great contempt for myself that I shd have gone so far and then not have sufficient courage to risk all to the end. But I have doubts

24. Miss Gladstone was sister to Helen Gladstone (then a Newnhamite, later one of Neville's pupils and later still a vice-principal of Newnham).

where I ought not to have doubts and it was better I shd write as I did and put an end to further uncertainty.

Fanny was at last convinced. The Diary for 6 November recorded her response: '"Your decision finds an echo in my deepest heart. … The only hardship is that a happy dream has ended but it is well it has ended so soon"'. The family at Brookside were enormously relieved. According to the Diary for 7 November: 'Harry writes – It is best so. I feel for both of you very much; all the more because I have had to play such a horrible part all along. I have written to Fanny'. Neville then talked at length to a sympathetic Annie: 'She says that if at the end of 6 months we both feel that we might love each other, she will do all she can to help us'. By then of course Fanny would be in her last term at Newnham and – given a few weeks of absolute discretion on the part of all concerned – scandal could presumably be avoided.

The exchange of letters was abruptly halted. Of course Neville saw Fanny at his lectures and at the Bonds' tea parties; but the uncertainties that had paralysed him in early November dispersed rapidly. On 15 November, for example, he wrote cheerfully: 'I went up to Brookside in the afternoon. Fanny Hoyle came in to tea and I was weak enough to stay. I could not help enjoying myself although we said very little to each other'. Anna Keynes came to stay with the Bonds for some days in mid-November and a week later Neville learned that, whilst in Cambridge, his mother had accepted Fanny's invitation to tea in her Newnham rooms, 'and was very pleased with her'. By then the fact that Fanny had made a good impression was of scant interest to Neville, and she was not again mentioned in the Diary until 6 December 1878, when he met a new Newnham student – a 'Baptist Minister's daughter' called Florence Brown – at a Brookside evening party. 'Fanny Hoyle was there', he wrote, 'and she talked even more wildly than she generally does. I think that is all over'. For him it certainly was. On 11 December he quoted a sententious passage from Fanny's end-of-term letter, full of gratitude to her teacher, in which she insisted: '"I believe I could be a friend that you would care to have; and it wd be good for me to have an interest in you, and you wd help me directly and indirectly to live a better and wider life and to put down sloth and selfishness!"'. Upon which Neville confessed that he agreed with Harry in wishing that the letter had not been written. When he met her again, at a large Newnham afternoon tea-party, he complained that 'she seemed ubiquitous'. At that point he felt grateful to Harry and Annie for opening his eyes to her character. 'The struggle at the beginning of term seems like a nightmare', he wrote, 'following a dream wh was pleasant while it lasted, but wh was only a dream. … I do still care for her very much as a friend, but now I know that my friendship is absolutely without any admixture of another feeling'. To each of her pleading letters which reached him during the rest of December 1878 he responded with unambiguous finality – as for example on 21 December, when he told her 'as plainly but as tenderly as I could my present feelings towards her. I should be very upset by a repetition of what she said in her last letter'. He was finally immune to her attempts to manipulate his emotions.[25]

4 THE COURTING OF FLORENCE

When Neville first met his future wife, Florence Ada Brown, at a Brookside evening party, in December 1878, she was then the youngest student ever to be admitted to Newnham College. Her father, John Brown was a scholar whose publications included a classic biography of John Bunyan and a monograph on the Pilgrim Fathers of New England. He was currently pastor of the congregational chapel at Bedford which he served from 1864 to 1903.[26] Her mother, Ada Brown – herself the daughter of a congregationalist minister and a schoolmistress – had established a school at the Manse where she educated her three daughters and a long succession of other Bedford girls. Their three sons went to Bedford Grammar School, a reputable boys' school. According to Florence's personal 'family biography', written and published when she was herself an octagenarian:

> Our mother had an active mind, unbounded energy and a full share of her own mother's passion for education. On my father's income – never more than modest – she set herself to provide for her daughters educational opportunities equal to the best that money could buy. ... Although Bedford was an educational centre the public schools were for boys only. ... Some of the masters, however, were willing to take outside work and thus it came about that we had from time to time visiting tutors for Latin, French, German, mathematics, botany, piano, musical theory – and even a drill sergeant for physical exercises – in addition to drawing and painting.[27]

25. After his initial sense of relief faded in the early months of 1879, Neville's references to Fanny Hoyle in the Diary dwindled into insignificance. Then, in April 1883 he heard from Harry Bond that 'Fanny Hoyle is introduced to Ernest Radford's friend Mr Rowe', and in August he and Florence (married for a year) gave Fanny a silver sugar sifter and bowl as a wedding present. The following summer the Rowes paid the Keyneses 'a short visit' and Neville took Mr Rowe to see Ely Cathedral. The last reference appeared in January 1889 when the Rowes visited the Frank Darwins and the Keyneses (and the James Wards) were invited to dinner. Mrs Darwin (Ellen Crofts) and Mrs Ward (Mary Martin) had also coincided as Newnhamites with Fanny ten years previously.
26. The congregational chapel in Bedford was known as Bunyan Meeting, because it originated in a barn where John Bunyan used to preach. See Neville Brown, *Dissenting Forbears: The Maternal Ancestors of J.M. Keynes* (Chichester: Phillimore, 1988), p. 80.
27. F.A. Keynes, *Gathering Up the Threads* (Cambridge: Heffer & Sons, 1950), p. 30.

The Manse school served Florence well, for in the summer of 1877, when only 16 years old, she passed the Cambridge Senior Local examination with sufficient distinction to win an Exhibition to Newnham College. Since she was too young to be admitted to college in 1877, John Brown sent her to lodge with the family of a Bonn Pastor, who ran a small finishing school designed to fill some of the gaps in the rather elementary education then available to German girls 'of good family'.[28] As the only English girl in residence, Florence was soon fluent in speaking and writing German, in which she had already acquired a basic grammatical grounding from the modern languages tutor at her mother's school. When, aged 17, she entered Newnham in October 1878, it was with a view to equipping herself with qualifications in subjects that she could usefully teach at the Manse school. She therefore read for the Cambridge Higher Local examination rather than for a tripos. At Newnham Hall she found herself in the ever-watchful care of Miss Anne Jemima Clough who 'threw out hints to friends in Cambridge indicating that the parents of her youngest student did not wish her to go out much'.[29] So it was not until the end of Florence's first term there that the most hospitable congregationalist family in the town obtained permission to invite her to one of their Sunday evening parties at 3 Brookside.

It was over two months before Neville again set eyes on the attractive new student who had first caught his interest in early December 1878. He was then feeling empty and depressed after deflation of the bubble of excited elation that characterized the last stage of his foolish infatuation with Fanny Hoyle. Above all, he was ashamed of his own failure to realize sooner that his emotions were being mindlessly aroused by a disappointed woman still in love with his best friend. Even in the second half of December he continued to receive troubled and troubling letters from Fanny, to which he responded with patient, discouraging, certitude – but without bitterness. Realistically, he blamed himself for the extent to which a manifestly superficial relationship had developed such high importance for him. By Christmas, Fanny knew exactly where they stood with each other. In a long letter, from which he quoted at length in the Diary for Boxing Day she confessed:

> 'You see now very plainly that I had no good and true feeling for you all along but only grasped at you as a drowning man grasps greedily. ... I shall always have on my conscience the painful experience to you that I was the cause of. – Such a letter as yours few men would write I am quite sure. ... And besides being true you were so kind; in return I have dragged you through the mud of my morbid mind – I regard you as someone very old and grave. ... At Newnham they think you are so young, I believe myself that you are not old in experience of character and of struggling humanity.'

28. Ibid., p. 35.
29. Ibid., p. 38.

This rambling apology marked the end of the affair-by-correspondence.

Back in Cambridge in early February 1879 Neville was conscious of a gap in his life and grateful for Annie Bond's attempts to lift his spirits and to keep alive the prospect of a new romantic relationship. The Diary for 7 February, for example, contains extracts from one of her letters of advice, concluding:

> 'I feel that you ought to have someone who will help you to develop what is in you, wh you dont give yourself credit for. May a maiden arise "nobly planned" for you! before many years are over – before you settle into a College Don. In the meantime, here am I, always ready to do any little thing that I can do for you and to be what little help I can.'

It was on Sunday 16 February, that chance and the congregationalist connection opened up a new window of opportunity at Brookside for the frustrated bachelor. That was when John Brown came to Emmanuel Chapel as visiting preacher and stayed, naturally enough, with the Bonds. Neville – at morning service as usual – listened with particular interest to the visitor's sermon and went to hear him again in the evening. The Diary reported:

> I met Mr Brown at the Bonds' at lunch and supper. Miss Brown, who is at Newnham, was also staying with them. I am hasty and the impression will probably not last long; but it seems to me that here is a girl who might make me a good and happy man. Yet this is not for me. I tried to talk to her today and only succeeded in making myself an intolerable bore.

Despite his feelings of inadequacy, and although it was some months before the 17-year-old Newnhamite appreciated it, Neville's courtship of Florence had begun.

The knowledge that John Brown had stayed overnight with the Bonds when he preached at Emmanuel Chapel must have encouraged the protective Miss Clough to let her youngest student accept more invitations to Brookside social events than she might otherwise have done. At any rate Miss Brown was there again twice before the end of the Lent term, as was Neville, with a hint from Annie. On 3 March, for example, the Diary recorded:

> Evening party at the Bonds', – including Miss Hoyle, Miss Martin and Miss Brown. With Fanny Hoyle I feel strange; I know her very well and yet I do not know her at all. Miss Brown did not shake hands with me when she came into the room and it was not until nearly supper time that I could get to talk to her. Then with Harry's assistance I was able to take her into supper and I was near her the rest of the evening. I was as much charmed with her as ever, but I did not seem to get to know her any better, as I so much want to do. She is very shy and nervous though not as awkward and clumsy as I am. Annie told me afterwards that she

informed May Geaves[30] she was afraid of the learned people she had to talk to – lecturers and the like.

Two weeks later it was Harry (rather than Annie) who ensured that when she was there again for Sunday lunch, Neville was also present. The latter wondered in the Diary that day whether she was:

> tired of always finding me there when she goes. But I very much want to see more of her and Harry is willing to help me as much as he can. Annie has gone for a week to Brighton. Harry, Miss Jeeves, Miss Brown and I had the drawing room to ourselves after dinner, being afterwards joined by Miss Hoyle, Mr and Mrs Bond. Miss Brown told me she has done the Grantchester grind at last – only yesterday, however. The subject of walks had been one on wh we had talked more than once. … She was more friendly and talked with less restraint than she had done before; and I was more charmed than ever. Harry reports that from what her Father said when he was at Brookside a few days ago, he thinks she will come for a second year to Newnham. I like the prospect of this. Miss Jeeves told me that Miss Brown is only just 18. I had thought she must be at least 19. I wonder if she thinks me an old fogy.

That Sunday was one of the pleasantest Neville could remember. Even Fanny Hoyle's malicious expressions of surprise at finding him sitting contentedly in the drawing room after lunch, instead of disappearing with Harry on their usual Sunday afternoon walk, did not spoil the occasion for him. Indeed he concluded his account of her taunts by remarking cheerfully:

> My correspondence with her seems now like a distant dream. What a contrast she and Miss Brown are! I wish Fanny and I could be good friends and no more. It was pure folly to think of our ever being more. But that is all over, and perhaps there is a brighter future in store for us all.

From then on, Neville was unable to get Miss Brown out of his mind and she recurs constantly in the Diary. Whenever he and Harry were walking together they talked about her; and he seems to have introduced her into conversations with most of his other walking companions who frequented Brookside. On 5 March, for example, after 'a pleasant walk with Hume Pinsent', Neville noted with relief that he was not the only admirer who found it hard to draw the shy young Newnhamite out in conversation. Occasionally (though not often) he saw her by chance – for example, at the Senate House on 20 March, when degrees were being conferred: 'Miss Brown was there. I suppose on account of Rose' he added, apparently envious of her

30. May Jeeves (misspelt in this entry) was staying with the Bonds. She later married Neville's London University College contemporary Alfred Dale, a classicist fellow of Trinity Hall who left Cambridge in 1899 to be principal of University College, Liverpool and become its first vice-chancellor as a full university from 1903 to 1919.

friendship with the brother of Miss Rose another Bedford Newnhamite. Fortunately Miss Clough's end-of-term 'At Home' on 29 March presented him with another informal opportunity to speak with her. Neville – gleefully anticipating the event – had already been warned by Harry not to talk too much to Miss Brown or Fanny Hoyle would draw mischievous attention to them. In the event, he was lucky from the outset:

> Miss Brown was standing near Miss Clough as I went in and the latter asked her to give me a cup of tea. This she did and then she took me to see the laboratory and the gymnasium. Fanny Hoyle came in and took me off to the top of the house … but Miss Brown presently joined us on the roof with Annie Bond and I was able to talk to her a little more. Not that that was much good for I was very nervous and awkward. … She did not seem to be so nervous as usual. It is foolish to allow myself to be so attracted by her as is the case, I wish knew her as well as that man Rose. … I told her I wished I could chaperon her and take her to see all the sights of Cambridge and neighbourhood, including the top of King's. … On our way down from the roof she told me her room was on the second floor. I laughingly begged to be allowed to see it; but that is of course against the rules. … I talked more or less foolishly to Miss Crofts, Miss Martin, Fanny Hoyle etc; but it seems to me that just now I am generally thinking of Miss Brown, whatever else I may be. I stayed till the last moment talking to Miss Crofts, and I was next door to being turned out of the house.

The Diary demonstrates that before the end of the 1879 Lent term Neville was in love with Florence Brown – more completely than he had ever been with anyone. On the day after Miss Clough's enjoyable party, for example, as he and Harry strolled back from Newnham to which they had jointly escorted Fanny Hoyle (after her usual Sunday tea with the Bonds), the two bachelors again discussed the special attractions of Miss Brown. According to Neville's account, it was Harry who wondered aloud:

> why it is that we are both much more drawn by her than by any other of the Newnhamites. He thinks it is partly because she is so womanly. I think I was first affected by her beautiful smile. No doubt she must be most attractive personally to everybody. But it is not that alone. I am beginning to think of her as my type of purity and sincerity and all that is lovely in women.

Circumstances conspired, however, to render her maddeningly elusive. For the next six weeks Neville saw her three times at most. At the very end of term he caught a brief glimpse of her in town – a chance sighting which left him 'quite excited'. Immediately after the Easter vacation, he and Pinsent, walking on Grantchester meadows, passed 'a girl who I feel sure was Miss Brown gathering kingcups'. Later still, on 4 May he saw her afar at the Emmanuel service and groaned desperately to the Diary: 'It doesnt seem as if I am going to have an opportunity of speaking to her the whole term'. Worse still, it was possible that she might leave Newnham for good, after sitting the Higher Local examination in the early summer. On 8 May Neville wrote:

> Mrs Bond tells me that Miss Brown is afraid she will not be able to return to Cambridge in October; she thinks that she ought to stay at home to help her Mother in her school. Mrs Bond seems anxious that we shd have more opportunity of seeing each other; and I am grateful to her.

Mrs Bond spoke from the heart and did her best for him. On the very next Sunday, Neville – duly alerted – found Miss Brown taking tea at Brookside again and reported more cheerfully:

> She was I think more friendly than she had been at all before. … She said she would be glad to have lunch with me next Saturday and go to the races afterwards. I had somehow been afraid that I shd get a refusal. … I walked down to chapel with her and Miss Jeeves. I mentioned incidentally that I hoped she would stay up at Newnham another year and take another group [of subjects] and she let the remark pass.

Having persuaded her to join the first of his May Week parties, however, Neville pronounced himself thoroughly happy 'for a change'. He was optimistic about his chances of arranging a succession of relatively free and easy meetings in the traditionally festive atmosphere of the Easter term. There were, however, two personal anxieties clouding his horizon. The first was the possibility that Miss Brown (he still referred to her thus formally in the Diary) might go down from Cambridge before he had had time to establish any kind of sustainable relationship with her. The second was the tragedy then threatening the domestic happiness and social reputation of his friends the Bonds. On the day that Neville returned to Cambridge after the Easter vacation, he had been horrified by Harry's confession – made in the course of a walk to Coton – that he and Daisy Duncan 'were quite unsuited to each other'. The news so astonished Neville that he hardly knew what to say. According to the Diary:

> My only advice to Harry was not to do anything hastily: and to tell Annie everything as he had told me. They were engaged hastily, after seeing very little of each other; but that was under circumstances in wh it could hardly be otherwise if they were to be engaged at all.

The underlying problem was that the circumstances constraining young male dons in their social contacts with women students of the university made it almost impossible to develop a natural friendly relationship in advance of a formal commitment.

Neville was the first of Harry's friends or relations to be told that the engagement was falling apart. Some members of the Bond family probably suspected as much already; a note in the Diary for 22 April recorded: 'His people remark on how gloomy Harry is'; and later, on 21 May – several weeks before Harry had been persuaded to talk frankly with Annie – Neville wrote in some embarrassment:

> Annie spoke to me very seriously about Harry's behaviour to Miss Duncan at Easter. He seems to have been irritated at nearly everything she said. ... He has not himself told Annie how he feels with regard to Miss Duncan and so I could not say much about it. She regrets that she and Harry really know so much less of each other than a brother and sister should.

As for Daisy she was probably having a wretched time, for as early as 14 May Neville heard that Miss Clough had referred to 'that sad affair of Miss Duncan's' – and at the same time cast doubt on the idea that Annie could be considered a sufficient chaperon for Newnham girls. Nevertheless, it was not surprising – apart altogether from the perennial Bond family frictions – that Harry hesitated either to confide in Annie, or to break openly with Daisy, before the latter had written her Higher Local examinations. He knew as well as anyone that his family's long-standing ambitions to bridge the gulf between town and gown in Cambridge were threatened by any infringement of the university's severe sexual code of behaviour that might be associated, directly or indirectly, with an individual member of that hospitable household.

May Week began on 14 May, on the day Anna Keynes arrived from Salisbury to stay with the Bonds. Over the next two weeks Cambridge came alive, as it did every year at that season, with parties revolving around the river boat races and the college rivalries. On 17 May Neville borrowed T.H. Orpen's rooms[31] (which were grander than his own set) and gave a lunch party for three Newnhamites, Miss Jeeves (a house guest of the Bonds since the previous summer), five young men and two chaperons (his mother and Mrs Bond). The seating plan in the Diary shows the host at the head of the table between Miss Brown and Mrs Bond. At the other end sat John Cox, between Miss Jeeves and Mrs Keynes. After lunch Neville toured his guests around Pembroke and tea was then served in the fellows' garden. At about 5 p.m. most of the younger members of the party walked down to the river where Neville had hired a boat so that they could row downstream to the stretch of the river where the races were then in progress. Mrs Bond and Mrs Keynes went back to Brookside, and the boat party was joined by Harry Bond as an oarsman, and Mrs Pinsent as the chaperon without whom the Newnhamites – Miss Brown, Miss Crofts and Miss Martin – would have felt obliged to walk decorously away from the mixed company. Neville reported the rest of the day's highlights at length in the Diary, for example:

31. Orpen had resigned his Pembroke fellowship to marry and take up a living, Neville had been promised his rooms for 1880/81.

> I was delighted at the interest wh Miss Brown seemed to take in everything. She learned the colours of the different clubs with surprising quickness. … The Newnhamites returned with us to Brookside to tea. On our way back from the boats I ventured to speak to Miss Brown about coming back to Newnham in October. She said that it was a great trouble to her to decide what to do. … She said she might never again be so much wanted at home as she will be during the next year. What could I reply to that? … Harry walked back to Newnham with Miss Martin and Miss Crofts; and I followed with Miss Brown. I was rash enough to ask her to join our party again on Tuesday. She did not give a decided refusal; but said she was afraid her work would not allow her … it was not merely the time that she lost, but she felt so dissipated next day. Perhaps I was foolish to ask her and she may resent it. Harry thinks not, but says she wont come because of propriety. I believe that she has a sort of respect for me, but that she finds me a bore and annoyance, and that this might develop into a positive dislike. Feeling this why am I so infatuated as to want to see more of her and so risk boring and annoying her more?

Neville's second party took place on 20 May and involved more guests than the first. The group occupied two boats down river to the races. Miss Brown was there, having been coaxed by a special letter from Annie Bond, and it was not difficult to ensure that she travelled in Neville's boat, along with other Newnhamites (one of whom was Fanny Hoyle) and his mother. According to the Diary: 'Miss Brown steered us back. I walked towards Brookside partly with her alone and partly with her and Mother. She said that Miss Clough appeared much shocked when she told her in the morning that she wished to go again to the races'. This time the climax of the evening was a supper party which Neville gave in C.H. Prior's rooms and again he sat between Miss Brown and his mother. Evidently the awkwardness between them was fast diminishing in the festive atmosphere, for the Diary continued:

> Conversation flows much more easily between us now. She has not read many novels and I have recommended a course of George Eliot after her examination. … After supper we migrated to Orpen's rooms and had some music. Miss Brown does seem a little interested in Pembroke and in Orpen's rooms, partly I hope because I am going to have them. Bond walked with Miss Richmond to their cab and I followed with her. … I thought she shook hands and said goodbye in a very friendly way and I went to bed in a happy state of mind. I am beginning to imagine a future that seems almost too delightful to be capable of realisation. But I dare say I am deceiving myself from the outset … she can hardly dislike me, or she would not have accepted my second invitation.

Encouraged by what he hoped were friendly signals, Neville then invited Miss Brown to join the party he and the Bonds had organized to view the boat procession, an annual event celebrating the results of the rowing competition. As usual she replied hesitantly, this time indicating that she had had an alternative invitation to which she was not yet committed. Neville was therefore particularly delighted when she joined his group on Clare Bridge and did not stray, even after greeting other friends on the bridge. In general, however, it proved a disappointing encounter – partly because it offered almost no opportunity of one-to-one conversation, partly because he himself had to depart early, to a Trinity Feast, when he 'might have had a little more time with her', but most of all because she 'said good afternoon very coldly indeed'. He remained sadly ignorant of what the quiet young girl thought of the attentions she was getting from an extraordinarily nervous bachelor don. Not until a year later – after Neville had finally plucked up courage to propose marriage – did he hear her side of the story. According to the Diary for 20 May 1880:

> F. actually thought for a long time after she knew me that I was engaged to Miss Hoyle – that being I suppose the current report at Newnham … but about this time last year she came to the conclusion that she must be mistaken about me and Fanny Hoyle. She says that she went to the races with me last year … thinking that I had asked her out of pure philanthropy.

Later still, on 21 July 1880, she was to elaborate on her past feelings in terms which suggested that it was actually when watching the 1879 boat procession that she first began to suspect that her host's intentions towards her were not as disinterested as she had originally supposed. According to the Diary:

> We talked … of a year ago. She said that her old feelings towards me were sometimes very strange; now and then she felt that she hated me, e.g. the boat procession day. … It was only quite at the end of the '79 May that she thought at all that I cared.

By the end of May Week 1879, Neville was in a state of high excitement. Florence had accepted three personal invitations from him; and he expected to see her socially at least twice before term ended – first at a Brookside tea party and second at a Newnham garden party. He was further encouraged when his mother (who was leaving Cambridge the next week) told him that Florence had deliberately lingered after the Sunday evening service to say goodbye to her. Meanwhile the Bonds watched his mounting excitement with a mixture of sympathy and anxiety. First Harry and then Annie warned him not to be hasty or rash. It was unlikely that Miss Clough suspected kind Mr Keynes of being a potential danger to any of her girls.[32] On the other hand,

32. Much later, when the engagement was known to all, Miss Creak told a breakfast party hosted by Neville on 31 October, that Miss Clough had said to her: 'Mr Keynes cannot have seen much of Miss Brown at Cambridge for he only came to Newnham two or three times while she was up and he never lectured to her!'. Noting this in the Diary, Neville wondered whether Miss Clough was deluded or hoping to delude others.

she was concerned to control the number of invitations that the youngest of them should be permitted to accept. At lunch on 29 May, the day of the Bonds' tea party, Mrs Bond showed Neville a letter from Miss Brown saying that Miss Clough did not think that she ought to come. According to the Diary, Annie came to the rescue:

> She called on Miss Clough and persuaded her to let Miss Brown come in the evening. She asked me in return to be careful how I behaved and not to walk back to Newnham with her. … After tea we walked in the garden and I devoted myself exclusively to Fanny Hoyle.

Later, in the drawing room, in the course of a 'long and pleasant' talk with Miss Brown, he made it as plain as he could that he was very interested in whether or not she returned to Cambridge.

At the Newnham garden party on 31 May, mindful of Annie's warnings (repeated the previous day in the course of a walk in the Botanical Gardens), Neville began by keeping a discreet distance from Florence, who 'had a hat with a large red ribbon and looked more charming than ever'. Eventually, with Harry's and Annie's connivance, he drew close enough to enter into casual conversation with her, but when saying goodbye he sensed that he took her hand with such warmth that 'she appeared to object'. The Bonds were not, of course, alone in observing how fascinated Mr Keynes was by Miss Brown and rumours were gathering momentum in Newnham. The Diary reports, for example, that at Brookside the next day, Fanny Hoyle (present as usual for Sunday tea) 'remarked that she had scarcely seen me yesterday and she had heard several others say the same'. Presumably Miss Clough's young ladies – especially the nonconformist element, who valued their regular visits to Brookside – were careful to insulate her from such rumours. In any case, Florence was allowed to accept invitations from the Bonds for each of the next two Sundays. On both occasions Neville raised with her the question of her return to Cambridge. He could think of little else. On 8 June – having heard her say that she did not expect to return to Newnham in October – he urged her to stay longer than usual with the tea party, instead of leaving early to attend the evening service. According to the Diary: 'After a slight hesitation she consented to stay'. Braced by that promising signal, and having discovered that Florence was unfamiliar with the novels of his favourite author, George Eliot, Neville tried to initiate a suitable correspondence with her. He lent her his copies of *Romola*, *Silas Marner*, and *The Mill on the Floss* – sending them with a letter of apology for his own awkwardness in conversation and adding the somewhat superfluous information that he counted on seeing her at Brookside in October. The initiative fell flat, however. As he never tired of noting in the Diary, she was quite unlike Fanny Hoyle; and the only response was: 'a friendly note from Miss Brown thanking me for sending the books but not making any reference to what I had said in my note'.

On 16 June, the last Sunday of the term, they were both at Brookside for lunch and again Neville raised the question at the top of his mind. This time her answer caused him to rage against Miss Clough, who must often have wished that the teenage daughter of the Manse, to whom she was officially *in loco parentis*, was less sought after. Neville wrote with unusually egotistical fury:

> I can only call Miss Clough a malignant and stupid old lady. She has quite given Miss Brown the impression that she does not want her back at Newnham next year. 'Well, my dear, if your mother wants you, you had better stay at home. Perhaps you will be able to return to Newnham in two or three years time'.

The fact was that – as his (and her) friends never tired of reminding him – Florence was only just 18.

> I wish there was not so much difference in age between us

He reflected gloomily in the Diary:

> … people will say she is too young to be engaged. But what does it matter what people will say. It only matters what she feels and I cannot tell much what that is from her manner. I was fancying that she was beginning to care a little about me, but Annie seems to think not.

As he was to learn a year later (in the course of a conversation with Florence which he reported in the Diary on 21 July 1880) she was actually so unnerved by the intensity of his behaviour towards her that she 'wanted to run away'. Her reaction may have been apparent to Annie, who wrote a sensible letter that reached Neville a few days later in Salisbury: '"She is so young and unformed at present it will be more necessary for you both to grow slowly into it. I will do my best to give you opportunities of seeing her"'. Although Neville respected Annie's judgement he found it hard to come to terms with her assessment of the situation. 'I dare say she is right', he confided to the Diary, 'but … I feel that I shall not be properly living this summer'.

Neville's dejection was obvious to his friends. Several of them told him how pale and thin he looked and he fretted about his loss of weight. That sunless summer of 1879 – reportedly the coldest and wettest in England for 60 years – matched his mood. To add to his depression, the Bond family were appalled in July by Harry's broken engagement to Daisy Duncan, whom they had all taken to their hearts, and Neville shared in the sadness affecting all who cared for the unhappy pair. Meanwhile, Fanny Hoyle, evidently hoping to extract confidences about his feelings for Florence, had written him one of her insidiously sympathetic letters from which he quoted on 25 June with wry amusement: '"I wish you wd trust me more. … Mr Keynes how can people *help* liking you"'. No longer capable of being deluded, however, by what he sarcastically described as Fanny's 'genius for letter writing', he commented: 'I do not wish to indulge in comparisons; but it is as clear as noonday to me that only Miss Brown can I really love, and it is she who can make me far the better and happier man'. He had by then confided in his mother (though not as freely as he often did to Annie), and the bracing maternal response was accordingly less than perceptive. 'I have told her partly how I feel with regard to Miss Brown', he wrote. 'I know it gives her pleasure that I shd not show myself reserved towards her. With a mother's partiality she thinks it extremely unlikely that I shd be declined'.

Over the next ten months Neville's hopes were alternately lifted and dashed. On 13 July, for example, they were briefly raised by the arrival of a letter from Mr Brown to the Bonds: 'thanking them very warmly for their kindness to his daughter Florence. He says he hopes that she will return to Cambridge'. Mrs Brown apparently thought otherwise. The news that Florence had passed her Higher Local examination – with a first-class result in Group A (including distinction in English language and literature), and a third class in Group C (with distinction in arithmetic) – gave Neville an excuse to write her a letter of congratulation. Her reply, quoted in the Diary for 13 August, hit him hard. Florence wrote:

> 'It is still very improbable that I shall return to Cambridge for anything more than a visit. When I went home my Mother – very unnecessarily I am sure – thought I was looking tired and wd not I think consent to my returning to Newnham. For my own part I am still vain enough to think I am needed at home.'

Neville's spirits drooped, but it was hardly surprising that Ada Brown, with a school to run and five other children at home (their ages ranging from under one year to 15), should have needed the help of her eldest daughter at that juncture. A few days later (as Neville, his mother and the Bonds travelled from Cambridge to Dover on the first stage of their joint Swiss holiday) his hopes soared at Annie's news of a letter from Florence hinting that she might return to Newnham after Christmas. This welcome information plunged him into paralysing uncertainty, however; for whilst there remained a possibility that Florence might return as a Newnham student, Neville dared not compromise his (and the Bonds') reputation in the university by attempting a direct approach to her. As it turned out, he did not see her again until late November, in effect representing a gap of more than five months since their last, relatively relaxed, conversation at Brookside. All he could do in that restless intermission was to urge Annie to keep in touch with Florence and, especially, to invite her to come for as long a visit to Brookside as possible during the October term. As ever Annie was cooperative, but the answer was slow in coming. As late as 1 November, for example, Annie showed him a letter from Florence which neither accepted the invitation to Brookside nor indicated whether she expected to return to Newnham. At which Neville wrote miserably: 'she can hardly care about coming', whilst desperately hoping that she did care. A few days later the Diary reported: 'I have twice met her friends, Miss Burges and Miss Sallitt this term. They have once or twice seemed to twinkle to each other in a comic sort of way when they have seen me; but I think it is very likely my fancy'. In the end, Annie's persistence was rewarded. On the evening of Sunday 16 November, after he had visited Brookside with James Ward, Neville noted: 'Mrs Bond spoke about Miss Brown's coming on Tuesday and I was amused to observe that Annie blushed while I did not'.

Florence stayed with the Bonds for a full week from 18 November. Neville turned up daily, at times for the merest glimpse of her. On the first evening he reported: 'She seemed shy and nervous but I thought her as charming as ever … she must to some extent know that she is not to me as other girls are'. In fact, however, although he noted obsessively every sign of friendliness or frigidity in her manner towards him, he had no sufficient reason to suppose that she had the slightest idea of how strongly he felt about her. They were rarely able to converse privately for more than a matter of minutes, and on those occasions, as he confessed to the Diary, he was so full of things he wanted to say that he 'was awkward and said practically nothing at all'. He rejoiced that she was now thoroughly at home with his friends, the Bonds, and still more cheered by the readiness with which she discussed with them her hopes of returning to Newnham after Christmas – in spite of Miss Clough's doubts whether there would actually be a room available for her in the Lent term. By the sixth day of her visit to Brookside, Sunday 23 November, Neville was in a happier frame of mind. Annie had written to tell him about Florence's 'very nice talk with Miss Clough yesterday. She was most kind she says and thinks she will try and manage to take her in'. Inevitably, however, Annie's letter concluded with a severe warning: '"If you come on Sunday afternoon leave before Fanny Hoyle comes. I think it better. Please"'.

Of course, Neville came on the Sunday afternoon. The Diary reported euphorically:

> Miss Brown shook hands with me in a different sort of way from what she wd with an ordinary acquaintance. She is more at home with the Bonds than she ever was and this afternoon she seemed more charming than ever. She sat at one end of the sofa playing with a peacock fan and Minnie sat on the ground leaning against her. They were chaffing Minnie about being so old and her about being so young. Miss Martin was there and Fanny Hoyle came half an hour earlier and before I had gone. I left a little after 4.

He returned a discreet few hours later (when Fanny had gone) and, according to the Diary:

> We talked together both before supper, at supper and after supper. We were able to say far more to each other than we had done during all the rest of her stay at Brookside. It seems that she as well as Mr Bond rather objects to Sunday morning breakfasts[33] but she did not appear much shocked at hearing that I had made Tripos papers on a Sunday. She did not express any decided objection to the theatre. We talked a good deal about our respective families and I gave her some idea of my prospects up here and hinted at the possibility of my finally going to practise at the bar. It seems that there will be room for her at Newnham next term only if some student who now expects to return does not. I am afraid the chance is a slender one but she seems really anxious to come back and says that she shall not let Miss Clough forget her promise. She thinks she must not go at all to the races if she does happen to be up next term. It seems that Miss Clough tells downright stories about the number of times she went out last term. … We talked about the George Eliots I lent her of wh she liked Romola the best, about the Lakes, and about the weddings she had been to in the Long etc. She was quite friendly throughout and I enjoyed the time immensely. The only drawback was that at saying goodbye she shook hands more coldly than usual.

The next day, Annie and her cousin from Birmingham (also staying at Brookside) accompanied Florence to tea with Neville at his rooms and Harry came in a little later. According to the Diary: 'She was exceedingly jolly. … I was with her alone in my back room for about a couple of minutes and perhaps I might have taken the opportunity of hinting at my feelings'. But he did not – partly in deference to Annie's dire warnings and partly because he feared to ruin his chances with Florence by being too hasty. He continued to indulge in wishful thinking; for example telling himself: 'she must recognise that I am more than a little attracted by her', and: 'she continues decidedly friendly in her manner'. He and Harry jointly walked her back to Brookside. By the time he wrote up his Diary that night, he believed not only that they had made 'tolerably rapid progress towards knowing each other' over the past two days, but also that she intended to return after Christmas. She had said, for example, that she was not at all satisfied with her poor result in mathematics and that, if no other room was available at Newnham she expected to be allowed to share with Miss Sallitt. The next day she returned to Bedford, leaving Neville to face a few more weeks of anxious uncertainty. When he left Cambridge himself in mid-December he took Annie to Salisbury to spend Christmas with him and his mother. On the way she told him that Florence had written to say that she needed to pass in another Higher Local Group in order to get the teaching certificate she wanted: 'another reason why Miss

33. Neville's invitation to Annie, her cousin and Florence was originally to Sunday breakfast with him, but on Annie's advice he changed it to a tea party.

Clough shd make an extra effort to find room for her', he noted with satisfaction.

Harry's letter carrying the 'exceedingly good news' that *she* was coming up this term arrived on 7 January. A week later Annie enclosed Florence's letter saying that 'Miss Clough will be delighted to have me back', with her own letter setting the ground rules for a suitably covert courtship:

> I'll trust you to be very wise for us as well as yourself and her, for you know it just would not do for us if it were at all known at Newnham. I am so thankful that Minnie likes her – it's a great point. I think she ought to come once or twice in the term when you are not in, for appearance's sake. Well you and Harry will have to manage it between you. I am so very glad about it.

By the beginning of term, however, the matchmaker was in a state of high alarm. According to the Diary for 20 January:

> Annie is afraid that Mrs Cox[34] has discovered that I care for Miss Brown. This is strange. … I do not think she has ever seen us together. Annie says, however, that John Cox was on the roof at Newnham when Miss Brown and I were there and she saw him give a twinkle. … But no doubt Fanny Hoyle is Mrs Cox's informant. Annie thinks I am to blame for having asked Miss Brown twice to my rooms last May term.

The lesson that Annie drew was that Neville must 'pay the penalty by being … extra cautious'. So, although he saw Miss Brown at Emmanuel on the first Sunday of term, he was forbidden to appear at Brookside that day because she had been invited to tea. This was particularly hard in that Neville could envisage no other prospect of meeting Florence in circumstances that might allow him to engage her in meaningful conversation. Worse still, as it turned out, Annie herself was away from Cambridge for the whole of the Lent term, which meant that Minnie was effectively in charge of issuing the family's invitations to Newnhamites. Unfortunately Minnie disapproved in principle of her sister's matchmaking proclivities and it soon transpired that she was positively 'rebelling at the way in wh Harry in person and Annie by letter are insisting on her inviting Miss Brown more'.[35]

In consequence there were only two social occasions that term which offered Neville an opportunity to converse with Miss Brown. The first of these was on 15 February, when the Diary records:

34. Mrs Cox, Annie's close friend (Caroline Bulley), had married John Cox then warden of the ill-fated Cavendish College. See P. Searby, 'A failure at Cambridge: Cavendish College 1877–92', *Proceedings of the Cambridge Antiquarian Society*, Vol. 72, 1982/83.
35. Neville did not learn the reason until 13 May when Annie told him: 'why Minnie objected to help me to see as much as possible of Miss B. The "responsibility" of giving any two people a lift on the road to matrimony is too great and she wonders how Annie can undertake it as she does'.

> a thoroughly enjoyable time at Brookside. It is very pleasant merely to be able to look at her and feel her presence near and besides that … a good deal of talk together. She was quite friendly and not shy, but I cannot persuade myself that she shewed the slightest sign of caring for me more for instance than … for Harry. … She rather wanted to leave before tea but Minnie would not let her. … I am afraid that I shd have made efforts to walk to chapel with her. But Harry wd not let me. … She talks a good deal about [A.] Caldecott of St John's who seems to have been visiting at Bedford.

In fact, as Florence confessed some time later, she now knew that she was being courted and her references to Caldecott and other young men were wholly mischievous.[36] It would have done much for Neville's self-confidence had he grasped then that he was being teased; but he was still agonizingly dubious whether she had noticed his interest in her. The second Lent term party to which they were both invited took place a fortnight later. According to the Diary for 29 February:

> I went up to Brookside a little before 4 and in the drawing room I found only Harry, Miss Buchanan and Fanny Hoyle. … Presently, however, there was a little knock on the door and in she came. She was very delightful. … I cant help thinking that she likes me a little. … After tea Harry and Fanny Hoyle and she and I sat for some time in the drawing room without gas but with a bright fire burning from which we shielded ourselves with fans. I dont think we talked much but I felt quite happy. About a quarter to seven she left for chapel.

On that occasion the ubiquitous Fanny Hoyle was in difficult mood. She deliberately needled Harry (who was currently focusing on Miss Maggie Johnson), and embarrassed Neville – who was prevented from slipping unobtrusively into a seat that became vacant beside Florence by Fanny's loud announcement that that was the chair he would find most comfortable.

When Neville returned to Pembroke on 10 April for the Easter term he knew that he was unlikely to get more than a fleeting glimpse of the object of his affections (in chapel perhaps or in the street) until Annie returned to Cambridge in a couple of weeks time. On Sunday 16 April he poured out his frustration into the Diary:

> 11pm. It is too absurd. All this afternoon I sat in my rooms trying to read Williams on Real Property and inwardly fuming and fretting because I did not know when I should have an opportunity of seeing Florence Brown. Then when I got to chapel in the evening Harry told me she had been to tea at Brookside!

36. The Diary entry for 31 October 1880 quotes a letter from Florence: 'Something told me that you did not altogether care to hear about him and Mr Haddon and so – horrible confession – I sometimes talked about them much more than I otherwise shd have done. You must not … suppose I wanted to make you jealous … it was simply a spirit of mischief that prompted me'.

Harry had simply forgotten to alert his friend in time. Outside the chapel she shook hands with them both – which was better than the distant bow Neville got the previous week – but he was inconsolable: 'It does seem hard that loving her as I do I shd not yet have had the opportunity of speaking to her this term'. The following Sunday he went up to Brookside at about 4 p.m. to find Miss Creak, Miss Pinsent, Fanny Hoyle, Minnie and Harry taking tea. He had hoped, though hardly expected, to see Florence, but according to the Diary:

> At half past four she came in with Annie. I believe the latter had been so awfully good as to go to Newnham on purpose to fetch her. I thought I had never before seen her looking so pretty and charming. … She wore a simple dress without ornaments of any kind. I wonder that everybody is not madly in love with her. Well I am and that's enough. We had a good deal of talk together. She spoke as if she were looking forward to May week and I am sure I am. Then perhaps I may tell her … how much I love her. … I walked down to chapel with her and Annie and Miss Creak but did not go in myself.

Neville was convinced that if he did not succeed in effectively communicating his intentions to Florence during the festive fortnight in late May, his chances of persuading her to marry him could vanish. For she did not intend to read for a tripos and would certainly leave Newnham as soon as she had achieved the Higher Local results that would earn her the desired teaching certificate. He spent sleepless nights 'thinking of Florence Brown'[37] and responded crossly (on 3 May) to Annie's 'serious lecture as to whether Miss Brown and I know each other well enough for me to think of asking her to be my wife'. The only occasion preceding May Week when he might expect to meet her was Miss Clough's annual garden party. That, however, was ruined for him by a nervous note from Annie which reached him just as he was setting out for Newnham. He quoted it in the Diary: '"You must be extremely careful this afternoon. Harry hears (from Fanny Hoyle) that you and FB are much talked about in Newnham and it wd soon get to Miss Clough's ears. They will be watching you. It is horrid"'. Neville agreed:

> It is damnable. … For her own sake as well as for Annie – who is very fearful of being talked about as a matchmaker and of Brookside getting again into Miss Clough's bad books – I must be careful. But it was dreadfully hard. Soon after I got to Newnham we just met and shook hands.

He then walked discreetly away and strolled aimlessly about the garden, talking to all the Newnhamites he knew, except Florence, although (the Diary recalls):

37. It was not until April 1880 that he began referring to her as Florence Brown rather than as Miss Brown in the Diary.

> I think I always knew whereabouts she was. … I do trust my manner shewed her I had been acting a part when I seemed to avoid her … my conduct must have seemed that of a brute. … The only thing to be glad of is that if any people were watching our behaviour towards each other they must have been thoroughly well sold. … Annie says that if she cares for me she has at any rate more command over herself than I – that I have a telltale face, that anyone carefully observing me last time we were at Brookside together might have told I cared … from the way in wh I looked at her.

Two days after this disappointing event, Neville encountered Florence briefly at Brookside where, according to the Diary: 'I cannot say I enjoyed myself. … She remarked that I had treated her very badly on Saturday hardly saying a word to her', to which he stammered:

> a lame answer … [which] … made things worse instead of better. … We were left alone together in the dining room for a minute or two. … I said nothing. She left rather soon. … Since coming back to my rooms I have written … asking her to join my party for the races this day fortnight; and then I went on to tell her that I spent a wretched afternoon on Saturday and really wanted to be with her. I said more … and in conclusion I begged her to write … telling me that she excused my writing as I had done. I wonder if she will. I cannot settle down to any work this evening.

Florence's reply, which arrived by the midday post on 12 May, put him out of his misery:

> She says that she shd 'like very much indeed' to join my party for the boats … then continues 'I am sorry I troubled you by saying anything about Saturday. I never thought for a moment that you avoided me because you did not think it worthwhile when so many other people were here.' I think this is sufficiently kindly to shew that she is not very angry with what I said in my letter.

He could now plan a strategy for his May Week party at which he was absolutely determined to propose marriage to Florence.

Florence's letter contained the warmest response that Neville had had to any of his invitations to her. So, on Sunday 16 May, after noting her distinctly friendly bow (on coming out of both the morning and evening services at Emmanuel), he wrote hopefully: 'She must know now … that I care … and I cannot help feeling sanguine that she cares for me a little. But I cannot go on much longer in this state of uncertainty'. Meanwhile both Annie and Fanny Hoyle did their best to discourage him from trying to resolve the situation in haste. Annie again walked him round the Botanical Gardens to warn him of impending scandal, and to name some of those who were either spreading or reacting to the rumours linking the youngest Newnhamite and the eligible Pembroke don. As ever, he worried to the Diary:

> It seems that the talk at Newnham dates back from last May term when I was certainly rather rash. Miss Magill is at the bottom of it. She was at the party at B'side during Mother's visit when I walked back with F as far as Pembroke. Then she noticed that I was 'paying marked attentions to Miss Brown' and at the Senate House … honorary degrees … 'her suspicions were confirmed'. … Miss Merrifield is also good enough to interest herself in the matter, although she cannot personally have noticed anything. She is concerned 'for the sake of the cause'.[38]

Fanny's letter on the same theme carried the following warning:

> You will have to undergo a great deal of obloquy in the end I am afraid and so will the Bonds; and for them especially I am sorry and for their friends here. … I hope you know what is best … and have thought thoroughly about everything. … However things go, Miss Clough might be so indignant as to refuse to let any more students be introduced to them.

Whilst frankly dismayed at the suggestion that he might bring his Brookside friends into ill repute, Neville was unimpressed by Fanny's advice and suspected her of exaggerating 'through fear for herself'. He noted complacently:

> At any rate Miss Clough cannot have the remotest idea of anything at present. I have just had a very kind note from her in wh she says that she will be glad to come to supper with me next Wednesday and will go to the races with us too if a chaperon is really wanted.

The party to which Neville had decorously invited Miss Clough took place on the first night of the 1880 May races, when he had 24 men and women to supper (in the Pembroke lecture hall above his own rooms) – following a river party for which he had hired three boats to take 21 of them to the races. Among the guests were three married ladies (apart from his mother), so that it was unlikely that Miss Clough would feel obliged to play chaperon. Meanwhile Florence had been invited to the second race party, on 20 May, which started with tea (given by Harry) before taking to the boats (organized by Neville). That was the day when Neville – having manoeuvred Florence to the fringe of a merry May Week jaunt – managed at last to declare his love for her, whilst everybody else's attention was concentrated on the river events. The Diary entry describing the occasion ran to nearly five pages, of which the gist was:

> It was some time after the 2nd division races were over before I could get to be alone with F. though she did not seem to be trying to avoid me. … I could not summon enough courage to say what I wanted to say to her. … When I did begin

38. The 'cause' that Miss Merrifield had in mind was the cause of women's higher education in Cambridge – which might have been threatened by the development of a relationship between a male lecturer and a woman student.

to say a few words I was so confused that hardly anything could have been intelligible to her except my desire to tell her that I cared for her. She too seemed troubled, even distressed and nervous … she wanted hastily to rejoin the others. At last I did express myself, but how clumsily. … I felt truly that I was made of clay. … If I had been absolutely alone with her I think I could have got on better. … However, she did not repel me and she did say Yes when I implored her … [to] … tell me whether she could care for me. She went on to say that it seemed strange and unreal, that we knew so little of each other, that she was so young and that she was afraid I did not understand her and that I shd not find her sufficiently companionable. I protested that I knew enough of her to trust my happiness absolutely to her … and that if she would only love me I felt I could undertake to make her happy and that her love for me would make me altogether and more worthy of her. I got her to say that although she could not feel that she knew me at all well, yet she did feel that she could trust herself to me. She was surprised and annoyed that certain Newnhamites were already talking about us … and we agreed that I could not even write to ask her Father's consent till she had left Newnham. She said it was horrible to think of what Miss Clough wd say if she knew all. … I told her Annie knew how I felt … and she wanted particularly to know if she thought we were suited to each other. We went on talking all through the 1st div^{n} races of which of course we saw nothing. We had a quiet row home and then I walked with her from the boathouses to the end of Pembroke when she and Fanny H. returned to Newnham, Annie … with them. … We talked more freely than we had done by the river, though the talk was not so direct. I told her among other things what trouble the thought of her possibly caring for Rose, Caldecott or Haddon had sometimes caused me. … She would not tell me exactly what she thought about my avoiding her at Miss Clough's party; but she apparently noticed that I was talking a good deal to Miss Sharp. She knows now my real reason for avoiding her. … I went back to supper at Brookside. … I told Annie hurriedly of the talk F and I had … and Harry has a vague notion. I have not yet told Mother. After returning … I wrote to F telling her rather better than I had done by the river how I felt towards her. I hope before very long to get something in reply. I can hardly believe yet in my happiness, that she really cares for me at all as I care for her.

Florence must have got the letter confirming Neville's proposal of marriage on Friday 21 May. He waited impatiently for her reply. On the Sunday, for example, he wrote: 'She was at chapel this morning but wd not look at me coming out. … Have I been deceiving myself? … is she angry with my letter? … this state of uncertainty is horrible'. Still, she had already accepted the invitation to join his Monday boat party. According to the Diary:

I did not walk with F to the boats nor did I speak to her much on the river though we were in the same boat. I just asked her if I might walk with her back from the boats and she said Yes. Then I asked why she had not written. She replied that … she was intending to do so only she hardly knew what to say. She said she hardly knew her own mind; yet she sometimes let me speak as if it were all settled. Indeed I told her that I could hardly endure the thought of giving her up now, though I could see no reason why she should care for me. She said she did not like the idea of me giving up so much for her. … She has told Miss Sallitt, for naturally she wanted to have

> someone to talk to about it; and she seems sadly to want to talk to her Mother. We got back to my rooms a little before the others and I did so want to give her a kiss but I thought she had hardly said enough to justify me in that yet. She sat next to me at supper and during the rest of the evening seemed very lively and happy. She said that she had hardly remembered that my rooms were so nice.

Three agitated days later Neville reported her letter of acceptance:

> She says that she did not write before because she wanted to be quite sure of herself before doing so. 'When you spoke to me first I was bewildered and hardly knew what I thought or felt. I have been thinking about it ever since and now have quite made up my mind to tell you that I am quite willing for you to write to my Father whenever you think it will be wise to do so. It is such an important thing for both of us that we cannot think too much about it. I know you have been thinking for a long time and I am quite prepared to trust myself to you'.

They were both convinced that until Florence had left Newnham they must meet as strangers, and the pretence was easier to maintain now that she was knowingly involved in it. The Diary for 30 May, for example, describing a Brookside Sunday tea party, noted: 'Annie much admired F's self-possession when she came into the garden and held out her hand to me this afternoon and said "How do you do Mr Keynes?". She maintained that I shd not have been nearly so self-possessed'. Thereafter the ban on their meeting again that term at Brookside was total, with Annie, an assiduous go-between, keeping them in touch. Florence stayed up at Newnham until her Higher Local examinations in Latin and mathematics were over but Neville left Cambridge on 12 June to preside over the Higher Locals taking place in Plymouth during the following week. It was while still at Plymouth (invigilating his own political economy papers), that Neville wrote to John Brown to ask his consent to their engagement.

'I did not write a particularly good letter', Neville admitted on 19 June, but he did explain, as transparently as he could, the current state of his own shifting religious views. The reply was gratifyingly immediate. On 23 June, when back in Salisbury, he transcribed

> the kindest possible letter from Mr Brown. He says – 'We truly feel as we have said to Florence, that the real responsibility of decision lies with herself. I have too deep a sense of the sacredness of such fellowships in life not to feel that interference from without, even from nearest friends, shd only be when the union is so manifestly imprudent and incongruous as to call for serious protest. Florence has been such a dear good child to us all her life and we think her qualities of mind and heart so sterling and real that we cannot but receive with affection anyone that appreciates her work and values her love. To pass to the other matter you mention – I greatly appreciate the honourable feeling wh has led you to speak so frankly on the question of Christian faith.' And he then goes on to express the broadest and most liberal views on this point.

As Neville admitted, receiving such a cordial and open-hearted response from his future father-in-law, a man whom he already admired for his charismatic moral force and intellect, should have made him 'the happiest man in the world'. Yet, typically, Neville could not shake off the tension and depression that had built up during more than a year of frustrated courtship. Florence would soon discover that he had an infinite capacity for worrying.

Fortunately for both of them, Florence was more resilient. Her cheerful letter delivered the next day, signed (for the first time) 'Yours very affectionately', diluted his depression by insisting that 'everything is coming right' and inviting him home to meet her parents on Saturday. Accordingly, on his way through London, Neville bought a ruby and diamond engagement ring and arrived at Bedford the next day, around noon. But, even after a 'very nice talk with Mr and Mrs Brown', he still could not believe that she loved him as unreservedly as he loved her. He wrote:

> In the afternoon Florence and I were left alone together; but even yet I am awkward and cannot say all that I want to say. And I cannot just now feel that she fully loves me. When I offered her the ring … I got yesterday she would hardly take it. I believe she said 'It seems dreadful'. At last however she put it on her finger; and then we gave each other our first kiss. O she must grow to love me. … I returned to Cambridge in the evening. We dont want our engagement to be known yet; so Mrs Brown and Alice walked to the station with me instead of F.

He now had something delightfully positive to anticipate, however. Florence and her parents had already planned a holiday tour in Switzerland and, at their invitation, Neville decided to join them in Paris and to travel with them through the Engadine.

Between Neville's first visit to the Bedford Manse on 26 June and 28 July when he joined Florence and her parents in Paris, their engagement was kept secret from all except immediate family and close friends.[39] This meant that the pair still saw less of each other than they would have wished, though they could, and did, exchange frequent letters. There were three occasions when Neville visited Florence at home in Bedford and when his in-laws allowed them a degree of space and privacy in which to get to know each other. It was not until 12 July, however, that a letter from Florence addressed him as Neville, and not until 21 July that she confessed openly that she loved him. After that blissfully happy day – when he responded by telling her that it was merely her extreme youth that still worried him – he recorded her reply that 'at any rate she hoped she was old enough to know her own mind'. He added

39. Apart from the Bonds, only two of Neville's friends knew of his engagement at this stage. One was Arthur Spokes who had to know why Neville withdrew from their planned continental holiday. The other was Alfred West to whom Spokes would undoubtedly have leaked the news.

hopefully: 'I talked about our getting married two years from now, when she will be twentyone; but she insisted that we must wait 3 years. Well we shall see about that'.

The holiday in the Engadine lasted four weeks, long enough to transform their relationship by expelling the shyness and misunderstandings that had so often distanced them over the past fifteen months. The couple spent many happy hours in each other's company – walking, climbing, sightseeing, dancing, reading, and discussing a great variety of topics. They revelled in glorious Swiss scenery. They exchanged a multitude of confidences – intimate and otherwise. They talked about their religious beliefs, their relatives and their shared friends. Neville was able to introduce his beloved to his undergraduate contemporary and friend John Lord (still exiled in Switzerland with tuberculosis), whom they met (with his mother and aunt) at Pontresina and St Moritz. There were, of course, some uncomfortable features of the joint holiday. Even relatively luxurious continental travel and hotel arrangements could be upset by unforeseen circumstances – as was evident in some of Neville's earlier holiday journals. In summer 1880, however, the trip was organized by John Brown, whose annual stipend as a congregational minister (with a wife and six children to maintain), was less than the bachelor's earnings from his college, teaching and examining functions.[40] So it was not surprising that when (back in Castle Street on 24 August) Neville counted up the costs of his latest holiday, he calculated that it was 'the cheapest trip I have ever had – travelling expenses from Salisbury to Salisbury (31 days) coming to less than £32'.

It had certainly been an economical tour, in which bedrooms were shared – Florence with her mother and Neville with her father – and in which the connections between places visited were made by public scheduled transport services rather than by expensively hired carriages. Sometimes they chose to walk part of the way from one place to the next – once at least with unwelcome consequences. On 3 August, for example, they had walked over the Albula Pass, hoping to complete their journey by diligence, but found, after waiting two hours, that it was full and could not accommodate them:

> When we got to the Wessenstein Inn we had walked 12½ miles and climbed 3185 feet and it was evident that it wd not do for F to attempt any more. … We could get no respectable conveyance to take us on. So we had to stay at this cheerless place.

Worse than that, the bed-sheets were damp and they felt obliged to lie fully clothed on them. 'I did not sleep much', Neville added gloomily, 'Mr Brown snores horribly and F was quite ill in the middle of the night'. It proved a

40. In addition to his professional earnings Neville had a private investment income derived from his father's bequest. See below, pp. 182–9.

testing expedition in many ways. No doubt the Diary enabled Neville to relieve the irritation caused by Mr Brown's frightful snores and Mrs Brown's 'incessant talking' or propensity to 'drop her "hs"'. Nevertheless, it was on their Swiss tour that their future son-in-law learned to appreciate the genuinely benevolent qualities of Florence's parents. On 18 August, for example, he wrote:

> I have by this time a warm admiration for Mr B's unfailing good nature and geniality. He is very widely read and takes a keen interest in all kinds of things. He has too a remarkable memory. Mrs Brown also is extremely good natured and kindly.

On their side the Browns were to accept him as their future son-in-law without further reservation. Back at home, on 6 September, Neville reported his pleasure at receiving 'a very kind letter from Mrs Brown' who wrote '"We are no longer strangers and having seen so much of you, when the time comes I shall have perfect confidence in entrusting the happiness of my daughter to your keeping"'.[41]

Happily, the fact that the engagement remained a close secret until after Neville had spent a continental holiday with Florence and her parents effectively stifled the scandalous rumours that the university community in Cambridge might otherwise have attached to either Newnham College or 3 Brookside. It certainly tranquillized Miss Clough. On 10 September Neville reported anxiously that Florence had 'written to Miss Clough to tell her the news. What will her reply be like? I do hope that Brookside will not get into disgrace through our sin'. On 15 September he was relieved to read:

> Miss Clough's letter to F.! 'I was much surprised at the contents of your letter. I have a great regard for Mr Keynes and send you my best wishes. I have always liked Mr Keynes very much and I am glad that the engagement was arranged while you were with your parents. It will be pleasant for you to help your Mother and be at home for a time and I suppose we shall sometimes see you in Cambridge'.

Neville commented cheerfully:

> This is on the whole more cordial than we had ventured to anticipate. It was very characteristic and I think faithfully reflects the mingled feelings with which the

41. During the early weeks of their engagement when Florence was sometimes frightened by the intensity of Neville's approach, the sympathetic attitude of her parents towards him was probably crucial to the success of his courtship. On the eve of their wedding, when both Florence and her mother were weeping together over her impending departure from the Manse, he confessed to the Diary: 'Mrs Brown … believes that in the earlier stages she could certainly have persuaded Florence out of any engagement. Certainly she would have been successful in our case. The first days were bad ones'.

> dear old lady would receive the news. F. writes: 'I think we may congratulate ourselves that she has taken my news very mildly. I have been having such nice letters. … Miss Gladstone's best of all … delightfully motherly! She says "I suppose you may have to wait, but as you were so lately our baby, perhaps it will not be altogether a bad thing for you"'.

Henry Fawcett's reaction to the news of young Keynes's engagement was characteristically mischievous. They had coincided, as usual, in Salisbury where each was visiting with his family in the week before term began. According to the Diary for 20 September:

> I had a short walk with Professor Fawcett, who is down here for a few days. He says that I shall never be able to persuade people that Florence did not attend my lectures, and he at once fastened on the Bonds' house as our meeting place. Unfortunately he is a great gossip. He says he always *was* of the opinion that the establishment of Newnham and Girton at Cambridge wd give rise to an *enormous* number of marriages. He looks forward to the time when an undergraduate will call on a Newnhamite to go for a walk just as a Trinity man wd now call on a Johnsman!

Two days later, according to the Diary:

> I dined at old Mrs Fawcett's meeting the Postmaster General and his wife. The latter [Millicent Fawcett] is unusually cautious, absolutely refusing to congratulate me until she knows something of 'the lady'! Fawcett advises me to stay on at Cambridge, saying that I shall be sure to find something definite to do sooner or later. He also advises me to set about building a house at once!

Once their engagement was public knowledge, the couple could openly enjoy the affectionate relationship they had developed during their Swiss holiday, share the congratulations that flooded in to each of them and begin to make plans for their home in Cambridge. Neville confided to the Diary that he now felt better in health than at any time over the past six months. He fell into the routine of visiting Florence at the Bedford Manse every two or three weeks, and they exchanged letters frequently – Florence delighting him by signing herself 'Yours with all my heart'. After term began he reported that he had 'called on Mrs Sidgwick and Miss Clough. The former was very cordial and said she was *glad* to hear of my engagement. The latter was very stiff "Mr Keynes you have my good wishes. I always thought Miss Brown a very nice girl"'. It seems to have been taken for granted that the wedding should be postponed until after Florence had reached the age of 21 (on 10 March 1882). The couple then faced – at first with equanimity and later with increasing signs of stress – a long engagement. It was almost six months after Florence's 21st birthday that they were actually married. Neville had hoped that the long wait could have been enlivened for them by another Swiss holiday (in summer

1881), accompanied by his mother. When he broached the idea to Florence, at Bedford on 7 November, she was clearly attracted by the scheme, but doubted whether her parents would approve. At the end of December 1880 he was disappointed to learn that her fears were justified. John Brown could not then afford to send his eldest daughter on another Swiss tour, but would not hear of either Neville or Anna Keynes meeting her costs.

Although the engaged pair fell more deeply in love during their long wait there were times when it proved a strain on each. Any attempt to interpret the causes or character of their recurrent attacks of depression or emotional conflict must be speculative, however, in view of the fact that the Diary for the years 1881 and 1882 is significantly incomplete – significantly in that a considerable number of pages have been deliberately excised and that entries relating to some of the most painful episodes in the courtship have been lost.[42] During the early weeks of their engagement Florence sometimes flinched from Neville's urgent demonstrations of affection, or ignored burning questions in his letters, to such an extent as to leave him doubting the strength and durability of her love for him. On the other hand, by the end of 1880 she was evidently reponding to his kisses with uninhibited warmth; and during most of 1881 his quotations from her letters reflect the patient persistence of her efforts to shake him out of his black moods of depression and self-criticism. Neville had long suffered from migraine when stressed and the two-year engagement apparently increased its incidence. The stressful quality of some of his letters to Florence is reflected in his extracts from her soothing replies. For example, on 7 July 1881: 'Florence writes – "I too do sometimes have misgivings but I am not fond of gloomy thoughts. … I have no fear for the future if I see we are really coming together as time goes on. I am sure we have done so yet, and I see no reason why we should stop here"'. At which he resolved to 'have patience and try to put aside misgivings and gloomy thoughts if they arise'. It was in that summer of 1881 that they shared a fraught holiday at Barmouth – the relevant entries for which have been excised, but which is retrospectively mentioned in several later entries. On 27 August, for example, he reported after reading a letter from her:

42. The volume in question was not received in the Cambridge University Library until 10 June 1983 and is prefaced by a note (signed by Geoffrey Keynes) to the effect that the remainder of the Diary had been deposited in the Library in October 1970. It is easy to assume that Geoffrey made the excision, but one must reserve judgement on this point. It could have been made by the diarist himself, who frequently reread (and occasionally amended) his entries; or it could have been Florence who died nine years after Neville himself. What is clear is that most of the excisions relate to fraught episodes in the engagement. They begin in late January/early February 1881 and end in the first fortnight of July 1882. Since the pages in the original volume were numbered, the missing pages are readily identifiable. For the year 1882 Neville actually kept two parallel diaries – one in the same cover and same expansive style as for 1881 and the other a largely factual and extremely concise record of events.

> She has never been in a temper with me; but depressed – Yes. She says that at Barmouth for two or three days I hardly spoke to her and she feared almost that I cared for her no more. I had to confess that I treated her badly – that I sometimes have my bad moods – I may even behave badly again. ... She protests that she loves me entirely and always.

Partly in view of his migraines, and for other (unexplained) reasons also, Neville worried continuously about his health in relation to his suitability as a husband. On 22 September he wrote: 'I sometimes feel I ought not to marry Florence; and yet what could I do without her', and followed this dismal thought with a long quotation from Goethe ending: 'nothing is less easily reasoned away than such hypochondriacal anxiety'. On 29 September he consulted a London surgeon and the Diary reported cryptically: 'In surgery as in other things it is possible to jump from the frying pan into the fire. It is my age: and I shall certainly be alright when I am married'. Following a visit to a Cambridge GP on 6 October, his laconic Diary entry was even less informative about the doctor's advice: 'Be of good cheer and do not fear to marry. Active measures might do more harm than good'. His mother, as ever, believed her son was 'delicate'. As for Florence, she reponded briskly in a letter which he quoted on 28 September: '"I wish you would not run yourself down as you do. You belong to me and I cannot let anyone abuse you – not even yourself. You know father was very delicate until after he was married and now he needs no one's pity"'.

In early October 1881 the couple began house-hunting and on 3 November Neville reported that he had arranged to have a house built in Harvey Road: 'Not two as I had thought of doing, as Mother would rather I did not build a house for her just at present'. Thereafter he referred frequently to the builders' progress on their new home. By 25 June 1882 he and Florence were selecting chimney pieces, table cloths and so on – to say nothing of 'a wedding dress in wh she is to be married and a wedding dress in wh she is not to be married' – and planning a honeymoon in Switzerland. In July the wedding presents began to arrive. On 15 August they were married and the Diary records with relief: 'we did not find the ceremony anything like so trying as we had anticipated'. They spent that night at the Lord Warden Hotel in Dover en route for their continental honeymoon. Eventually, on 15 September Neville wrote:

> Now we are at Dover again after a most delightful time in Switzerland. We both had excellent health throughout, and *my* enjoyment at least was unalloyed. I think I may say the same for Florence. For about 10 days we travelled about with Cozens Hardy and his wife and enjoyed their company. They were married the day after ourselves.

V Career of a moral scientist

1 FIRST UNIVERSITY LECTURER IN MORAL SCIENCES

When he stepped out of his Pembroke fellowship in 1882, Neville had, at the age of 30, effectively hitched his future career to the new pattern of opportunities implicit in a redistribution of finance and influence from the colleges to the university. At that stage he saw himself primarily as a university teacher. Although, a year ago, he had coveted the part-time post of Pembroke's treasurer (which would have carried a fellowship for as long as he held it), running the finances of such a small college was not of itself a particularly attractive prospect. So, after resigning himself to the fact that the Pembroke fellows were unlikely to vote a young nonconformist moralist (however popular personally) into such a prominent position within the college, he looked to the university for income-earning opportunities. He had already applied for, and got, in March 1881, the post of assistant secretary to the Local Examinations Syndicate; and he now knew not only that the objectives and organizational challenges associated with this fast-growing university department suited his temperament, but also that his administrative talents were evidently superior to those of the then secretary to the Syndicate.[1] Accordingly, he set his sights on succeeding the latter as the Syndicate's principal officer. Meanwhile, as far as his long-term career objectives were concerned, the most important feature of the 'general academic reorganization'[2] unleashed by the 1882 revision of statutes lay in the revolution it was designed to achieve in the teaching of undergraduates who aimed at honours degrees. In October 1883 the General Board of Studies set up to oversee and direct the changes, submitted its plans for discussion by the Senate.[3] Henry Sidgwick, who was a prime mover in the reforms, sat on the General Board of Studies as well as on the Board of Moral Sciences.

1. The secretary was G.F. Browne.
2. The phrase is Sidgwick's: for example, in a letter to a friend on 18 December 1883, reprinted in (A. and E. Sidgwick), *Henry Sidgwick; a Memoir* (London: Macmillan, 1906), p. 370.
3. The Senate consisted of all MAs of the university whether resident in Cambridge or not. On non-controversial issues the formal discussion of policy-related reports attracted a small fraction of resident MAs. On controversial issues where policy hinged on a vote, most resident and many non-resident MAs would attend.

It was he who explained to the Senate in congregation that the system (already practised in the history and moral science faculties) of requiring a university lecturer to offer personal tuition to any of his pupils who might need it, was now intended to apply generally. In Sidgwick's view, according to the published record: 'no provision that could be made was worth making from the University funds unless the system of instruction to which it was given could seriously aim at rendering private tuition unnecessary for industrious students'.[4] After almost seven years experience of teaching logic and political economy to moralists, on the lines Sidgwick advocated, Neville had reason to hope that he would be in the first batch of lecturers appointed by the University of Cambridge and financed out of the Common Fund into which the annual levy from the colleges was to flow. Sidgwick himself encouraged this expectation. On 30 July 1883, for example, the Diary reported hopefully: 'Sidgwick seems to have a scheme for making me University Lecturer'. It was not, however, until 1884 that the General Board was ready to appoint its first 23 university lecturers and three readers. According to the Diary for 29 April, Sidgwick leaked the news that Neville had been elected unopposed to the moral science lectureship, during a Newnham dinner party given by Miss Clough, at which both the Sidgwicks and the Keyneses were guests. 'From the way he spoke', the Diary went on, 'it was clear that he had originally had me in mind in arranging for this lectureship'.

During the two academic years Neville waited for this good news, his pattern of life had not greatly changed – except that he was now married and living at 6 Harvey Road. He had kept his college rooms until the end of 1882 when, for the last time, he took a share in the college dividend.[5] He remained a member of Pembroke's senior combination room, without time limit, and enjoyed the associated social and dining rights. He now carried a more substantial and varied intercollegiate teaching load than ever before. He lectured on logic and political economy to men reading for the tripos and to Newnhamites (whose lectures were arranged by Sidgwick); he coached Girtonians reading political economy and from 1883 to 1893 he gave a 'specially adapted course on political economy' to Indian Civil Service candidates. He examined political economy and/or logic papers written in connection with the moral sciences Special examination,[6] the Trinity and John's scholarship examination and the Higher (and Senior) Local examina-

4. See *CUR*, 24 October 1883, p. 120, which printed the discussion on the first report of the General Board of Studies, dated 13 June 1883.
5. The 1882 revision of statutes limited the future dividends of college fellows to a maximum of £250 per annum. The Pembroke dividend had been £394 in 1880 and £390 in 1881.
6. Men who had failed to reach honours standard in the tripos examination could take the Special in order to qualify for an ordinary degree.

tions. In addition, on 16 April 1883 the Diary noted his appointment as examiner in political economy for University of London MA and DSc candidates. At the same time he wrote and published his first book. All of this must have enabled Sidgwick (chairman of the Moral Sciences Board and recently elevated to the Knightbridge Chair of Philosophy) to ensure that the one and only university lectureship in moral sciences went to Keynes.

At this stage of his career, Neville was dedicated to becoming an effective teacher. He read widely for his lectures and worked hard at expounding them clearly and accurately. He spent hours composing suitably testing question papers and in one-to-one discussion with students who had submitted written answers for him to assess. The Diary regularly recorded his impressions of the reception students gave to his latest lecture, and he deliberately sought comments on his performance – either directly from his auditors or indirectly through other dons to whom they may have confided their frank impressions. Each summer vacation he devoted much time and effort to clarifying his exposition – in the light of such critical comments, or of the levels of understanding revealed by his reading of class papers or examination scripts. There is no evidence that the earnestly unassertive, young Neville Keynes was ever a charismatic lecturer. On the other hand there is ample evidence in the Diary to suggest that women students, as well as ambitious honours men, found his methodical, clearheaded approach to formal logic particularly helpful when preparing for examinations. They were often explicitly grateful for the time and effort he put into giving advice and detailed explanations to puzzled individuals. Partly as a result of the relative scarcity of moralists competent to teach logic in Cambridge, most of his lectures during his early years as a fellow were in that area. True, he could have resumed his political economy classes for women after Marshall married Mary Paley and migrated to Bristol in 1876 with Newnham's resident lecturer in the subject. But he was so obsessively concerned to perfect his logic lectures that, in 1877, when Sidgwick invited him to lecture on political economy to Newnhamites he refused. It was not until 1880 that Neville felt ready to extend his range by offering regular courses on political economy as well as logic. By the early summer of 1883 the concentration of effort had paid off and he felt sufficiently in control of his material on formal logic to write a students' manual which he described in the Diary as his 'small book of Problems and Exercises'.

2 FIRST BOOK: *STUDIES AND EXERCISES IN FORMAL LOGIC*

It took Neville less than a year to get his first book into print. Much of it had been systematically thought through (if not fully written out) in the course of the seven years, during which he regularly coached, lectured and examined in the area. Besides the men and women who intended to sit the tripos in moral sciences, he also taught logic to a small stream of Newnhamites proposing to offer it in the Higher Local examinations – which then served either as a qualifying test for women proposing to enter for the tripos, or as part of a certificate of competence for would-be teachers or governesses. Most of those who attended his lectures took advantage of the invitation to write answers to questions set by, and personally assessed by him. As a byproduct of these one-to-one sessions with students, as well as of his annual involvement in tripos, Higher Local and college scholarship examinations, Neville acquired useful expertise in identifying problems and exercises that were likely to be most effective in clarifying the subject for individuals with a severely limited mathematical education. It was these students, and their teachers, that he envisaged as the readers of his first book. According to the Diary entry for 5 July 1883, for example, he began writing it immediately after completing that year's stint examining the logic papers for the Higher Locals. By the end of the vacation he had almost finished the book and with his wife's help in improving its style, as well as in producing handwritten fair copy, he was able to get the main text (apart from the preface) to the Press by 22 November. The publisher was Macmillan but it was printed by Cambridge University Press. This was a convenient arrangement for Cambridge authors. They could deal directly with the printers, get first proofs rapidly to colleagues and friends and make extensive changes in response to informed criticism. The *Formal Logic* proofs were read in full by John Venn (who was both encouraging and constructively critical), and in part by James Ward, who was bluntly discouraging: 'the best thing he would say was that it was *accurate* and that the Germans do these things much better' wrote the downcast diarist – who had never learned to read German. Two of Keynes's former pupils also read and commented on the proofs and were warmly acknowledged in the preface. One was Alfred Caldecott, a fellow of St John's since 1880. The other was Mary Martin who won a first class result in the 1879 tripos (at which Neville was examiner) and to whom he had lent his lecture notes when she took over from him as Newnham's lecturer in logic in 1880. James Ward, who had also been among her tripos examiners, was to marry her in 1884. The preface also announced: 'the writers on logic to whom I have been chiefly indebted are [A.] De Morgan, [W.S.] Jevons and Venn', and added: 'To Mr Venn I am peculiarly indebted not merely by reason of his published writings, but also for most valuable suggestions and criticisms while this work was in progress'. There are a number of affectionate references in the Diary (though not the preface) to Florence's hard work on the manuscript and proofs.

Publication day was 13 February 1884. The next day, letters of thanks and congratulation began to arrive at 6 Harvey Road, from recipients of the 63 copies sent straight from the Press to the author's friends, colleagues and potential reviewers. Marshall (who had small interest in formal logic) responded blandly as soon as his copy reached him in Oxford. The Diary noted his comment on 16 February: '"So far as I can judge, it seems to be a beautiful specimen of thorough Cambridge work"'. Sidgwick took time to read the book critically and was characteristically candid. According to the Diary for 22 March: 'He says that he thinks very highly of the work in it but he is not sure of its form. After the dogmatism of the ordinary textbooks the student may find my somewhat isolated and critical discussions rather difficult'. Disappointed, Keynes commented sarcastically: 'he seems to be of the opinion that I am not sufficiently dogmatic'. Ward, on the other hand, who had been discouraging after skimming some early chapters, reacted generously to the finished product. The Diary reports that when the two friends walked back home together after a pleasant dinner party at the Sidgwicks' on 20 May:

> Ward talked in the highest terms of my book which he has now read thro'. He said that in his opinion the fourth part of the book shd entitle me to my doctor's degree. This was more gratifying coming from him than it wd have been from anyone else – especially after what he said about the earlier chapters. He holds, however, that it was a mistake to put so much original work into a book of problems.

The first signed review was by Venn, who had actually shown Neville a first draft of the article he was commissioned to write for *Mind* (a leading learned journal in the field), and even deleted a criticism which the reviewee was able to convince him was an 'absolute error'. As eventually published, in April, Venn's review seemed both authoritative and laudatory. It put *Formal Logic* in context as follows:

> This work belongs to the same class as Jevons's *Studies in Deductive Logic*. It is not so much a systematic treatise on the theory of the subject as a systematic collection of examples illustrating all the points in that theory. To Jevons must be assigned the credit of having been the first to introduce into the study of Logic this important aid to intelligent instruction, familiar as it had long been in the cognate science of mathematics; but the present work seems to me in several respects to represent a decided advance on its predecessor. The range of examples in itself is better, the main principles of the science seem more clearly and consistently conceived, and are not marred by the few unfortunate crochets with which readers of Jevons will be familiar. Moreover, in the latter part of the work, which deals with those generalised problems which have not hitherto been attacked without the aid of mathematical symbols, Mr Keynes shows constructive capacity and skill of a high order and has, it seems to me, given us a real advance on anything hitherto effected.

After listing especially valuable features of the book and approving 'the variety and ingenuity of the examples devoted to the illustrations of the portions of the science which are very commonly neglected', Venn concluded:

> [T]he part of the work which will probably excite most interest is that which deals with complex propositions. Mr Keynes has shown that examples of a degree of intricacy which I should not have supposed could be grappled with except by the aid of some kind of algebraic or symbolic procedure may be solved by generalisations of the common processes.

Over the next few months the anxious author was buoyed by a stream of congratulatory letters, or favourable press notices, from the recipients of complimentary copies. Reactions from individuals ranged from vaguely polite to positively effusive. Rival authors could be aggravatingly dismissive, as was illustrated in the Diary entry for 11 April: '[A.] Bain did not consider his "little volume of Essays" at all equivalent for my "very elaborate volume of Logic". Is that "very elaborate" ironical?' Most recipients whose enthusiasm rang true were actively teaching in the field. For example he heard in October from Henry Luries, a lecturer on logic and mental philosophy in the University of Melbourne, whose gratitude for having so 'excellent a Manual' placed in his hands seemed genuine enough. Substantial signed reviews of the first edition were rare. F.Y. Edgeworth, then London University's lecturer in logic at King's College, signed his in the June issue of *The Academy*. After describing it in the Diary as 'friendly though perhaps a trifle flippant', Keynes welcomed it as 'the most satisfactory criticism I have read next to Venn's in *Mind*'. It was certainly livelier than Venn's and more sharply focused. Neville was sufficiently flattered and intrigued to copy long extracts into the Diary, for example:

> 'Mr Keynes's contributions to Logic are of three species: studies, exercises and an original method. … The studies may be described as short pithy disquisitions upon controverted points. … A clear recognition of the work of others enhances the terse enunciation of his own. … Mr Keynes does not proceed so methodically as [G.] Boole; he relies more upon ingenuity and happy conjecture. … This very absence of method may conduce to mental training. … In short Mr Keynes's system is a gymnastic apparatus: Boole's may be a scientific instrument. The one is like an academic outrigger adapted to the sports of youth; the other a ship equipped for the discovery of some North-West passage between widely separated regions.'

Not surprisingly most of the extracts that Neville copied out of reviews into his Diary were favourable. In particular, he quoted most of the first paragraph of an unsigned review that appeared in a United States periodical (*The Nation*) which compared *Formal Logic* with the text Keynes saw as its closest rival – Jevons's *Studies in Deductive Logic* (1880):

> 'The two books are very similar in plan. ... That of Jevons is more elementary but comes nearer to covering all the ground; in that of Keynes the discussion is more exhaustive and usually more satisfactory; there is no shirking of difficult points, and there is a praiseworthy avoidance of metaphysical subtleties. If one has occasion to refer to a brief and perfectly clear statement of the view held on any subject by the English writers on logic (the author makes almost no allusion to German writers) he cannot do better than to take up this book. Admirably clear, for example, are the discussions of connotation and denotation and of the extent of a negative term. There is an excellent criticism of Jevons's very weak treatment of composition and of his unfortunate answer to the question, What is the precise meaning of the assertion that a proposition is false? ... The numerous examples are very well chosen and very instructive.'

Thereafter the tone shifted and after, making the point that '"the book has too much the air of being intended as an examination drillbook but it answers that purpose to perfection"', the review became scathingly critical. The Diary then noted the '"serious blemish"' found by his critic in '"the very large amount of space given to the syllogism"' but passed over the ferocious concluding peroration beginning: '"In spite of its many excellent features the greater part of Mr Keynes's book cannot be considered as anything more than a final effort to perpetuate the dark ages of logical method – an exhibition of wasted ingenuity which it is painful to contemplate"'.[7] However, on 24 August, after quoting from 'a friendly review of my book in yesterday's *Spectator*', Neville wrote: 'It is amusing that the treatment of the syllogism shd be spoken of as cursory, while according to the Nation the book would really be excellent if it were not for the excessive amount of space given up to the Syllogism'.

Keynes used his new book as the basic text for the first course on formal (that is, deductive) logic which he gave as a university lecturer. On 8 December, he was pleased to report that his class of 15 men and seven women (more than twice the size of audience he had been accustomed to address) had kept up till the end of term. Thus encouraged, he set about rewriting his lectures on inductive logic for the Lent term and began to contemplate the possibility of working them up into 'a small volume of studies on Inductive Logic'. This project was abandoned, however, following a conversation with Venn in January 1885. According to the Diary:

> Venn says that in consequence of my book he has given up the idea of writing a Formal Logic. He thinks the work is done better than he could do it; but he is anxious that in a second edn I shd make it a more systematic and complete treatment. He himself is now writing on Inductive Logic.

7. I am indebted to Professor Daniel Merrill of Oberlin College for the information that the author of the review in *The Nation* was Christine Ladd-Franklin (1847–84) a pupil of C.S. Pierce at Johns Hopkins in the early 1880s and a brilliant logician.

As it turned out, Neville's workload during the academic year 1884/85 was too heavy to permit him to more than dream about either writing a second textbook or revising the old. He taught political economy to Newnhamites and Girtonians, as well as to Indian Civil Service candidates and to Oxford students in the Easter term. His logic commitments were heavier than ever; his administrative duties at the Local Examinations Syndicate expanded steadily. Moreover, after Henry Fawcett died, and in 1885 Marshall returned to the Cambridge chair of political economy, the Moral Sciences Board's teaching needs changed dramatically. Fawcett had never aimed his courses at honours men; so his replacement by Marshall (plus Mary Paley's return to Newnham), transformed the quality and quantity of Cambridge economics teaching. At first Keynes found it hard to accept the implications of this shift. After complaining of overwork in the Diary for 29 January 1885, he wrote irritably:

> Sidgwick is anxious that I should consider my University Lectureship as being in Logic and not in Political Economy. This is no doubt in reference to Marshall's position. I tell him that I consider myself in the hands of the Board and will do that work wh seems most needed. I am rather coming to the conclusion that Sidgwick is open to the charge of wanting to regulate too much.

Nevertheless, although unwilling to be relieved of his duties as an economics lecturer, Keynes rejected Sidgwick's suggestion that he should retain his Newnham lectureship on political economy into the 1885/86 academic year. According to the Diary for 11 November:

> [Sidgwick] said he was not quite sure that Mrs Marshall would be a success; he fancied she was too cut and dried. I told him that I had gone too far to be able to draw back; also that I was really very anxious to reduce the amount of lecturing work I had in hand. When he found that I intended to give up lecturing at Girton he seemed content. I was gratified to find that he really did put a rather high value on my teaching: but I think that his estimate of Mrs Marshall is wrong.

Macmillan's accounts for the first 15 months or so after *Formal Logic* first appeared, showed only 310 copies (out of 750 printed) still in stock at the end of June 1885. By then it had displaced Jevons's *Studies in Deductive Logic* on the Moral Sciences Board's reading list for 1885/86. At the end of June 1886, only 85 copies remained unsold and the Diary for 30 September noted Macmillan's belated call for a second edition. Two days later they set out terms proposing the usual half-profits arrangement and a print run of 1250, but – to the author's regret – no reduction in price. He accepted the offer, taking nine months to complete the revised edition. The preface (dated 22 June 1887) summarized his revisions, for example, 'In Part II a distinction is adopted for which I am indebted to Mr W.E. Johnson; and the treatment of the existential import of propositions has been both expanded and systematised'. He also reduced the number of exercises in Part IV and expanded the text. When the new volume reached him (on 27 July 1887) the first edition had been out of print for several months and the publisher had actually raised the print number of the second edition to 2000.[8] There were more favourable reviews – including an unsigned one in *The Academy*, which Neville suspected was by Edgeworth. He quoted from it in the Diary for 14 January 1888: '"Probably the most important additions have been made to the fourth part where the author, leaving the beaten road, strikes out a new path in that comparatively untrodden region which Boole added to the province of logic"'. The publishers were wise to raise the print number substantially, for the second edition rode the crest of the first edition's success for a full five years. By 30 June 1892, the stock had dwindled to 206 copies. The book was then yielding its author an annual profit of about £50.

Meanwhile, an annoying incident had occurred which probably contributed to a slump in sales in 1892/93 by putting a cheap rival on the crammers' market. On 23 October 1891, an outraged entry in the *Diary* reported:

> [James] Welton has published a manual of Logic for the University Correspondence College. So far as I can judge from a first glance there is hardly any originality in the book. He reproduces pages from my book and others, somtimes giving the very same illustrations and without specific acknowledgment. Now and then comes a criticism which shows complete misunderstanding. Altogether I feel very angry about the book. I am returning the copy sent to me by the Correspondence College.[9]

The slowdown in sales may have reduced Neville's incentive to produce a third edition, designed to be 'a decided improvement on the second'; but the impression left by the Diary was that he was too heavily involved in administration, examining, teaching and writing a book on political economy (alongside a full family life revolving around three lively children) to complete the major revision he had in mind before the middle of 1894. At last, in September of that year he returned to Cambridge, refreshed by a family holiday, to find a copy of the third edition awaiting him. 'It is such a noble looking volume', he confided to the Diary, 'that I feel it wont sell … as a

8. Keynes had learned from the printer that the publisher had decided to increase the print number of 1250 (agreed earlier with him) to 2000. In view of the fact that publication was undertaken on a half-profits basis, he had grounds for being annoyed that he had not been consulted before the order was given to the printer.
9. The self-styled University Correspondence College was an independent institution used mainly by students cramming for Higher Local and college scholarship examinations. After taking a borderline first class at the 1891 moral sciences examination (where Keynes had been one of the four examiners), Welton had plagiarized the texts he read as an undergraduate to create a crammer's manual for the Correspondence College.

textbook'. It then ran to 494 demi-octavo pages, having become a teachers' standby rather than a students' manual. Its average annual sales for the 1895–1904 decade barely reached 200 per annum. In October 1895 Macmillan, recognizing that it had become a relatively advanced exposition, invited Neville to write a more elementary text aimed at Indian university undergraduates. He declined on the grounds that he already planned to write another elementary logic text 'on somewhat different lines'. Certainly the third edition was a more useful text than its predecessors as far as Cambridge honours students were concerned. It went out of print before the end of 1904, having yielded its author a net profit of about £200 and was replaced in 1906 by a fourth edition – again extensively rewritten, enlarged and further improved. The preface to the fourth edition, after specifying the more important modifications, emphasized the author's debt to H. Sigwart's *Logic*, and reiterated his continuing indebtedness 'to Mr W.E. Johnson, who by his criticisms has enabled me to improve my exposition in many parts of the book and also to avoid some errors'. It also acknowledged 'valuable help from Professor J.S. Mackenzie and from my son J.M. Keynes'.

One of Maynard's terse asides, quoted in the Diary, sheds some light on why the 1906 textbook[10] became a classic of its kind, to be reprinted twice – in 1917 and in 1928: '"The worst of your book is that when one is reading it everything seems so hopelessly obvious and uncontroversial"'.[11] Much later, in 1950, the following appraisal of the book appeared in an *Economic Journal* obituary of Neville Keynes:

> It is an extremely good book, far and away the best which exists in English on the old-fashioned formal logic and its main developments in the nineteenth century. Keynes settled a number of ancient and troublesome controversies by drawing the necessary distinctions and embodying the results in clear definitions. In this respect his contribution in the discussion of connotation and of existential import and his distinction between what he called 'conditional' and 'hypothetical' propositions were particularly valuable. Another admirable feature of the book is the treatment of logical diagrams, with its clear recognition that Euler's diagrams have certain existential implications which need to be made explicit if fallacies are to be avoided. ... [Keynes's] originality consisted in devising and clearly formulating simple elegant and powerful methods of treatment which involve no technical mathematics and depart to the least possible extent from the traditional logic of 'simple' propositions.[12]

10. John Neville Keynes, *Studies and Exercises in Formal Logic; including a generalisation of logical processes in their application to complex references*, 4th edn (London: Macmillan & Co., 1906), xxiv, 548pp.
11. Maynard was then a postgraduate reading for the Civil Service exams. The comment is in a letter to his father, reprinted by D.E. Moggridge, *Maynard Keynes: An Economist's Biography* (London: Routledge, 1992), p. 106. The original is in King's College's Keynes Papers.
12. C. Broad, *Economic Journal*, vol. 60, 1950, pp. 405–6.

3. MARSHALL'S RETURN TO CAMBRIDGE

Alfred Marshall had left Cambridge in 1877 to become principal of University College, Bristol and acting professor of political economy. Whilst there he published *Economics of Industry* (1879) – in collaboration with his wife – and began work on his *Principles of Economics* (1890). In 1883, when the death of Arnold Toynbee opened up a vacant lectureship in Oxford, B. Jowett, Master of Balliol, invited Marshall to fill that gap and join the Balliol fellowship. The Oxford chair of political economy (as also the Cambridge chair) was then occupied by a man who had neither the ability, nor the inclination, to advance the discipline he professed. Since the Oxford incumbent, Bonamy Price, was in his late seventies and the term of his tenure was scheduled to end in 1888, Marshall's prospects of winning that chair within four or five years appeared promising. In contrast, Fawcett was then under 50 and could be expected to occupy the Cambridge chair for most of the next two decades. In a letter to Keynes dated 30 April 1883, Marshall justified his decision to accept Jowett's offer:

> We had a yearning to be with our old friends at Cambridge and to try to help on the Cambridge Tripos, which we like better than any exam at Oxford. But after all Oxford is a rich and nearly empty field in economic work and we are sure we are right in making our choice.[13]

While Marshall was away from Cambridge, a cordial correspondence flowed between him and Keynes – the pupil who had amused his tripos examiners (particularly Jevons) by deploying Marshallian curves in answering the 1875 tripos papers. In September 1880, when preparing a new set of economics lectures for the following academic year, he confessed to his Diary that he intended to 'base them as much on Marshall as on Mill'. Listed, in autumn 1882, to give a course to final-year honours men on advanced economic theory, he had focused on teaching the mathematical techniques of analysis that characterized what contemporaries were already beginning to call 'the new political economy'. He did not succeed in charming his audience. 'My 7 men come to my lectures on Advanced Pol. Econ. at Pembroke very regularly', he wrote on 17 November, 'but I am very doubtful if they quite follow all I say'. Still, he was relieved to be able to confirm that the numbers had kept up well until the end of term; introducing the new political economy was evidently not easy. In the Easter term of 1882/83, he abandoned another set of advanced economic theory lectures –

13. Letter dated 30 March 1883, in Cambridge Marshall Library. The original is reproduced in J.K. Whitaker (ed.), *The Early Economic Writings of Alfred Marshall 1867–90*, Vol. I (London: Macmillan, 1975), p. 22.

this time on the application of curves to international values – 'because no men came to them'.

As it happened, the Cambridge chair fell vacant first, when Fawcett died suddenly in November 1884. There, even more than might have been the case in Oxford, Marshall was clearly the strongest candidate in the field. Keynes welcomed the Marshalls' return warmly, in spite of being aware that it must inevitably reduce his own prospects of teaching in an area which – now that *Formal Logic* was published – had become central to his current research and teaching interests. It does not seem, however, that he had yet fully taken into account the implications, for himself in particular and the Cambridge moral science faculty generally, of the potential for conflict between two dynamic professors – in spite of certain earlier incidents that should have alerted him. For example, on 9 February 1881 a letter arrived from Marshall (enclosed with a glowing testimonial supporting Neville's own application for the London chair of political economy), which complained:

> 'Foxwell says that you are helping Sidgwick with his economic book.[14] Sidgwick and I differ on some questions of literary morality, for one thing we could not agree on … the use wh he (not you) wd be at liberty to make of your notes of my lectures and on hearing that he had asked you to help him with his book I asked Foxwell to give you my views on the subject.

Upon which Neville commented anxiously in the Diary: 'I am immensely sorry for all that this implies. Personally, however, so far as I can remember I have never shown Sidgwick anything of what I regard as Marshall's original work'. Sidgwick had actually invited all members of the faculty to 'help him with his book' when, in April 1880, he presented successive chapters for discussion at the Moral Science Club he had set up; and as soon as proof sheets were available, he passed them to Keynes and F.W. Maitland for detailed comments, When Sidgwick's *Principles of Political Economy* eventually appeared, the preface, dated March 1883, acknowledged the author's debt to Jevons's *Theory of Political Economy* (1871), J.E. Cairnes's *Some Leading Principles of Political Economy* (1874), A. and M. Marshall's *Economics of Industry* (1879), as well as Marshall's privately published paper on theory of value and his unpublished manuscript on foreign trade. The acknowledgement to Keynes (and Maitland) referred simply to 'suggestions and help at proof stage'.

It is unlikely that Keynes then had any inkling of the explosive confrontation between the two professors that occurred within a week of Marshall's election and was described by Sidgwick in his Journal for 22–26 December 1884:

14. The book in question was H. Sidgwick, *Principles of Political Economy* (London: Macmillan, 1883).

> The story begins on December 13, when we elected Alfred Marshall Professor of Political Economy. He came here on December 17, called on us, heard my view of the lectures required, then suddenly broke out. I had produced on him the impression of a petty tyrant 'dressed in a little brief authority' (Chairman of the Board of Moral Sciences) who wished to regulate, trammel, and hamper a man who knew more about the subject than I did. I tried to explain, and we parted friends; but the explanation was imperfect, correspondence ensued, and on Tuesday (23) I received from him a long and very impressive letter, analysing my academic career, and pointing out that the one source of failure in it was my mania for *over-regulation*. The result of this had been that my energies had been frittered away in details of administration and on the effort to give a wretched handful of undergraduates the particular teaching that they required for the Moral Sciences Tripos. He contrasted my lecture-room, in which a handful of men are taking down what they regard as useful for examination, with that of [T.H.] Green, in which a hundred men – half of them B.A.s ignoring examinations – were wont to hang on the lips of the man who was sincerely anxious to teach them the truth about the universe and human life. I have left out the partly courteous, partly affectionate – for Marshall is an old friend – padding of the letter, by which he meant to soften the pressure of these hard truths.[15]

Characteristically, Sidgwick took this bitterly personalized criticism philosophically, without anger or arrogance. Reflecting on his personal aims and motives, he concluded:

> As for 'over-regulation' … I have no desire to have my own way – not knowing sufficiently which way is my own; still less to coerce others. But I have a great desire in all social relations for definite understandings; not knowing which road is best for humanity to walk in, I want all roads that claim to be roads to be well made and hedged in.[16]

Neville was away during Marshall's aggressive visit to Sidgwick on 17 December, and when the Marshalls called (together) at 6 Harvey Road, they found that the head of the house was overseeing Senior Local exams at Caversham in his capacity as assistant secretary to the Local Examinations Syndicate. Florence's letter giving her account of their visit reached Neville next day and he transcribed chunks of it into the Diary for 18 December:

> 'I must first of all tell you that I do not at all wonder at your enthusiasm for him. He *is* a most delightful man. You need not be jealous husband, for the chief reason why I speak so warmly of him is because he said such nice things about you and seemed to be genuinely interested in all that concerned you. He came about this post at Oxford he is giving up. It seems that [William] Cunningham is going in. … He feels that in persuading you in any way to consider it he is acting most unselfishly because there is no one he is more anxious to keep here – but at the

15. A. and E. Sidgwick (1906), p. 394.
16. Ibid., p. 396.

same time he is not altogether satisfied with your position here (he does not like you to be spending your energies on the Local Exam work) while there is such a fine career there for the right man. ... The pay is merely nominal – £120 for the Indian students[17] and £80 for the rest. ... Still there is a good chance of a Professorship to come. ... The Master of Balliol who has a good deal of influence on the matter has been questioning Mr M. [Marshall] about possible candidates and he told him that yours was the finest mind he knew – or something to that effect. ... Of course we shd both very much dislike the thought of leaving Cambridge – but your work must be considered first of all ... you wd be able to devote yourself to Political Economy wh is the subject I believe you are really most interested in. And so long as we had each other and the boy[18] we could get on happily anywhere. ... Mr M. does not wish it to be known that the first suggestion came from him.'

Neville was not so easily bewitched by Marshall's flattery, however, and discussed the matter with Alfred West (with whom he was currently lodging at Amersham School whilst supervising the Local examinations). His own comment on Florence's letter was: 'I cannot at present feel that my chances of success at Oxford are sufficient to warrant me giving up what I have at Cambridge. This is also Alfred's opinion'.

Back in Cambridge, on 20 December Keynes recorded a peremptory telegram from Marshall: '"Have just had important conversation – think strongly you shd seriously consider being a candidate – Write soon to Dr Markby[19] – This cannot hurt. You may be glad"'. On 22 December another long letter from Marshall urged him to become a candidate and added: '"I have described you minutely to Dr Markby. ... I think that either you or Cunningham will be asked to come here. Each has his own claims. I know and perhaps Dr Markby guesses wh I think the stronger"'. The following day there arrived 'a pleasant letter from Markby' (to whom Keynes had duly written for information) telling him that Marshall's lectures were 'having a very important effect upon the study of Political Economy in Oxford'. Neville replied on Christmas Day that he did not intend to be a candidate for the Oxford post. At once, on 29 December Marshall's barrage of telegrams and persuasive letters resumed. By 30 December the onslaught was giving its victim a migraine and the Diary reported:

Letter from Marshall saying he feels that I am *the* man wanted at Oxford and that if I go there and succeed I shall probably be the Professor in three years time. 'With your singular power of lucid exposition you wd certainly get hold of the

17. The 'Indian' students were the candidates for the Indian Civil Service. Neville had been teaching Cambridge ICS candidates since 1881.
18. Maynard was then a toddler of about eighteen months old, and Florence was pregnant with their second child, Margaret.
19. William Markby, Reader in Indian Law, was in charge of the Oxford courses for Indian Civil Service candidates.

best of the men. If you have any lack of rhetorical power – and on this point I have no information beyond what Mrs Keynes has said – it wd only influence the numbers at the fag end of your class. I pray you then to consider whether you could not give Oxford a six month trial. … If you do go to Oxford you will have the formation of a very considerable part of thought and feeling of the English people in your own hands'.

Before Neville found time to answer this the Diary referred, on 31 December, to:

Another letter from Marshall urging that I shd take the Oxford work temporarily. 'Consider whether anyhow you wd not be wise in giving up the Local Exam^{n} work. But if you find any difficulty in answering this, then dont worry yourself over it. Too much worry of that kind wd upset you. Then try if you can to make temporary arrangements.

There followed, on 5 January, a letter from Markby (prodded no doubt by an impatient Marshall) making Keynes a definite offer of the Oxford work for two terms. The recipient then sought impartial advice. According to his Diary:

In the afternoon I had a good talk with [James] Ward on the subject of Oxford. He had already discussed the matter with Sidgwick, who had been asked by Markby to express his views concerning Cunningham and myself and who had on the whole summed up in my favour. Ward himself thinks I am not the man best suited for Oxford, that I am not sufficiently viewy or enthusiastic, and that is quite my own opinion. He says that there is the probability that I shall some time have the opportunity of succeeding Browne; and on the other hand that there may be some chance of my getting a readership. At Oxford all is uncertain. Ward was very sympathetic and I am sure he gave me wise counsel. He expressed himself very kindly as to his personal wish that I shd not leave Cambridge. I called on Sidgwick; but he was away from Cambridge. I have written to him.

This time, Keynes did not wait for Sidgwick's reply. He had heard what he wanted to hear from Ward and on 8 January he wrote to Markby declining the Oxford offer.

Marshall had not given up, however, and sent his wife to exert a direct attack. The following Sunday, Mary Marshall visited Cambridge, alone, and called at 6 Harvey Road. 'She and her husband had evidently set their hearts on my going to Oxford', the harassed diarist wrote on 11 January. A postcard from Marshall, next day, presumed that he had capitulated, but it was instantly followed by a telegram saying: '"Mary writes – wishes I could talk with you. This useless if mind made up; but if still least doubt, telegraph and I return tomorrow – quite convenient in every way. Please speak frankly"'. Keynes tried to end this wearing flood of communications by instantly telegraphing that his mind was quite made up. Two days later he got a calming letter from Sidgwick: '"I am glad that we are not to lose you, and hope you have decided rightly for yourself and society. The decision seemed a difficult one, as the post at Oxford seemed to offer great opportunities, though of a rather indefinite kind"'. There was then the briefest of pauses before Marshall himself returned to Cambridge, later in the month, and managed to persuade Keynes to give a weekly course in Oxford (choosing his own topic) during the following summer term. Marshall's personal influence with Markby and the Master of Balliol was sufficient to clinch the deal with Oxford. On 10 February the Diary reported: 'It is practically settled that I am to go to Oxford once a week during next term. They will give me £40'. This was followed on 16 February by a note to the effect that: 'I have decided to lecture at Oxford on The Method of Political Economy; and I have an idea of writing a small book on the same subject'.

It was not until the end of March that Keynes began preparing the lectures. He delivered them twice; first in Cambridge to a typically small class of 7 tripos finalists and secondly in Oxford on Saturdays to an audience that varied between 35 and 41 students. The Oxford lectures provided a much-needed boost to Neville's confidence in his lecturing ability. After they were over he was gratified to hear from Markby, on 17 June: '"so strong an opinion was expressed of the advantages of your lectures that it was determined if possible to continue them"'. Pleased though he was Neville declined firmly to consider the offer. He was further flattered, a few days later, by a typically effusive letter from Marshall that began:

> 'I have been staying at Balliol with the Master. He and everyone spoke very warmly of you: said you had been a great success; and that they were very anxious you shd go on for the next three terms on the same plan as in the last term. … Markby was full of apologies as to the small pay offered. And I told him that you wd understand the situation; and that if you declined it wd not be on account of the smallness of the pay; but I very much hope you wd do it. Popular gossip says that there is pretty sure to be a vacancy in the chair of PE [political economy] at Oxford in less than 3 years; and that if you go on as you have begun your chance will be a very good one. Of course gossip must be taken only for what it is worth; but it is worth something. … I dont want to make invidious comparisons between you and others who might be asked to do the work if you declined. But considering the particular lacuna there is in Oxford teaching and Oxford Economics I feel strongly that you are the right man to fill it; and on public grounds I am very very anxious you shd fill it. Phelps was among those who spoke warmly of you and hoped you wd go on.'

Neville was absolutely determined, however, not to continue commuting to Oxford. He had not enjoyed the weekly visit that swallowed up most of Friday and Saturday, at the end of a heavy week of Cambridge teaching, when he longed to spend more time at home with a beloved wife and their enchanting firstborn. The lectures themselves had gone well enough – though it was not until the seventh and last in the series that he escaped from the dauntingly large Balliol Hall into an ordinary lecture room, with a blackboard on which he could entertain his audience with exotic Marshallian curves. After the second occasion, on 2 May, for example, he wrote in the Diary with some satisfaction: 'There were 41 men at my lecture (against 36 last time). … I lectured on the Deductive Method of Pol. Econ. with some illustrations and seemed to keep the attention of the class. A large audience is certainly pleasing and this is the largest I have had'. But the prospect of attentive audiences was not enough to convince Neville that Oxford would be an attractive ambiance in which to live and work. The Balliol fellows had made no effort to welcome the stranger at their table and the only Oxford don who struck him as tolerably companionable was L.R. Phelps. Oxford seemed a social and intellectual desert. Nor was he persuaded by Marshall's flattery either that he had a public duty to take the 'new political economy' to the heathen, or that doing so would improve his chances of being elected to the Drummond Chair. On the contrary, he was realistically convinced that his chances of election to a chair in political economy – wherever and whenever a suitable opening arose – would hinge crucially on his having published a scholarly book in the field. There was, of course, no better place than Cambridge in which to write a monograph on the new economics. Meanwhile, even if he never rose above the status of Cambridge University lecturer, his prospects of succeeding Browne as chief secretary to the Local Examinations Syndicate were both promising and attractive. Most important of all, family life in Harvey Road absorbed a great deal of his time and energy, and the fact that he had at last persuaded his mother to leave her Salisbury home and settle in Cambridge may also have rendered a move to Oxford a peculiarly unattractive option at that stage of his career.

The letter that arrived at 6 Harvey Road on 23 June suggests that Marshall was resigned to his failure to recruit Neville to the post he had vacated at Oxford. He wrote: '"I am very sorry. However, I expect they will now ask Foxwell. If he consents, well. If not, I shall puff and blow at you again on public grounds"'. The reference to Foxwell was probably rhetorical, for the latter – who was already juggling the competing commitments of a John's fellowship and a London professorship – was highly unlikely to be attracted to a poorly paid, part-time lecturing appointment in Oxford. In any case, once the disquieting prospect of Cunningham filling the vacancy had faded,[20] Marshall could afford to wait until the Oxford chair came up for election again in 1888, before renewing the conspiracy to get his nominee in place. Meanwhile Neville

20. William Cunningham's lectures on economic history and political economy were subject to the History Board. Marshall, who became a member of that Board, when he returned to Cambridge, found that Cunningham's lectures treated economic theory as a virtual aside to his economic history course.

had broadcast his determination to expand his Oxford lectures into a monograph on the method of the new political economy which, if published within the next three years, would unquestionably strengthen his candidacy.

4 METHODOLOGICAL DEBATE IN POLITICAL ECONOMY

It was at a Trinity dinner on 2 June 1885 that Neville discussed with J.S. Nicholson his plans to write a book on method. According to the Diary his ex-pupil and colleague (then Edinburgh's professor of political economy) scoffed and said '"anyone could write such a book as that. He says he is sick of disquisitions on Method and that what we want is useful *applications* of the right method"'. The problem for a conscientious teacher of the subject, however, was that the flood of 'disquisitions on method' against which Nicholson was understandably reacting, reflected an uncomfortable lack of consensus among leading economists as to what *was* the right method. J.S. Mill's *Principles of Political Economy* (1848) was still the starting-point for most undergraduates in English-speaking countries, but the classical economic theory that he there presented as received wisdom had been attacked from a variety of directions. The Ricardian model was criticized by policy makers and social reformers for what they saw as a doctrinaire adherence to the principle of *laissez-faire* and for its failure to address itself to the ethical problems of an industrial economy. Its individualist stance seemed irrelevant in a world where humanity and justice demanded more rather than less government intervention in economic affairs. Middle-class commentators were repelled by the notion of inevitable socioeconomic conflict inherent in the Ricardian theory of value and distribution – such as the conflict of interest between landowners and the rest of the community, and the conflict between capital and labour inferred by most socialist writers. More fundamental were the attacks from academic and philosophical quarters on the abstract methodology of the Ricardian school and on the excessive confidence of its devotees as to the existence of universal economic laws. 'Happily', Mill asserted in a much-quoted sentence from his *Principles*, 'there is nothing in the laws of value which remains for the present or any future writer to clear up; the theory of the subject is complete'. Yet, in spite of his personal recantation of the wage-fund doctrine in 1869,[21] the last (1871) revised edition still insisted that trade unions had a strictly limited scope for raising the general level of wages at the expense of profits – beyond these limits, increasing wage costs would increase unemployment. Such inconsist-

21. Mill's recantation was published in the May 1869 *Fortnightly Review* in the course of a review of W.T. Thornton's *On Labour* (1869).

ency in a revered textbook had the effect of putting its author in the direct line of fire from activists in debates on theory – although in other passages Mill had shown himself to be far from a doctrinaire exponent of classical economic orthodoxy.[22] During the mid-Victorian boom – which conventional wisdom associated with a world-wide shift towards relaxing tariff barriers – the notion that abstract theory was capable of generating testable scientific laws of economic behaviour was rarely unchallenged in Britain, the main beneficiary and advocate of free trade. When prosperity waned, however, teachers and writers on political economy could be disconcerted by a lack of consensus among leading authorities, either on its fundamental principles or on the scientific validity of its analytical methods. The resulting methodological debate then developed from two opposing directions – historical and mathematical – and opinions tended to polarize.

Two issues were crucial in distinguishing the historical school's critique of classical economic analysis – the first was the relativity of economic theory and the second was the role of facts in formulating and validating that theory. Typically the members of the historical school rejected the presumption that economists had, by virtue of introspection, an innate knowledge of the strategic determinants of economic behaviour; they poured particular scorn on that figment of the economist's imagination, the 'economic man'; and they insisted that so-called economic laws had no meaning outside the highly specific legal, institutional, cultural and historical context to which they were relevant. The only starting assumptions they regarded as acceptable in a process of economic reasoning were those that could be inferred from the facts of history (including the most recent history) and the only valid test of an economic theory was to confront it with either historical or contemporary empirical data. The founders of the historical school were scholars with a bias towards the study of history and especially of economic development. This was a notable feature of the German school, which was able to build on a powerfully reputable historiographical tradition. In Britain, where the academic prestige of historical research had been less impressive, the influence of historicist studies and research findings was assisted in the 1870s and 1880s by an upsurge of interest in two related streams of thought. One was the systematic positivism associated with August Comte and Herbert Spencer, which pinned its faith on human progress through intellectual enlightenment: the other was the social Darwinism (already foreshadowed in

22. See the introduction by Donald Winch to *Mill: Principles of Political Economy*, Books IV and V (London: Penguin Classics, 1970), for example, pp. 28–9: 'Throughout the *Principles* Mill performed a delicate balancing act, reaffirming and expanding the Ricardian framework while at the same time generously incorporating new ideas and taking account of evidence which others considered to be antagonistic or damaging to the Ricardian system'.

Spencer's 'development hypothesis'), which became influential after the publication of Charles Darwin's *Origin of Species* (1859). Both sets of ideas favoured a comparative-historical approach to the explanation of economic events and both stressed the essential unity of scientific method.

The evolution debate may have lifted the confidence of economists ambitious to emulate scientific method, not merely because it exhibited natural scientists openly disputing fundamental principles, but also because it indicated a line of defence against the historicist critique of classical political economy. On the one hand, the Darwinian theory, though based on twenty years of painstaking empirical research, was a prime example of hypothetico-deductive reasoning. On the other hand, both Darwin's theory of organic change by natural selection and Spencer's *System of Synthetic Philosophy* (1862–93), with its individualist and *laissez-faire* doctrines, resonated with the classical economists' ideological bias towards free trade and their theoretical assumptions of free competition and the economic man. The result was to strengthen economists' belief in the scientific validity of their theorizing and to suggest ways of adjusting their traditional analytical methods, so as to deflect or absorb the most damaging criticisms of both positivists and historicists. Theorists favouring a more rigorous and explicitly mathematical approach to economic theory also found their arguments falling on more fertile ground in the 1870s; the traditionally high prestige of mathematics in British universities made it more likely that this route to a reform of the classical methodology would attract into the discipline first-class graduates committed to the search for economic truth within a rigorously defined analytical framework. At the same time, the twin presumptions of (a) the inexorable progress of human society (associated with Spencerian doctrines), and (b) adaptive improvement as the driving force in institutional change (implicit perhaps in Darwin's theory of natural selection), offered a rationale for incorporating history into political economy as an illustration to, rather than as a source of economic theory – in effect by providing historical flesh to clothe the bones of pure theory. The way was then open to convert economic history into a branch of applied economics. The first task, however, was to reconstruct economic theory on lines which would command a consensus among leading economists.

Jevons, a natural scientist by training, had sketched his mathematical theory of political economy early in the 1860s and noted in his Journal that, when he presented it to the 1862 meeting of the British Association for the Advancement of Science, his paper was received 'without a word of interest or belief'.[23] By 1871 the climate of ideas had changed, however, so that – when

23. Journal of W.S. Jevons, 31 December 1862, in *Papers and Correspondence of William Stanley Jevons* Vol. I, edited by R.D. Collison and Rosamond Konekamp (London: Macmillan, 1972), p. 188. The paper in question was printed in full in the *Journal of the Royal Statistical Society*, June 1869.

stimulated by the appearance of Fleeming Jenkin's articles on 'The graphic representation of supply and demand' – he sent his *Theory of Political Economy* to press.[24] Unlike the historicist critics of classical political economy, Jevons did not reject the whole corpus of economic theory. Having already won a reputation as an applied economist, with two well-received publications – *A Serious Fall in the Value of Gold* (1863) and *The Coal Question* (1865) – he adopted a constructive approach. His aim was to reconstruct orthodox economic theory on sound mathematical foundations. By reformulating the laws of supply and demand in terms of the concept of marginal utility, he helped to pioneer the transformation in economic ideas that later historians of economic thought dubbed the 'marginal revolution'. The preface to his second (1879) edition, revised in the knowledge that he had made a decisive impact on contemporary economic debate, introduced a new research programme in what he chose to call economics rather than political economy:

> [A]s all physical sciences have their basis more or less obviously in the principles of mechanics, so all branches and divisions of economic science must be pervaded by general principles. It is to the investigation of such principles, to the tracing out of the mechanics of self-interest and utility that this essay has been devoted. The establishment of such a theory is a necessary preliminary to a definite drafting of the super-structure of the aggregate science.[25]

5 THE SCOPE AND METHOD OF POLITICAL ECONOMY

When Keynes began his monograph on method in the mid-1880s, he was among the rising generation of economists – inspired by Jevons and taught by Marshall – who believed they had inherited a logical system of ideas that was steadily advancing in explanatory power. His friend and colleague H.S. Foxwell, for example, described recent developments in economics for an American learned journal.[26] There he interpreted 'the new school of political economy in England' as a synthesis of the most fruitful ideas generated by past classical political economists and their recent critics – whether mathematical or historical in their approach. He claimed that, since the publication of Jevons's *Theory of Political Economy* (1871): 'the standard of economic instruction has been raised in remarkable degree and the amount of interest and activity in economic study is greater than at any

24. See the preface to the 4th edition of Jevons's *Theory of Political Economy*, written by his son. Jenkin was a professor of mechanical engineering at Edinburgh.
25. W.S. Jevons, *Theory of Political Economy* (1879), ed. by R.D. Collison Black (Penguin edn, 1970), p. 50.
26. H.S. Foxwell, 'The Economic Movement in England', *Quarterly Journal of Economics*, October 1887.

previous time in our history'. He then went on to assert that no living writer had 'done as much as Alfred Marshall to bring about this advance. ... Half the economics chairs in the United Kingdom are occupied by his pupils and the share taken by them in general economic instruction in England is even greater than this'.[27] In the event, Marshall's pupils could adopt the essentials of Jevons's marginal analysis, for example, without dismissing both Ricardo and Mill as 'wrongheaded'. Similarly, they could agree wholeheartedly with the historicists that it was necessary to test the hypotheses and conclusions of economic theory against historical facts and statistics, whilst pointing out that even historical economists were forced to use deductive techniques of economic analysis to give shape and direction to their research. More important still, they were comfortably aware that, in occupying the middle ground of the methodological disputes, they were in distinguished foreign company. Economists such as A. Wagner in Germany, C. Menger in Austria, L. Cossa in Italy and R.T. Ely in the United States had gone on record in advocating a judicious mixture of empirical and theoretical, deductive and inductive techniques of analysis, as the foundation for a scientific political economy.[28] In short, the Marshallian vision of a continuity of ideas stretching back through Smith, Ricardo and Mill, of a broad consensus among the international community of economists, and of the analytical potential of rigorous mathematically-structured theorizing, gave them a robust confidence in the scientific credentials of their discipline. They could thus easily override the 'waves of disputation' which Sidgwick had feared were 'in danger of submerging the really sound and valuable results of practical thought.'[29]

For Cambridge economists already under Marshall's spell, his inaugural lecture represented a manifesto for a progressive research programme, founded on a narrow core of pure, deductive, politically detached and mathematically rigorous economic science.[30] According to Neville's Diary for 24 February 1885: 'Mother went with me to hear Marshall's inaugural lecture, wh I thought a decided success. I hear, however, that he caused (for different reasons), displeasure to Sidgwick, Cunningham and Ward'. Cunningham's hackles were inevitably raised by Marshall's marginalization of the contribution of history to scientific economics. The only lesson of history the new professor of political economy acknowledged was 'that our present economic

27. Ibid., pp. 91–2.
28. See A. Wagner on the present state of political economy, *Quarterly Journal of Economics*, October 1886; L. Cossa, *Guide to the Study of Political Economy*, ed. W.S. Jevons in an English translation of 1880; R.T. Ely, *The Past and Present of Political Economy*, Johns Hopkins University Study, 2nd series, III (1884).
29. Sidgwick (1883), p. 7.
30. A. Marshall, 'The present position of economics', in A.C. Pigou (ed.), *Memorials of Alfred Marshall* (London: Macmillan, 1925).

conditions are quite unlike any that have existed before'.[31] Indeed he deduced:

> [T]he economist must be suspicious of any direct light that the past is said to throw on the problems of the present. He must stand fast by the more laborious plan of interrogating facts in order to learn the manner of actions singly and in combination, applying this knowledge to build up the organon in dealing with the economic side of social problems. He will thus work in the light of facts, but the light will not be thrown directly, it will be reflected and concentrated by science.[32]

In the event, Sidgwick, the current chairman of the Moral Sciences Board, confidently expected a full account of Marshall's inaugural lecture from Ward and was not himself present. His own expectations were frankly conditioned by his earlier confrontation with the newly-arrived professor, who had angrily declared that the subject he had been elected to promote deserved a more important role in the moral sciences tripos than the current regulations prescribed. Sidgwick summarized his own views of the lecture in his Journal on 24 February 1885:

> Marshall gave his inaugural lecture containing the threatened declaration of war against me and my efforts at University organisation. I did not go to hear him, but I am told that it was courteously expressed, though unmistakable to the initiated. I have come to the conclusion, without – I think – pique or undue despondency, that I must abandon my efforts. Too many forces are against me – [B.F.] Westcott, [John] Seeley and now Marshall. [Henry] Jackson who is the only member of the [General Studies] Board who cordially and strongly agrees with me, avows that he is quite hopeless. And after all, it is easy to overvalue organisation, and at any rate well to know in time when a line has to be abandoned.[33]

Nevertheless, as far as the Moral Sciences Board was concerned none of its members, apart from Marshall, was inclined to create organizational problems for their chairman. The economists who were Marshall's disciples relaxed in the belief that the inaugural lecture justified their own research and teaching activities. It encouraged them to take for granted the progressive character of their science without presuming that it gave its practitioners either a licence, or a responsibility, to pontificate on practical policy issues. Marshall maintained, for example 'that part of economic doctrine, which alone can

31. Ibid., p. 169.
32. Ibid., p. 171.
33. Sidgwick, *Journal* reprinted A. and E. Sidgwick (1906), pp. 401–2. The 'Board' referred to in this quotation was the General Board of Studies. The 'declaration of war' lay in Marshall's contention that the abysmally small output of good Cambridge economists was due to the structure of the moral sciences tripos, for example, 'many of those who are fitted for the highest and hardest economic work are not attracted by the metaphysical studies that lie at the threshold of that Tripos'. See Marshall 'The present position', in Pigou (ed.) (1925), p. 171.

claim universality, has no dogmas. It is not a body of concrete truth, but an engine for the discovery of concrete truth, similar to, say, the theory of mechanics'.[34] This was the analytically-orientated vision that his pupils passed on to their students and to the wider audience of applied economists, policy makers and others, who had been disconcerted by classical political economy's loss of public credibility. Half a century later, Maynard Keynes restated it as the distinctive formula of the Cambridge school in his introduction to the Cambridge Economic Handbooks series. His interpretation ran: 'The Theory of Economics does not furnish a body of settled conclusions immediately applicable to a policy. It is a method rather than a doctrine, an apparatus of the mind, a technique of thinking, which helps its possessor to draw correct conclusions'. It survived in the editorial introduction to the Handbooks, signed by C.W. Guillebaud and Milton Friedman, in the 1950s.[35]

In effect, Keynes's *Scope and Method* represented a ground-clearing contribution to the Marshallian research programme. It proved a more challenging task than *Formal Logic* and took over five years to complete. Its long gestation was partly due to its author's teaching, examining and administrative commitments which grew heavier in the 1880s. Another reason for delay was the success of his first book – *Formal Logic* – which by October 1886 was rapidly selling out. The publisher's pressure to get copy for an instant reprint confronted the author's determination to revise it thoroughly. Consequently *Scope and Method* was put aside until July 1887. It was again delayed, in October, by the proofs of Marshall's *Principles of Economics*. 'My spare time is now being given to Marshall's proofsheets', groaned Keynes to his Diary on 26 October. They were still arriving when he wrote on 13 January 1888: 'Bonamy Price died a few days ago and so there is a vacancy in the Oxford professorship'. By then he had only two chapters of *Scope and Method* in first proof. Marshall, after glancing hastily through the copies sent to him, at once passed them on to the Master of Balliol and Robert Giffen, in the hope that they would add weight to his favourite candidate's qualifications for the Oxford chair. Much to Neville Keynes's relief, the chair went to Thorold Rogers, an economic historian. He made no attempt to disguise his satisfaction when he reported the news in the Diary on 11 April. No doubt Neville recalled Foxwell's letter of 16 January (when responding to his request for a testimonial):

> Pray dont go. It is much better that a study should be conducted in a particular place. There arise many of the same advantages in the localisation of an industry. Your departure would leave a nasty ragged wound in our Moral Sciences organi-

34. Ibid., p. 159.
35. See, for example, R.C.O. Matthews, *The Trade Cycle*, Cambridge Economic Handbooks, ed. C.W. Guillebaud and Milton Friedman (Cambridge: Cambridge University Press, 1959), p. vii.

sation. What is the use of being a settled family man if you are to drift from your moorings in this fashion! Think of the effect your move may have on your son. He may grow up flippantly epigrammatical and end by becoming the proprietor of a Gutter Gazette, or the hero of a popular party; instead of emulating his father's example, becoming a clearheaded Cambridge man, spending a life in valuable unpretentious service to his kind, dying beloved by his friends, venerated by the wise and as unknown to the masses as true merit and worth mostly are. Let me as earnestly as a bachelor can, appeal to your feelings as a father. Can you hesitate?

With the unsettling matter of the Oxford chair behind him, Keynes could concentrate on writing a second book, and on discussing problems of definition and principle – at length and as they arose – with his contemporaries. Two of them – J.S. Nicholson and W.E. Johnson – read and constructively criticized successive chapters in proof. So too did Alfred and Mary Marshall, the former's comments being extensively transcribed in Neville's Diary. He was an admirer of Mary Marshall's writing style, so it can be supposed that her corrections were also taken very seriously. However, there is no doubt that Marshall's influence on the substance and thrust of his pupil's *magnum opus* was predominant. He had been sending Keynes draft chapters of his own *Principles of Economics* well before the Oxford lectures were planned. The two books thus developed side by side, as it were, with the pupil continuously indoctrinated from the outset, and highly sensitive to the master's criticisms – even when he chose not to take his advice. As representatives of what Marshall called 'the new generation of economists',[36] both were impatient with current controversies on method. Marshall preferred to consign them to oblivion lest they should cloud his own message. Neville's perspective was that of a teacher rather than a prophet, and he was persuaded that if his students were to avoid unnecessary confusion they needed a detailed and orderly methodological statement that was judicious instead of polemical, moderate rather than extreme, and expository rather than argumentative. Hence the tone of the *Scope and Method* Preface:

I have endeavoured to avoid the tone of a partisan and have sought in the treatment of disputed questions to represent both sides without prejudice. Whilst making no attempt to bring about a complete reconciliation between opposing views, I have been able to show that the nature of the opposition between them has sometimes been misunderstood and its content consequently exaggerated.[37]

36. In 1896 Marshall addressed the new Cambridge Economics Club on the subject of 'the relation in which the work of the older generation of economists, which is drawing near the close of its activity, stands to the work which appears to be before that coming generation to which most of the members of the club belong', later published in 'The old generation of economists and the new', *Quarterly Journal of Economics*, October 1897, p. 115.
37. J.N. Keynes, *The Scope and Method of Political Economy* (London: Macmillan, 4th edn reprinted 1930), p. vi. The publishers listed 1890 as the date of the first edition but according to the Diary it appeared on 17 January 1891.

Neville Keynes's reactions to Marshall's comments on his proofs were volatile, partly because the latter's comments tended to be devious. The Diary for 18 February 1888, for example, quoted from Marshall's letter: "'I have glanced rapidly through your proofs. I think them excellent. The only general suggestion that occurs to me is that I shd prefer references of a controversial nature to the opinions of individuals being relegated to footnotes'". These were the proofs that Marshall intended to rush to Oxford, and Keynes added: 'On Marshall's advice I have modified my remarks on Bonamy Price, reducing the personal allusions to a minimum'. But that was merely a tactical issue. On 21 April a conversation with, and another letter from, Marshall gave his disciple (readily shamed by his inability to read German) the first of many sleepless nights. According to the Diary:

> Marshall writes – 'A new book on the subject ought to be very German and based more on "new school" difficulties as felt in Germany and in America and England. Too much prominence is given to the doctrines of writers who are sinking out of memory, too little in comparison is said in anticipation of the difficulties of the coming generation'.

A day later, after a talk with Florence had braced her husband's self-confidence, he revealed a more buoyant state of mind:

> I think he has hardly done justice to the good points of my book. I think I can claim for it clearness and definitions. Another thing is that I never can rely much on Marshall's judgment. His views are nearly always exaggerated on one side or the other. My great comfort is, as usual, my darling wife with whom I can talk the whole thing over as if I were talking with myself.

Perhaps Mary Marshall also intervened, for a week later (28 April) the Diary records:

> I was unduly depressed after my conversation with Marshall. He and Mrs Marshall have kindly read through my chapters again and he writes more encouragingly – 'The more I look at your proofs the more I think that they are excellent, but that they can be made better – I think there is most excellent material in these two chapters but I dont think you have made the most of them. They are a sort of introduction and introductions have to be rewritten many times. I have no doubt that the book will be best in the subject and will have a large circulation even if you bring it out as it is'.

In time, however, Marshall's aggravating mixture of criticism and encouragement proved surprisingly effective. Fortunately Florence was fluent in German and there are frequent references in the Diary to her translations of relevant texts. For example, on 8 September 1888: 'Every evening Florence reads me some pages of Menger on the method of Political Economy'; and on 13 July 1889: 'Florence has been reading to me Schmoller on Menger and is now reading to me Menger on Schmoller. He is very abusive and makes us roar with laughter'. At last, on 5 September 1889, the Diary quoted a letter in which Marshall gave his final verdict on that most contentious first chapter:

> I think your Chap I is excellent now. I do not mean that on every part I shd say exactly what you have. But it represents excellently your point of view; and my own differences from it are never more than half the breadth of a hair. And it is not useful to hairsplit.'

In the end, Marshall's *Principles* appeared first – in July 1890 – and Keynes's *Scope and Method* on 17 January 1891. After reading the last of his pupil's proofs, Marshall had sent generous congratulations on the book as a whole. 'I know there is great exaggeration here', Neville confided to his Diary on 4 October 1890, 'and that out of kindness and friendliness Marshall writes in a style of exaggeration in order to encourage me. Still on the whole he cannot think the book contemptible or as bad as I am sometimes myself inclined to think'.

Marshall had been didactically right to concentrate his most persistent fire on the first two chapters, for they contained the nub and justification of *Scope and Method*. They deserved to be 'rewritten many times'. Chapter I reviewed the recent methodological debates in terms of two polar views of the scope and method of political economy – one seeing it as a positive abstract and inductive science; the other as an ethical, realistic and deductive science. Neville then set out to show that it was all of these things by distinguishing three types of economic inquiry:

1. 'a positive science', that is, 'a body of systematized knowledge concerning what is';
2. 'a normative or regulative science', that is, 'an art as systematized knowledge relating to criteria of what ought to be and concerned therefore with the ideal as distinguished from the actual';
3. 'an art as a system of rules for the attainment of a given end'.

The object of this classification scheme[38] was to distinguish assumptions and findings about what *is* (which constitutes the scientific core of political economy) from, on the one hand, statements about what ought to be (which also have a scientific validity in so far as ethics is a rational discipline, a moral science), and, on the other hand, prescriptions for achieving desired ends. It permitted the economic theorist to insulate his or her fundamental theorems from accusations of ideological bias, or immorality, or relativity, as

38. Ibid., pp. 34–5.

well as from failures in economic policies derived from these theorems. In effect, the normative science and the art of political economy provided a protective belt for the hard core of neoclassical theory that emerged from the marginal revolution. The protective belt could absorb the attacks of historicists, socialists and nationalists, and so shift the battlefield of doctrinal or methodological dispute away from fundamental principles. According to Keynes:

> If political economy regarded from the theoretical standpoint is to make good progress it is essential that all extrinsic or premature sources of controversy should be eliminated; and we may be sure that the more its principles are discussed independently of ethical and practical considerations, the sooner will the science emerge from the controversial stage.[39]

As Marshall insisted frequently, in the letters he wrote on reading successive instalments of Keynes's proofs, *Scope and Method* was not the kind of book he would have written himself. At one point, for example, he remarked that (since he had a positive aversion to hard and fast demarcation lines): 'I am not a good judge of the views expressed by your more orderly nature'.[40] He made essentially the same point about his pupil's propensity for clear-cut definition and classification in a letter dated 20 September 1890:

> You make all your contrasts rather too sharply for me. You talk of induction and deduction methods, when I contend that each involves the other and that historians are always deducing and that even the most deductive writers are always implicitly at least basing themselves on observed facts.[41]

The truth was that Keynes was essentially a logician in his approach to his subject and did not share Marshall's readiness to fudge issues that could be marginalized. He was more interested in the validity of the analytical techniques associated with the new economics than in its political or philosophical implications. Nor did he share Marshall's fascination with competing philosophical systems or respond sympathetically to his dialectical propensities. Keynes's way of resolving conflicts of principle inherent in methodological disputes was to begin by systematically clearing confusion and bias from his identification of the issues and then to redefine terms so that they fell naturally into the synthesis indicated by the new political economy. He was determined, above all, to leave no loose ends in his own reasoning.

Perhaps because it was so painstakingly unprovocative in attack and so impeccably logical in its objectives, the book attracted few antagonistic

39. Ibid., p. 52.
40. In an undated letter, no. 66 in the Marshall Library, JNK Papers.
41. No. 74 in the Marshall Library, JNK Papers.

reviews. It was guaranteed a sympathetic reception from the 'new generation of economists'. Edgeworth who reviewed it twice – first in *Nature* and then at some length in the *Economic Journal* – set the tone for many later reviews which welcomed it as the definitive methodological text for the economic science contained in Marshall's *Principles*. Keynes was particularly heartened by the *Nature* review. The Diary for 28 February 1891 described it as 'a most enthusiastic review, given a prominent position by the Editor' and quoted proudly:

> 'Altogether it is a matter for rejoicing that the cost of connecting and supplementing all the authorities on all the methods has devolved upon one so widely read, impartial and exact. On a subject which it is undesirable to be always reopening, it may be hoped that Keynes's work will prove final.'

Edgeworth made the same point more bluntly in his *Economic Journal* review. After describing Keynes as the 'Hallam of methodologists' he concluded with the hope that

> Mr Keynes' later logical treatise may also resemble his earlier one in its popularity. We could wish for it indeed a monopoly of favour, and such finality as in political economy is attainable. For we cannot conceal a certain impatience at the continual reopening of a question on which authorities appear to be substantially, if not in phrase, agreed. [42]

Scope and Method was widely reviewed internationally, for example by Dr Stephan Bauer of Vienna,[43] and by Simon Patten in the *Annals of the American Academy*. Patten lauded it as a 'marked success' in pouring oil on the troubled waters of methodological dispute, and criticized it for focusing too narrowly on the English school. For example: 'He seems to regard the English writers as creators of positive doctrines while other economists are viewed merely as critics of these doctrines'.[44] The most substantial of the unfavourable reviews appeared in the Oxford *Economic Review*. There Phelps, whilst conceding Keynes's impartiality and moderation, dismissed the notion that such a conciliatory statement could reduce methodological conflict. It was Phelps who came out abrasively with the criticism lurking below the surface of other, politer, reviews – that *Scope and Method* was a boring text:

> The besetting sin of analytical writers is a certain lack of humour, which whilst it helps them to steer past the Scylla of paradox, runs them dangerously near the Charybdis of commonplace. I could wish that Mr Keynes had been more success-

42. F.Y. Edgeworth, *Economic Journal*, Vol. I, 1891, p. 423.
43. In the 1891 *Jahrbücher für Nationalökonomie. Dritte Folge II*, pp. 274–8.
44. Simon Patten, *Annals of the American Academy*, April 1891, p. 690.

> ful in avoiding this latter danger. This book is careful, accurate and clear but it is not distinguished by ideas.[45]

Keynes, who was particularly sensitive to the accusation that his book was 'commonplace' commented sadly on this review in the Diary for 27 October 1891: 'Not favourable, but I think in the main just. It might perhaps have been a little less contemptuous in tone; but then it hails from Oxford where they hold works of an analytical character in very light esteem'.

Although Keynes's monograph rapidly displaced J.E. Cairnes's *Character and Logical Method of Political Economy* (1875) on undergraduate reading lists, it drew such an authoritative line under the debates on economic method that it became superfluous – except for students of the history of economic thought who needed to see precisely where the neoclassical orthodoxy scored over its classical predecessor. Some sixty years later, Dennis Robertson recalled the total lack of interest in methodology that characterized his contemporaries' reading for honours in economics towards the end of the first decade of the twentieth century:

> To us, I think, it seemed (what sort of study economics is, and what it is all about) more suitable for discussion by Germans than by Englishmen. There was on our reading list what I have since come to regard as a good if dry book about it, J.N. Keynes's *Scope and Method of Political Economy*, but to be quite honest I doubt if many of us read it. We thought we knew pretty well what sort of things we wanted to read about and were glad enough to take the counsel given by Marshall himself near the beginning of the *Principles* 'the less we concern ourselves with scholastic enquiries as to whether a certain consideration comes within the scope of economics the better'.[46]

6 OTHER MORALIST PUBLICATIONS AND INTERESTS

After the publication of *Scope and Method*, the Diary offered no indication that Neville Keynes intended to write another book on economics. When the third (much-expanded) edition of his *Formal Logic* appeared in late summer of 1894, he quoted in the Diary for 22 September a letter from J.S. Mackenzie congratulating him on the new volume and adding: 'The book strikes me now as rather too ambitious for an elementary textbook. Wd it not be worthwhile to bring out a smaller edit^{n} bearing much the same relation to this as Marshall's Elements to his Principles?' We have seen that he declined Macmillan's invitation to write an elementary textbook of logic (for students

45. L.R. Phelps, *Economic Review*, October 1891, pp. 570–1.
46. D.H. Robertson, 'Utility and all that', *Manchester School of Social and Economic Studies*, May 1951, pp. 111–12. The passage quoted by Robertson is on p. 23 of Marshall's *Principles*, 8th edn, 1952 reprint.

in Indian universities) – on the grounds that he had already decided to write an 'Elements of logic'. On the other hand, it is hard to say how seriously he entertained that project for it was not again mentioned in the Diary. He was to produce another expanded and revised *Formal Logic* in 1895 and two relatively lightly revised further editions of *Scope and Method*. Well before then his two well-received books had effectively established his reputation for accurate, unpretentious scholarship in logic and political economy – and put him on the fast track for his coveted award of a Cambridge doctorate. Thus, encouraged by both Marshall and Sidgwick, Keynes applied early in May 1891 to the Moral Sciences Board, which appointed referees whose reports were tabled at the next General Board of Studies meeting. It was G.F. Browne (his superior at the Local Examinations Syndicate) who gave him the news that his application was unanimously approved and told him that he would have been 'extremely gratified' if he could have heard the referees' reports. Browne was tantalizingly discreet, however, and failed to identify the names. After the formal announcement in the *University Reporter*, a stream of congratulations poured in to 6 Harvey Road from ex-pupils, old friends and academic colleagues. James Ward, never lavish with his praise, was one of those who had urged him in 1884 to apply for the degree on the strength of his *Formal Logic* alone;[47] his screed arrived on 15 June and the Diary noted his humorously cryptic comment: '"I am congratulating myself that you have become Dr. I had been feeling a good deal like the fox who lost his tail"'. On 18 June, W.E. Johnson deputized at short notice (as invigilator at the Higher Local examinations), so that the new DSc could be presented ceremonially by Sidgwick to a 'most impressive' vice-chancellor at a Senate House congregation. Neville's pleasure in the occasion shines out from the Diary – marred only by the fact that Florence, then confined to bed with influenza, was unable to join the family group at the ceremony. On returning home to tea they heard four-year-old Geoffrey 'enquiring most anxiously when he should see Dr Keynes. But when he saw me in my ordinary costume he thought there must be some mistake'. Family pride climaxed on 9 October when Neville took delivery of his scarlet gown – 'so gorgeous that I can hardly imagine myself appearing in it in public'. It was a birthday present from his mother who *had* watched the ceremony.

Thereafter writing for publication accounted for a relatively small proportion of Neville Keynes's work in moral sciences. He continued to write concise, definitive articles for Palgrave's *Dictionary of Economics*, as well as

47. Foxwell was another who had persistently urged him to apply for the DSc degree. (See the Diary for 27 November 1887.) It should be noted that JNK's DSc represented recognition by his peers of his competence to teach in a particular field of knowledge whereas a modern Cambridge doctorate, such as a PhD, recognizes a specific contribution to knowledge in the relevant field.

articles or reviews for the *Economic Journal*; and he conscientiously fulfilled Sidgwick's deathbed commission to complete and see through the Press the partially revised edition of the latter's *Principles of Political Economy* (1901). From 1891, however, Neville chose to promote the two moral sciences in which he specialized by trying to improve the quality and effectiveness of his role as a teacher and examiner, rather than by breaking new ground in logical analysis or contributing to current debates on economic policy. He agreed to serve on the Council of the new British Economic Association (later the Royal Economic Society), whilst stubbornly resisting Marshall's pressure to edit its *Economic Journal*. It was not at all surprising – given his brief experience of teaching at Oxford in 1885 and the results of his uneasy candidacy for the Drummond Chair in 1888 – that when Thorold Rogers died in October 1890 Keynes did not even mention the idea of re-entering the lists. Moreover, although he was clearly gratified (on 5 January 1895) to get a letter from Professor J.L. Laughlin offering him a professorship at the University of Chicago – 'in the most polite and flattering terms' – he was uninterested in the proposition. Similarly, just over a month later, the Diary acknowledged his pleasure at being invited to serve as vice-president of Section F of the British Association for Advancement of Science in connection with its Ipswich meeting: but the result was the same. Aware that acceptance would have committed him to preside over the Section F programme in 1896 he refused. On the other hand, when the University of London needed a new registrar at the end of 1895, Neville thought seriously of applying for the post. On 7 January 1896, after noting in the Diary that R.D. Roberts (his colleague at the Local Examinations and Lectures Syndicate) had decided to apply, he added: 'I am very much exercised in my mind as to whether I shall be a candidate too. Florence rather urges it upon me'. Sidgwick, with whom he discussed the matter on 8 January, encouraged him with the opinion that he was better suited for the post than Roberts. However, by the mid-1890s his primary ambitions lay clearly in administrative directions.

The three Keynes children (1895)

VI Late-Victorian family life

1 FAMILY EXTENSIONS

The house which Neville built, and moved into with his bride in November 1882, was a substantial, semi-detached, three-storied brick residence over a basement (of which the front windows were partly above street level). At the back was a secluded garden where the family could relax on sunny summer afternoons. Visitors climbed ten stone steps to reach the main front door, situated between two bay windows. Tradesmen descended to a second front door beneath the steps. In this dwelling – big enough to accommodate a family with three young children, at least three live-in servants, and sometimes as many as three overnight guests – Neville and Florence lived contentedly for the rest of their lives. According to their younger son Geoffrey, writing in the 1970s:

> The house and small garden were without charm or character, but the place suited our unexacting standards, and my mother died there 76 years later at the age of 96. ... The walls of the rather dark dining-room were clad in deep blue and crimson Morris paper of such quality that it never needed renewal during our tenancy.[1]

It was the unstinted welcome extended to friends, relatives, colleagues, students and assorted visitors to Cambridge that gave 6 Harvey Road its distinctive character. From 23 November 1882 – when Neville and Florence gave an informal supper party to thank more than 40 workmen who had built it – until the late 1930s and 1940s (when their grandchildren were as free to invite their friends to take Sunday lunch or tea in it as their children had been in the first decade or so of the century), their home maintained an unbroken tradition of friendly, unpretentious hospitality.

It soon became the social centre for an extended Victorian family. When Neville decided to build (in October 1881), he already hoped to persuade his 60-year-old mother to move to Cambridge. It was obvious that his marriage would have disruptive implications for the Salisbury household, of which he had himself been the absentee head since his father's death in

1. The paper was hung in the summer of 1884. See essay by G. Keynes, in Milo Keynes (ed.), *Essays on John Maynard Keynes* (Cambridge: Cambridge University Press, 1975), p. 26.

1878 and where Anna Keynes still lived with her husband's sister Mary (ten years her senior) and two female servants. It was his widowed mother for whom Neville felt directly responsible. As far as Aunt Mary was concerned, he knew that she would be welcomed into the household of his stepsister, Fanny Purchase, whom she had mothered as a child and nursed through various domestic emergencies (including each of seven pregnancies) at Kington. So, when telling his mother that he intended to build a home for Florence and himself, he suggested building for her another house in Cambridge. Her response, in a letter that reached him on 17 October 1881, was hesitant, perhaps disappointed by his failure to invite her to share his new home. She wrote: 'I hardly know what to say about your building a house for me. I shd like to see you settled and visit you in your own home before I decide what to do'. Meanwhile, she continued to display her profound emotional dependence on her only son. On the day they parted affectionately in London in January 1882 – after sharing a three-week continental holiday[2] – Neville groaned to his Diary: 'I know that my marriage will be in some respects a heavy trial for her'. A month later, Anna Keynes underlined her feelings for him, whilst signalling that she might easily be persuaded to move house: 'I often wonder if I shall come to live in Cambridge, but I feel I must be nearer to you. You are *everything* to me. I thank God for such a son. You *do* make up in great degree what I have lost in your beloved Father'.

There were many excisions from the 1882 Diary, and it contains no further reference to the question of his mother's future home until after the honeymoon, when it transpired that Florence had never explicitly encouraged her mother-in-law to move to Cambridge. On 13 October Neville quoted from another of his mother's letters: '"Do you think Florence wd be pleased for me to live in Cambridge? She has never *said* she shd like me to do so – neither has Mrs Brown when I have been talking about it to her"'. When reading this plaintive passage in the privacy of his Pembroke rooms, however, he was wholly preoccupied by the knowledge that Florence (then visiting her parents in Bedford) was already pregnant. His comment in the Diary was then rather dismissive: 'It does grieve me that Mother shd feel as indicated here. I know she is wrong'. The next time the newly-weds were living under the same roof was at Brookside – where the Bonds had invited them to lodge while the builders put the finishing touches to the new house. At that point they had more urgent and exhilarating topics than Anna Keynes's future abode to discuss whenever they were alone together. Nev-

2. JNK had hoped to take Florence as well as his mother on this trip but John Brown could not afford to finance another continental holiday for his daughter, so soon after their Swiss holiday in the summer of 1881; and neither he nor Florence would consent to her travelling at either Neville's or his mother's expense.

ertheless, Neville was still determined to settle her in Cambridge. With that in mind, he decided to buy no. 5 Harvey Road (the house attached to no. 6) – borrowing the £2000 purchase price by a mortgage on both houses at 4 per cent. He now (January 1883), cherished the hope of persuading his mother to live next door to him. Meanwhile, Fanny was already making arrangements for Aunt Mary to reside permanently in the Purchase household at Kington. On visiting his Salisbury family home at the end of March, Neville found his stepsister gently uprooting Aunt Mary from the Castle Street house where she had been usefully domiciled for four decades. Although the old lady's sadness at being forced to leave life-long friends and familiar places was understandable, it was not hard for Fanny to persuade her that such a move was 'for the best'. Anna Keynes, however, was younger, more independent and keenly sensitive to her position as mother-in-law. Neville confided ruefully to the Diary in March 1883: 'So far I dont get any encouragement for my scheme for Mother's living next to us'. It was the birth of her first full grandchild, in June 1883, that finally persuaded her to make her home in Cambridge.

On the other hand it soon became clear – in spite of Neville's myopic reluctance to come to terms with the fact – that Florence dreaded the prospect of having her mother-in-law settled next door to them. Eager to view the new baby, Anna Keynes had arrived when it was barely a week old and stayed on as house guest for almost four full weeks. On 8 July, the day before she left, the Diary described a tense situation:

> Mother is slightly more inclined to come next door. Florence does not altogether like the idea, but she admits its advantages and is trying to reconcile herself to it. When I was talking to her on the subject this evening I surprised her with tears in her eyes and it troubled me a good deal. I only want to do what is best for the happiness of both of them whom I love the most. They love each other too; but Mother still thinks Florence a little undemonstrative … and on the other hand Florence is worried by implicit criticisms on small matters which Mother does rather keep on about. I am sometimes worried myself for the same reason.

His mother must have summed up the situation; for, less than a month later, Neville regretfully accepted her final decision not to move next door and arranged to let the property to the new professor of anatomy. Henceforth relations between mother and wife were restored to an equable norm and Anna Keynes became almost as frequent, and as welcome, a guest in Cambridge as Ada Brown. Best of all, she was invariably willing to move in to take charge of the Harvey Road household, and especially little Maynard, whenever Neville and Florence chose to spend a few days in London enjoying theatres and galleries or visiting friends. Ada Brown, who had a young family of her own as well as a school to manage, was rarely free to act as minder to her grandchild.[3] In August 1884, Anna Keynes even persuaded the young parents – now expecting their second child – to leave Maynard (and his nursemaid) with her in Salisbury, whilst they enjoyed an unencumbered three weeks in Devon and Cornwall. She then invited a delighted Aunt Mary back to her old Castle Street home to share the pleasure of minding the toddler.

Although both Neville and Florence searched diligently for a Cambridge house that might suit his mother, almost another year passed before a property came on the market that the widow liked well enough to sell her two Salisbury houses. On 15 July 1885 Anna Keynes arrived at Harvey Road, to spend the few days until her furniture arrived and could be unloaded and arranged in her new home at 54 Bateman Street. Moving house was evidently women's work. Neville, who spent the time working on his new book, doing a little logic teaching at Girton and trying to improve his tennis, successfully detached himself from the removal process. He referred to it briefly in the Diary for 18 July: 'Mother and Florence are fatiguing themselves at Bateman Street. Mother is very delighted with the welcome she has received from Florence. I am playing tennis very badly'. A few days later, he wrote: 'Mother is disgusted with the operation of moving house', and he wondered miserably whether he had been wise to persuade his mother to leave the Salisbury home in which she had enjoyed a rewarding social life for almost three decades. However, when he and Florence left for a Swiss holiday that summer, they left a 'rather naughty' two-year-old boy with his baby sister at home in Harvey Road (with a full domestic staff), and thus transformed the situation for the grandmother by giving her a pleasant, but hardly burdensome, responsibility. Anna Keynes was well-consoled by her daily visits to Harvey Road. She greeted the returning travellers there a month later, and the next day Neville wrote cheerfully: 'We had supper with Mother. Annie Neville [a niece] is staying with her but leaves tomorrow. Her house looks capital and she seems much more content with it'.[4] Inevitably, it took time for the elder Mrs Keynes to construct an independent life in a new town, but for the next 22 years she lived, barely a mile from Harvey Road, entertaining a wide circle of friends and relatives, until she died in August 1907, at the age of 86. Meanwhile Neville was rewarded by an outcome which enabled him to maintain intimate contact with his mother for the rest of her life.

Neville himself had been born and reared in an atypically small Victorian family, but his familial horizons were extending even before he married. As early as his ninth year, his sister Fanny had left the Castle Street household to

3. The last of Ada Brown's children, Kenneth, had been born in 1879 when his mother was 42; so he was still under school age in 1884.
4. Only three weeks later, for example, she was complaining bitterly to her son about her loneliness in Bateman Street: 'She says that at the end of her lease she thinks she shall give up housekeeping. At the same time Florence feels strongly that it wd not be the right thing for her to come to live with us' (see Diary for 27 September 1885).

marry Edward Purchase, a grocer who set up business in the small market town of Kington on the borders of Shropshire and Herefordshire. Over the next decade and a half there was much coming and going between Salisbury and Kington while Fanny gave birth to four sons and three daughters. Neville's relations with his sister and her family were always warm. During school or university holidays he regularly visited her Kington home to join in the activities of his nephews and nieces and to take a positive interest in their education and welfare. In August 1875, for example, during his final honours year, he went directly from Cambridge to Kington to celebrate his 23rd birthday with them. As usual Fanny met his train, on this occasion accompanied by her four eldest children (Keynes, John, Matilda and Alice), leaving the two younger boys (Frank and Herbert) and the infant Mabel at home, in charge of the ever-devoted Aunt Mary. It was a particularly memorable reunion according to the Diary and, two days later: 'Father and Mother arrived from Salisbury in the evening, completing the family. 17 slept in the house overnight' – a number which presumably included three or four live-in servants. It must already have been a commodious residence, but one of the first things Edward Purchase did after their legacy from John Keynes relaxed the constraint on the family budget, was to extend the house. His next option opened up by the new affluence was to dabble in stocks and shares.

From the beginning, of course, Neville was more than ready to share his own more extensive knowledge and direct experience of the money market with his brother-in-law. The two men spent many wet afternoons at Kington discussing such matters; while Neville did his best to restrain Edward's impulsive propensity to sink his liquid assets in high-risk ventures. On the whole, however, Edward went his own way, and Neville's anxieties concerning his brother-in-law's wilder speculations continued to recur in the Diary. For example the entry for 20 July 1882 reads:

> To London for the day to meet Edward. He has been speculating wildly in Egyptians but has come out with only a moderate loss. I was always afraid that some day he would go too far. Unfortunately Mr Sprague had gone with him and lost his all – £500 – the laborious saving of years. They must both have had some bad moments.

Neville found Edward's underwriting problems the more worrying because it was his own example that had first induced his brother-in-law to become a Lloyd's name, through the agency of Frank Tiffin. In the event, Tiffin, Neville's boyhood friend, let down all his names, partly through sheer carelessness or incompetence, but also as a result of his growing drink problem. Fortunately by the time it was obvious that both brothers-in-law needed to be extricated from Tiffin's alcoholic ineptitude, John Purchase, the cleverest of Edward's sons, was an established London solicitor whose experience and city contacts enabled him to assist both Neville and Edward in minimizing their losses when closing their Lloyds' accounts.

Florence's numerous relatives provided the other major set of ramifications in the extended family[5] frequenting the Keynes household in Harvey Road. She herself was the eldest of John Brown's six children – three girls and three boys. Her mother, Ada Brown, had six siblings – of whom four survived to attend Neville's wedding to their niece. Bedford was near enough and the train service regular enough to permit a frequent exchange of visits between the Bunyan Manse and Harvey Road. A speedy postal and telegraphic service kept adult family members in constant touch with each other. On Monday 9 October 1882, for example, Neville – returning at the beginning of term from a weekend at the Manse – brought with him Alice (next in age to Florence) to take up her place at Newnham College. That was some weeks before he and Florence moved into their new home. The Saturday after they did so, Mrs Brown came to visit her daughter in college and to spend the Sunday with Florence and Neville – as she was to do on countless later occasions. During the next three terms, Alice regularly took Sunday lunch and dinner in Harvey Road and spent several days there during each vacation. Henceforth the Brown family treated 6 Harvey Road as a second home. John Brown spent Saturday nights there before the two or three Sundays each year when he was visiting preacher at one or other Cambridge congregational churches. His daughter Jessie and his three sons regularly spent part of their school holidays there. Kenneth, the youngest of the Brown children, was only a year older than Maynard of whom he became an early playmate.

Ada Brown's visits to Harvey Road were generally briefer as well as more purposeful than those of her husband or children. Often she came and went within the day. Her considerable personal experience of the problems and perils of giving birth made her an invaluable source of advice and practical support in each of her eldest daughter's pregnancies. When Florence was first afflicted by morning sickness in early October 1882, for example, it was her mother whose instant diagnosis astonished both of the newly-weds. Eight months later Mrs Brown arrived on the first Saturday in June to spend the week-end in Harvey Road when she judged Florence's confinement to be imminent. She returned to her school at the Manse early on Monday morning and caught the last train back to Cambridge that same night. Roused from her bed at 5 a.m. on 5 June, Mrs Brown took charge of a fast-developing situation. She got Neville to telegraph to the nurse standing by for the occasion and, a couple of hours later, sent him running to fetch the family doctor, Dr Wherry.

5. Neville Brown, *Dissenting Forbears: The Maternal Ancestors of J.M. Keynes* (Chichester: Phillimore, 1988) provides a mass of information on the Brown family and its ancestors.

It proved a gratifyingly smooth delivery. At 9 a.m. Neville was banished from the back bedroom where Florence was in labour and at 9.30 he listened at the door while his mother-in-law (then acting as midwife) and the doctor brought the event to a speedy conclusion. At 12.30 p.m., Neville began to write to his mother a blow-by-blow account of that morning's happenings – with the following climax:

> Florence was giving a slight groan every now and then (they say she was very brave) and at 9.45 I heard such a hullabaloo and Mrs Brown came to the door and said it was a boy. (This was rather a blow. I had wanted a girl but I think *you* will be satisfied.) Everything went well, except for a little tear, wh Wherry sewed up. Just before eleven I went in to see her and I thought she was looking very bonny. They say that the boy is the image of me. It's ugly enough. But Mrs Brown says I'm wrong there. It has our little finger. ... Now what do you think of *John Maynard* for a name? That is what we propose. We shd call him John. ... Florence looks very comfortable.

The nurse duly arrived soon after 1 p.m. and at about 9 that evening, according to the proud father: 'Mrs Brown and I ventured out to a party given by the fellows of St John's and I felt myself the lion of the evening. Miss Clough, Miss Gladstone and Mrs Sidgwick were particularly interested'. The following day he continued the story in the Diary: 'Florence is getting on nicely, though she looks very white. She will be able to nurse the child herself. The little man is improving in appearance – but indeed I am already getting fond of him notwithstanding his ugliness. I feel that I could sit and look at him for hours'. By then the nurse, who had seemed 'rather old' on first appearance, had won Neville's approval by allowing him to admire the baby for almost as long as he chose. Within the next 24 hours the new parents had decided to call John Maynard by his second name. After such an uncomplicated delivery, Dr Wherry's bill for 7 guineas, which arrived about three weeks later, seemed a small price to pay. The infant was duly christened by his grandfather (John Brown) at the Bunyan Meeting on 13 January 1884.

Accordingly, when Florence again began to suffer from morning sickness, only six months after Maynard's baptism, Neville viewed the prospect complacently: 'We did not want the little sister quite so soon', he wrote in the Diary for 15 June 1884, 'but she and Maynard will be nice companions to each other'. Florence seems to have taken the next eight months in her stride for there is no evidence in the Diary to suggest that either prospective parent was worried. Her mother took charge as usual. When Neville spent a couple of days in London in early January, for example, Mrs Brown bustled over to Harvey Road 'as it would not do for Florence to be left with only the servants just now'. A little later, during the week preceding the expected delivery date, Neville seems to have been more concerned by his own state of health than by his wife's. 'I have had shooting pains in my chest and back lately', he wrote in the Diary for 1 February 1885, 'and last night and today I very much worried myself about them. I began to speculate on how long I had to live. … Florence wd cheer me if I could talk to her about my fears; but I dare not worry her in her present condition'.[6] Although Dr Wherry's thorough examination (the next day) found nothing wrong, Neville continued to insist that his pains were getting worse until, on the morning of 4 February, Florence went into labour and he was instantly distracted by a fast-moving sequence of events. Margaret was born at about 10 a.m. and her birth was to precipitate a traumatically stressful episode. After Neville (leaving Florence in the care of doctor and midwife) had telegraphed the news to Bedford, Salisbury and Kington his natural propensity for worrying was intensified by a dreadful prognosis. According to the Diary:

> Mr Wherry made me frightfully anxious. He said she was terribly exhausted and he feared failure of the heart's action. … At 12 I sent for some Brand's Essence of Beef and after this she was better and Wherry left, giving directions for her to have brandy, milk or essence of beef every fifteen minutes. I went in to see her. At 1.45 Wherry returned. He said the rapidity of the confinement was alarming, and he did not think he had ever seen any one more thoroughly exhausted.

He then departed. At 3.30 Mrs Brown arrived with the nurse she had engaged for her daughter in Bedford. At 5.30 Wherry reappeared to 'sew up' another little tear, after which he departed, together with the midwife, leaving instructions that he must be recalled immediately if the patient showed 'the slightest signs of heart failure'. Doctor and nurses all made a point of impressing on Neville that his wife had almost died on this occasion and he was profoundly shaken. It certainly took some weeks before she recovered her energy and her rosy cheeks. Not until 13 March did the Diary report that she was 'sitting in an ordinary chair to meals and walking about from room to room', although, according to her mother, she still looked very ill. Meanwhile, Neville's chest pains seem to have vanished[7] and on 22 March he noted cheerfully in the Diary: 'I am feeling remarkably well just now. Is it the malt extract? We have

6. With hindsight – given that both Neville and Florence lived into their late nineties – these fears of an early demise seem comical, but deaths among their contemporaries were reported with sad frequency in the Diary.
7. They recurred in the summer of 1885 and on 10 August JNK sought medical advice a few days before he and Florence set off for a Swiss holiday: 'He says my lungs are quite sound and he attributes my pains to muscular rheumatism. He advises me not to put too much strain on my heart by climbing in Switzerland'. After that the pains were not mentioned again in the Diary. However he consulted Dr Wherry again the following December, because he was 'feeling rather out of sorts'. On that occasion he was given some medicine with the suggestion that: 'leading as I do a sedentary life I ought not to have three meat meals a day'.

been for a Family Walk today'. The emergency was over but Neville had learned that childbirth was a life-threatening process and, being ever risk-averse, he was ready to settle for a complement of one boy and one girl.

Early in August 1886 Neville found a recurrence of Florence's morning sickness a more disturbing portent than he was prepared to admit. Significantly the Diary offers no further reference to the impending event until late February 1887 when an irritated outburst against his mother-in-law exposed a cauldron of repressed emotions. After one of her many weekend stop-overs in Harvey Road, he wrote:

> Mrs Brown [as he invariably called her] protests how terribly anxious she is about Florence's confinement; and I believe she thinks me wanting any even decent feeling because I do not respond. I believe I am at least as anxious as she is, but I cannot talk about it. And for Florence's sake it is important that we should try to appear as little anxious as possible. I do trust Mrs Brown does not talk to Florence at all as she talks to me. Even the thought of her doing so makes me angry; and I am sorry that I can never feel complete confidence in her discretion.

Two days later, when Florence confessed to feeling as she had the night before Margaret was born, he ran to warn Dr Wherry 'to be ready in case of need'. It was actually more than three weeks later before the birth, by which time nurse Jackson had been sleeping for seven nights at 6 Harvey Road. Happily, baby Geoffrey achieved an even smoother entrance into the world than his brother had done. Florence awoke at 6 a.m. on 24 March and gave birth to a 10-pound boy two hours later. 'All went well from the beginning and Wherry stayed quite a short time', wrote Neville, 'O it was a relief to me and a cause for thankfulness not to have a repetition of last time's experience'. A telegram to Mrs Brown brought her to her daughter's bedside before 11 a.m. and the two children were allowed to see the baby and their mother that afternoon. The Keynes family was complete.

2 UPSTAIRS DOWNSTAIRS

The servants who enabled the family to maintain their comfortable and sociable way of life in Harvey Road were Florence's problem. They were seldom mentioned in the Diary, except in the context of a domestic crisis, and the rarity of such references testifies to Florence's ability to manage her staff without involving her husband in hiring or firing decisions. She could, of course, draw on her mother's practical experience in organizing a large household and wide personal contacts among employable women and girls. When John Brown went to Bedford in the early 1860s, he and his wife (herself the daughter of a congregational minister) already had two daughters to educate at home. Sons, of course, merited a grammar school education and their three boys went to Bedford Grammar School. Ada Brown, however, followed her own mother's example by starting a school for girls at the Manse. In November 1882, when Florence needed a housemaid and a cook to live in at 6 Harvey Road, Mrs Brown's personal links with relevant sectors of the labour market proved invaluable. It was up to Florence, however, to find out for herself whether young inexperienced maids were trainable. Neville's first Diary reference to their domestic staff was on 22 January 1883, when he noted: 'Lilla left us today and the new housemaid Ellen, engaged by Mrs Brown, has arrived'. Later, when Florence's first confinement was imminent, he recorded appreciatively that his mother-in-law had secured them the services of a professional nurse to take care of mother and infant during the crucial early weeks after the birth. Meanwhile Florence had hired a second maid, Alice, to help her in caring for the baby when nurse had moved on to another confinement. So, when Maynard was under three weeks old and the 'tremendous thunderstorms' of 24 June 1883 flooded the basement of 6 Harvey Road to a depth of two inches, there were two willing girls – then Mary and Alice – available to clear up the resultant mess.[8]

Nurse departed in mid-July, leaving Mary, Alice and another housemaid, Austin, to serve a household which entertained (often overnight) an endless succession of relatives and friends eager to visit the couple's new home or to admire their firstborn. It was a socially agreeable time for Neville and an anxious one for Florence, who now assumed major responsibility for nursing her infant son and for developing an efficient and humane regime downstairs. Occasionally, servant problems erupted into the Diary. The entry for 31 October, for example, recorded 'another anonymous letter about Mary and her young man – and although we have the greatest confidence in Mary and I know the letter is full of lies, it worries us'. Alice's character, of course, needed to be above reproach because it was she who looked after Maynard. When the baby was six months old, Neville wrote:

> We are again a good deal worried about our servants. Alice has quarrelled with the other two; and their statement is that we cant believe a word she says and that she is not kind to baby. At first we thought of giving her notice at once – but Mary and Austin cannot give definite proofs of what they say and we have decided to do nothing in a hurry. At the same time Florence has given Alice some hint of what we have heard.

Alice was still with them when a telegram announcing the death of her father took her home to Ireland for the funeral in March 1884. 'So little Maynard sleeps with us once more', remarked the pleased, if weary, father, 'and

8. According to the Diary the flood was aggravated because: 'A wretched bricklayer broke off one of the drainpipes which he said was blocked. Of course he could not replace it'.

Florence is obliged to give up coming to my Newnham lectures for the rest of term'. They gladly welcomed the young nursemaid back two weeks later; but on 18 April Mrs McAlister (their tenant at no. 5 Harvey Road) persuaded Florence to reconsider the position by confirming that the rumours about Alice's treatment of the baby were justified.

Emma, their second trainee nursemaid, replaced Alice shortly after Maynard's first birthday (when Florence was again pregnant) and was apparently an instant success. Neville marvelled on 24 August at how fond Maynard had become of her:

> Every afternoon while she is having her dinner he plays in the Dining Room – then when she has finished, she just knocks on the door and opens it a little without coming in. Although he has been very happy with us, he at once walks straight out and we hear him no more.

At the end of August, Florence felt sufficient confidence to leave Maynard in Emma's care (at his grandmother's house in Salisbury), while his parents spent four relaxed weeks in Devon and Cornwall. As ever, Anna Keynes was an assiduous correspondent. At Tintagel, for example, on 6 September, Neville quoted cheerfully in the Diary from his mother's latest letter announcing that she was 'more and more pleased with Emma'.

During the early weeks of 1885, when Florence's second pregnancy was approaching its term, Neville had been under stress for reasons other than his wife's condition. Sidgwick had made it clear that Marshall's return to Cambridge would restrict Keynes's university lectureship to logic for the foreseeable future. At the same time, Marshall was putting unwelcome pressure on his most reliably orthodox disciple to fill the gap left in Oxford economics teaching by his own election to the Cambridge chair. Neville thus faced crucial shifts in his personal career options at a time when he did not feel justified in calling on Florence's reassuring commonsense to help him make appropriate choices. In these circumstances, given his hypochondriac propensities, the relatively frequent Diary references to minor health problems – such as migraine, diarrhoea, chest pains or 'feeling seedy all this week' – are unsurprising. Nevertheless, by the summer of 1885 Neville had adjusted to the changed patterns in his professional and family way of life. His self-confidence had been boosted by the success of his Oxford lectures and by the fact that they provided the basis for a book on the scope and method of political economy. Such a scholarly publication must improve his academic standing if he chose to apply for the Oxford chair of political economy when it became vacant.[9] He was still enthusiastically and effectively teaching the

9. Bonamy Price, Drummond Professor at Oxford (since 1868), was in his late seventies. Keynes, who had worked with him on London MSc examinations – for which they were

subject to Indian Civil Service candidates[10], having confidently resigned his Newnham lectureship in favour of Mary Marshall, in spite of Sidgwick's suggestion that she was not a fully satisfactory substitute. He remained obdurately deaf to Marshall's insistence that he was 'throwing himself away' on the administrative and examining work he positively enjoyed doing for the Local Examinations Syndicate. Meanwhile his beloved mother had at last been persuaded to settle in Cambridge. Now obsessively devoted to his two-year-old son – 'a regular chatterbox, but not all that he says is intelligible' – as well as enchanted by his 'good and sweet baby daughter', Neville strewed that summer's Diary with references to the shared pleasure and satisfaction which both he and Florence derived from their two small children. In late June he rented a house and garden at Hunstanton for himself, Florence, Maynard, Margaret, Emma and Austin. There he began working on his new book by reading J.A. Blanqui's *History of Political Economy in Europe* (1885) and by learning to read German under Florence's instruction. But much of their time was spent either on the beach (where Maynard was blissfully 'equipped with sandshoes, spade and pail'), or in entertaining friends and neighbours (day-visiting from Cambridge), or in taking excursions (aboard a four-in-hand) to historic estates such as Sandringham or Holkham Hall. The overall cost of this, their first seaside family holiday, came to ten guineas for the fortnight.

The family at 6 Harvey Road in the last few months of 1885 generated enough work to keep three servants occupied. Summer faded suddenly that year and heating the upstairs rooms by open coal fires involved a laborious daily chore. Emma continued to take care of baby Margaret and of an increasingly self-willed Maynard, who was sometimes disobedient enough to merit the traditional last resort of 'a whipping' – which custom required should be administered by his extremely reluctant father. Austin and Cook made it possible to entertain a variety of visiting relatives and friends. Anna Keynes – still inclined to feel depressed and isolated in her new home – ate frequently at Harvey Road. On 13 November Neville wrote:

> I cannot bear to think of her being so lonely and fancying that we do not love and care tenderly for her. Florence agrees that if this goes on we must ask her to come and live with us, though we fear that not having a house of her own to manage she wd chafe at there being too little to do.

both examiners in political economy in 1885 – was well aware of his weakness. The Diary references to Price are uncharacteristically caustic: for example, on 24 June 1885 he wrote: 'Bonamy Price has very little clear understanding of the real nature of the exam^{n}. He is too old for his work and I should have thought also for his professional duties'. It was reasonable to suppose that the chair would become vacant within the next few years and that Marshall would support his pupil's candidature.

10. His pupils annually achieved relatively high marks in the political economy papers of the national examination for ICS candidates.

Some members of Florence's much larger family also lived near enough to drop in for occasional meals. Her parents, for example, came to Cambridge for a political meeting (in connection with the forthcoming general election) at which John Brown 'made a very good speech' on behalf of the Liberal candidate. On 11 October, Neville and Florence gladly welcomed to Sunday lunch her recently matriculated Langdon-Down cousin, whom they encouraged to bring undergraduate friends to future such occasions. Among the numerous overnight visitors, Edith Creak (one of the original five Newnham students) held the record for length of stay.[11] She had arrived in early November to spend a three-day half-term holiday with Florence and Neville, joining Alice Brown who was there for a similar reason. However when, a few weeks later, Alice returned to her teaching duties at the Bedford Manse, Miss Creak remained – 'laid up with a sore throat', which developed into a severe quinsy. So ill was she that her hosts first brought in a night nurse from Addenbrooke's hospital and then sent for her mother. Mrs Creak, who arrived on 18 November, stayed to nurse her daughter for a further ten days – until Dr Wherry pronounced the invalid well enough to be moved back home to Birmingham. Within less than a week another two ex-Newnhamites had arrived 'to spend a few days' at Harvey Road.

The domestic staff of three survived until July 1886 when Emma left to get married and was replaced by Hetty. Neville and Florence much regretted losing Emma. According to the Diary: 'She has managed the children well; and we always felt her to be thoroughly reliable'. Nevertheless, Hetty fitted in rapidly with her young charges and, a few days later, Neville observed with surprise: 'Maynard and Margaret seem to miss Emma hardly at all'. That was also the month when the Diary reported the bizarre episode of

> Cook's strange infatuation for the fishmonger. It is combined with a religious mania and we are doubtful whether it will be safe to keep her even for a month. Florence has already given her warning. We are very sorry for the woman herself; we had looked upon her as settled with us for years.

According to the Diary, the day before Cook's notice expired,

> [She] handed a most strange epistle to Florence; 'The lion shall lie down with the lamb and a little child shall lead them. But there is more to follow.' At one time Florence was a little doubtful whether she was doing the right thing to send her away. But now she is glad that she did not change her mind.

11. Edith Creak was at Newnham from 1871 to 1875 and took both the maths and the classical triposes. She went on to achieve a first class London University BA and was the first headmistress of King Edward VI High School for Girls (Birmingham) from 1883 to 1910.

In mid-August, Neville, Florence, the two children, their grandmother Keynes and Hetty set out for a month's holiday in Wales, leaving Austin with the task of shutting up the house before taking a holiday herself. As they were about to depart, Florence was alarmed to hear from Austin that Cook intended to stay in the empty house and insisted that she must leave on schedule, while Neville worried to his Diary about what would become of the poor woman. They returned to Cambridge on 11 September to find that she was 'undoubtedly out of her mind'.

The only occasion when Neville was personally confronted by servant problems occurred in the aftermath of Florence's third pregnancy when he was sleeping apart from his wife and absolutely determined not to disturb her convalescence. Their resident staff then consisted of Austin the housemaid who had been with them for four years, a cook who had moved in the previous September, Hetty who was looking after Maynard and Margaret, and Nurse Jackson in temporary charge of Florence and the infant, Geoffrey. The latter was born on 25 March 1887 and on the next evening the Diary recorded: 'rather an upset. Mrs Brown discovered that there was only one blanket on Florence's bed and quite a thin coverlet. Mrs Jackson at first put the blame on Austin; but it rather seems that the mistake was her own. The discovery made us feel anxious and uncomfortable'. It also destroyed Neville's (though not Florence's) faith in Nurse Jackson. A week later it was his own mother's intervention that exposed the unsuspected passions and frictions simmering downstairs. On 7 April Neville reported at length, and in unusually laborious detail in the Diary, the beginning of a sequence of events that was to give him sleepless nights for the next few weeks. He began:

> The day before yesterday Mother took a piece of our silver that was tarnished for her maids to make bright; she said they had very little to do. They grumbled and began making remarks about the time Austin had for seeing the young man who came to see her. Austin heard that this had been said and came to see me last night quite spontaneously to say that it was entirely false, she had been in the house for four years and had never done anything that she wd be ashamed for me or her mistress to know about.

Neville wanted to believe the girl who had been part of his household for over four years and who had never caused him to doubt her integrity. His mother, however, was not so easily satisfied and after questioning her own servants she 'brought a more circumstantial account of what was alleged to have been going on'.

Neville then embarked on a series of interrogations designed to extract the truth of the matter. He spoke again to Austin who stood by her story and then to Cook who corroborated it. He also cross-questioned Hetty again and reported:

> She told a quite different story and seemed on the whole glad to be able to relieve her mind about it. ... Cook's cousin, a lad of only 17 has been coming to see Austin for months at least once a week if not oftener; he frequently stays to tea and is often here until 10°/c at night ... and he and a friend were here to tea at least once while we were away at Christmas; Austin herself told Hetty that on this occasion she went to her bedroom to look after the fire she had there and he went with her.

Neville now began to doubt both Austin and Cook. After dinner (this time with Alice, Florence's sister, present as an observer) he interviewed them separately and together. According to the Diary:

> They denied repeatedly that Cook's cousin had been more than once in the house since November when Florence found he was here and requested that he should not come again. Cook could not admit to even this once, but said it must have happened on a Thursday after^{n} when she was out. Austin could not remember how long it was ago; and she then took the opportunity to tell him he must not come again. I then confronted them with Hetty – Austin had been to her in the meantime, told her what they had said and that she must say the same thing. Hetty gave circumstantial details and asked them if they did not remember that he was here last Monday evening, once the week before and also the day before baby was born. They contradicted themselves once or twice but still persisted there was no truth in all this. Thereupon I gave them both a month's warning. Austin then begged to see me alone in the study and when we got there asked if she might not stay at any rate a few months. She admitted she had told lies but was sincerely sorry. It was so dreadful to be dismissed for telling lies; and her mother and father would feel it so. I said I would speak to her again next day; and there the matter rested for the night.

The following day, 8 April, was Good Friday and Florence, oblivious of the ongoing drama downstairs, relaxed in her blue dressing gown on a couch – outside her bed for the first time since Geoffrey's birth – whilst Neville continued to be harrowed by Austin's deceitful behaviour. That evening he interviewed the housemaid again, confirmed that she would have to leave, but was sadly convinced by her tearful insistence that 'since Cook had been here she was not the girl she used to be'. Feeling guilty because neither he nor Florence had suspected that Cook might have been leading the girl astray, he talked to her again 'very seriously but kindly' on the following day. He reported: 'she was again in tears and seemed very repentant; but Mrs Jackson tells me that at supper she was laughing, said she had had it out with the Master and was jeering at Hetty for telling lies'. Florence had previously given Austin leave to go out with Cook on Easter Sunday and Neville, touched by the weeping girl's penitence, and unconvinced by Nurse Jackson's story, did not feel justified in revoking that promise. He was dismayed, therefore, to see the two of them leave in a dog-cart driven by Cook's errant cousin and another young man. That evening he talked again with Hetty, now the only servant whose sincerity he trusted, and wrote:

> She talks very frankly sensibly and nicely. What happened at Xmas was that Austin remarked that she must go and look after her fire. He [Cook's cousin] said if you do I shall go too. When she got to the first landing, she found he was following her; but she went on and he went with her into her bedroom. This is Austin's own account. What may have happened then or at any other time of course we do not know.

Further cross-questioned, Hetty said that 'She herself often heard him when she came to fetch the children to go to bed. … Hetty says that Austin cries a good deal now, yet she braves it and keeps making plans as to what she will do along with Cook when she has left'.

Neville was profoundly disturbed by his ignorance of the motivation and behaviour of the young women in their service. The neighbours (informed by their own servants) seem to have known exactly what was going on downstairs at 6 Harvey Road. Still seeking enlightenment, he talked to his mother again. 'Mother tells me', he wrote on Easter Sunday, 'that Cook told one of her servants how kind her mistress was, and that she let them do as they like in the kitchen!' After re-interviewing Cook on Easter Monday, he reported:

> [S]he admitted that she had told a falsehood in order to shield her fellow servant. She was very plausible, and spoke of her affection for her mistress and yet I believe that she was telling me more untruths. I may be wrong; but she seems to me now an altogether different person from what I thought her before.

He also interviewed Austin's mother and her sister and Austin herself yet again; and after this last meeting he lamented: 'The girl is evidently very unhappy, but I really hardly know what to believe'. No doubt Florence would have handled the crisis more perceptively and resourcefully, but it was not until 21 April – after he had engaged (with his mother's help) a new housemaid with well-attested references – that Neville felt able to tell his wife the dismal story. 'She was very much surprised', he wrote, 'but it was a relief to her to have so much of it over. And for other reasons she was glad that Austin was going. She has for some time been neglectful of her duties'. That night Florence also tossed sleeplessly and was pale and tired next day. Nor were their problems over, for Austin and Cook still had to work out their notice, and Nurse Jackson, who was 'strongly of the opinion' that Cook had been unjustly blamed, was now keeping Florence, as well as Neville, fully informed of Harvey Road gossip on Austin's misdemeanours. According to the Diary for 22 April, for example:

> Mrs Jackson says that Austin is telling everybody that she gave me notice and is spreading all sorts of reports on Hetty. She has had a friend with her today from 3.30 to 9.30 (a girl who is a barmaid at a small public house near the Guildhall); and this very much annoyed us. But we thought it better not to take any action in the matter. Cook goes about her work most industriously as she has always done; and so far as I can see all the visitors are to see Austin not her.

Goaded by Mrs Jackson to find out for himself about the 'gossipping going on in the road', Neville again sent for Hetty, who proved a mine of hearsay evidence about 'the goings-on' at no. 6, for example:

> Mrs Lock's servants say that at Christmas they saw Austin with a man in the nursery; and Mrs Boughey's servants say that what went on at Xmas was disgraceful. Hetty says that she herself knows that Austin's friend is actually a girl on the town; and she has heard of two or three young men saying that if they wanted to have a girl they could have one in Harvey Road.

Neville was 'mightily worried', but was no longer in a position to shield Florence, who insisted on hearing all. After talking it over with her he wrote: 'I think now that while Hetty spoke the truth of what she had heard, in the gossipping the worst was made of everything and surmises treated as established facts'.

On 29 April, although Florence was clearly reluctant to lose a capable and industrious cook, they engaged a replacement – 'who admits to be 48 and looks still older', to Neville's great relief. Both Austin and Cook left on 5 May but, according to the Diary: 'Austin left a final sting behind her, telling Florence that on two occasions Hetty had had a young man from the Salvation Army to see her and on one occasion they were in the breakfast room together'. Florence was now strong enough to follow up this piece of gossip and Neville's reference to it in the Diary was gratefully brief:

> Hetty entirely denies that her young man has ever been into the house to see her. Unfortunately Mrs Jackson heard precisely the same story from Cook some time ago. One does not know what to believe. Mrs Jackson says she has never been in a house in which so much feasting went on downstairs. At any rate we dont think our new cook will allow that.

The following day Nurse Jackson also left and Neville, after claiming that he no longer disliked her, added uneasily: 'She has however her faults and is I fear rather a mischiefmaker'. Henceforth, Florence seems to have kept the domestic establishment at no. 6 free from the kind of reputation that had made it the talk of Harvey Road in early 1887, Neville could retreat contentedly into normal academic detachment and his Diary references to servant problems were rare and laconic. From mid-1887 to 1889 the household accommodated four live-in servants – two nursemaids, one housemaid and a cook. Evidently the key to harmony downstairs was a suitably mature and responsible cook. Such women were hard to find. The cook who was taken on in May 1887, for example, decided to leave in June 1888 because she could not get on with Hetty. In November 1888, all four servants left and although it was easy to replace the three maids they were without a cook for some weeks. Neville wrote cheerfully in the Diary for 23 November: 'Florence is becoming quite an enthusiastic cook'. At last, in 1889 she was able to solve their servant problem by engaging as cook, Jane Handley, who remained a valued member of the household until she retired 22 years later.

3 BRINGING UP CHILDREN

Although Florence was only 22 when she had the first of her three babies, she was already experienced in bringing up children. The eldest of six siblings, she had been nine when her brother Walter was born, twelve when Harold arrived and 18 when Kenneth completed the Brown family in 1879. It is inconceivable that her mother could have effectively combined the two occupations of busy minister's wife and headmistress (as well as principal teacher) at a girls' secondary school, had Florence not proved capable of assuming much of the daily responsibility for minding, instructing and caring for the young family at the Manse. Neville, on the other hand, had neither shared a home with young children nor taught them. To begin with he could only marvel somewhat helplessly at the fascinating infant his wife produced on 5 June 1883. On 6 June, for example he confided to the Diary: 'I could sit and look at him for hours. I love the contortions of his little face and his little hands'; and on 8 June he joked: 'Maynard is 3 days old. I have bought him a new book of Swinburne's wh contains some charming roundels about babies. He has himself sent another copy of the book to Marjorie Dale'.[12]

Gradually, however, Neville's love for his firstborn developed into an intensely personal attachment. It was actually the Dale baby, born a few days earlier, who first aroused the fiercely competitive spirit that always characterized his feelings for the boy, and later for the man. After tersely noting on 1 October 1883: 'We hear that baby Dale is much more intellectually advanced than Maynard', he disposed firmly of the rumour three weeks later, by visiting the Dale household and recording confidently that their offspring 'does not in any way come up to our youngster'. Henceforth the Diary charted the

12. Dale, a fellow of Trinity Hall and Neville's undergraduate contemporary had met his wife (Miss Jeeves) at the Bonds' home in Brookside. The Dale baby arrived a few days before Maynard.

stages in Maynard's progress in relentless detail. By 24 February 1884, for example, it records that the infant, now 'crawling fast', liked his father to play on the floor with him; by May he was 'showing a good deal of self will and some temper'; by 15 July at the age of 13 months and 10 days Maynard had taken his first steps while five days later he was 'very much at home on his legs'; and by December 1884 he could name twelve animals. Even after Margaret was born (February 1885), Maynard's prowess still dominated the Diary, as soon as the traumatic aftermath of confinement was over. On 22 March, for example, the proud father added to his account of a family walk the information that Maynard 'now goes through in pantomime the whole story of the Frog who would a wooing go'. Two months later, the Diary reported another family walk, adding; 'Maynard is delighted to have Margaret in the perambulator. He is now beginning to put words together'.

It is hardly surprising that Maynard dominated Keynes's Diary. Not only was he born within the first year of an enduring love match, he also projected a forceful personality from a very early age. He was brave, affectionate, self-willed, precociously articulate and intellectually adventurous – as well as worryingly vulnerable to childish ailments. He seems to have suffered more than either of his siblings from early teething problems and from the colds and bilious attacks that recurred with depressing frequency at 6 Harvey Road. The epithet most often applied in the Diary to Maynard, as a small boy, was 'naughty' and once he was described as 'thin and crabbed'. Margaret, on the other hand, was repeatedly referred to as 'bonny' or as 'good and sweet' and envisaged by her father as a 'radiant person'. On Sunday 29 November 1885, when, for the first time, Maynard and Margaret took tea together with their parents in the dining room, the Diary reported: 'Florence tries to make out that she is more forward than Maynard was at her age; but looking back at my diary for March 1884 we found that it is rather the reverse. I think however she is the more robust of the two'. Certainly Maynard lost an abnormal proportion of his school days to illness, his feverish attacks struck with legendary frequency and at six he alarmed his parents by developing 'dreadful twitchings about the eyes' which Dr Wherry diagnosed as 'a slight touch of chorea (St Vitus' Dance)'. As for 'dear little Geoffrey' (born March 1887) he exhibited a most winning personality from birth. According to his father he was 'the sweetest little man in the world', who walked unaided earlier than either Maynard or Margaret and who captivated family and strangers alike with his brilliantly blond hair, blue eyes and happy smile. The Diary quoted with approval Maynard's view that 'Geoffrey and Mother are quite the most precious things in the house'. Even Geoffrey's sudden childish rages were comically endearing. They appear to have started when he was about 2½. According to his father:

> He is quiet – no screaming – but he throws out his arms and flings his cap (if it is that he is not allowed to go out) or his crust (if he is told he must not eat any more) or whatever it may be, violently from him. He is, generally speaking, as amiable as ever in the space of about one minute.

On 29 December 1888 Florence, Neville and their three children plus Lizzie, Geoffrey's nursemaid, went to Bedford to see in the New Year at the Manse. As usual, Neville and John Brown, discussed politics – especially Irish Home Rule, the issue currently troubling liberal nonconformists. Young Maynard, then 5½, listened quietly and at bedtime interrogated his father, who recorded their conversation in the Diary, whilst insisting that he had not prompted the boy in his choice of names:

> 'Does Mr Gladstone want Ireland to have a separate parliament?'
> 'Yes.'
> 'Does the Queen?' 'No.'
> 'Does Lord Salisbury?' 'No'.
> 'Do you?' 'No.'
> 'Does Lord Hartington?' 'No'.
> 'Does the Lord Mayor of London?' 'I am not sure. I dont think he does.'
> 'Well' contemptuously 'I dont think Mr Gladstone can do much against all these.'

The last entry in the Diary for 31 December 1888 testified uniquivocally to the writer's heartfelt sense of married bliss. It began by quoting the first sentence of a thank-you letter (from a recent visitor to Harvey Road) that began: '"When I called upon you and Mrs Keynes it seemed like entering an ideal household – you seemed to possess domestic happiness in unusual perfection"'; to which Neville added:

> Florence and I often tell each other that now must be our happiest time. But indeed all our six years of married life has been almost unalloyed happiness – and if our children always continue to give us the pleasure that they now give us we shall in truth be among the most enviable of mortals. And never before have I loved my darling wife more than I do now.

Neville and Florence took their responsibilities in the matter of bringing up children with the utmost seriousness. In accord with their own family traditions they resolved to inject a distinctive religious component into the educational process at the earliest feasible stage. So, until their children were old enough to accompany them regularly to Sunday morning services at Emmanuel Chapel, a short daily session of family prayers was instituted in the dining room of 6 Harvey Road. According to the Diary, Maynard was first brought down for morning prayers in January 1886, at the age of three and a half when 'the prayers soon exhausted his patience'. By mid-March the child was so accustomed to the daily ritual – at which Neville read from the Bible and Florence recited a prayer – that he failed to notice his mother's absence until his grandfather began the prayer.[13] At that point, the Diary records, Maynard 'burst into a passion of tears and would not be comforted until I took him upstairs to see his Mummy'. By early 1889 all three of the children were expected to sit through family prayers, though Geoffrey (not yet three years old) often had to be removed before the end of the session. Meanwhile Maynard had persuaded his parents to take him, each Sunday, to Emmanuel Chapel – although he was far from ready for such a lengthy performance, On 2 December 1888, for example, Neville confided to the Diary: 'he gets rather bored when he is there. Today as he was returning home – other members of the congregation with us – he cried out in his loud clear voice "It is the prayers that I dislike the most"'.

Education, for the Keynes children, began naturally enough in the home. It gathered momentum for Maynard when he had graduated from the nursery to a small bedroom of his own, adjoining his parents' room. The fact that he and his father both tended to wake early gave them ample opportunity to talk together before the rest of the family were stirring. Neville always responded with interest to his children's views and pastimes, and the Diary is studded with references to young Maynard's probing questions. As early as 10 September 1887, for example, we read: 'Maynard is very anxious to see a hen lay an egg. I told him that I had never seen that operation performed. "Then how" said he "do you know that they lay eggs at all?"' By September 1888, Neville was reading Charles Kingsley's *Water Babies* to his son and by October 1889 they were both enjoying *The Boy Hunters*. At that stage, being read to by his father was one of the six-year-old's 'three favourite things'; the two others were 'being with Mother' and 'being with Geoffrey'. As for Margaret, she almost certainly absorbed much information from her talkative elder brother, although his condescending logic was not always inspiring.[14] The Diary for 5 June 1889, for example, records:

> In the nursery a day or two ago Alice heard Maynard arguing with Margaret and reducing her to tears by proving that she was a *thing*. 'She wouldnt like to be a nothing', he said, 'and if she was a something she must be a thing.' We were telling this story in Maynard's presence to W.E. Johnson who tried to provoke him – 'You call Margaret a thing. But can things talk? Is this table a thing?' 'Yes.' 'Well, if it cannot talk and Margaret can talk?' The answer was ready in a moment. '<u>Some</u> things cant talk but <u>some</u> things <u>can</u> talk' – with clear emphasis on the words I have underlined.

13. John Brown had been preaching in the Victoria Road Chapel the previous day (Sunday) and, as usual on such occasions, had spent the weekend at 6 Harvey Road.
14. It was Florence who observed with amusement how 'extremely condescending' were 5-year-old Maynard's efforts to instruct his 3½-year-old sister. See Diary, 17 August 1888.

The head of the Harvey Road household, whose job it was to administer the ultimate, and thoroughly distasteful, discipline of corporal punishment found himself accused, from time to time, of spoiling his firstborn. As early as 17 April 1885, for example, he wrote angrily: 'Mrs Hunt has had the audacity to report at Bedford that I spoil him, that he is naughty directly I go to the nursery'.[15] A year later when Maynard was not quite five, he too was outraged at the suggestion that he was spoilt and his views were duly relayed to the Diary:

> 'Marjorie Dale's nurse asked Hetty if you spoilt any of us and Hetty said "Yes, the eldest."' The young gentleman rather resents the idea that we spoil him. Certainly Hetty is a more severe disciplinarian than we are. He is not always quite so prompt and obedient as I should like. But on the whole he is a very good boy indeed and we by no means let him have his way without restraint.

This partisan assessment was independently confirmed, a year later, by Maynard's first infant school report (April 1889), which rated his conduct as 'Very good and obedient'.

Each of the three children were given their first lessons in reading, writing and arithmetic by their mother. On 26 October 1888, for example, the Diary reported: 'Florence now teaches Maynard and Margaret for about an hour every morning in the diningroom. I like to see her seated at the table with one chick on either side of her'. Their first school, however, was the Perse kindergarten which took them five mornings weekly (from 10 to 12 a.m.). Maynard started when he was five and a half in January 1889, and Margaret entered the following September. After two years of infant school Maynard was taken away to have lessons at home. According to the Diary for 21 January 1891: 'This week his Mother will teach him and then Miss Beatrice Mackintosh will begin her work. Two hours a day. Half a guinea a week. At present Maynard is longing for the lessons to begin'. Florence took over all the teaching when Miss Mackintosh fell ill. In January 1892, in his ninth year, Maynard was sent to St Faith's (a preparatory day-school headed by Ralph Goodchild), as was Geoffrey four years later. Unlike her brothers, Margaret did not attend preparatory school. It was an era when the education of daughters usually followed a less formal pattern than was conventional for sons. Nevertheless, in an academic household where both parents were actively concerned to foster their children's full potential, there is no reason to suppose that a girl with intellectual interests and ample access to books would be disadvantaged by being taught at home rather than at school. Margaret's education was certainly not neglected. She enjoyed the support of

15. Mrs Hunt was the Bedford nurse who had spent almost two months at 6 Harvey Road in the fraught aftermath of Margaret's birth.

a mother who was an experienced school teacher and a father who actively encouraged her many practical interests and achievements. After leaving infant school she was taught by her mother, by a series of live-in governesses (the first of whom, Miss Laxton, arrived in January 1892), and by Hattie and Fanny Johnson[16] who ran a small Dame's school. Fanny Johnson described ten-year-old Margaret to Florence, in March 1895, as 'a clever and good little girl with a decided sense of humour'; and on 7 May Neville noted with satisfaction in the Diary that his daughter was first in her class at Miss Johnson's. By this time a German governess, Fraulein Rottmann, was in residence at 6 Harvey Road, and – when tested in conversation by Harry Bond's German friend – Margaret displayed a better grasp of the spoken language than either of her brothers. In December of that year the three Keynes children all sat the German paper for the Preliminary Local examination and Margaret again excelled, by passing with distinction. At the same time, she was in her element in a variety of manual and artistic pursuits. She learned to milk cows during the family's summer holidays on a Yorkshire farm, for example, she was a forthright and energetic editor of the in-family journal *The Gem*, she became an efficient cyclist faster than any other member of the family, and (according to her father) she was already 'fond of doing little paintings that I think show true ability'.

It was Florence who worried continuously about Margaret's scholastic progress, and her concerns surfaced from time to time in the 1897 Diary, in terms which suggest that her husband took a relatively complacent view of the matter. For example, on 19 June, Neville wrote: 'Florence is I think a little worried in her teaching of Margaret because the little woman is so harum scarum. She will not stick to anything long enough and is untidy in her work as well as everything else. No doubt, however, she will improve in these respects'. Similarly, on 29 July, he wrote: 'Margaret is a most fascinating child; but just now she is rather trying to her mother and me. She will no doubt grow more methodical and manageable'. Florence, however, was impatient to stimulate an improvement. She persuaded Margaret Verrall – a Newnham lecturer in classics – to coach Margaret systematically.[17] The twelve-year-old welcomed her high-powered tutor and they began their sessions on 17 January 1898. On 27 January, however – after noting: 'The little maid seems to like her work with Mrs Verrall and Florence says she is working more industriously than she has ever known her to do before' – Neville

16. The Johnson ladies were sisters of Willie Johnson, Keynes's colleague and close friend in the moral sciences faculty and were friends of the family in Harvey Road.
17. Margaret Verrall (nee Merrifield) was a contemporary of Florence as well as one of the small band of Newnhamites who married Cambridge dons. She took the classics tripos in 1880. Her husband was A.W. Verrall, also a classicist, later appointed Edward VII Professor of English Literature in 1911.

reported cheerfully that his daughter was 'now a birdfancier'. Ever ready to encourage his children's hobbies, he gave her two canaries and a breeding cage for her 13th birthday and commented with amusement: 'We are soon to have young canaries which are to be sold at an enormous profit'.[18] Mrs Verrall's first report on her charge was copied into the Diary:

> 'Her Algebra and Arithmetic are certainly good. She does not take to her Latin so kindly. She strikes me as a very clear headed child and so I think her Latin will go on fast when she has made a start. But her vocabulary is small and she has not as much aptitude for language I fancy as for mathematics. She is a very interesting and pleasant child to teach and I hope she likes her lessons with me as much as I do.'

By June 1898, however, Mrs Verrall's patience had been severely strained by Margaret's light-hearted approach to her studies, and she made it clear that she did not intend to continue their tutorials after the end of the year. It was at that point that Florence and Neville concluded that their daughter needed the discipline of a sound boarding school if she was to advance her education. On Mrs Verrall's advice, they set their sights on Wycombe Abbey school, and the goal of reaching the required entrance standard seems to have energized Margaret and her teachers (Florence during the summer months and Mrs Verrall during the autumn). In December 1898 she passed the Preliminary Local examination with third-class honours (again with a distinction in German but a failure in history); and on 18 January 1898 her parents and two brothers saw her on to the train from Cambridge which was to take her on the first stage of the journey to boarding school. According to the Diary, she embarked in high spirits – largely no doubt because three girls with whom she was already friendly, were travelling with her to Wycombe Abbey.

Neville's relaxed approach to his daughter's education contrasts vividly with his close and continuous involvement in Maynard's schooling. Throughout the period that the latter spent at his preparatory school – from January 1892 until he sat for the Eton scholarship examination in July 1897 – Neville watched over Maynard's programme and progress with passionate intensity. It was as if his own youthful academic ambitions had been reborn in the person of a son with superior intellectual talents, but without the low self-esteem which had always shadowed the father's prospects. Maynard himself soon impressed his teachers (and gratified his father) by the enthusiasm with which he tackled his school work and the concentrated determination that he applied to problem-solving exercises. When a 'troublesome cough and cold'

18. See Diary, 4 February 1898 where Neville wrote of his daughter: 'She is full of devices and enjoys herself greatly. She is certainly not over-industrious: but Mrs Verrall seems on the whole to think well of her abilities'. The canary's four eggs were not hatched.

prevented him from sitting the end-of-term examinations in March 1892, he was so downcast, according to the Diary, that: 'Mr Goodchild has sent him a couple of papers – one in Latin and one in Arithmetic. He is very keen to settle down to them … it is clear that he is very much more advanced than I was at his age'. Despite losing many school days to illness, and being put in a class where most of the other boys were aged between ten and eleven, the nine-year old was ranked among the top three in his second term and had already been identified by the headmaster as a high-flyer. Goodchild wrote in his end-year report (copied into the Diary for 7 August):

> 'I am anxious to have Maynard in my lower division next term, but I shd like to hear what you think of this proposal. He will take Caesar and probably begin Greek and Algebra. I shd also like him to come for evening preparation, namely from 6 to 7°/c. He is decidedly the brightest boy in his division and I am surprised to see his place in the class.[19] He has been most brave at the river but it will be some time before he learns to swim.'

Unfortunately Maynard continued to be highly vulnerable to infection and his parents were alarmed by the headmaster's attempts to pressure his star pupil into tasks that were beyond his childish grasp. On 11 February, for example, Neville grumbled to the Diary: 'Maynard is being pushed rather too rapidly. He has work that he does not really understand and without Florence's assistance he would hardly be able to do anything with his homework'. More specifically, after discussing Maynard's programme with another headmaster, Neville reported:

> He thinks Maynard is being pushed a good deal too fast. He is not yet 10 and in Euclid he has finished Bk I, in Algebra doing Quadratics, in Arithmetic stocks etc, in Latin Ovid and continuous prose, in English Samson Agonistes. It is only by protesting that we have prevented his beginning Greek.

Finally, after Maynard's 1893 summer term was again cut up by illness, Florence insisted on taking him away from St Faith's for the autumn term and sent him instead to the Manse at Bedford where her mother set up a less ambitious programme for him. He returned to St Faith's in January 1894. Evidently the parental interference was justified, for, at the end of the summer term, on 31 July, the Diary rejoiced at Maynard's 'very handsome prize for being first in his class. It is a great pleasure to us, especially as he has been doing his work lately with so little effort'.

19. He was second in his class for the term but third in the exams. Goodchild seemed to have expected more of him. According to his father, however: 'He is 9 years and 2 months old: the boys who have beaten him (by very little) are both 10 years and 10 months'. Diary 7 August 1892.

For the next three years Maynard easily held his position at the top of his class and his health ceased to represent a constant source of anxiety to his parents. In late 1896 when they pondered his next school move, the prospect of his winning a scholarship to one of the large public schools looked extremely favourable. Goodchild had assured them that 'Maynard is head and shoulders above all the other boys' at St Faith's and after Charles Smith (the vice-chancellor and Eton examiner) had lent Neville a recent set of scholarship question papers, it seemed wholly appropriate that the boy should try for the school with the highest national reputation. By mid-April, Goodchild was telling Maynard's parents that their son was 'the best boy all round that he had ever had in his school'; but Neville was already worrying whether aiming at the most prestigious school was actually the safest strategy. 'I have got Maynard and his school very much on my mind just now', he confided to the Diary for 15 April, 'It worries me at night and in the early morning'. Early in June he and Maynard began a regime of rising early each morning so as to put in an extra hour's work before breakfast. On 23 June he was able to report that both R.W. Shackle and S. Turner, who were then coaching Maynard intensively for the maths and classics papers, respectively, 'give an excellent account of Maynard's work and just now we feel rather sanguine as to the success provided nothing untoward happens. He has been stammering a little more lately and he must slack off work at the end of the week'.[20] Meanwhile, the Eton scholarship examination had been scheduled for early July and Geoffrey (having developed mumps in mid-June) was hastily banished from home, to lodge with his grandmother in Bateman Street, lest he pass on the untimely infection to Maynard. From then on Neville assumed his customary attitude of expecting the worst. On 3 July he fretted to the Diary: 'Maynard has a slight liver attack that is worrying. Florence says that I am unduly anxious and that I shall make him nervous. But I wish she would back me up a little more in avoiding all risks. It is surely worth while just at this crisis'.

On 5 July 1897, Neville 'in a fearful state of worry', and Florence, wisely trying to reduce unnecessary family tensions, accompanied their 14-year-old son to Windsor where they had rented lodgings in the High Street for the duration of the Eton scholarship examination. That evening, according to the Diary: 'Maynard went to bed a little after 8.30 and at 10.30 1 found him still awake, and again at 11.15. We then went to bed ourselves but we were worried at the idea that Maynard might still be staying awake. To sleep seemed hopeless'. The exam started the next day. There were 62 candidates for 17 papers – all of which were in maths or classics (except one general

20. Maynard's tendency to stammer was first mentioned in the March 1895 Diary when Florence took him up to London to consult her uncle Langdon-Down a leading doctor. But when he was there 'the perverse boy would not stammer at all'!

paper and an essay). Their ordeal stretched over 3½ days beginning at 7 a.m. and ending at 5 p.m. – except on the final day when it ended at 1 p.m. The Diary listed each paper, whether it suited Maynard, how often he walked out early and even niggled over a suspected misprint in one of the maths questions. It also chronicled Neville's agonies concerning late-night High Street revellers, or navvies breaking the road at 4.30 a.m., who might disturb the examinee's sleep. Maynard himself showed no signs of being unduly nervous. His only complaint was that 'the days seem dreadfully long'.

The results were out in less than a week, during which Neville was beside himself with worry. So was Goodchild, to whom Neville had posted the question papers. The latter's response reached father and son in London on 19 July.[21] It concluded: 'My review of the whole is that Maynard has not done himself justice in any paper, but there is hope'. As for Maynard he offered his father a typically laid-back impression 'that he did as well as he would under any circumstances be likely to do the same papers'. Back in Cambridge, on 10 July Neville pestered the vice-chancellor for news. According to the Diary the vice-chancellor admitted that the examiners had met but refused to put the importunate father out of his misery by divulging the relevant results. 'He avoided the subject and seemed less genial than usual and I was discouraged'. Two days later, however, he sent a splendidly terse telegram which Neville quoted in the Diary: '"Maynard tenth CS [Charles Smith]." This was I think the most delightful telegram I have ever received. My own successes never gave me anything like the pleasure this has done'.[22] The boy's place as a King's Scholar at Eton was assured.

Geoffrey's school career followed the same path as Margaret's (via Perse kindergarten and a Dame's school run by the Johnson sisters) until September 1896 when he joined Maynard at prep-school. He was then nine years old. His big brother (four years older and almost a foot taller) was a sixth-former with an enviable reputation for all-round brilliance, who was already being groomed for the Eton scholarship examination. Not surprisingly, the headmaster's first end-of-term report on both boys (quoted in the Diary for 23 December), focused on Maynard's strengths and future prospects and dealt with Geoffrey, the new boy (then eighth in his class), almost as an aside. It is fair to say that the progress report on their elder son was then of overriding concern to the parents; but Neville's interest in Geoffrey's school career –

21. Keynes was a member of a deputation summoned to present, on 20 July, the university's loyal address to the Queen on the occasion of her Diamond Jubilee. So, after leaving Windsor on 8 July, he and his son spent a couple of nights in London before returning to Cambridge.
22. When, a few days later, Keynes called on the provost of King's and Charles Smith the vice-chancellor (examiners both) to get advice on a suitable tutor for Maynard at Eton, he learned that the boy was bracketed first in maths with one other candidate, and that he won his scholarship primarily because of his strengths in that area.

J.N. and Geoffrey Keynes (1897)

though lacking the anxious urgency and personal competitive edge with which he watched Maynard's – never wavered. Re-reading the headmaster's report a few days later, he commented: 'Goodchild seems pleased with Geoffrey also. I have been looking again at the little man's marks and find them more satisfactory than they looked at first sight … four of the seven who beat him were a year older or more'.

As a new boy at St Faith's, Geoffrey might have found it hard to follow in the footsteps of such a remarkable brother, but neither he nor Margaret seem to have felt diminished by Maynard's achievements. On the contrary the Diary consistently indicates a united family rejoicing at, and taking pride in the elder boy's serial triumphs. On the day the telegram arrived announcing Maynard's success in the Eton scholarship examination, for example, Neville commented: 'It is delightful to see how pleased Margaret and Geoffrey are. Geoffrey is fired with ambition to go and do likewise'. Five years later, in December 1901, Margaret responded joyously from High Wycombe to her father's telegram announcing that Maynard had won the coveted King's College scholarship: 'that brother of mine is a marvel and I'm proud of him'. Eight decades later, Geoffrey's own autobiography was to look back on his boyish relationship with his brother in the following terms:

> All my young days were … lived under the shadow of a far more forceful and intellectual character than my own. Not that Maynard was ever unkind or domineering; our relation was the natural result of the elder leading not so much by virtue of being a few years older as by inborn advantages of mind. We were not close friends and my view of him was more that of an eminent acquaintance to whom I looked up as a superior and somewhat distant being.[23]

In retrospect Geoffrey was to describe his own school career as 'more humdrum' than his brother's. His prep-school reports indicated an intelligent, shy, warm-hearted, industrious pupil modest in respect of his own intellect, but endowed with a transparent honesty of purpose. Within the family, according to his father he was seen as 'a constant ray of sunshine' and as 'a sensitive loving little creature'. Although the Diary regularly reported his marks and position in class, it carried no hint that either of his parents was troubled by their younger son's failure to rise much above the middle of the class order in his early years. Neville's usual assessment of Geoffrey's prep-school results was 'satisfactory' and, on the solitary occasion when it was diluted to 'not unsatisfactory' that was glossed by a reference to the boy's youth as compared with his classmates. At the end of his second year, Neville and Florence called on the headmaster to discuss Geoffrey's prospects for

23. Geoffrey Keynes, *The Gates of Memory* (Oxford: Oxford University Press, 1981), pp. 19–20.

entry to a public school and were undeterred by the information that, although making good progress, he was unlikely to win an open scholarship to the kind of school they had in mind for him. Having already decided to send Margaret to Wycombe Abbey school they were now seeking advice on the most suitable school for Geoffrey. Eventually – after a year in which Goodchild applauded a marked improvement in his classical work[24] – they applied to Rugby. There he passed the entrance examination in July 1901 and his grandmother Keynes at once promised a substantial contribution to his annual fees.

Well before he left St Faith's, however, Geoffrey had developed an intelligent interest in certain scientifically-orientated hobbies, each of which brought him into instructive personal contact with Cambridge natural scientists and their museum assistants and stimulated his ambition to specialize in natural sciences at secondary school and university. It was his father who introduced him to the hobby of collecting butterflies and moths and a schoolfriend's father who encouraged both boys to excavate and articulate the skeletons of semi-fossilized prehistoric animals that could be found in sites around Cambridge. Geoffrey's own autobiography describes and evaluates these boyish expeditions in quest of entomological, geological, archaeological and ornithological specimens. As far as Neville was concerned, his younger son's lasting commitment to what had originally been simply a summer holiday pastime designed to amuse an active young family, represented a particular bonus. The first mention of butterfly-hunting in the Diary was in August 1895 when Neville took Margaret (aged ten) and Geoffrey (aged 8) to Bottisham on an abortive search for butterflies: 'but the weather was not propitious'. By 1898 all members of the family were enjoying sunny excursions to butterfly-rich locations around Cambridge. Two years later (June 1900) Neville observed in the Diary: 'A Puss Moth has emerged today. Geoffrey now sets up the moths and he does them quite well, or better than I should'. It was the start of a joint activity which was to fascinate father and son for at least another decade; for both were endowed with the research drive and the qualities of mind needed to convert a congenial shared hobby into an absorbing scientific enterprise.

On 26 September 1901, after putting 14-year-old Geoffrey on the train for Rugby, Neville confided to the Diary that Florence was feeling 'anxious about the dear little man' – and reminded himself that it was time to drop the affectionate diminutive. Since their firstborn had settled so readily at boarding school, Florence no longer felt obliged to escort the two younger children to their schools. In any case, Neville was able to report that Geoffrey's first letter from Rugby was

24. JNK, Diary, 7 June 1900.

> thoroughly cheerful. … He says: 'I have got a study with a chap called Bell. … My form master is very decent. … I think the whole place is ripping and please give Grandma my express thanks for enabling me to come. I'd rather be here than Charterhouse or anywhere else. … I am Sampson's fag'.

In effect, the move to Rugby was to transform Geoffrey – physically as well as mentally. Following a routine medical examination the doctor ordered him to go to the gymnasium daily 'for development', the matron allowed him milk and biscuits each morning because she did not think he looked as robust as he should, and he regularly played rugger three days weekly. He found another new boy who shared his passion for butterflies and he went to 'a ripping lecture about spiders', on which he was actually glad to have to write an essay. By the end of term his place in class had risen to fifth, his examination results included a first in classics as well as in natural sciences, he was seven pounds heavier, his chest girth had expanded by an inch and he had grown a quarter of an inch. Henceforth his school reports were predominantly good (not simply satisfactory) and his opportunities to pursue studies and hobbies of special personal interest had broadened. On 23 May his father wrote confidently in the Diary: 'Evidently we sent him to the right school'.

By the first full academic year of the twentieth century then, each of the three Keynes children was a boarder in a reputable public school. From 1897 onwards extracts from their letters, or accounts of termly school visits by parents (or of the children's home leaves) regularly enlivened the dwindling entries in Keynes's Diary. It was Maynard, who in October 1897, started the tradition of a weekly (Sunday) letter from school. He crammed it with news and anecdotes illustrating the relatively exotic way of life of a late-Victorian Etonian. His parents were both relieved and entertained by the great good humour with which Maynard adapted to the frenetic pace, curious conventions and restrictive routines of a tradition-bound school community without losing any of his critical acumen, or his boyish enthusiasm for games, or his competitive approach to examinations. His long letters helped to put the two worlds of school and home into a coherent personalized perspective and to update individual family members on those aspects of his experience that were most likely to interest them. He supplied his father with a running commentary on his teachers, work programme and marks – as well as on the performance of his closest rivals in a system which was constantly testing and grading its pupils. He kept his mother punctiliously – and reassuringly – informed about his frequent colds, influenza, mysterious fevers, or liver disorders. The first of his brotherly letters to Geoffrey explained the famous Eton Wall game; and he teased his sister with a letter in French. By the time his sister and brother were ready to enter boarding school, Maynard's letters had opened up adventurous prospects that outweighed their anxieties about leaving home.

The whole family were gripped by Maynard's vivid accounts of his reactions to people (especially teachers), to sporting, social or other events (involving cricket, football, boating, singsongs or debates), and to special occasions (such as the royal functions where Eton schoolboys played a traditionally ceremonial role). In May 1899, for example, Maynard told the story of an occasion when the boys gathered to celebrate the presence of their neighbour, Queen Victoria, which ended: 'After we had sung and serenaded and seen the Queen's white cap bobbing up and down (as she was having her breakfast) she came to the window and stayed bowing and looking at us through opera glasses for a long time'. Again, in November that year Maynard was one of the Eton boys who lined the roadside for the German Emperor's visit to Windsor. After commenting on: 'a great deal of waiting without which no royal function is complete' that Sunday's letter observed that 'his imperial majesty was well worth waiting for, as I was much impressed by his really kingly bearing and his moustache was quite up to expectations'. Occasionally Maynard spiced his letters home with the latest schoolboy gossip and jokes,[25] explained how it was to be a fag (or to have a fag at his disposal) and offered glimpses of the role of a sixth-form prefect. '"I have very much enjoyed my week of praepostership"', he wrote in a letter extracted to the Diary for 11 November 1901, '"The long lies I have of course appreciated and it has been most interesting going round the school summoning malefactors and then standing behind the Head's chair while he rebukes them. He is a dear old boy"'.

Finally, the weekly letter raised the problems on which parental advice was needed. During the Boer War, for example, at the end of January 1900, Maynard reported a stirring oration from the headmaster on the Eton Volunteer Corps.

> For once his words have had effect and people are joining or being coerced into joining in throngs including all the Sixth Form and the greater part of the College. Am I to join? I am not keen and the drills will be a nuisance but I am perfectly willing to do so if I ought. It would be unpleasant to be almost the only non-shooter.

His parents' characteristic response to this dilemma was: 'We have said that on the whole we should prefer his not joining; but we pronounce no veto; he may join if his not joining would make him feel very much out of it'.[26] On

25. An Eton spoonerism which Neville delighted in passing on to his fellow guests at a Trinity Hall feast in November 1898 ran: 'Mr Spooner has started sleeping in a hammock and he finds that banging his head from wall to wall is very conducive to a goodnight's sleep'.

26. When Geoffrey asked his parents' consent to his joining the Rugby Volunteers in January 1903, they seem to have had no hesitation in agreeing. Perhaps the fact that the prospect of his being involved in a war had receded, altered the context of their decision.

matters related to Maynard's work programme, however, Neville failed to maintain a deliberately self-effacing stance, because he was too obsessed by his ambition for a son who so obviously had the talent to scale intellectual heights that had been beyond his own reach. During the academic year 1900/01 Maynard was torn between the competing claims made on his time by H. Hurst, his main mathematics teacher, and S.G. Lubbock who taught him classics. Hurst took the view that if the boy were to specialize entirely in mathematics he would be capable of winning a scholarship to Trinity (still the most prestigious of the Cambridge colleges), and of figuring among the first twelve wranglers in the tripos. Mathematics was currently the boy's strongest subject but Lubbock believed that his excellent progress in classics was such that if he specialized in it he could easily qualify for a King's scholarship and 'would be safe for a first class' in the classical tripos. A voluminous correspondence flowed between father and son on this issue. Maynard himself did not want to abandon classics or history or English essay – although he dropped French cheerfully enough in October 1900. Nor was he attracted to the Trinity option. He and his father seem to have taken it for granted, from the moment he entered Eton, that he would aim at King's College. Originally that assumption stemmed from the special relationship between Eton and King's which made it easier for an able Etonian to win a scholarship to King's than to any other college. According to Maynard's October 1901 letter, however, he had become altogether wedded to the idea. True, he went on to add: 'Besides Trinity is all too risky'; but this may have been included more to please his risk-averse father than because it had weight in his own scale of preferences.

To his father the allocation of Maynard's time between maths and classics was essentially a problem of long-term examination strategy. The boy was planning to sit three examinations in 1901. In June he faced the competition for the Tomline prize, which hinged on excellence in maths; in July he was expected to sit for the Schools Certificate covering a wide choice of subjects; but the third, most crucial of the hurdles, was the King's scholarship examination, scheduled for the first week in December. In that test, candidates could specialize in mathematics or classics or a combination of the two. Hurst advised abandoning classics altogether; on which Maynard wrote: 'His jealousy of Classics is most curious and interesting'. Meanwhile, Neville sought advice from his friends at King's on whether the combined option would damage the boy's prospects – given that he was spending more than half of his time on maths and that Hurst's teaching was 'unsystematic'. 'I often worry whether we have done the right thing' he groaned on 12 March; and after interrogating Maynard at the beginning of the Easter vacation he worried even more about Hurst's failure to insist on basic bookwork. He therefore did his best to persuade his son to focus on gaps in bookwork over the vacation. On 11 March 1901, for example, he wrote proudly in the Diary: 'Maynard is working steadily about 3 hours a day under my direction. I feel quite like a trainer, as if I were training him for a race or a prize-fight'. In the event, concentrating heavily on maths was evidently the right strategy for the Tomline and the Schools Certificate, in both of which Maynard topped the list. After that he went back to his classics and did well enough at the third hurdle to win an Open (not merely an Eton) Scholarship to King's.

The stream of correspondence between boarding schools and home, supplemented by mid-term parental visits and pupils' holiday breaks, were a source of enormous pleasure and satisfaction to both Neville and Florence and helped to sustain the intimate relationship they had always enjoyed with their children. When Margaret's Sunday letters from Wycombe Abbey were added to Maynard's from Eton, their parents' pleasure doubled. On 1 February 1899, for example, the Diary reported eleven-year-old Geoffrey's amusement at the number of times his parents – '"Curious old Creatures!"' – read and reread Maynard's and Margaret's letters. On Monday 27 February, after a ten-hour day which began with a long Council meeting (for the minutes of which he was responsible as secretary) Neville wrote: 'I am tired and driven, but my children's letters are refreshing'. What made them especially welcome was the fact that each of them positively enjoyed the boarding school experience. Only Margaret sometimes signalled a degree of homesickness – as on her first vacation (Easter 1899) when she told her mother that being at home was 'like heaven. Not that she did not like school, it was very nice, but still so different from home'. On the other hand her letters were almost invariably cheerful. The truth was that in spite of the boring impact of routine, examination-orientated lessons, boarding school had a multitude of compensations for an outgoing, high-spirited girl, with a tremendous zest for physical and artistic activities and a keen sense of humour. Margaret rapidly found warm friends among her contemporaries and her social skills endeared her to the house mistress. Her first postcard, written on the day she arrived at Wycombe Abbey happily informed her parents: 'Several of the girls are already on speaking terms with me' – a message that must have greatly tickled Maynard, for it triggered a postcard, which arrived a couple of days later from Eton, to the effect that: 'Several of the boys are already on speaking terms with me'. Three weeks later (February 1899), Margaret wrote urgently:

> My dear, dear, dear Mother: Drill is awful fun, so is carpentering and gardening. I like my gym suit. As to going to Miss Scott's house next term, I want to, so please will Father write to Miss Dove immediately or else I may not go in. We are doing Prop 35 in Euclid. I know it and I love you for it, though perhaps you dont love me for it. I should like another of those big nice letters. [To which she added, less convincingly:] Science and literature are very interesting.

Most convincing was her constant delight in new physical skills, such as tree climbing or gymnastic feats. For example, in a letter written in June 1899 she told her parents: 'one of our achievements is to stand on our heads. It is a lovely feeling, although your face becomes rather pink in colour'.

It took another two years, however, before Margaret could be induced to inject enough of her time and boundless energy into schoolwork, to satisfy most of her teachers and win the approval of Miss Dove, the formidably severe headmistress. Meanwhile Neville's extracts from his daughter's letters home made it abundantly clear that her ready enjoyment of boarding school hinged more on her lively circle of friends than on an ambition to impress her teachers. What happened on the playing fields or in the gym was evidently more exciting and newsworthy than her place in the class order or in the examination lists. On returning to school for the autumn term 1899, for example, the fact that she had been '"moved up for Lacrosse"' took higher precedence in her letter home than her relatively high score in arithmetic. Margaret's mathematics was always strong relatively to that of her classmates – largely no doubt as a result of the early tuition by her mother – though it was often marred by carelessness. Even Miss Scott, whose report to her parents in December 1899 described her as 'A very bright and cheerful member of the House', felt obliged to add: 'Margaret must learn when and how to put a check on her own enjoyments and not let them lead her into neglect of work or other duties'. By the following year, however, an improvement began to show in her termly reports, so that in May 1901 Neville and Florence even contemplated taking her away from Wycombe Abbey and sending her to Roedean. That plan was abandoned because Margaret herself was totally opposed to leaving Wycombe. Happily, the improvement in her work continued, so that in August 1902, after a year in which Margaret had at last been allowed to take options which were of keener interest to her – such as German,[27] drawing and music – Miss Dove's rating had risen to 'Thoroughly satisfactory'. That was the year when she sat the Schools Certificate examination and her father recorded in his Diary for 29 September that she was first in the school for all the mathematical subjects but was let down by her French composition. As usual Margaret took the result philosophically – team failures on the lacrosse or hockey field were a great deal more disappointing. In her letter home on the subject she remarked cheerfully: 'If I had passed in French I might have got a scholarship; but then I suppose somebody else would not have done so'. Overall it would seem that four years at Wycombe Abbey served Margaret's education well. When she left at the age of 18 she had won an 'excellent' final report from both Miss

27. Miss Dove was not persuaded earlier that Margaret could cope with an additional subject and would not hear of her making time for German by abandoning Latin.

Dove and Miss Scott. She had also gathered some creditable distinctions in art and design, while the teacher from whom she had been getting special drawing lessons described her work as 'very good, very clever and inventive'. Florence was far from satisfied, however, and she arranged for her daughter to finish her education in German – as she herself had done – by sending her to spend six months with a private family at Wittenberg from October 1903 to March 1904.

Geoffrey also left school at 18, with a glowing report both from his housemaster – who described him as 'a useful member of the house and a most pleasant pupil in all ways' – and from his headmaster who applauded his 'excellent record in every way'. That was in December 1906 after Geoffrey had won a scholarship to Pembroke, his father's old college, to specialize in the area that had caught his imagination before leaving prep-school – that was, natural sciences, which led naturally to a medical career. Neville and Florence could therefore feel content at the outcome of the education they had set up for their three children.

Geoffrey himself was to add to that satisfaction by thanking his father for sending him to Rugby. 'He says', wrote Neville in the Diary for 20 December 1906, 'that it is the cleanest and most moral school in England'. Geoffrey's autobiography sets out, in some detail, his later recollections of what it was like to be a Rugby schoolboy in the early years of the twentieth century. It also contains his personal testimonial to the parents who sent him and his siblings to boarding school:

> Our parents as I now look back on them had a lovable aura of perfect integrity and goodness without stuffiness or pomposity; they were affectionate without sentimentality and were careful not to interfere with the personalities of their children, while always ready to foster any worthwhile interests as soon as they discerned them.[28]

4 FAMILY FINANCES

It is clear that the Keynes family budget was comfortably unconstrained by financial pressures throughout over seven decades during which it occupied 6 Harvey Road. When John Keynes died in 1878 he had left a sufficient capital sum to his wife and son, which – if well invested – should enable each of them to live, independently, in a manner commensurate with their familiar life style. As an economist with an active interest in the investment opportunities provided on the Victorian Stock Exchange, Neville responded readily to the challenge to build on his legacy and was able to generate an investment

28. G. Keynes (1981), p. 19.

income which outweighed anything he could hope to earn as a Cambridge academic. Characteristically he was an extremely cautious investor although, in early 1880, when his Salisbury contemporary and close boyhood friend – Frank Tiffin – became a Lloyd's underwriter, he was persuaded to become the first of the latter's 'names'. Thus, on 10 April 1880, Neville broke his journey (from Salisbury to Cambridge) in London to sign up with Tiffin at Lloyd's and to open an underwriting account at the London and County Bank. 'Frank seems in good spirits', he wrote, adding hopefully, 'There have been some heavy losses lately, but he began too late to come in for them'. The Diary does not specify how much Neville had so far committed to Tiffin's agency, but on 22 November 1880 he was able to report: 'Frank sends me a cheque for £500 and continues to speak well of the underwriting'. Over the next few years, however, his involvement with Lloyd's was to cause him more anxiety and irritation than any of his other investment decisions.

Neville obviously expected to get regular reports from Lloyd's on how his insurances were faring, and the first hint that all was not well was in October 1881 when Tiffin warned his names that losses from a recent gale might amount to as much as £500 for each of them. At his first opportunity Neville called at Lloyd's in search of more detailed information and was told airily that: 'Bad storms are followed by high premiums and in that way we score'. To which Neville added somewhat uneasily: 'He is very busy and in good spirits'. A couple of weeks later another inconclusive and unsettling letter arrived from Tiffin to the effect that:

> We have come through last Sunday's gale very well, but there are lots of overdue ships and steamers some of which are hopeless. *All* the October gale losses are not only settled but *paid*, I dont think our figures are very bad – and if we can meet about 45% at the end of the year I think we ought to have a decent year.

By July 1882 Neville was more worried for his brother-in-law Edward Purchase (another of Tiffin's names), whom he suspected of 'speculating wildly' and who was so enraged by Frank's dilatory and unsatisfactory communications that he was talking of giving up underwriting altogether. So it went on, with Tiffin responding to requests for information by a scatter of vaguely optimistic messages alternating with gloomy predictions, until in January 1883 Neville – now a married man whose wife was expecting their first child – became restive. It was then that he wrote severely to Tiffin suggesting that if he was so busy at Lloyd's as to be unable to provide useful reports he would be wise to abandon the brokerage business. To which the latter replied shortly 'that from every point of view it would be unwise to give up the brokerage'.

Neville was annoyed and irritated, but not seriously alarmed until, on 3 April 1883, he received from his father-in-law, John Brown, a long letter which he transcribed into his Diary. It began: '"There is a matter of considerable importance on wh I feel I ought to write to you at once. You will please to consider the source of information – for obvious reasons – as *strictly confidential*'". The source was Mrs Brown, recently returned from a visit to her sister Mrs Dixey, whose son Alick was a junior employee at Lloyd's. John Brown's letter told at length the story his wife had heard from Alick Dixey. It alleged, for example, 'that Tiffin is badly given to drink, that he is hardly ever to be found on his stool during office hours as other underwriters are … and that he signs recklessly. Young Found [another Lloyd's junior from Salisbury] told Alick that Tiffin gave his name to 116 insurances in one day'. And so it went on. After repeating in detail the miscellany of office gossip, John Brown concluded positively 'It wd be well to take steps at once'. No doubt Neville would have followed this advice in any case, but – later the same morning – a letter arrived from Frank Tiffin's mother, which sharpened his concern. It announced that

> [The Tiffins] had just had a letter from Frank saying that he was going to be married immediately to a girl in a lower position than himself, but one whom he had loved for 5 or 6 years. They were very much troubled by the news. The two things together quite bowled me over. I remembered that I had hardly had a line in Frank's own handwriting for 5 or 6 weeks. … I determined to run up to London tomorrow.

The following day, at Lloyd's, Neville interrogated Tiffin who hastily summoned a colleague to testify on his behalf. The latter denied that Frank's office behaviour justified the gossip retailed by Mrs Brown, but personally undertook to make independent enquiries. Neville added in the Diary:

> With regard to his marriage Frank said very little. The girl has been a barmaid at the Grosvenor. … I asked enough about her antecedents to feel that I was on dangerous ground. … There are things I wd rather not know. I got him to promise to run down to Salisbury next day to see his people.

The next day he had a letter from Tiffin's supportive colleague, who insisted that his further enquiries had failed to produce 'the slightest reason for even the semblance of such an accusation against our friend'. He also got a furious letter from Tiffin himself: 'Since you left it has occurred to me that your private intelligence amounts to a serious libel … *you* shd demand justification of it … let this report be traced to its *original* source'. With unhesitating candour Neville then wrote to Alick Dixey and to John Brown 'to tell them what had transpired'. Later the same day he plucked Frank off the London train (en route to Salisbury), had supper with him and – before sending him on his way to visit his family – warned him that he did not wish to extend his underwriting commitments. According to the Diary: 'He agreed with me that I must not risk more than a moderate loss and that if there appeared any chance of its exceeding £2000 I ought to stop at once'.

Neville's forthright approaches provoked agitated repercussions. First came a letter from Mr Dixey to say: 'My son has just handed me your note, the contents of which have quite upset him. ... You seem to have had a very exaggerated account. ... My son personally knows very little of the gentleman to whom you refer'. After replying to Mr Dixey and informing his father-in-law what had occurred, Neville was most distressed to read a letter which Florence got from her mother by the last post that day. According to Mrs Brown:

> Neville's letter has worried me considerably. I so felt sure of his caution that I told all at once. If I thought he wd have gone straight to Tiffin, of course, I shd not have done so. ... Very likely Alick will lose his position in Lloyd's for revealing the secrets. The moral is – let those that are dearest be ruined but say nothing. I feel so upset I hardly know how to go to my work.

Neville copied this letter into his Diary, adding: 'I at once wrote to Mr Tiffin, Leslie, Mr Dixey and Mr Brown stifling further investigation. I told Tiffin and Leslie [his colleague], what was contained in Mr Dixey's letter – that the account I had was a very exaggerated one'. A second letter from Mr Dixey reinforced his first: 'You really must not attach any importance to anything said by Alick during Mrs Brown's visit to us ... as he is only a boy. I dare say he expressed himself indiscreetly from impressions rather than facts'. Neville also noted

> a nice letter from Mr Brown. 'I am afraid that nothing more can now be done since you have spoken out on the matter to the party concerned. I know that it was your own honourable feeling wh prompted you to this course. Yet I do not think it wd have been *dis*honourable under the circumstances to have found out privately whether there was any evidence to bear out the rumours wh reached you. If so speak out, if not remain silent yet keenly watchful. ... In any case the matter for the future is one of anxiety. ... It is not as if it were a case of limited liability. Unless you have absolute confidence and certainty you may be entirely cleared out and have no redress whatever'.

Unfortunately Mrs Brown (whose own mother was also 'taking sides') continued her indignant letters to Florence, and Neville worried miserably to his Diary, for another three pages, on 9 April 1883. He began to wish that he had cross-questioned young Dixey himself before talking to Tiffin but there is no doubt that his confidence in the latter was severely shaken. 'I have almost decided to give up underwriting', he wrote a few days later, 'The anxiety is too great'. Meanwhile, he felt obliged to complain frequently to Frank about his dilatory, incomplete and unsatisfactory reports. The March figures which arrived on 23 April, for example, revealed only that the loss on the 1880 account 'shd not exceed £1000', that 'there may be a profit of £1000' on the 1881 account and that '1883 has opened very badly'. A hasty exchange of letters between the two men brought their friendship under severe strain. Tiffin's answer which arrived on 26 April said sadly and incoherently: 'If you cease underwriting at once I trust we shall still be as formerly (altho' our walks in life are in different paths and *socially speaking* must diverge) sincere friends'. Tiffin was married early in May 1883 and in a letter thanking Neville and Florence for their wedding present, he wrote: 'The marriage yesterday was, of course, of the quietest description, but we had a fine day and it went off satisfactorily. The two Aunts were at the Church'.[29]

Neville's underwriting account for 1880 was finally settled on 9 May 'showing a net profit of £450 after deducting entrance fee and Frank's commission'. This was good news in itself, if not altogether encouraging, and it was actually not until a week after Maynard's birth that Neville finally decided to withdraw from any further unlimited liability commitment with Lloyd's. The Diary for 12 June 1883 reported:

> I have written to Tiffin to say definitely that I mean to give up underwriting at the end of August. I have said 'The way in wh this year opened had not been encouraging, and judging by my little experience the chances of profits do not seem sufficient to balance the worry and anxiety that are inevitable. The arrival of my little son has made me feel this more strongly. We have enough to live upon comfortably but no considerable margin to bear losses and I am anxious not to jeopardize the future. Another thing that weighs with me is a desire to know precisely what my income is. The possible gains and losses of underwriting interfere with this'.

By this time he was taking Edward Purchase with him in his interviews with Tiffin and they jointly decided to withdraw from the end of August. Their existing commitments were not the same, however, and Edward had evidently speculated unwisely; in any case neither of them found it easy to interpret the significance of Tiffin's devious accounts. In November 1883, Neville wrote irritably: 'Edward and Frank are disagreeing over the negociations [sic] for giving up Edward's underwriting. The one is unbusinesslike and the other unnecessarily hard'. On Easter Sunday of the following year the Diary reverted to Neville's own problems with Frank's opaque financial procedures: 'I worked at the underwriting a/cs wh are getting rather into a mess. I am very glad that I am getting out of this business'. Later that year he met an urgent call from Tiffin by sending him a cheque for £300. In the end it was not until early 1889 that the mess was finally cleared

29. The wedding present was a silver sugar bowl with tongs and sifter. It would appear that neither of Frank's parents were at the wedding ceremony.

up. By then Tiffin's drink problem had so far overtaken him that he was virtually out of action. On 12 May 1888, Neville had reported that, having written twice to Tiffin without getting an answer, he had begun to correspond directly with the latter's assistant – Walter Found – about the matter of his underwriting accounts. 'So far as I can make out', he wrote, after hearing from Found, 'I shall not be involved in any considerable loss. I am sorry to say it is otherwise with Edward. Tiffin has at last sent him his a/cs and asks for a cheque for £1339. … I gather, however, that of this only £615 represents net loss'. Fortunately Edward's son John, now a solicitor with reliable contacts at Lloyd's, found the time and the patience to deal with his father's affairs in an intelligent and businesslike way. 'John finds it difficult to get Tiffin to keep his appointments', wrote Neville on 27 May, 'He says that he looks like a man who is really past business'.

By 1 August 1888, Neville had been able to report with relief that Walter Found 'is now definitely undertaking the final settlement of my underwriting affairs', and on 31 August that 'Tiffin has promised him to write me a formal letter winding up everything. But even this letter has not come'. Finally after a joint City meeting on 4 January 1889, with Tiffin, Found, John Purchase and another Lloyd's officer, Neville reported the final settlement on 8 January: 'wound up my underwriting a/c by sending John a cheque on Tiffin's a/c for £24. On balance I nominally lose about £60. But for some time I had the use of a good deal of money and if I take this into a/c I am something to the good'. It was actually not until 17 March 1890 that he noted in the Diary: 'At last Tiffin has been obliged to give up all his work at Lloyd's and Found has stepped definitely into his place. What he will do in the future I cannot think'. Neville himself called at Lloyd's a couple of weeks later to enquire from Found what had become of their old Salisbury friend and was told that he had gone to live at Margate and that: 'At present they are allowing him something out of the brokerage business'. From then on Tiffin dropped out of touch with friends and family. He never wrote to them except to ask for money.[30] Anna Keynes continued to hear from the Salisbury Tiffins and it was she who conveyed the news in Cambridge that Frank's wife had died suddenly in 1895 and that Frank himself died equally suddenly, of pneumonia, in May 1901.

The Diary does not set out a systematic record of the Keynes family's financial affairs and most references to such matters relate to particular changes in incomes and outgoings. When Neville married Florence in August 1882 his annual stipend, as assistant secretary at the Local Examinations Syndicate, was £200 and in December of that year he collected his final dividend as a fellow of Pembroke – now capped by the 1882 statutes to

30. On one occasion Frank wrote to ask Neville for a loan of £10 and was sent a gift of £5. Diary, 4 April 1893.

£250.[31] In addition he earned various ad hoc fees for examining, invigilating, coaching or lecturing which were then unlikely to have amounted to more than about £30. In March 1883 his Locals stipend was raised to £250 and in the next academic year he began to draw a university lecturer's annual stipend of £50, which subsumed most of the miscellaneous teaching fees he had earned in earlier years. It is plain that the family at 6 Harvey Road was already heavily dependent on its investment income, for Neville had developed the habit of regularly auditing the family accounts. In July 1883 he reported, for example: 'Florence and I went through our accounts for the first half year. We spent £600 but we reckon that nearly £300 of that was extraordinary expenditure in connection with our new house'. At the end of the year, after deploring the recent fall in Stock Exchange prices, he concluded: 'We have saved a little but that only keeps us where we were in January last'. That implied a net worth of about £16,100, for on 4 January 1885 he reported the result of his end-1884 audit thus: 'We have saved £400; but the depreciation of securities is such that after writing up furniture by £100 I calculate that we are only worth £16,000 as against £16,100'.

In the second half of the 1880s a 'strong upward movement' on Stock Exchange prices raised the family's 'net worth' to £16,800 at the end of 1886 and to £17,300 at the end of 1887. For the next two years Neville recorded enough information in the Diary on his investment income and academic earnings to demonstrate that investments provided more than 60 per cent of the family's annual income.[32] During the late 1880s his two regular university stipends together amounted to £300, which could be supplemented by examining, invigilating and teaching fees generating up to about £250 per annum as the opportunities presented themselves and he could spare time for them. By 1890, time was becoming the scarce factor, as G.F. Browne absented himself more and more from Syndicate Buildings and left to Keynes an increasing proportion of the responsibilities of chief secretary for Local examinations. The result was to squeeze his assistant's casual academic earnings.

31. Before the 1882 revision of statutes limited fellowship dividends to an annual £250, Keynes's annual Pembroke dividend had usually varied between £390 and £400.
32. The results of end-year audit calculations mentioned in the Diary for the late 1880s suggest the following rough breakdown:

	1888 £	1889 £	1890 £
Income from investments	866	860	
Earnings	556	491	
Total income	1,422	1,351	1,409
Expenditure	1,023	951	1,019
Saving (*circa*)	400	400	400
Capital at end of year (*circa*)	18,000	18,800	18,800

In early 1891 the Syndicate, prompted by Browne, recognized the fact that the assistant secretary was carrying a heavier burden than had been expected of him and raised his stipend to £350 per annum. It was not until March 1892 that Browne formally resigned and Keynes was appointed chief secretary for Local examinations at an annual stipend of £500 rising to £700 by increments of £25. In the same year, Keynes was appointed unpaid secretary to the Council, a task which took up increasing amounts of his spare time, so that the variable component in his academic earnings rapidly dwindled.

On the other hand, the value of the family's capital stock continued to accumulate and already exceeded £24,000 at the beginning of the twentieth century. The annual saving on current income and expenditure continued to average £300 or £400 and while Neville's university stipend stuck at about £750 per annum from 1901 to 1910 (when he was appointed university registrary), his investment incomes went on rising. In October 1903, for example, when Keynes was offered the post of chief inspectorship of schools with a stipend of £1200 plus a life-time pension, he commented in his Diary: 'It is a flattering offer and in many respects attractive. But I do not feel inclined to accept it. Florence is more disposed than I to think of it seriously'. In 1907, when his mother died, Neville was the chief beneficiary of her will, and on 3 January 1908, he recorded: 'I have now finished my Audit of Securities and find that we are worth about £38,000. Last year we saved £400'. Thereafter Neville rarely referred in the Diary to the results of his annual audit of accounts but it is clear that he was able to make generous gifts and allowances to individual members of his own and his sister's family. In autumn 1909, for example, although Maynard's annual income from his fellowship, lecturing and coaching activities had reached £600 his father continued to add to it a regular allowance of £100.

VII Academic administration

1 LOCAL EXAMINATIONS AND LECTURES

Neville Keynes's first administrative appointment in the university was as assistant secretary to the Local Examinations and Lectures Syndicate, which had organized examinations throughout England for schoolboys (since 1858) and schoolgirls (since 1865). It also arranged associated extension lectures in some of the localities from which candidates were drawn and operated a schools inspection service. The schoolchildren's examinations, held annually in December, represented the Syndicate's most important and onerous responsibility. In June 1869 it ran its first 'Examination for Women' (later called the Higher Local examination) which had been promoted by Henry Sidgwick (among others) with a view to 'improving female education by providing examinations for governesses'.[1] When Newnhamites and Girtonians were first allowed to be examined and classed at Cambridge tripos exams the Higher Local examination served them as a qualifying test, analogous to the Previous or 'Little-Go' which undergraduate males had to pass before taking a tripos examination. Better still, a first class in the Higher Locals virtually guaranteed a scholarship in a women's college. Keynes was himself an experienced examiner at college and university level and had both examined and invigilated in the school-leaver examinations in 1878, 1879 and 1880 and in the Higher Locals in 1879 and 1880. He was therefore familiar with the operational details of the Syndicate's examination system, and enthused by its extra-mural objectives, before he applied to join its responsible staff.

When Keynes succeeded William Cunningham[2] as assistant secretary for examinations in March 1881, the Syndicate's office staff consisted of a chief secretary (G.F. Browne), two assistant secretaries (the second of whom – R.D. Roberts – organized the extension lectures), three full-time clerks and two graduates of the university regularly hired as back-up during the seasonal peak of activity arising out of the December Local examinations. Browne, chief secretary to the Syndicate, was the son of a proctor in the York Ecclesi-

1. See A.S. and E.M. Sidgwick, *Henry Sidgwick: A Memoir* (London: Macmillan, 1906), which quotes from Sidgwick's letter to his sister dated 13 November 1867.
2. Cunningham was to distinguish himself as an economic historian and a professor of divinity and became the leading critic of Marshallian economics in Cambridge.

astical Courts who had been impoverished by speculation in the railway mania of the late 1840s. Fortunately the boy then held a four-year secondary school scholarship providing tuition, board and lodging in an era when (according to his autobiography), 'Yorkshire men had a county right to scholarships and fellowships' at St Catharine's College.[3] He therefore came to Cambridge with a classical scholarship in 1852 – the year Neville was born. There was, as it happened, no vacancy in the St Catharine's fellowship when Browne graduated in 1857 and it was not until 1863 that he was offered one. Meanwhile, he had made the first move towards an ecclesiastical career by taking holy orders in 1858 and he accepted a schoolmaster's job at Glenalmond in Scotland, where he was to fall deeply in love. When he married in 1865 he was of course in need of a steady source of income, but the college rules were such that he lost his fellowship. So, in 1869, he accepted a country living which maintained the newly-weds until Browne returned to Cambridge as secretary to the Local Examinations and Lectures Syndicate. That office brought him into close personal contact with some of the most influential members of the academic community and he was subsequently elected to the Council of the Senate. In these circumstances, in 1877, Browne was also appointed secretary to the Cambridge University Commission empowered to negotiate the extensive statutory reforms which came into effect in 1882/83 and which revolutionized the relations between the university and its colleges. This was the man to whom Neville was to act as assistant, and often as deputy, for eleven years. They enjoyed a generally comfortable working relationship for, although Browne lacked Keynes's orderly approach to management, he had a personality that made friends easily and enemies rarely.

Since 1871, the Syndicate's offices were located in the set of college rooms which Browne then occupied as a minor officer of St Catharine's. This constrained accommodation was later supplemented by another set, rented from the college. A college lecture room was also made available during the Christmas vacation when extra space was needed to accommodate examiners' meetings in each subject section, as well as to send, receive and sort question papers and scripts to or from hundreds of centres and examiners at home and abroad. At Neville's appointment, the increasing number of candidates was already causing severe pressure on space at peak periods. In December 1881, 6986 candidates were entered at 110 centres for boys and 96 for girls; and in the June Higher Local examination 882 candidates sat in 19 centres. By 1883 the December examinations involved 8290 candidates at 124 boys' centres and 115 girls' centres. The office accommodation problem reached crisis proportions in 1882/83 because the new statutes obliged Browne

3. G.F. Browne, *The Recollections of a Bishop* (Smith & Elder, 1915).

to resign his college office so that he was no longer entitled to rooms at St Catharine's. Thus driven, the Syndicate rushed a report to the Senate, dated 13 February 1884, stressing the urgency of its need for custom-built offices. The report spelt out the practical problems that had faced the assistant secretary for examinations (and his aides) ever since his appointment in 1881:

> They find that for the last 2 or 3 years the space at their disposal had not been really sufficient for preparing the parcels of exam^{n} papers for the Presiding Examiners and for unpacking and sorting the answers returned from the centres of examination. Various devices have been resorted to for getting through this work but the inconvenience and the risk of error have been considerable and the present accommodation will not bear any greater strain. It may be mentioned that in preparing for the examination last December 50 yards of desk was required for distributing each of the examination papers into separate bundles for the several centres: 250 parcels had to be arranged for the Presiding Examiners, each parcel requiring 5 square feet of desk; and the answers of the candidates weighed over 3 tons and had to be sorted according to the subjects into 98 separate piles.[4]

Browne had welcomed the appointment of a new assistant secretary for examinations with open relief in March 1881. After confiding that 'his head has been feeling like a boiled sponge', he disappeared – a fortnight later – for several weeks holiday, leaving Neville to correct, and put through the *University Reporter*, the detailed statistical tables of 1880 examination results. From the outset Keynes was obsessively concerned to improve the organization of each of the subject examinations – for example, by actively ensuring that examiners produced suitable question papers and recorded marks accurately, by responding personally to the varied concerns of individual schoolmasters and mistresses, and by carefully monitoring the work of the clerks. At first he found ample time to spend on the time-consuming minutiae involved in bringing the system up to his own punctilious standards. On 2 February 1882, for example, according to the Diary, he spent a whole morning 'putting right the markbook of the Religious Knowledge section. Every possible mistake, even 9 in a single subject. … Their neglect of duty is *immoral* in my view, rather worse than lying or stealing. Religious Knowledge of course!' Well aware that the new assistant secretary for examinations was extremely conscientious and methodical in his work, Browne felt free to spend more time on his own rather varied activities. According to the Diary for 28 November 1881: 'Mrs Browne had told Prior that I relieve him of a good deal of trouble. He is able to leave many details to me that he could never leave to anyone before without fearing lest they go wrong'. Neville seemed unruffled by Browne's long spells of absence from the office – although, as time went on, references in the Diary to the difference in their respective salaries suggested

4. *CUR*, 29 February 1884, reproduces the Syndicate's report.

a certain irritation. On 4 May 1883, for example, he referred to a Syndicate meeting at which:

> Roberts's salary is raised from £100 to £200 and mine from £200 to £250. Browne wishes that the ultimate position of the Secretary shd be discussed in detail. His view is that the salary shd be £1000 (it is now £700). I agree but I think also that he shd do less outside work than Browne now does. He shd not require to supplement his income in other ways. Any lecturing or other work that he might do because congenial shd be completely subordinated to his work as Secretary to the Syndicate.

The fact was that the assistant secretary for examinations had set his sights on the chief secretary's job, which he believed he could handle more efficiently than Browne, who tended to be overwhelmed by the seasonal peaks of activity – partly (Keynes judged) 'because he has put off things that might have been done before'. Nevertheless, Browne, although often wearied by the burdens of office, needed the income and was unlikely to resign as secretary until he was offered an ecclesiastical preferment with prospects of advancement. Neville, after his first child was born in 1883, and another was on its way, also began to ponder possibilities of adding to his income without subtracting from his teaching, writing or family time. On 4 December 1883, for example, he wrote ambivalently:

> I am just now having a longing come over me for leisure to do some really useful work – also Browne has succeeded in having the position of the 'Locals' Secretary discussed and a proposal for an ultimate pension will no doubt be assured. This no doubt means that he intends to make it his life work; and it will be a good thing for the university if he does so. We could, however, hardly afford at present to give up the stipend of the assistant secretaryship and I am afraid it is possible that if I had more leisure I might merely waste it.

On the other hand, although Keynes welcomed the organizational challenge implicit in his current responsibilities, he seems – after a series of disappointments as eccleciastical vacancies arose and went – to have recognized the grim possibility that Browne would never go. For example, on 7 December 1885 he wrote: 'It is rumoured that Browne will be Dean of Worcester. He will certainly be disappointed if he gets nothing; and so shall I'. When that too failed, he wrote sadly: 'I have given up all hope of preferment for GFB'. A few weeks later he grumbled: 'I have been for the last week or two in a state of mind in which I find the Local work burdensome and long to have the time to give to my own work. But doubtless these feelings will pass off as they have often done before'.

His spirits certainly rose when the Syndicate's new buildings in Mill Lane were completed in September 1886 and he escaped from the claustrophobic offices at St Catharine's. A few weeks before he had shown R.W. Lockhart, the secretary of the Oxford 'Locals', over the new premises and then boasted to the Diary that he had probably 'filled his soul with envy. He has only one room for everything'. Putting order in his spacious new office on 13 September gave Keynes immense satisfaction and he went to work cheerfully throughout that October term. No doubt a more commodious environment raised spirits and speeded operations for all concerned; at any rate he was able to report in January 1887 that they were further ahead than usual in the examination process. On the other hand, on 21 February, he resisted a proposal by the Local Examinations Finance Sub-Committee that his stipend should be raised from £200 to £300 on the grounds that 'If this were done I should feel obliged to be more hours at the office; and this I do not want to be. I therefore expressed to Browne my desire that the proposal should not be made'. The reason was that he was desperate to find time for his book on *The Scope and Method of Political Economy*, whilst being continually badgered by Marshall for 'throwing [my]self away on administration'. As it happened, Keynes had little choice over the demands on his time, for the examination workload continued to expand and Browne's efforts to advance his own career increasingly took him out of Cambridge. Although, in November 1887 Browne's elevation to the Disney Professorship of Archaeology brought him a meagre additional stipend of £112 per annum, it was limited to a five-year term and carried no future prospects of advancement. It simply provided the chief secretary with another set of reasons for leaving his assistant in effective charge of Syndicate Buildings. By December 1888 the number of schoolboy and -girl candidates was in excess of 10,000, the Syndicate had introduced yet another examination (leading to a Commercial Certificate); and Keynes was spending an average of 34 hours a week on Locals work.

It was not until late in 1890 that Browne reverted to the matter of Neville's salary. According to the Diary for 8 November:

> To my surprise GFB said that he had for some time been feeling very uncomfortable about my stipend and that he intended to propose to the Financial sub-Committee to raise it to £350. He spoke very nicely and kindly about my value in the office and the large proportion of the work that I did. He said that I should not be expected to give up more of my time.

This time Keynes accepted the rise. *Scope and Method* was then virtually complete and he decided that he would no longer invigilate at the Higher Locals for which he had always earned a small extra fee.[5] He continued

5. The many hours Neville spent annually invigilating examinations provided the kind of relatively uninterrupted peace which was difficult for him to find at Syndicate Buildings and enabled him to read for his lectures or his book or to correct proofs.

however, to set and mark the senior political economy papers (for which there were 231 candidates in December/January 1891). At the next meeting of the Syndicate (which Neville was unable to attend because he was invigilating for the Moral Sciences Board), the proposal to raise his stipend was agreed. At last, unexpectedly, in January 1891, Browne obtained a part-time ecclesiastical position which could be expected to prove a stepping stone to a future bishopric. He was elected Canon of St Paul's, a post which entailed three months' residence in London annually. He did not, however, choose to resign at once. The Syndicate agreed (according to the Diary of 14 February):

> that Browne's Secretaryship should terminate on Lady Day 1892. There are to be appointed in his place two Secretaries (one for Examinations and one for Lectures). There seems to be no doubt that Roberts and I will be the Secretaries but the question of stipends and that of a pension for Browne remain undecided.

On 28 February 1891, Neville recorded with evident satisfaction: 'GFB goes today to London to be in residence during the month of March. So I shall be in possession at Synd. Buildings'. At the March meeting of the Syndicate, Keynes was elected secretary for examinations from Lady Day 1892, with a salary commencing at £500 and increasing by £25 a year up to £700. Although destined to be overburdened for another year, Neville admitted his relief to the Diary that the office was not thrown open to competition and that the stipend was set at an acceptable level. Since the Syndicate also decided to appoint two assistant secretaries in 1892, he could look forward to a substantial reduction in his Locals workload.

Browne finally left Syndicate Buildings on 26 February 1892. A month later Keynes became the nominal as well as the acting chief secretary of examinations and confessed to the Diary that his long-standing interest in the work had been positively increased by the fact that he was now master at Syndicate Buildings. Having spent several years silently disapproving of the haste with which Browne rushed the Syndicate through its meetings, the new secretary at once set about trying to introduce more order and deliberation into its proceedings. One of his first achievements was to get the previous year's academic accounts agreed in the October term, before the office work had begun to rise to its December peak. Browne's practice had been to shelve the audit until February when the clerks were exhausted and their memories of last year's transactions had faded beyond recall. On 9 February 1892, for example, Neville complained to his Diary: 'I must say that GFB manages his accounts wretchedly and he presents them to the auditors in an entirely uncompleted state'. Ten days later he wrote: 'I discovered GFB and Thomas beginning to go through the whole of the accounts again. I felt sure that the error must be in the Bank Book and I soon discovered it'. Determined to avoid such unnecessary crises he began preparing the ground for the next audit in September 1892, so that the accounts could be conclusively balanced before the end of October. In consequence the 4 p.m. meeting with the auditors on 16 November was concluded well before 7, upon which Neville recorded smugly: 'the auditors clearly thought the accounts presented in a more satisfactory form than in previous years'.

The new assistant secretary for examinations, J.H. Flather (a fellow of Emmanuel with a first in the 1875 classical tripos) began work on 6 April 1892. Neville, who would have preferred to see C. Geldard (a fellow stamp-collector and good friend) elected, was initially disappointed when the Syndicate chairman's casting vote decided Flather's election. The disappointment was shortlived. He soon settled into a companionable working routine with a new colleague of his own age, who had already acquired significant administrative experience, first as tutor (1878–88) then as principal (1888–91) of the ill-fated Cavendish College.[6] The number of candidates for examination in 1892 – Keynes's and Flather's first year in harness together – amounted to a record 10,375, including 794 taking the Highers in June and 221 in December, plus 17 seeking the Commercial Certificate. Partly no doubt because of the increase in clerical staff at Syndicate Buildings, but largely because Flather shared Keynes's passion for orderliness, the examination work went more smoothly after March 1892 than ever before. On 7 October Neville confided to the Diary: 'I feel now very distinctly the advantage of having Flather at the ofice. The work I have had to do is much lighter than it was this time last year'. In spite of the unprecedentedly large number of candidates, and of a scatter of scarlet fever outbreaks disrupting the examinations, as well as of the accommodation problems posed by an increase in numbers of secretarial and clerical staff operating in Syndicate Buildings,[7] the December examination class lists were available before the end of February. The *Cambridge Daily News* published them, with the comment (quoted in the Diary for 28 March):

> 'These are the first lists of this exam by Dr Keynes of Pembroke who has succeeded the Rev. Canon Browne as secretary and it is to be noted and appreciated by candidates and their friends that this is the earliest date for at least the last 15 years that the result has been declared, and it is at least a week earlier than last year.'

6. Cavendish College (1877–92) was founded on a shoestring to permit a poorer class of male undergraduates to enter Cambridge. It failed to raise sufficient funds to survive, but 358 men matriculated under its auspices before it was declared bankrupt. The story is told by P. Searby in *Proceedings of the Cambridge Antiquarian Society*, Vol. 72. (Cambridge: Cambridge University Press, 1982–83).
7. The Syndicate's case for doubling accommodation at Syndicate Buildings – *CUR*, 21 February 1893 – was accepted by the Senate without opposition.

In the event, R.D. Roberts did not accept the post of chief secretary for extension lectures when it was offered to him. His domestic circumstances had changed in so far as he had married in 1889 and stepped out of his Clare fellowship. The stipend offered for an extremely time-consuming and difficult organizational post[8] was unattractive, and he probably judged it wiser to seek alternative earning opportunities in London – where he had doubled, since 1887, as secretary to the Delegacy for the Extension of University Teaching. Keynes regretted Roberts's departure from Cambridge, for they had been appointed together and had collaborated harmoniously over the past decade. In contrast, the new secretary for extension lectures – Arthur Berry (a fellow of King's), and his assistant Stanley Leathes (a fellow of Trinity) were relatively young men who slotted less smoothly into the Syndicate's operational mode than either Keynes or Roberts had done. Berry, the 1885 senior wrangler, had attracted Marshall's attention whilst attending the latter's lectures in 1886 and he became King's College lecturer in mathematics in 1889. By the early 1890s, Marshall had persuaded him to lecture on mathematical economics under the auspices of the Moral Sciences Board. Keynes was to suffer sleepless nights when he and Berry disagreed, for he believed the two chief secretaries and their assistants should operate as a team at Syndicate meetings. On 5 May 1892 he worried to his Diary: 'Berry and Leathes want to go ahead too fast and are very impatient of the control of the Syndicate and the Senate. I find myself in opposition and feel a good deal worried on the subject'.

For his part, Berry was dismayed to be chief secretary for extension lectures at a time when the demand for them was falling. His first annual report (November 1893) explained his anxieties:

> The existence of science classes of all kinds carried on by the aid of County Council grants and open to students gratuitously or on payment of extremely small fees, has rendered it difficult for Local Committees to sell tickets for courses of Local Lectures at reasonable prices. ... The fact that grants can be obtained from Counties and Town Councils for a course on science, but not on history or literature has in many cases induced a Local Committee to choose a subject not desired by the majority of the usual audience or the more serious students. Not only have literature and history thus suffered, but courses on branches of science not of obviously practical utility (such as Astronomy) have tended to be replaced by more 'technical' subjects.[9]

As if this were not bad enough, in December 1893 Berry had outraged Alfred Marshall by appointing a Girton history lecturer – Ellen MacArthur – who

8. Edwin Welch, *The Peripatetic University* (Cambridge: Cambridge University Press, 1973) contains a brief history of the Cambridge Local Lectures movement and of the contribution of successive secretaries from 1873 onwards.
9. *CUR*, 15 November 1893. Berry had himself given extension courses on astronomy before becoming chief secretary.

had established an undeniably sound scholarly reputation, but whose gender disqualified her in the eyes of those who took a reactionary stance on the question of women in Cambridge.[10] As it happened Marshall's protests to the Syndicate via its chairman, the vice-chancellor, were not effective in overturning Berry's decision. In its 21st Annual Report on the Local Lectures, the Syndicate defended its secretary on the grounds that since practical experience at both Oxford and London universities had

> suggested the desirability of employing women as lecturers (particularly at centres where the large majority of the students are women) and of increasing the field from which competent lecturers can be drawn, the Syndicate have during the past year for the first time placed the name of a woman on their list of available lecturers. The student selected was a former student of Girton college who had been placed in the first class of the historical Tripos Examination and had had several years of experience of lecturing and other teaching.

It concluded diplomatically, however, that: 'Some time must elapse before the Syndicate can judge definitely of the success of such appointments, but they do not at present anticipate that it will be found advisable to appoint women as lecturers in other than exceptional cases'.[11] Berry knew, of course, that Marshall's views on women academics were widely shared, and that the professor was an unforgiving antagonist whose ill will could threaten the career of a young academic. In July 1894, when Keynes heard an overworked and dejected Berry talking seriously about resigning his secretaryship, he persuaded him not to act hastily; but by October the younger man was obviously at the end of his tether. According to the Diary for 8 October: 'Berry now seems definitely to have made up his mind to resign the Secretaryship. Marshall talks of indicting the Syndicate for appointing women lecturers'. Neville promptly invited Roberts to lunch at Harvey Road, and established that he might be induced to return to Cambridge as Berry's successor. At its next meeting the secretarial sub-Syndicate agreed to offer an invitation to Roberts who, after seizing the opportunity to negotiate a higher stipend, was warmly welcomed back to Syndicate Buildings by Keynes and his other former colleagues on 18 January 1895.

The problems that had defeated Berry did not vanish when the more enthusiastic and experienced man took charge of Cambridge extension lectures. The fact was that the Technical Instruction and Local Taxation Acts of 1890 had provided county councils with funds enabling them to organize courses of lectures on technical and scientific subjects only. The short-term impact of this competing development was not only to reduce demand for

10. The story is told by Rita McWilliams-Tullberg in *Women at Cambridge* (London: Gollancz, 1975), pp. 105–6.
11. *CUR*, 13 November 1894, p. 198.

university extension lectures but also to narrow the range of subjects generally available for adult students. The first report to the Syndicate from Roberts (October 1895) offered an incisive analysis of the current situation together with a set of suggestions for action at the university level:

> There can be no question that the whole movement has reached a critical stage in its history. From whatever point of view the work is regarded there are indications that it is passing through a period of depression. The number of Centres taking courses of Lectures has been decreasing; a certain measure of disheartenment is discernible amongst Local Committees and the number of experienced lecturers free to take full work has been growing smaller. The last condition is due to the fact that almost all lecturers have entered into permanent engagements at Cambridge, London or elsewhere.

He concluded by advocating three remedial policies: (1) the establishment of a permanent fund to finance four or five 'Lecturing Fellowships or Superintendent Lecturers' at stipends of £200 annually; (2) 'representations to Government in favour of widening the scope of the Technical Education Act' so as to allow local authorities to subsidize courses in literature, history and economics as well as in science; and (3) the establishment of a Diploma for external students based 'on a scheme of work involving both Higher and Local Examinations and the Local Lectures'.[12] Although Keynes lent his support to these proposals he was well aware that they were unlikely to attract widespread support in a university which was perennially short of funds, where extension lectures were essentially a fringe activity and where the problem facing the Local examinations department was one of rising rather than falling demand. In 1895, a new examination (preliminary to the junior and senior school leavers' exams) brought the number of school children examined by the Syndicate to a new high of almost 13,600. Plainly it would be an impossible task to persuade the Senate to divert more of its scarce funds to a Syndicate which already spent more per annum than the average small Cambridge college.[13]

At that stage, even Roberts seemed to flag in his enthusiasm for the cause of creating local centres of higher education where serious students who were too poor to contemplate residence at a university could have access to a broad range of lectures and classes provided by academically-qualified graduates. On 31 December Keynes noted with alarm: 'Roberts talks of being a candidate for the Registrarship of the University of London'. As for Keynes himself, he was then feeling excessively burdened by his Locals workload, and, after

12. *CUR*, 22 October 1895, p. 106.
13. In the academic year 1900/01 the total expenditure of the Local Examinations and Lectures Syndicate amounted to £20,000, compared with Pembroke College's total expenditure of under £13,000.

groaning to the Diary that he had spent all of his time on Local examinations during the Christmas vacation he wrote on 7 January 1896: 'Roberts has decided to be a candidate for the vacant Registrarship in the University of London and I am very much exercised in my mind as to whether I shall be a candidate too. Florence rather urges it upon me'. The following day he sought advice from Sidgwick who was, as ever, gravely impartial and offered the encouraging opinion that Keynes was better qualified than Roberts for the London registrarship. Over the next three weeks Keynes wrestled with the problem of whether or not to apply for the top administrative position in the University of London. He wrote, or talked, to old friends such as Alfred West and Harry Bond, and to colleagues such as James Ward, H.S. Foxwell, E.J. Routh and R.T. Wright. He even began to seek references, for example from G.F. Browne (then Bishop of Stepney), and from his colleagues on the Council of the Senate such as the vice-chancellor, the Master of Christ's and the Provost of King's. As the number mounted of those predicting that his prospects of a successful application were promising, and as the Locals workload began its seasonal decline, he became less depressed and less inclined to desert Cambridge. What eventually turned the scale was his realization that those heads of houses on the Council of the Senate who had most reason to appreciate his administrative talents were appalled at the notion that their secretary might migrate to London. On 24 January, he reported with surprise:

> Letters from the VC, Master Xts [of Christ's] and Provost of King's strongly deprecating my leaving Cambridge and both suggesting that my stipend as Locals Exam^{n} Secretary be raised! This was a new idea to me and I dont think it influenced my decision. I have asked that the point may not be raised at any rate at this juncture. I have finally decided not to stand for the London Registrarship.

Roberts did apply for the London appointment but without success. Meanwhile the only one of his departmental proposals that attracted substantive support on the Syndicate was the external diploma project. Drafting a workable scheme proved a slow and contentious process, but by 24 November 1897 the Syndicate was ready to sign a unanimous report to the Senate. It was discussed at a congregation in the Easter term of 1898. At the discussion the scheme was strongly defended by such university heavy-weights as the vice-chancellor, Richard Jebb (the professor of classics and the university MP), and H.M. Butler (Master of Trinity), as well as by Keynes and Roberts. It was attacked by speakers whose limited vision reflected the parochial perspective of most members of the Senate; and it was comprehensively defeated at the vote on 28 May. W. Ridgeway (the Disney Professor of Archaeology), for example, argued:

> The University should remember that the class on which it mainly relied for support was the middle class and that what was necessary was to retain its hold on

> the public schools. By granting such a diploma as proposed the University would seriously degrade itself, and the public would confuse the holders of diplomas with graduates.[14]

More scornfully, but equally verbosely, L. Whibley (a Pembroke classicist) asserted: 'The scheme was framed in the interests of the Local Lectures system … an attempt to supply an artifical stimulus to a declining movement', and he could not see 'how it was called for either by the Examination System or in any legitimate manner by the Lecture Organization, while it was contrary to the interests and the dignity of the University'.[15]

After the rejection of the diploma scheme, Keynes confessed to the Diary that he was 'sick and angry'. He went on: 'RDR [R.D. Roberts] is I think more resigned than might have been anticipated. I do not myself mind the rejection of the scheme in itself; but I very much dislike the defeat which the Syndicate has sustained'. The retiring vice-chancellor referred to it obliquely in his address to the Senate on university events during the past academic year (1897/98):

> Changes in the organisation of the studies of the University have been but few. Certain proposals have been made by Boards and Syndicates and rejected by the Senate; showing that the system of legislation by *referendum* upon which the government of the University is based is a guarantee against any rapid or extensive changes in its organic life. Its development is likely to be in the future, as in the past, a gradual process.[16]

Evidently university administration was not a career for academics in a hurry to reform the institution. Perhaps the diploma scheme was too revolutionary to stand any chance of success. It certainly made no headway. On the other hand other developments were successfully piloted through the Syndicate by Roberts and Keynes, without raising the kind of opposition that called for a vote on principle. In the month of August 1900, for example, the Local Lectures staff celebrated the millennium by organizing a summer meeting of university extension students, which attracted about 750 participants, including some distinguished lecturers and students. According to the vice-chancellor, who presided over the occasion (the theme of which was 'Life and Thought of England during the Nineteenth Century'):

> [T]he quality of the lectures was unusually excellent and the Local Examinations and Local Lectures Syndicate hope that they succeeded in arranging them on a more systematic and connected scheme than was possible on previous occasions.

14. *CUR*, 3 May 1898, p. 727.
15. Ibid., pp. 727–8.
16. *CUR*, 4 October 1898, p. 8.

> Special interest was given to the meeting by the presence of A.J. Balfour who delivered the Inaugural Address in the Senate House on August 2.[17]

Meanwhile, Roberts was inspiring the development of university extension colleges in Exeter, Nottingham and Colchester, and arranging scientific courses within the technical institutes that had been established since 1890 – many of which had set up permanent buildings. He took comfort from the fact that the legislation then being steered through parliament by Balfour, among others, would in principle permit these local authority funded institutions to finance courses in literature, political economy and history as well as scientific subjects. By then also the Syndicate had begun to appoint a small number of experienced teachers as staff lecturers on a fixed stipend.

Before the Education Act of 1902 came into force, however, Roberts was offered and accepted the relatively high-powered appointment of registrar to the new Board for University Extension of the University of London, established in 1901 as part of the reconstitution of the University of London. These constitutional changes had already severed the long-standing connection – which Roberts had done so much to maintain – between the Cambridge Locals Syndicate and the London Society for the Extension of University Teaching. In Cambridge, Roberts was replaced as chief secretary for Local lectures by D.H.S. Cranage, a clergyman–schoolmaster who had graduated at King's and been a Cambridge Local lecturer in history and architecture. Keynes nursed the new man through his first year as secretary and found him an efficient, hardworking and persuasive colleague. They constituted a mutually-supportive team until he himself retired from the Syndicate in 1910. As for Cranage he held his post until 1928, when he retired to become Dean of Norwich Cathedral.

2 COUNCIL OF THE SENATE

In October 1892, Keynes was approached by his friend Alfred Dale – then canvassing for the 'liberal ticket' on the Council of the Senate – to persuade him to stand at the November election. The Council was the university's supreme governing body. It consisted of four college heads (one of whom was the vice-chancellor), four university professors and eight other resident MAs. Although hesitant, as usual, about either his suitability for the role, or his prospects of being elected, Neville accepted nomination to fill a vacancy among the resident MAs who were neither heads of houses nor professors. In the event, on 7 November, he became one of four newly elected councillors

17. *CUR*, 2 October 1901, p. 13.

(among the eight who were in his category) – his tally of votes being second only to that of Henry Jackson, the justifiably popular and respected Trinity classicist.[18] References in the Diary to those ultra-conservatives (such as Charles Searle, then Master of Pembroke) who wrote to Keynes promising him their votes, demonstrate that his support was not limited to voters who normally embraced the 'liberal ticket', and that he had already earned the affectionate trust of a wide range of academic colleagues. He was to extend that broad support over the next three decades, for his election was never in doubt and his name generally figured on both the conservative and liberal 'tickets'.

Elevation to 'cabinet rank' in the university Senate committed the 40-year-old moral scientist to an expanding schedule of meetings each term. It was opportune that the restructuring and expansion of Local Examinations Syndicate staff, after the departure of G.F. Browne in March 1892, had appreciably lightened Neville's Locals workload by appointing an effective assistant secretary for examinations as well as enlarging the clerical establishment to whom the routine operational work in Syndicate Buildings could confidently be delegated. The Council itself generally met at least twice weekly during full term and nominated its members to serve on the various boards and committees responsible for managing university departments and executing university policies. In his first month on the Council, for example, Keynes was put on the Times-for-Tripos Syndicate (which drew up the annual examination timetables that had to be coordinated with each board of studies) and on the Syndicate which managed the Cambridge University Press – an unusually complex business that spawned its own multiplicity of separate sub-committees. 'Alas!' he was to write in the Diary a year later, 'I am now in the following sub-Syndicates: Business Details; Partnership; Secondary School Books; French and German Books'. Within his first year, he was also put on an appointments committee for geographical lecturers and on the committee managing the Cambridge Training College for Women.

During the 32 years Keynes served continuously on this elected governing body he was to become its most trusted, well-informed and influential component. He had established his credentials for sound common-sense, reliability and integrity before the end of his first six months on the Council and was accordingly asked to replace its secretary Donald MacAlister (his neighbour in Harvey Road and a medical university lecturer) who then wanted to escape from an intolerably heavy workload. Keynes admitted in the Diary for 24 April 1893: 'The proposal took me by surprise – but on thinking it over I am

18. Jackson, who was to succeed Richard Jebb as Regius Professor of Classics, was a Trinity fellow, one of the new generation of dons who had offered one-to-one teaching and convivial hospitality to successive generations of men reading for the classical tripos since the mid-1860s.

glad I accepted. If I can do the work decently it will give me justification for being on the Council at all'. In fact this unpaid office carried considerable responsibility and called for administrative talents of a kind that few academics cared to cultivate. They included: a methodical analytical approach to university policy problems; an impartial determination to implement the policies preferred by a Council majority even when he had himself voted with the minority; a capacity to identify and assess the agenda or the strategy essential to effective executive action; and the ability to draft unambiguous, concise and accurate minutes (or official notices) and to define lucid policy recommendations for validation by members of the Senate in congregation. Neville Keynes was not only relatively well-endowed with such talents; he positively enjoyed deploying them. Moreover – having already published two successful and respected texts on his academic specialisms and being saddled, at the time, with a conveniently light teaching load as university lecturer in moral sciences[19] and no college commitments – he had the leisure as well as the inclination to develop his administrative skills.

At the beginning of October 1893, John Peile, Master of Christ's, completed his two-year stint as vice-chancellor and gave way to his successor Austen Leigh, the Provost of King's. Henceforth Keynes normally spent each Saturday morning in term with the vice-chancellor, discussing and listing detailed agenda (and relevant papers) for the 11 a.m. Monday morning Council. The papers circulated to Council members had to be prepared by the secretary on Saturday afternoons. On 9 February, for example, the Diary reported with resigned surprise: 'The preparation of next week's Grace paper has taken me some time – 94 Graces!'[20] Monday morning Council meetings were sometimes preceded by a steering committee meeting and frequently lasted until 2 p.m. or later. Before the end of each Monday, the secretary was expected to record that morning's decisions, amend the reports that were destined for discussion at the next Thursday congregation, and arrange for their advance printing in the Wednesday *University Reporter*. He was also responsible for writing full formal minutes of Council proceedings, so that from 25 April 1893 onwards, the massive Minute Volumes of the Council of the Senate were penned in Neville Keynes's elegantly antiquated copybook hand. His first Council minutes took just an hour to complete. On 25 April, according to the Diary: 'I am indexing the Council Minute Book. It hadnt been done since last June, but after this I shall try to keep it up to date'. It has to be said that his predecessor, Donald MacAlister, had been (as Neville himself noted in October 1893), 'certainly very businesslike and efficient'.

19. Keynes lectured and read papers in logic for moral science students and in political economy for Indian Civil Service candidates.
20. At that time Graces were painstakingly penned by the secretary to the Council before being printed in the *CUR*.

So it was with understandable pride that he reported to the Diary, in April 1894, Bond's information that F.W. Maitland had described him as 'an even better secretary of the Council than MacAlister'.

Membership of the Council was not always an unalloyed burden, of course, and the Diary reflects the naive pleasure which Neville (and often his family) got from the public occasions in which 'cabinet rank' involved him. As early as 27 February 1893, for example, he described his enjoyment of a foreign royal visit:

> 3.45. To King's Lodge to a Reception arranged for the Empress Frederick who was spending the day in Cambridge. She did not stay more than a few minutes but the impression I formed was exceedingly favourable. Her smile and manner were extremely pleasant and unaffected. A few of the guests were presented to her and most of them looked exceedingly uncomfortable. The day must I think have been most fatiguing for the Empress.

Then there were the ceremonial events associated with the award of honorary degrees each year (regularly in May or June but also at other special occasions). The initial Council discussions on awards often raised delicate or controversial issues. Such matters were rarely mentioned in the secretary's personal Diary, but the Council minutes are more informative. For example, they record the names of persons who either refused a Cambridge honorary degree, or were rejected by Council vote – without divulging the underlying reasons. It was different, however, when Arthur Berry, the other chief secretary at the Local Examinations and Lectures Syndicate, signalled his intention to oppose the award of an honorary degree to the Duke of York when the Grace came before the Senate in congregation. Keynes was appalled. The Diary reported on Thursday 24 May: '12. Council to consider what action if any shd be taken in consequence of Berry's non-placet of the Duke of York's degree. We decided to go on with the Grace. 12.30 Congregation. Placet 137 non-placet 6'. On the following day, presumably after confronting Berry, Keynes wrote: 'Berry now regrets his non-placet: he recognises that there is danger of injuring University Extension'. In the event, when the royal party (including the Duke of York and the Prince and Princess of Wales) came to Cambridge for the ceremony, Neville met them at dinner at King's on 26 June and at a Trinity reception (with Florence) on 27 June and was able to arrange that his mother, stepsister and her husband, plus 12-year-old Maynard, could watch parts of the grand occasion (as well as the subsequent Trinity fireworks display) from convenient vantage points.

Although both the vice-chancellor and the secretary were new to their respective roles in 1893/94, the Council business seems to have proceeded smoothly during that academic year. Austen Leigh's traditional year-end speech to the Senate on 1 October 1894 concluded with the usual expressions of thanks to all who had assisted him in his presidential task but singled out the secretary for special credit, as reported in the *University Reporter* on the following day:

> [I]f I were obliged to name one member of the Senate to whom I owe more than any other it would – I think – be Dr Keynes. All the members of the Council are able to appreciate his work as their Secretary; but only the Vice-Chancellor can estimate how many more mistakes he would have made, and how much more time he would have spent in making them, if he had not had the help of one whose memory, judgment and industry are unfailing.

Without doubt Keynes had approved the text of the speech (whilst protesting at its 'peroration') before it was delivered. 'Fortunately for my blushes', he noted with evident pleasure, 'I was not myself present in the Senate House'.

Austen Leigh served the customary second year as vice-chancellor before retiring on 1 October 1895. His successor Charles Smith, Master of Sidney Sussex, was duly escorted through Cambridge streets (from the Senate House to his College Lodge) by a colourful procession of Council members robed in their grandest academic gowns. Neville Keynes was among those sporting their doctoral scarlet. He soon warmed to the new vice-chancellor as a kindred spirit. On 19 October, for example he confided to the Diary: 'The present V-C seems to dislike public speaking almost as much as I do'. By then, however, he was feeling pressured by the multiple commitments that fell on him as secretary to the Council. On 4 November he mentioned the Monday morning meeting – for the first time in irritable terms:

> 11. Council. I thought everybody seems rather cantankerous, but perhaps it is only that I have myself an attack of the nerves. I am feeling rather oppressed. ... Mother to dinner. She is rather inclined to complain that we (i.e. Florence and I) are now so busy that we neglect our social duties. Perhaps we do.

But worse was to come. On 13 November the vice-chancellor had a bicycle accident that temporarily immobilized him and magnified the direct responsibilities of the Council's secretary. According to the Diary: 'Mrs Smith writes to me at once. I go to see her and the Provost of King's to decide on a plan of campaign'. To Neville's great relief, Austen Leigh (the previous incumbent) agreed to accept appointment as deputy vice-chancellor. Meanwhile: 'Mrs C. Smith is going about saying the most extravagant things of the help I have been to them. She has borne up well but she is in a very excitable state'. The provost was not willing to act for more than two weeks, however, and on Friday 29 November a weary secretary was taking the Master of St John's (Charles Taylor who had been vice-chancellor in 1886) through the details of the next Monday's Council agenda.

Charles Smith was back in the chair at the first 1896 Council meeting – in spite of Neville's gloomy prediction (after briefing him on the Council agenda the previous Saturday): 'It does not seem to me that he will be able to do much work this term'. The early Council meetings of the Lent term were always comparatively heavy but at the meeting on 3 February a major controversial issue arose which was to haunt the agenda for the next five terms. It was triggered by a private meeting of dons sympathetic to the women's cause, called by Peile at Christ's Lodge on 7 December, to consider the question of women's degrees. Keynes, according to his Diary: 'spoke in favour of the titular degree only – with certain privileges. The decision was to memorialize the Council to nominate a Syndicate to consider the question and report – all details (membership of the Senate etc) to be left to the Syndicate'. Inevitably the composition of the Syndicate (which had to be validated by the Senate) proved an extremely divisive issue. Very reluctantly Keynes allowed his name to be included on a provisional list agreed by the Council on 24 February whilst noting apprehensively in the Diary: 'So far as we have gone the Syndicate is no doubt too one-sided (on the advanced side). Austen Leigh and [A.R.] Forsyth are very angry'. The following day after an angry discussion in the Senate, he joined Peile, Sidgwick, Jackson and Wright at another private meeting in Christ's Lodge to talk over the problems of composing a generally acceptable Women's Syndicate. Keynes anxiously tried to avoid nomination, but since his name attracted minimal resentment he stood little chance of escape. 'Florence is angry with me for having allowed my name to be voted upon' he groaned to the Diary, 'The whole thing worries me'. Indeed, for the rest of that Lent term the 'Woman Question' recurred in heated college combination room arguments as well as on the Council agenda. The Diary for 7 March reported wearily: 'The *Cambridge Review* criticizes the Women's Syndicate, on the ground (1) of its antiquity, and (2) that there is an excessive number of members of Council'. At a Senate congregation on 12 March another list of members proposed by the Council was defeated by 186 votes to 171 and Neville confessed: 'I feel rather upset about it but rather as a member of the Council than as a member of the rejected Syndicate'. The battle was resumed at successive Council meetings in the Easter term until, at a congregation on 4 June, a revised list of names (still including Keynes) passed through the Senate without opposition.

The next Council election was scheduled for November 1896 and, characteristically, Neville discounted his prospects of being re-elected. Liberal Council members such as Wright, Jackson and Forsyth assured him that he was indispensable and on 26 October the full liberal caucus sent MacAlister to persuade him to accept their nomination. 'The election is rather on my mind', he confided to the Diary on 27 October, adding 'I understand that an anti-women caucus is to be held on Thursday'. As it turned out, however, the conservative 'ticket' was identical to the liberal 'ticket' except that it included the Master of John's instead of the Master of Downing. On election day (7 November) Neville suffered an 'attack of megrims of the worst kind'. His anxiety was misplaced, for, as he wrote later, the conservative caucus had 'agreed not to oppose me on the grounds that I was indispensable to the Council'. On this occasion his tally of votes was exceeded only by such academic heavyweights as the Provost of King's, the Master of St John's and Jebb (then Regius Professor of Greek and Member of Parliament for Cambridge). The new Council met on 9 November to indulge in a stormy meeting. Peile, the longest-serving member of them all, judged it a poor substitute for its predecessor, 'the best working Council he had ever known'. There is no doubt that the 'Woman Question' – fraught as it was by conflicting ethical and atavistic undercurrents – continued to sour relationships between responsible members of the university. The Syndicate issued questionnaires to collect evidence and opinions from university teachers, college tutors, headmasters and mistresses, and other interested parties in the October term; and in the Lent term published its report recommending the formal award of degrees to women qualifying for honours without granting full undergraduate status to women students. Given the strength of the feeling against women in the university this seemed a suitably cautious compromise. Meanwhile, the Report was publicly debated in the national press and the *Cambridge Daily News* as well as formally by members of the Senate at three crowded congregations – on Saturday 13, Monday 15 and Tuesday 16 March 1897. Maitland's speech on the Saturday, according to the Diary was 'extraordinarily brilliant' and on Monday Neville judged that, on the whole, 'the speaking maintained a high level of excellence'. He did not himself speak, but on 12 May, after the second of two further campaign meetings of the pro-women committee, he undertook 'to write a good many letters' to prod voters in a liberal direction.

Voting on the Council's recommendations was postponed until the last term of the academic year. The opposition proved both numerous and hostile – cheered on, as it was, by the rabble of undergraduate poll men as well as most of the popular press. On 15 May, after a meeting of Newnham College Council, of which he and Peile were both members, Keynes confessed to the Diary:

> There is I think no doubt that Mrs Sidgwick feels regret (as Florence and I do) that the Women's Degree question has been raised. The outlook is not very pleasant whatever the result of the voting next Friday. The Master of Christ's [Peile] is suffering badly from insomnia. Many moderate supporters (especially tutors) are alarmed at the atttitude taken by the undergraduates and it must be in many ways disagreeable for the women's colleges.

At the Council of the Senate on 17 May, according to the Diary: 'Sidgwick raises the question as to withdrawing from the fight on Friday. He feels very much depressed about the result. I oscillated in my view and felt much worried.' Later that day at another meeting at Christ's College: 'there was a very strong feeling for going on with the fight'. What supporters of the women's cause seem not to have reckoned with was the excited army of non-resident MAs who were only too ready to turn up at the Senate House in order to vote against any radical change in the exclusivity of their *alma mater*. On 21 May Neville recorded with bitter brevity: 'Vote on the question of titular degrees for women. It is no use attempting a description of the scene. Placet 662. Non-placet 1713'.[21] Meanwhile, provoked by the publication of an ill-informed letter to the editor of *The Times*, Keynes despatched an authoritative correction. He was infuriated by a dismissive response on 24 May to the effect that: 'The Editor regrets that your letter which reached him today is now out of date and that he cannot find room for a continuation of a controversy about the Grace for titles of degrees for women which was rejected on Friday'. The issue of degrees for women was thus effectively killed at Cambridge until after the First World War. Indeed, the Council's recommendation to admit women to titular degrees and membership of the university did not pass the Senate until half a century after its comprehensive defeat in 1897.

The other troublesome issue that encouraged wrangles among the more cantankerous Council members during Charles Smith's stint as vice-chancellor was what action, if any, the university should take to influence legislation arising out of the Royal Commission on Secondary Education that had reported in August 1895. Given his long experience on the Local Examinations and Lectures Syndicate, as well as a spell on the Teacher Training Syndicate (in the late 1880s), Keynes had special expertise on questions of secondary education and teacher training and his informed advice carried due weight. In his retrospective review of the Council's decisions over the academic year 1895/96 the vice-chancellor reported to the Senate on 2 October 1896:

> By a Grace which passed the Senate on December 12 I was authorised to invite on behalf of the University, representatives of the chief educational authorities and institutions in England to meet at Cambridge in order to confer on questions arising out of the Report of the Commission on Secondary Education. The Council appointed a Committee to arrange the necessary details and the conference was held in the Senate House on April 21 and 22.[22]

21. See McWilliams-Tullberg (1975), for a vivid description of the scene as well as details of the campaign leading up to the 1897 vote and beyond.
22. *CUR*, 2 October 1896, p. 6.

Inevitably Keynes was put on the organizing committee and nominated as the university's official representative at the conference, which attracted more than 200 participants qualified to speak with authority on educational questions. He also drafted the set of crucial resolutions that were discussed and put to the vote at this nationally representative assembly. The consensus which emerged, and was deliberately designed to influence government legislation on secondary education, approved the main recommendations of the 1895 Royal Commission whilst offering a constructive critique of two Bills (relating to the educational registration of teachers) which were then under consideration by the House of Commons. A full report on the conference was published by Cambridge University Press and the two Bills were subsequently withdrawn by the government – an outcome which gave credibility to the vice-chancellor's assurance that 'the proceedings of the Conference will not fail to exert considerable influence when legislation with regard to secondary education again occupies the attention of the Government'.[23] A few weeks later, the Council reported that a Memorial – listing the resolutions 'submitted at the conference and agreed to either *nemine contradicente* or by a very large majority' – had been presented on behalf of the university to the Duke of Devonshire as Lord President of the Privy Council. The resolutions put great stress on the need for professional training and registration of secondary school teachers.[24] Nevertheless it took several years before these representations began to be reflected in legislation. Lord Salisbury's government introduced a Teachers' Registration Bill in 1898, but did not find time to carry it into law. The 1899 Board of Education Act gave the Board's Consultative Advisory Committee the task of forming and maintaining a register of qualified teachers, and it was not until 1902 that a Teachers' Registration Council was set up.

The major problem which recurred with increasing frequency and urgency in Council discussions during the last decade of the nineteenth century was that posed by the university's limited financial resources. In the 1880s and early 1890s, most members of Council were still largely college-orientated in their approach to the university's financial problems. For example, when Searle (Master of Pembroke) retired on 1 October 1889, he expressed the sentiment of the majority on the Council in his final speech to the Senate:

> While fully sympathising with the General Board of Studies in their desire for adequate provision for the teaching of the subjects under their care by the appointment of additional Readers, Lecturers and Demonstrators, as well as of suitable buildings and material appliances for carrying on their work, I am nevertheless strongly persuaded that the revenues of the Colleges cannot meet these require-

23. *CUR*, 24 November 1896, p. 10.
24. *CUR*, 24 November 1896, p. 35.

> ments, and that the incidence of the present contribution is already so oppressive that means must be found from other sources for supplying the present needs of the University.[25]

Clearly the colleges were then either unwilling or unable to part with funds on a scale sufficient to finance the schemes designed by boards of studies with a view to improving the range and quality of teaching and research in the disciplines they were concerned to promote. Not all the colleges were poor, of course, and there were a few dons who were willing and able to back their ambitions for the wider university community by supplementing the limited resources of the university with personal donations. H.M. Butler, Master of Trinity (Searle's successor as vice-chancellor), announced at the end of his first year in office, in October 1890, for example: 'At a moment when it seemed doubtful whether the proposed new building for Physiology could be erected simultaneously with the building for Human Anatomy, Dr Sidgwick came forward with a timely gift of £1500 that enabled a much needed work to proceed'.[26] Given the regressive system of taxation imposed by the 1882 statute revisions, the plight of the 'financially depressed' colleges continued to be a live issue on the Council. Significantly, in 1890/91 when the Council proposed a Statute to grant relief to the poorest colleges by reducing their annual rate of contribution it was defeated by the opposition of ten of the relatively rich colleges who had no intention of footing the bill.

Before the end of Neville's first quinquennium as Council secretary, however, it was plain that the scale of the shortfall in the university's financial resources had risen beyond the point at which a 'timely gift' of one or two thousand pounds could make a difference to the policy problems faced by its governing body. As the number of students admitted by colleges continued to grow and as boards of studies expanded the range of academic subjects in their honours examinations, the university was faced with intolerable pressure on the small stock of buildings and personnel at the disposal of the central administration. There were acute shortages of teaching officers, lecture rooms, laboratory space, examination and business rooms. Even the Council had to meet in rooms borrowed from colleges or from Syndicates that were also short of space, so that its secretary spent a great deal of time renegotiating such provisional arrangements. Moreover, the fact that the number of students reading for the natural sciences tripos had recently been

25. *CUR*, 1 October 1889, p. 6. When the Cambridge commissioners drew up their schedule of taxes, whereby the colleges were to supply funds for university purposes from 1882 onwards, they imposed a flat rate which fell with particular severity on poor colleges. By contrast in Oxford the scale was graduated. See *Report of the Royal Commission on Oxford and Cambridge*, Cmd 1588 (1922), p. 23.
26. *CUR*, 2 October 1890, p. 34.

rising faster than for any other honours examination meant that a shortage of essential expensive equipment was exacerbating inter-faculty frictions over the distribution of resources. In effect, every scheme to improve the quality or extend the range of university teaching or research services was inhibited by the need either to divert funds from other worthy activities, or to raise funds from external sources.

The central funding problem was first confronted squarely in 1897. In his address to the Senate on 1 October Charles Smith, Master of Sidney Sussex, the retiring vice-chancellor, reported a

> largely attended meeting … held in the Lodge of Trinity College to which all the principal officers of the University together with the representatives of the different colleges were invited. It was resolved at this meeting that steps should be taken to lay a statement concerning the financial conditions and requirements of the University before the members of the University and the public generally. A careful statement of the resources of the University and of the urgent need of many new buildings and also of considerable additions to our Teaching Staff was accordingly drawn up, and was published in all the leading newspapers with an introductory letter of his Grace the Duke of Devonshire, Chancellor of the University. It is hoped that by this means the erroneous but widespread belief that the University is a very wealthy body may be dispelled. … It cannot be too strongly emphasized that what we require at the present time is not so much donations for the founding of special prizes and scholarships, as benefactions for general purposes.

He went on to welcome the first such untied benefaction – £2000 in four instalments (one of which had already been received) – from an anonymous friend of A.J. Balfour.[27]

Inspired by the collaborative exercise of defining and costing the university's most urgent requirements and fired by the prospects of attracting external resources to fund these aims, members of the three overlapping governing bodies – the Council, the General Board of Studies and the Financial Board – developed a shared ethos. The prime objective was to create at Cambridge a national university generating a stream of 'thoroughly educated men' and providing the essential facilities for advanced scientific research. As a working member of two of these bodies, Keynes – who had been elected to the General Board from January 1898 and whose administrative responsibilities at the Local Examinations and Lectures Syndicate had stretched over a decade and a half – was himself wholly committed to the idea of Cambridge University's national role. From the late 1890s, the formal end-year speeches of vice-chancellors regularly commented on

27. *CUR*, 2 October 1897, p. 5. A.J. Balfour – a Trinity MA and brother of Eleanor Sidgwick – was an influential friend of Cambridge. He became prime minister from 1902–06 and chancellor to the university in 1917.

the outcome of what became an ongoing appeal for funds to promote the general purposes of the university. Although the Financial Board seized every opportunity to acquire central and inexpensive land, wherever available, public funding was slow to materialize on the scale needed for major building projects. In October 1898, for example, Vice-Chancellor A. Hill, Master of Downing, reported:

> The admirable and central sites which have been purchased by the University during the last 3 years are still entirely unoccupied although many departments of the University are either overcrowded or inadequately housed; but at the desire of our Chancellor steps have been taken which may it is hoped bring in the funds for the erection of buildings which are urgently required. A very influential committee of University men has been formed for the purpose of organizing a 'Cambridge University Association' the members of which will be kept informed of and will be pledged to make known the needs of the University.

It was not that Cambridge lacked generously loyal *alumni* but that their allegiance attached to their colleges, or academic disciplines, rather than to the nebulous idea of a university. Accordingly, after acknowledging the most recent benefactions and gifts, including a handsome bequest of £10,000 for the establishment of a scholarship or prize, Hill reiterated the crucial message: 'at the present time there is a greater need for the endowment of teaching posts and the provision of buildings for University purposes than for the encouragement and stimulation of students'.[28]

By the beginning of the twentieth century, limited progress had been made on the teaching front. Five new university lecturers were appointed in subjects on which no teaching had hitherto been officially provided (that is, agricultural chemistry, bacteriology and preventive medicine, ethnology, physical anthropology and Russian); and Syndicates had been appointed to prepare plans for the Botany School, the Law School and Library, the Medical School, a new Museum of Archaeology and of Ethnology, and new buildings for the University Press. According to W. Chawner, Master of Emmanuel, speaking at the end of his first year as vice-chancellor:

> Many subjects are taught inadequately, or not at all, for lack of means to pay the stipends of the Professors, Readers or Lecturers required. Of the teachers whom we have, no Reader receives the full stipend of £400 from the University; and many University Lecturers who hold no fellowship have to be content with the minimum stipend of £50 per annum, which is only a recognition and not in any sense a remuneration of their work.[29]

28. *CUR*, 4 October 1898, p. 9.
29. *CUR*, 2 October 1900, p. 11.

In 1903/04, for example, the Senate approved proposals for the new economics tripos when the only university-appointed teacher on the core subject was Alfred Marshall, the professor, who paid (out of his own pocket) a lecturer's annual stipend of £100 to Pigou. It was not until June that the Worshipful Company of Girdlers offered its grant of £100 a year over three years to pay a university lecturer to teach economics for the tripos. That was the year when the Financial Board calculated that the university's expenditure would exceed its income by about £1800 even before taking account of the £20,000 needed to complete new buildings. The shortfall had to be financed by taking out a loan. 1903/04 was also the year when the King and Queen paid a formal visit to Cambridge, the first visit to the university by a reigning sovereign for 56 years. On that occasion, Edward VII encouraged the Cambridge Association's fundraising efforts by affirming: 'the older Universities must receive new endowments if education within my realm is to be kept at its proper standard of efficiency'. On the other hand, nobody – inside or outside the university – suggested that government might contribute to these much needed endowments. That had to await a revolution in the climate of ideas precipitated by the First World War. Before the year 1919, no state aid was given to either Cambridge or Oxford – apart from the small sums paid by government departments (such as the Boards of Education or Agriculture or the War Office or the India Office) in return for specific teaching or examining activities supported by those departments.

By 1903, Neville Keynes had been the Council's secretary for a decade, actively participating in the process by which an evolving concern for the university's role as a national institution ensured that its central administration would effectively override its collegiate counterparts. In these circumstances, it reads curiously that, for three or four weeks early in 1903, Keynes apparently contemplated the possibility of being elected Master at Pembroke where he had ceased to be a fellow over twenty years earlier. Searle – Master since 1883 – had fallen seriously ill at the beginning of 1902. Since resigning as fellow Neville had developed a cordial relationship with his old tutor. On 3 May, after visiting the invalid at Pembroke Lodge, he wrote gloomily: 'I could not understand what he said. It is very sad to see him so ill. I owe a great deal to him'. When Searle died on 30 July 1902 he was smoothly succeeded by Sir George Stokes, an eminent theoretical physicist, whose Jubilee as Lucasian Professor of Mathematics had been proudly celebrated by the university in 1899. Unfortunately Stokes died just six months later and the Pembroke fellowship was abruptly confronted with the unexpected and unwelcome dilemma of making another choice. Whilst they deliberated in secret, wild rumours flew around Cambridge. After lunching with his mother on 10 February 1903, an amused Neville reported that she was 'rather excited because people have been talking to her about the appropriateness of my being elected Master of Pembroke'. There was then no obvious candidate apart from the senior tutor, W.S. Hadley, whom Neville himself regarded as a suitable choice. 'There are, however, rumours of a hitch', he wrote on 11 February, 'I wish I could find out what is going on'. Five days later he noted his mother's opinion that 'I should be elected Master … if I were not a nonconformist. No doubt my nonconformism is a final bar'. By 18 February he confessed himself in 'rather a state of excitement', which recurred in early March when he copied into his Diary a paragraph from the *Educational Times* to the effect that 'Dr Keynes is undoubtedly the strongest member of the College but his work has for many years been outside the College walls'. When it was eventually announced that an outsider from the fellowship – the Reverend Professor A.J. Mason – had been elected, Neville commented sourly on 10 March:

> He is I am afraid not a man with whom I shall feel particularly cordial but I must do my best. Of course they would never elect me and yet there is just a faint tinge of disappointment now that the question is settled. The whole situation makes me regret Neil's death more than ever.[30]

It was of course inconceivable that an ancient Anglican college with the traditional Cambridge reverence for the disciplines of mathematics and classics, would have been ready in the early 1900s to elect a nonconformist moral scientist as its head. It is equally hard to believe that Keynes would have chosen to be nominated in the mastership election, since his own interests and ambitions were firmly located in the university administrative service – which occupied most of his working hours, either as chief secretary to the Local Examinations Syndicate or as unpaid Secretary and member of the Council. Vice-chancellor after vice-chancellor had gratefully acknowledged that his advice and direct participation had been vital to the efficient operation of the university's supreme governing body. So, when the Council tried to pre-empt the possibility of yet another Royal Commission being appointed to modernize the two ancient English universities – by setting up its own Syndicate 'to consider what changes if any are desirable in the studies, teaching and examinations of the University, to confer with any persons or bodies and to submit a Report or Reports before the end of the Easter Term 1904' – Keynes was obviously a key member of this body.

On 30 September 1905, E.A. Beck, Master of Trinity Hall – one of the most perceptive and articulate of the vice-chancellors whom Keynes had initiated into what had become a complex and difficult office – surprised the

30. R.A. Neil, Senior Classicist in 1875, was a friend and contemporary of Keynes at Pembroke to which they had both been elected fellows in 1876. He died in 1901 from appendicitis and would certainly have been the most popular choice for Master of the college after Stokes.

audience at his first end-year speech as vice-chancellor with the following pointed reference to the Council's secretary:

> But there is one man in particular who does a burdensome and inconspicuous task with a quite phenomenal grasp of principles and of details, and with a lucid order that seems almost automatic. I do not think it is acceptable to us that this secretarial work of the Council, which is quite exceptional in amount, should remain without some substantial or public recognition. Nor is it wise. I know Dr Keynes will be annoyed with me when he reads this and that he likes to work for love. But it is always precarious to get work done for love. It is but once in a way that you will find a man who from pure sense of duty and passion for labour will so long do for nothing a work that is worth so much.[31]

Neville himself did not attend the formal annual occasion at which the speech was delivered, believing that – as usual – he already knew its content. On first reading the unexpected passage he reacted with a mixture of gratification and irritation. On 4 October he admitted to the Diary: 'I am of course pleased at these appreciative words; but I should not at all like that this particular piece of work should be paid. I feel that its character would be altered'. The truth was that the work of the secretary was continuously shifting and expanding in ways that he was concerned to control. The effect, for example, of putting him on the new Studies and Examinations Syndicate – with the widest possible brief for exploring and proposing reforms to improve the quality and efficiency of the university's educational system – was to add substantially to his (as well as the vice-chancellor's) workload. Vice-chancellors, however, escaped at the end of a gruelling two-year stint; the Council's secretary had to initiate each new vice-chancellor into the delicate problems of reconciling faculty special interests and ancient academic prejudices so as to facilitate a progressive and orderly improvement in educational practice. At the end of his first year as vice-chancellor, Beck reminded the Senate of its three days fruitlessly discussing the 'Greek Question', which led to rejection of the Council's proposals to drop the requirement of Greek as a universal entry qualification. He went on to speak with passion against the 'one-sidedness' of those who were intolerant of change:

> Life and knowledge are so complex that an educated man cannot be brought up on Science alone, any more than on Literature alone. But it is the Mind of Man as a whole that is our charge: the history of its concentration, expansion and elevation; its imaginings and foreshadowings and its infinite aspirations. … The aim of a University must be comprehensive and must be humanising. … Without a tolerant union between apparently conflicting interests, I believe that hardly any man and no nation and certainly no great National University can long live greatly.[32]

31. *CUR*, 2 October 1905, p. 29.
32. Ibid., pp. 29–30.

Twelve months later, in his retirement address, he grimly dismissed the matter of reform by announcing:

> [O]n the grave of that [Syndicate] called 'Studies and Examinations', the summer having been as dry as the subject, the grass has not yet grown; and lest that Syndicate should rise and kill my successor as, seriously, it has nearly killed me, I will pass by on the other side.[33]

Beck's warning that the Council was exploiting its secretary, apparently fell on deaf ears. Given the university's chronic shortage of funds and the fact that the secretary himself clearly regarded his unpaid office as a challenge and a privilege from which he had no intention of resigning, the lack of response was predictable. When E.S. Roberts (Master of Caius who took over as vice-chancellor in October 1906), assumed some of the secretary's workload, his efforts were certainly not appreciated. On 6 May 1907, Keynes grumbled to his Diary: 'The late V.C. handed over to me the work he should have done. The present V.C. on the other hand tries to do too much himself and does not do it well'. A year later he repeated the criticism – this time after a particularly troublesome General Board meeting: 'I think the V.C. is partly to blame for having tried to arrange everything himself before coming to the General Board'. Plainly, the secretary was glad to regain the full weight of his personal influence on the Council when Roberts gave way to the new vice-chancellor, A.J. Mason, Master of Pembroke. 'I welcome the change of regime', he confessed with relief on 1 October 1908. Fortunately, he had by then acquired a positively cordial relationship with the head of his own college whose election he had noted so grudgingly five years previously.[34] So, although Mason was frequently absent in Canterbury on ecclesiastical business during the vacations, leaving Keynes to deal with the vice-chancellor's official correspondence and to take sole responsibility for drawing up the Council's agenda, the latter cheerfully accepted the resultant increase in his personal load. When the vice-chancellor expressed his gratitude (in his retiring address to the Senate on 1 October 1910) it was in terms which nicely reflected their joint roles in dealing with a complicated administrative system:

> Above all I thank the Secretary of the Council, Dr Keynes, for help and advice such as only his experience and sagacity could supply. Scarcely a day has passed

33. *CUR*, 2 October 1906, p. 40.
34. It took some time for cordiality to prevail. Keynes, who had successfully negotiated the Council's use of Pembroke Lodge as its meeting place in 1902/03, was at first incensed by the new Master's insistence on taking over his Lodge forthwith in March 1903 – thus showing (according to the Diary) 'a great want of consideration for the University'. In December 1904, the Diary was again critical – this time in relation to Mason's stance on 'the Greek Question' which was currently a bitter source of dissension between a would-be reforming Council and a reactionary Senate.

> without my seeking his help and whenever I have sought it he has given it with a smile, as if he had nothing else to attend to.[35]

During the first decade of the twentieth century, the Council and General Board presided over a series of piecemeal improvements in the quality and range of the education and research facilities available in Cambridge and a marked expansion in the numbers taught or examined. Nevertheless, given the vision and idealism of the leading academics who aspired to transform the university into a modern national institution of higher learning, as well as the amount of time and argument devoted to more fundamental or general reforms, the progress achieved was pathetically limited. True, there were significant additions to the Cavendish Laboratories and the University Library, for example, made possible by Lord Rayleigh's gift of his Nobel prize; a few much-needed new examination halls, lecture rooms and central administrative offices were built; there was a trickle of new appointments to the thinly spread cadre of university teaching officers; there were modest annual improvements in tripos or diploma or school exam options alongside an appreciable increase in the numbers of students and examinees (internal and external) involved at Cambridge.[36] Nevertheless, after the failure of the Studies and Examinations Syndicate – which had 'nearly killed' at least one vice-chancellor – concern for the 'reformation of the University' seems briefly to have subsided – as did the threat of a Royal Commission. Then, early in 1908, the Diary reported a 'meeting at [A.E.] Shipley's. Can we agree on a plan of reform?' Two weeks later, on 10 February, three new reform committees were set to work, the most crucial of which dealt with the constitution and government of the university and became a major preoccupation for Keynes over the next two to three years.

The fundamental obstacle to radical reform in the university, as we have seen, was the statutory requirement for each proposal to be approved by a Senate which included an army of non-resident MAs who could readily be summoned to vote against any change that conflicted with traditional prejudices – such as the admission of women to undergraduate status, the abolition of compulsory Greek in the Previous examination, or the admission of a Roman Catholic Hostel (St Edmund's House) to college status. In 1910, for example, the Council's conservatively formulated Report to the Senate on the Constitution and Government of the University was successively submitted, rejected, amended and resubmitted in diluted form. At no point was it possi-

35. *CUR*, 3 October 1910, p. 45.
36. The number of matriculated male undergraduates and women students in residence at Cambridge rose from about 3100 in 1900 to about 4000 in 1912, that is, by almost 30 per cent. See *Report of the Royal Commission on Oxford and Cambridge* (1922), p. 27. The numbers had been virtually static over the previous decade.

ble to carry the crucial change which would have limited the voting constituency to the resident members of the university and colleges who were directly responsible for teaching, research or administration. At last, in 1914, with the outbreak of the First World War questions of the long-term reformation of Cambridge University's constitution lost their immediate urgency and Keynes was finally freed from the time-consuming task of drafting and redrafting Council reports which were doomed to be rejected by the Senate's irresponsible non-residents. It was not until 1919 that the road to reform was reopened by the formation of a Royal Commission which reported in 1922.[37] Meanwhile, before the war began, the anomalous situation of the unpaid secretary to the Council had been unobtrusively rectified by combining that office with the permanent paid post of registrary to the university.

The university registrary whom Keynes succeeded in 1910 was John Willis Clark, a 77-year-old non-teaching, non-specialist don whose seniority in the University hierarchy of officials owed more to his having always been in the right place at the right time than to his scholastic record or administrative efficiency. Born in Cambridge in 1833, he was the son of the professor of comparative anatomy (the Reverend William Clark) and the nephew of another professor, Robert Willis, who had held the chair of applied mechanics since 1837 and became posthumously famous as the principal author of a famous architectural history of the University. J.W. Clark was schooled at Eton and graduated from Trinity College in 1856 with a low first in the classical tripos. He applied for, and won, a Trinity fellowship in 1858, a year in which there was an abnormally large number of vacancies open to competition. His first university appointment, in 1866, was as superintendent of the Museum of Comparative Anatomy, where he had already deputized over four years for his ailing father. It was a post that was soon conveniently consolidated with superintendent of the Museum of Zoology and secretary to the Museums and Lecture Rooms Syndicate. When Robert Willis died in 1875 he bequeathed to his nephew his massive unfinished manuscript and J.W. Clark won well-deserved credit for completing the *Architectural History of the University of Cambridge and its Colleges* which was published, in four volumes, by the University Press in 1886.[38] Whilst riding on that credit he accepted an invitation from Professor T.M. Hughes to collaborate with him in editing the geologist Adam Sedgwick's *Life and Letters*. By the time the post of registrary came up for election in

37. The war created a financial crisis in all the universities, which could not be resolved without state aid, and in 1919 both Cambridge and Oxford were given provisional grants of £30,000 annually on the assumption that they would cooperate fully with the inevitable Royal Commission.

38. He is said to have checked and amended, where necessary, this massive manuscript which Robert Willis had worked on from 1854 to 1875. Among Clark's notable additions was an architectural history of his old school – Eton.

1891, Clark was a familiar Cambridge character, generally perceived as a reliable, hard-working member of the academic community and on affable terms with most members of the relevant electoral roll.

The registrary – who commanded the university's central administrative headquarters (the Registry) – was its highest-paid official drawing a stipend exceeding that of most professors.[39] It was an appointment that was crucially important without being intellectually demanding. His principal statutory duty was 'to keep an accurate record of the proceedings of the University, to place in the Registry in due order of arrangement all letters, writings and documents delivered to him by the Chancellor and by all concerned in the University with knowledge of past transactions'. For these purposes he was expected to officiate at all congregations of the Senate, the courts of the Chancellor, the audits of university accounts, matriculations and all public proceedings of the university; he was also keeper and codifier of the university archives, he promulgated all university notices and played a leading part at royal and other public occasions of a ceremonial or disciplinary nature. In the 1890s the registrary was assisted in his many recordkeeping and clerical duties by a registry staff which consisted of an assistant registrary and a registrary's clerk. During the first decade of the twentieth century when the number of students rose by more than a quarter it became necessary to add an additional registry clerk. In a memoir published in 1911, Montagu James, Provost of King's, Clark's contemporary and friend, described the latter's distinctive approach to his duties as registrary:

> The work of the post was in many ways congenial; it brought Clark into contact with the whole of the personnel of the University and it gave him a voice in the arrangement of ceremonies and 'functions' which appealed to his instinct for stage-management. Much was also required of him in the way of codifying university regulations and investigations of records. Of the numerous publications issued by Clark as Registrary the most important is probably an edition of the 'University Endowments' which appeared in 1904. ... In university politics he was a liberal and a fiery supporter of every cause which he took up. His quickness of temper and freedom of expression involved him in many somewhat acute personal controversies; but the geniality which was his leading characteristic seldom allowed a quarrel to develop into an enmity.[40]

There are relatively few references to Clark in the Diary. They suggest that contacts between him and Keynes were always officially rather than socially

39. Most professors had salaries of £500 or less. Even the Cavendish Professor drew only £650 in the early 1890s.
40. *Dictionary of National Biography*, 2nd Supplement, p. 361. See also Christopher Brooke's reference to J.W. Clark as 'up to his elbows in every good cause in the University, lively, quixotic, irascible, universally loved', in *History of the University of Cambridge*, Vol. IV (Cambridge: Cambridge University Press, 1993), p. 590.

motivated and usually coloured by the fact that the registrary resented the Council's attempts to assert its control over the Registry or indeed over any department of the university in which he took a personal interest – including the Library (of which he was a Syndic). In February 1897, for example, Keynes was one of a committee of three set up by the Council to consider the duties of the staff of the Registry; the other two members were the Master of Christ's and the Provost of King's. After a series of stormy meetings the Diary reported irritably on 22 February that the Council 'was involved in a troublesome conflict with the Registrary'. There was an even more disapproving reference to Clark in March 1899 when Keynes reported an 'extraordinary interview with the Registrary', and concluded that: 'one can only regard him as a spoilt child with an ungovernable temper'. Then, suddenly, in December 1908, Clark's wife – to whom he had been happily married for 35 years – died and 'inflicted a shock from which he never recovered'.[41]

It was probably at some point within the next year that Keynes began to consider the possibility of succeeding Clark as registrary. It was not, however, until December 1909 that he referred to the matter in the Diary: 'There seems every probability that there will be a vacancy in the Registraryship and it makes me feel rather unsettled'. It seems that for most of 1909 the registrary had been so depressed as to render him barely competent to head his department. In these circumstances, responsible members of Council had evidently indicated that they favoured combining the two jobs when the expected vacancy arose. On 27 January, 1910, after noting that the registrary was unlikely to recover, Keynes worried characteristically to the Diary:

> If he could only hold on for 18 months or so his successor wd probably be appointed by the Council and that wd suit me well. Bond thinks that even with the Senate as an Elective Body no one has a chance against me and I believe Mollison [Secretary to the General Board] takes the same view – but I have my fears.

Meanwhile B. Benham, the deputy registrary, was already reporting daily to Keynes from January 1910 onwards and even Clark may have seen Keynes as his likely successor; for on 7 February the Diary records that 'J.W. Clark has written to ask me to call to see him. But Mrs Edward Clark [daughter-in-law] tells me that the doctor will not allow it'. Although too ill to act during the rest of that academic year, Clark did not formally resign until 1 October, though he gave notice of intent in mid-September – allowing Keynes to write almost a thousand letters to his friends calling for their support in the forthcoming election. In the event, after four weeks of hectic campaigning, an unnecessarily agitated Keynes was formally nominated by the Master of

41. According to the memoir by Montagu James, *Dictionary of National Biography*.

Pembroke for the office of registrary on 11 October. There were no other candidates. On 12 October he recorded in the Diary: 'I was elected Registrary without opposition. It is delightful the extreme cordiality with which my election appears to be received by everybody'. On 13 October he was inducted as registrary between the 1.45 Council meeting and the 2 p.m. congregation; at 3 p.m. that afternoon, members of the Senate attended the funeral of J.W. Clark who had died on 10 October.

For Neville Keynes the promotion represented a major watershed in his career. There was a certain overlap between the duties of secretary to the Council and the registrary so that combining the two posts did not bring so much extra work as might have seemed likely. Indeed the presence of an executive registrary who did not sit on any of the policy-designing bodies, and hence never hesitated to resist Council proposals for reform, tended to increase the secretary's problems. On the other hand, the registrary was generally precluded from holding other paid offices. For Keynes the new appointment involved retiring from his secretaryship at the Local Examinations Syndicate (at the end of December 1910) and from his university lectureship in moral sciences (at the end of the 1910/11 academic year). On 4 November 1910 – in the midst of the busiest term of his life – he wrote happily: 'What a quiet haven the Registraryship is in comparison with the Local Exam^{ns} Secretaryship'. After rejoicing on 17 December: 'The last Locals for which I have had responsibility have come to an end without catastrophe', he left Syndicate Buildings on 31 December, somewhat sadly, but predicted 'I shall enjoy my work at the Registry even more'. Over the next nine months he found time to bring administrative operations at the Registry up to his own meticulous standards. On 20 May, for example, after dealing with 'many mistakes on the part of Tutors and Praelectors' nominating their pupils for degrees, he observed with some satisfaction that he was afraid he would soon be the most unpopular man in Cambridge. On 22 June, grandly decked out in academical robes and court dress, he thoroughly enjoyed occupying one of the three seats allocated to Cambridge University at the coronation of George V, and 'saw everything of importance except the crowning and part of the homage'. On returning from a continental holiday with Florence at the end of July 1911, he settled down contentedly to editing the new edition of the Ordinances and took over as sole editor of the *Cambridge University Reporter*. It was the beginning of a new way of life for Neville and a transformation in the role of the university's registrary.

J.N. Keynes (c. 1905)

VIII Faculty conflicts and tripos reform

1 REFORMING THE MORAL SCIENCES TRIPOS, 1885–97

The controversies over the reform of the moral sciences tripos that erupted in the late 1880s, and again in the 1890s, were exacerbated by the presence of two would-be reforming leaders on the Board – one holding the chair of philosophy and the other the chair of political economy. At the same time, most of the lecturers teaching under the Board's auspices had already defined their areas of specialization within the broad range of subjects defined as moral sciences, and did not welcome programme changes that might either limit their own choice of courses or add to their workload. Indeed, when Marshall returned to take up his Cambridge chair in 1885, Keynes was the only university lecturer at the disposal of the Board and hence the only member of its teaching team over whom it had full authority. The others – apart from Sidgwick (who gave the main courses on ethics and philosophy) and Cunningham (the History Board's university lecturer who lectured on political philosophy and economic history) – were all college employees. They included two teaching logic, John Venn (Caius) and T.W. Levin (St Catharine's); James Ward (Trinity) lecturing on psychology and metaphysics; and Foxwell (John's) who had taken over most of the economics teaching when Marshall left in 1877 – but refused to teach women.[1] As for Keynes, he had held his university lectureship for less than a year when the arrival of Alfred and Mary Marshall transformed the quality and quantity of Cambridge's teaching resources in political economy. It was plain that only the Indian Civil Service candidates would still need his economics lectures.[2] Yet so deeply entrenched was the moral scientists' traditional right to design their own teaching programmes that even Keynes was vexed by Sidgwick's directive to consider his lectureship as being in logic rather than in economics.

1. Since 1881, when Foxwell succeeded Jevons in the chair of political economy at University College London, he had acquired heavy teaching and examining duties there. It is therefore not surprising that he opted out of the relatively time-consuming obligations involved in teaching Cambridge women – many of whom were not destined for the tripos, but who made full use of the privilege of personal tuition offered by their lecturers.
2. ICS candidates were outside the normal obligations of a college lecturer – as were women students. JNK (without college teaching responsibilities) was contentedly accustomed to lecturing on both logic and political economy.

There were two episodes in the late 1880s and 1890s when questions of tripos reform preoccupied Cambridge moralists. One began in early 1888 and was resolved in 1889; the other began in February 1894 and led to new regulations formally approved by the university in 1897. Keynes was the Board's secretary throughout and became the channel that Marshall usually chose to broadcast his own views on tripos reform. Sidgwick raised the issue formally in February 1888 by circulating a set of suggestions for change. A letter from Marshall to Keynes (enclosing a testimonial for the Oxford professorship) contained the following aside on Sidgwick's proposals: 'I am writing a line to Sidgwick to tell him my chief objection to his scheme and to say that I wd gladly revert to ye Tripos of 1873, or something of the sort'.[3] Marshall's views on tripos reform were primarily concerned with developing the role of economics in the moral sciences curriculum. When he left Cambridge in 1877, political economy had been one of four equally-weighted subjects – the others were moral and political philosophy, logic, and mental philosophy. Whilst he was away, in 1883, a reform masterminded by Sidgwick had divided the tripos into two parts, either of which could qualify for an honours degree. Part I contained, in addition to the original list of four examination subjects, two others (metaphysics and general philosophical essays) and permitted candidates to choose five out of the six. Candidates for Part II could specialize in two subjects out of the following six: advanced political economy; advanced logic; advanced psychology and psychophysics, and three areas in the history of philosophical thought. The effect, of course, was to increase the range and importance of philosophical subjects in the tripos.

Marshall's major objection to this pattern of options was not that candidates for the moral sciences tripos could bypass economics altogether. It was that it encouraged an unsystematic and superficial treatment of economic theory in Part I with the result that final year students attending his lectures on advanced economic theory were often inadequately schooled on basic principles. In a letter to Keynes on 18 February, for example, he announced: 'I am increasingly of the opinion that a short study of Political Economy seldom does much good and not infrequently does much harm. It is not till a man is about to take his degree that his work at economics generally becomes of any substantial value'.[4] Marshall then offered his own plan, which he invited Keynes to show 'to Sidgwick or any other member of the Board'. This plan combined advanced political economy with statistics, sidelined the early (pre-Adam Smith) history of economic thought (one of Foxwell's interests)

3. Letter printed in full in J.K. Whitaker, *The Correspondence of Alfred Marshall, Economist* (Cambridge: Cambridge University Press, 1996), Vol. I, p. 259.
4. Ibid., p. 260.

and was destined to attract lukewarm support, if not outright dissent, from the economists on the Board.

Sidgwick's proposals were discussed by the Moral Sciences Board at its meeting on 29 February 1888 and again on 28 April and revised for the meeting on 15 May when Sidgwick (seconded by Cunningham) moved to make the study of philosophy, including metaphysics, compulsory. The Board deadlocked on this occasion. Marshall had already expressed outrage at a scheme, 'in every way bad', which permitted candidates 'to take Part II on Moral and Metaphysical Philosophy alone without extending a similar grace to other subjects'.[5] In April he openly envisaged totally detaching political economy from the moral sciences tripos; for example, he concluded a letter to Keynes by asserting:

> I would rather see PE turned out of the MSc Tripos altogether than have the Tripos so manipulated as to cause the greater part of the students for it to give their third year – the only time when they are at all fit to see the bearing of economic questions – exclusively to Philosophy.[6]

Keynes's Diary reported the explosive Board meeting of 15 May with weary brevity:

> Meeting of the Moral Sciences Board to discuss proposed changes in the Tripos. The conflict of opinion between Sidgwick and Marshall takes a form that is very painful to other members of the Board. The question now is whether we shall put compulsory metaphysics into Part I (Marshall) or into Part II (Sidgwick). 3 voted for the former, 3 for the latter and 3 (including myself) did not vote. The question will be raised again at our next meeting.

The Diary does not explain Keynes's abstention, but there is no reason to believe that he cared where compulsory metaphysics appeared in the syllabus. What was clear was his relief that further formal discussion was to be deferred until October. A cold war simmered informally, however, for the rest of that Easter term. On 7 June he seethed at a Johnian feast where he 'sat next to Marshall who let out with his customary exaggeration about Sidgwick and the proposed changes in the Moral Sciences Tripos'. Evidently Keynes had not disguised his annoyance, and the next Diary entry quoted a pacific letter from Marshall saying:

> I shd like to add to what I said yesterday that I have no intention of making an attack on Sidgwick's method of conducting M.Sc. Board business unless I can help it. Also all my indignation against him is confined to a rather narrow area. It

5. Ibid., p. 264.
6. Ibid., p. 266.

is Sidgwick as a University politician and to some extent as a writer on economics that I quarrel with. All the rest of Sidgwick I expect I think of as highly as you do.

A fortnight later – after a private conversation with Sidgwick who confided thoughts of resigning his chair within the next two or three years – Keynes wrote miserably: 'But he would be an immense loss to us. I should dread having Marshall at the head of the school'.

The Board met on three Saturday mornings during the October term to discuss tripos reform. After the first meeting, on 23 October, Keynes reported gloomily: 'Ward thought he had succeeded in reconciling Marshall to Sidgwick's original scheme, but it did not seem like reconciliation'. After the second, on 10 November he admitted to a glimmer of hope: 'Moral Sciences Board. I am off the Board now but was present as secretary. Sidgwick proposed a compromise in his scheme of the Tripos which Marshall actually accepted!' At the third meeting on 1 December there was further argument, however, and on this occasion Keynes had a personal interest in the outcome: 'M Sc Board. Marshall wants one of the Advanced Logic papers to be taken in lieu of Metaphysics by PE specialists.[7] I rather hesitate to agree as it may mean that the Logic examiners will have difficulty in setting their questions'. At last on 31 January a Sidgwickian compromise seems to have broken the deadlock. The Diary entry for that day – after noting: 'We are now making fair progress with the new regulations' – spelt out Neville's personal feelings in more detail than usual: 'I get irritated with myself for feeling irritated with Marshall. One thing that annoys me is his constant references to his own lectures, and the class of men who are attending them'. It took two more meetings before the report of the Moral Sciences Board was finally signed for transmission to the university.

There were three principal speakers at the Senate House when the Board's report was debated on 7 March 1889 – one hostile, two supportive. The hostile speaker was William Cunningham, who had been bracketed Senior Moralist with F.W. Maitland in the 1872 moral sciences tripos, had failed as candidate for both the Oxford and Cambridge chairs of political economy and was now a Trinity College lecturer. His lecturing experience gave him authority to speak on both political philosophy and political economy. He was, however, a bitter critic of Marshall's 'new political economy'. The Diary makes it obvious that Keynes enjoyed a friendship with Cunningham (just three years his senior) which overrode methodological differences. On 15 March, when they were both awaiting news of the Oxford election, the entry reads:

No news from Oxford. This morning walk and talk with Cunningham. He is keen on being elected and also sanguine. He is anxious to have in his inaugural lecture

7. See Ibid., p. 283 for details of what Marshall had in mind with his proposals.

> an opportunity to deliver a manifesto from the historical point of view in opposition to Marshall and Sidgwick.

Later (when they knew that the Oxford chair had gone to Thorold Rogers), Keynes was Cunningham's guest at a Trinity dinner on 21 April. On that occasion according to the Diary: 'I attacked him for the way in which, in his last book,[8] he talks about Economic Principles. His reply is practically a denial of the possibility of an Economic Theory'. The 1889 Senate House debate on reform of the moral sciences tripos thus offered Cunningham a suitable platform from which to launch his threatened 'manifesto' against both Marshall and Sidgwick. According to the record in the *University Reporter*, his objections to the Board's proposals focused on its implications for the teaching of political economy. In particular, he opposed

> the regulation which allowed the substitution of Political Philosophy for Metaphysics in the case of Economic students who took up the second part of the Tripos. ... It seemed to him that ... so far as he could judge of the Political Economy in the present day there were a great many Metaphysical questions underlying it, and those who went out into the world as specialists in it should have some insight into the treatment of these Metaphysical questions. ... [for example,] the whole controversy of socialism ... in order to take a sound view with regard to socialism, there ought to be preparation in the study of Metaphysics. Similarly a great many of the burning questions in Modern Economics related to the appropriate method of study, and they could not be thoroughly treated without trenching on metaphysical problems as to the nature of knowledge.

Having made his point that specialists in political economy absolutely needed the intellectual discipline of metaphysics Cunningham remarked:

> A student with interest in Political Philosophy but not in Metaphysics was already encouraged to study Political Economy in conjunction with Jurisprudence and History for the Historical Tripos. Since that scheme had been so recently framed, it required very strong justification to start another examination with a similar arrangement.[9]

As leader of the new school of political economy, Marshall dismissed Cunningham's arguments on the significance of metaphysics. Granting that 'if a student who was making Political Economy his main subject, chose to read Metaphysics, he would be the better for it', he argued that 'Metaphysics was not adapted for compulsory study', and added pointedly: 'Looking at the history of Economics, one did not find that those who had approached it from

8. W. Cunningham, *Politics and Economics* (London, 1885).
9. *CUR*, 19 March 1889, pp. 593–6.

a Metaphysical standpoint had contributed very much to its progress'. He went on to claim that:

> There was a great deal to be said for separating to some extent these two branches of moral science, the mental metaphysical side, and the social side; though they had long been united in the Moral Sciences Tripos. Ere long a time might come when they would be ready to have a political sciences school. … Economic conditions were changing so fast and the rate of change was increasing so fast that the Economic student was more and more taken up with recent and contemporary history and had every year less time to spare for Medieval History. Therefore he could not admit that the wants of the ordinary Economic student could be met by an examination in which Medieval History was as prominent as in the present Historical Tripos. … He thought that the scheme now proposed for the Moral Sciences Tripos, though not altogether satisfactory, and though in many respects to be regarded as a transitional stage, was yet the best step on the whole they could take. The plan was not exactly what he himself wanted. He wanted to give more freedom of choice, but opinions on the Board differed and the plan now adopted seemed to be an excellent compromise.

However, Marshall admitted frankly that political philosophy had not been his favourite substitute for metaphysics. He would have preferred either a paper on economic history or 'a paper on Advanced Scientific Method with special regard to statistics, in order that they might be worked at by mathematicians who take up the study of Economics after their degrees … but he cordially accepted the decision of the Board'.[10]

Sidgwick's contribution to the Senate House debate was characteristically lucid, broadminded and unprovocative. He acknowledged that students of political economy would benefit by 'studying the theory of the nature and conditions of knowledge and of the relation of the individual to the universe included in the term Metaphysics', whilst agreeing with Marshall that it was

> a subject exceedingly well suited to men whose minds were adapted to it, but exceedingly bad when forced upon minds not so adapted; and he thought the rest of the Board were unable to resist the evidence brought forward by Professor Marshall from his own experience, to shew that there were students anxious to devote themselves to a full and complete study of Political Economy, and who might with advantage be encouraged to take up that subject, who still had very clearly an unmetaphysical turn of mind. Therefore after much deliberation and thought, he had come to the conclusion that the exact regulation here made was on the whole the best.

He then defended the Board's choice of political philosophy as an alternative to metaphysics – on the grounds that

10. Ibid.

> if a student took up Ethical Philosophy and Political Economy the study of Political Philosophy, connected as it was on the one side with Ethics and on the other with Political Economy was one that naturally and properly combined with the other two. ... He agreed, however, with Professor Marshall in thinking it probable that in the course of a few years they would feel a desire to construct a Political Sciences Tripos: and if they were moving in that direction, it seemed clearly advantageous that the subject of Political Philosophy should be maintained in the Moral Sciences Tripos.[11]

Neville's sympathies in the professorial confrontations of the late 1880s and early 1890s were generally (if not invariably) with Sidgwick rather than with Marshall. For him it seemed largely a conflict of personality. Marshall was a schemer who relentlessly pressured his disciples to structure their careers and plan their lectures in ways that would promote the new economics that he aspired to develop. As one of his most reliable disciples, Keynes had suffered persistent pressure – for example to carry the gospel to Oxford, or to become editor of the *Economic Journal* or to jettison the university administrative functions where he confidently believed he could operate more efficiently than most other academics. Sidgwick, on the other hand, though often open to the accusation of 'trying to regulate too much', could not be suspected of devious or egotistical motives, so that his proposals for tripos reform, or his advice to junior colleagues came across as impartial and sincere. Moreover Keynes himself was a product of the moral sciences tripos, a senior moralist of the 1873/83 era, when political economy, moral plus political philosophy, logic, and mental philosophy, were all compulsory and carried equal weight in the final result. He shared Sidgwick's concern with the relatively thin stream and low quality of undergraduates opting for the current moral sciences tripos. He had chosen to specialize in political economy and logic because these were areas in which he realistically believed he could make his most effective contribution as teacher and examiner – not because he regarded the philosophical subjects as less relevant to the basic training of a moralist. Although sympathetic in principle to Marshall's aim of restoring the weight lost by political economy in the 1883 tripos reform, he was more concerned by the currently poor quality of teaching in logic, where Venn – the senior lecturer – was failing to keep in touch with new writing on the subject. More important still, Keynes did not share Marshall's personal vision of a syllabus designed to provide the professor with his longed-for elite audience of undergraduate (better still graduate) males who had already demonstrated first-class ability in some other tripos (preferably mathematical or historical) and who could be trained to handle usefully the 'delicate

11. Ibid.

and powerful machinery of scientific investigation' offered by advanced economic theory.[12]

Five years later, when tripos reform next featured on the Board's agenda, Keynes reported gloomily on 6 February 1894: 'We are talking of further changes in the M.Sc. Tripos. Scene between Sidgwick and Marshall that was very painful. The former seemed more to blame than the latter'. As Board secretary he was instructed to draft a scheme to provide the basis of discussion at its next meeting on 27 February. By this time he was also secretary to the Council of the Senate and was glad to have to leave the Board meeting early, in order to officiate at a foreign royal visit to the university.[13] Marshall (with whom he had prudently cleared his draft) was also absent from that meeting and the next Diary entry complained that 'some definite resolutions were passed. This seems to me rather a pity in Marshall's absence'. As usual Keynes worried too much. The topic recurred on the agenda at widely spaced intervals over the next three years but the temperature of the debate had been substantially reduced. The only crucial decision noted by Keynes in his Diary for either 1895 or 1896 occurred on 28 February 1896, when the Board agreed 'not to require both parts of the Tripos for a Degree'.[14] In effect, what had changed since the disputations of the late 1880s was Marshall's strategy. Taking advantage of the fact that tripos reform was on the agenda of the History Board, as well as that of the Moral Sciences Board in the mid-1890s, Marshall carried his campaign for political economy to both of them. He was appointed one of four members of the Moral Sciences Board sub-committee set up on 27 November 1896, to draft detailed proposals on the political economy papers. The other members were Sidgwick, Foxwell and Keynes. On the History Board, he won the support (most unusually) not only of Oscar Browning, but also of his old enemy Cunningham, in persuading the historians to double the number of political economy papers offered as options in Part II of the tripos. That change was ratified in the Lent term of 1897. At the Senate congregation which discussed the History Board's proposals for reform, Marshall expressed his 'great gratitude for the concessions which had been made to the subjects in which he was specially interested. The subject of Political Economy should have two, it might almost be said three papers; since a paper was to be given to Economic History since 1688'.[15]

12. See P.D. Groenewegen, *A Soaring Eagle: Alfred Marshall, 1842–1924* (Cheltenham, UK: Edward Elgar, 1998), pp. 321–9 for detailed analysis of the size and composition of Marshall's classes 1885–1908.
13. The royal visitor was the German Empress Frederick in whose honour a formal reception was held at King's College Lodge.
14. It was crucial because allowing candidates to qualify for an honours degree on the strength of Part I tended to reduce the numbers of moralists willing (or financially able) to move on to Part II.
15. The Senate House debate on the History Board report was recorded in *CUR*, 9 February 1897.

The arguments on reform of the moral sciences tripos reached a conclusion in the spring. After a Board meeting on 30 April, Keynes rejoiced: 'We are making progress at last with the new regulations for the Tripos'. Four days later he noted another meeting: 'Marshall was not there and in a little over an hour we got through as much as we generally managed in two long evenings'. Presumably Marshall, never very convincing as a discussant, was finally resigned to the fact that his economist colleagues could not be shifted from their lukewarm attitudes to his proposals. By 6 May, Keynes had drafted the Board's report to the Senate, aided by Sidgwick who had contributed most of the persuasive preamble – and on 10 May the Board reassembled to agree its final submission to the university on reform of the tripos. According to the Diary: 'Marshall again absent. We settled our Report on the Tripos Regulations at a great rate after desultory discussions for two or three years'. Sidgwick's preamble defended the 1897 reform, on the grounds that it was designed to

> improve the whole course of preparation gone through by students of Moral Sciences whose bent lies in the direction of Economics; while at the same time it will meet the needs of students who have taken honours in other Triposes and of Advanced Students, better than the present arrangement.[16]

On 23 May, the day the report was tabled for discussion and ratification by the Senate, Keynes reported with relieved surprise: 'nothing is said. Marshall arrives just after we have broken up. We all felt happy at the contretemps'.

The fact was, however, that Marshall was devastated at the 1897 reforms of the moral science tripos but, having signed the Board's report, felt unable to speak up on 23 May. In two letters to Keynes, written during the long vacation, he agonized over his own want of resolution in accepting the outcome. The first (dated 15 August 1897) complained that the smothering weight of philosophy in the new Part I had 'rendered it impossible to have a respectable school of economics connected with that Tripos', and that '[until the] Report is superseded, or a Pol.Sc.Tripos is started, mathematical casuals will remain almost the only men worth teaching economics in Cambridge'.[17] The second (dated 30 August 1897) revealed his sense of betrayal:

> I had given a definite promise to sign the Report, if Part II were made suitable for economic students coming from other Triposes; and when my promise was converted into something different from what I had intended, by the resolution of the Board to make Part I so heavy that few men are likely to take Part I and Part II on the economic side, I ought boldly to have broken my promise. I do not say that the trap was designed: I am sure it was not. But I was caught in a trap and my promise

16. The text of the Moral Sciences Board report appeared in *CUR*, 18 May 1897.
17. Whitaker (1996), Vol. II, p. 192.

> was heavy on me. I shall never forgive myself for not having broken it; and, if challenged explained the whole history in the Arts Schools. ... It was difficult to know what to do. For Sidgwick was already incensed against me *re* women: and I dreaded to intensify and perpetuate the conflict. It was cowardly and I am deeply ashamed and sorry. It was one of those errors that enter into a man's life.[18]

2 CREATING AN ECONOMICS TRIPOS, 1897–1908

By the summer of 1897 it was plain to Marshall that there was insufficient support on the Moral Sciences Board for his personal mission to restructure the tripos on lines that could establish a starting-point for a modern school of economics at Cambridge. Among those who were professionally committed to political economy, only Sidgwick had sufficient intellectual vision, reforming zeal and personal charisma to persuade the university to promote a discipline which attracted so few students; and he was unlikely to do so at the expense of other moral sciences. The way forward was evidently to create a separate tripos for economics and associated subjects; and before Sidgwick died in August 1900 there was reason to suppose that he might support that solution. Marshall's letter of October 1900, to Oscar Browning (his ally on the History Board), revealed that, during the previous year, Sidgwick had indicated in conversation that he then favoured the creation of a Cambridge faculty of economics to rival the recently established London School of Economics.[19] As it turned out, however, Sidgwick's death terminated the prospect of a benevolent conspiracy between the two warring professors – leaving Keynes and Foxwell as the only moralists whom Marshall might hope to enlist in his campaign.

As far as Keynes was concerned, raising the status of political economy in the university had never ranked high on his personal agenda. Indeed, once the professorial disagreements on tripos reform had ceased to inject tension and disorder into the Board's meetings, its secretary gladly focused on less contentious and more urgent agenda – such as lecture programmes, book lists and appointments of examiners. The conflict had left its scars on his normally even temper, however. Although, for the rest of the 1890s, the Diary entries on Marshall related mainly to social occasions, they still reflected a chronic

18. Ibid., pp. 194–5. Marshall's reference to his other area of conflict with Sidgwick – the woman question – is revealing. It happened that the timing of the 1894/97 discussion on tripos reform coincided with a furious university-wide debate on women's admission to degrees. Indeed the evidence suggests that Marshall's 'want of resolution' in the final stages of his campaign for economics in the moral sciences tripos may have been due to his having spent most of his limited physical energy on an even more obsessive campaign – that of excluding women from membership of the university.
19. Ibid., pp. 289–90. Sidgwick's contribution to the Senate debate on moral science reform (quoted above, p. 231) also hinted at the desirability of a separate tripos.

irritation. In December 1899, for example, a reference to one of the professor's dinner parties ended:

> Marshall is the most exasperating talker I know. He will agree with nothing you say and argues and dogmatises so as to drive one wild. He is a keen pro-Boer and kept making innuendos, trying without success to draw us into an argument on the subject. F says we agreed with absolutely nothing that he said throughout the evening.

More significant for Marshall's campaign was the fact that Keynes became less and less involved in economics teaching. His last course on the subject was to Indian Civil Service candidates and ended in 1893, when a change of syllabus meant that his classes were no longer required – though he continued to give advice to ICS men and to examine them nationally.[20] Four years later, another circumstantial change ensured that his future teaching (though not examining) activities would be tied exclusively to logic.

In 1897 the university found the funds for its planned chair in mental philosophy and logic. Keynes and Sidgwick, who were among the electors, persuaded James Ward, the university's leading psychologist, to stand. Unfortunately, John Venn – Caius lecturer in moral sciences since 1862, one of Sidgwick's loyal supporters in the long battle to raise the scholarly credibility of the tripos, and Cambridge's senior logician with several reputable texts already published on the subject – expected to be elevated to the chair. However, respectable seniority as a logician was not a sufficient qualification for a chair which had been established primarily to promote mental philosophy. On 14 January, Keynes commented on a letter from Ward: 'It would probably be a relief to him if Venn were elected'. The result was predictable. When Sidgwick humanely cast one of only two votes for Venn, it was in the certain knowledge that Ward would win. Two days later, on 18 January, Keynes worried to his Diary that the electors' choice had not only alienated Venn but financially penalized Ward: 'Venn writes to say that he will now entirely cease to lecture. We hear Mrs Ward is on pecuniary grounds very upset at the exchange of Tutorship for Professorship'. Venn issued a battery of furious letters to his friends among the electors – to Keynes who was indebted to him for many past acts of kindness and to Sidgwick who had long been able to rely on his support at Board meetings. But it was clear that the right man had been chosen, and that Venn would abandon his lectures, leaving Keynes with primary responsibility for the tripos logic courses.

20. JNK continued to examine regularly in political economy inside and outside Cambridge. For example, he examined in the 1897, 1901 and 1902 triposes, frequently assessed Higher Local papers in the subject and remained external examiner in political economy for the University of London as well as for Victoria University (Manchester) among other places.

Neville's relations with Sidgwick remained close and almost invariably harmonious. They served together on several central university bodies, enjoyed each other's dinner parties and played golf together. True, Sidgwick as chairman of the Board, could still raise Keynes's hackles when allocating teaching duties. The Diary entry for 10 October 1899, for example, noted: 'Johnson to lunch. Sidgwick seems to encourage him to give lectures [in logic] in direct competition with my own, though it does not seem to be his own wish'. The irritation was, however, short-lived as well as unreasonable.[21] On 28 May 1900 Keynes was deeply shocked when Sidgwick called on him with 'very terrible news. He is to undergo an operation on Thursday, and after that the future is very dark'. Sidgwick, of course, resigned his chair instantly. At the end of June, Keynes was one of the electors saddled with the task of choosing his successor. This time their decision was uninhibited by personal considerations. On 25 July the Diary quoted Sidgwick's letter approving the outcome:

> He says 'I quite cordially acquiesce in the result; and I think that the work of the Chair and of the School will be quite safe in [W.R.] Sorley's hands … I cannot remember that he failed in anything he undertook – which is a great thing to say of anyone who has had so varied a career.' About himself he does not speak very hopefully.

Meanwhile Sidgwick had asked Keynes to complete the revision of his *Principles of Political Economy* and to see the final edition through the press. Sidgwick's death ended an era for the disparate faculty of moral scientists. It removed an eminent polymath and university reformer who was an intellectual and moral role-model with outstanding leadership qualities. In September, Marshall tried again to manipulate Keynes (now more committed to university than to faculty policy matters) in order to further his plans for economics. According to the Diary for 21 September:

> Marshall and Ward are getting very much awry with one another over the question as to who shall be Sidgwick's successor as Chairman of the Moral Sciences Board, Marshall wants to put me in, but he has managed very much to irritate Ward by the manner in which he has suggested it.

Keynes was resolutely determined to detach himself from faculty politics and in the end common sense prevailed. On 8 October, after the first meeting of

21. Given that JNK was then virtually monopolizing the logic teaching for honours men and that he was steadily extending the range of his university administrative commitments, it is not surprising that Sidgwick should have tried to bring into service W.E. Johnson, who had taken a first class in the moral sciences tripos in 1883, was a pupil and family friend of the Keyneses, and who had given much-valued help with more than one edition of JNK's *Formal Logic*.

the Board for 1900/01, the Diary finally disposed of the matter: 'We elected Ward Chairman. Marshall's long disquisitions are very tiresome'.

Marshall's relationship with Foxwell, his other potential ally on the Board, was altogether different. The substantial amount of extant correspondence between the two men (over the 34 years preceding Marshall's resignation of his chair) demonstrates the long-standing quality of their friendship.[22] They had met at St John's in October 1868, when 26-year-old Marshall took up his appointment as the college's second lecturer in moral sciences, and was asked to teach the relatively unpopular science of political economy to a group of freshmen – of whom Foxwell was one. Marshall (second wrangler in 1865) had spent barely two years browsing in the moral sciences; and it was not until 1871/72 that he finally decided to specialize in political economy.[23] So, when Foxwell (Senior Moralist in December 1872) became St John's junior lecturer in moral sciences in 1875, he inherited the teaching in psychology and philosophy. As fellows of the same college they became close colleagues. Two years later, the departure of Marshall and his bride (Newnham's lecturer in political economy) left an unprecedented resource gap in the teaching of economics. Marshall, of course, nominated his (and Mary's) preferred replacements. Consequently, after Keynes had lectured for just one year – in logic to men and women (separately) – Sidgwick invited him to teach political economy (instead of logic) to Newnham students. According to the Diary:

> The suggestion [wrote Sidgwick] came from Marshall who tells me that Political Economy is your favourite subject and who is anxious that you should not desert it for Logic. There is no doubt that it is the most important and also I am afraid the most laborious subject of the two, as regards the lectures for women; and if you do not mind taking it, we should all be very glad that it was in your hands.

At that stage, however, Keynes was not confident enough to work up a new course on political economy before he was fully satisfied with his first-year logic lectures. According to the Diary, J.S. Nicholson could have substituted for Mary Marshall: 'but Ward tells me that Marshall objected to him strongly, partly on the grounds that he was too self conscious to lecture well'. As for Foxwell, he was evidently happy to lecture on economics to the honours men, but he shared Marshall's view that lecturing to women students was a tedious chore. In a letter to Keynes written in October 1883 (by which time he was also Professor of Political Economy at London's

22. See, for example, J.R. Whitaker (1996), Vols I and II which prints over 150 extant letters from Marshall to Foxwell from 1874 to 1908: and these were only part of the total correspondence.
23. These dates were given by Marshall in a letter to James Ward dated 23 September 1900, in Whitaker (1996) Vol. II, p. 285.

University College), Foxwell justified his dismissive attitude to Cambridge women students thus:

> My college lectures are the only ones I take any real pleasure in, or in which I see the work of my hands proper. I believe this is principally because I am completely en rapport with the men. I have never found it the same thing when lecturing to women; but that is infinitely preferable to a mixed class, such as I have at UCL [University College London], which may be a higher form of development but is certainly not one to which I am adapted.[24]

Even before Marshall left Cambridge for Bristol in the summer of 1877, their mutual affection illuminated the correspondence with Foxwell. When clearing his St John's bachelor rooms in September, for example, he sent a favourite rosewood reading desk across to Foxwell's rooms with a note (read and approved by Mary) saying: 'I love it too much to sell it and I cannot use it at Bristol. You once praised it; so you may become fond of it'.[25] During the seven or so years of the Marshalls' exile, first in Bristol and then at Oxford, Foxwell's gossipy letters kept their link with Cambridge alive. His detailed comments on successive drafts of the Marshalls' joint book, *Economics of Industry*, were valued by both authors. He made persistent efforts to persuade St John's to offer Marshall a non-resident lectureship. A letter dated 25 October 1879 from Marshall to Foxwell, for example, began: 'I thank you for your kind letter. As to your offer to resign half your salary to me, it is just like you; but there is no consideration whatever that would induce me to accept that offer or anything like it', and ended: 'Yours everlastingly (in spirit as well as in length of letter)'.[26] It was well known that Foxwell and Marshall did not always agree. They differed publicly on policy matters such as bimetallism or tariff reform and more discreetly on teaching priorities such as the significance of pure theory or of the history of economic thought. As thinking practitioners of an inexact science with many political implications, they were destined to differ on a variety of issues which did not disturb the warm mutual respect then sustaining their friendship. Foxwell referred often to such differences in letters to Keynes. For example, in January 1891, he justified his refusal to write the political economy section of the *Cambridge Students' Guide*, on the grounds that he disagreed profoundly with the professor 'especially in

24. Marshall Library, JNK Papers I(23), October 1883.
25. Whitaker (1996) Vol. I, p. 43. Letter dated 11 September 1877.
26. Whitaker (1996), Vol. I pp. 116–18. See also Appendix III, 'Foxwell's Initiative', which prints two letters written in September 1881 from Foxwell to the new Master of St John's, in support of the proposal that the college should create a non-resident lectureship for Marshall when the latter resigned from Bristol in 1881. The initiative seems to have come to nothing, perhaps because a new Master was hesitant to push it on.

regard to Ricardo, Mill, Economic Method and Consumption'. Some years later, on 20 April 1897, Keynes quoted another of Foxwell's letters:

> 'I believe I generally agree with the core of Marshall's thought and opinion, except on politics, but I almost invariably disagree with his emphasis. I do not think his sense of proportion good; and I believe he is led away by an irresistible inclination to paradox, very characteristic of the smart intellectual set, [W.K.] Clifford, [J.F.] Moulton, etc among whom he mixed in younger days; ... Still he is a most excellent fellow, most able, honourable, and kindly, whom I for one am proud to have as my chief here. Even his weaknesses are amiable.'

As far as Foxwell was concerned then, the evidence suggests that the common ground between Marshall and himself – especially their joint interest in raising the academic status of political economy and their shared prejudice against women university students – outweighed any doctrinal or political differences.

There was, however, an in-built source of tension associated with the traditionally weak powers of control over their teaching programmes that the university boards of studies then deployed. When Marshall returned to Cambridge as its professor of political economy he had expected to lecture exclusively to students who had either been through a general first-year course taught by Foxwell, or had graduated from the mathematical or historical tripos. As a college lecturer rather than a university employee, Foxwell was, of course, free to design his own courses so long as they fell within the tripos syllabus. Since 1881 when he was appointed professor of political economy in London's University College, the weight of his lecture load for two institutions had encouraged him to repeat some of his London courses in Cambridge, to resign altogether from teaching Cambridge women and to opt out of the chore of setting and assessing question papers for honours men auditing his Cambridge lectures. In these circumstances, when Marshall asked Foxwell to give elementary courses in economics, and to assess students' written papers – in order systematically to prepare freshmen for the professorial advanced courses – he was met with a flat refusal. According to Marshall's account,[27] he appealed to Foxwell for help twice more – even offering to share the drudgery by himself taking the systematic elementary course (and letting Foxwell give the advanced course) in alternate years – only to be rebuffed again and again. In the end, Marshall developed his own solution to a burden he found intolerable. He first selected recent graduates, of whom he thought highly (such as J.M.E. McTaggart and Clapham), to assess question papers relevant to his own lectures – a task which was directly remunerated

27. In a long letter to Foxwell dated 14 May 1901, printed in Whitaker (1996), Vol. II, pp. 319–21.

out of student fees – and then he began hiring additional lecturers, chosen and paid by himself, to lay a basis for his advanced courses. In March 1900 he wrote in confidence to Keynes (still secretary to the Moral Sciences Board) to tell him that he had identified an 'ideal man' for the purpose – A.C. Pigou who had taken a first in Part I of the 1899 history tripos, was expected to take a first in Part II of the 1900 moral sciences tripos and should be ready to deliver the appropriate elementary courses from 1901/02 onwards. Meanwhile for the year 1900/01 he persuaded Bowley (tenth wrangler in 1891 and subsequent winner of the Cobden and Adam Smith prizes) to give a course of lectures on statistics and statistical method.[28]

By October 1900, Marshall's plans had been informally approved by the Board and he was using Keynes, its secretary, to inform Foxwell that his 12 noon lectures must clash with Bowley's during the ensuing term.[29] Foxwell accepted the time-tabling directive with surprising resignation. He was probably confident that the solemn young statistician was unlikely to entice away the liveliest members of his own audience. In any case, his letter of 6 October to Keynes, explicitly acknowledged that 'the Professor ought to be Head of the School and control the arrangements'. On the other hand, he seems to have felt threatened when Marshall hired Pigou as an additional lecturer in political economy, for he maintained:

> [I]t is not the case that I only get beginners at my general lectures; and I much prefer a salting of the better class of men; but I always fancy Marshall does not like them to come to me: for we have had a good many differences on these matters: culminating in his having engaged Pigou to deliver an elementary course: a man, of all I have known, least qualified to deal with a general class, as he is such a prig![30]

In May 1901, when the timetable for Pigou's lectures in the following academic year was being negotiated, the rift between Marshall and Foxwell widened. True, they were still cooperating in the campaign to establish an economics tripos; but the mutual trust no longer coloured their relationship. Marshall – whose temper was sorely frayed by the lecture-clashing problems involved in his determination to ensure that Pigou's lectures were listed by both the History and the Moral Sciences Board – complained bitterly to Keynes about Foxwell's behaviour (in a letter dated 22 May 1901):

> It seems to me the story of the wolf and the lamb. Foxwell refused for 15 years to set papers, though he knew his not doing so was regarded by me as a great oppression. Then when at last I had got arrangements wh would (i) free me from a

28. Letter dated March 1900, Marshall Library, JNK Letters.
29. Marshall to JNK, 6 October 1900, Marshall Library, JNK Papers.
30. Foxwell to JNK, 6 October 1900, Marshall Library, JNK Papers.

> disagreeable position (ii) enable the better sort of beginners to have a systematic general course from wh people who want quick and really advanced teaching wd be excluded and (iii) enable a proper advanced course to be given; wh has never been done yet – then he instantly cuts in before Pigou and duplicates in anticipation a part of the course ... wh Pigou has been preparing himself to give. ... Pigou and I care for the men; and I think I may truly say for the men only. Foxwell does not seem to be able to understand this sort of aim. ... I know you are *absolutely* unselfish; and I have always loved you for it. So I unburden myself to you.[31]

Keynes referred wearily and briefly in his May 1901 Diary to the lengthy letters he was getting from Marshall about the latter's strained relations with Foxwell. The evidence suggests that Neville sympathized with Foxwell's reluctance to tailor his well-established and arguably useful lectures to the professor's curricular ambitions. Another stream of communications harassed Keynes early in 1902. On 31 January he groaned to the Diary:

> Marshall is starting an agitation for the establishment of an Economics and Politics Tripos and he has written a paper on the subject with which I am in considerable disagreement. We are having a correspondence that bothers me and I am sure worries him considerably. I want to nip it in the bud if possible.

The paper to which he referred was Marshall's *Plea for the Creation of a Curriculum in Economics and Associated Branches of Political Science*, which was widely circulated in draft for comment in Cambridge and elsewhere during January and February.[32] In his comments on the first draft, Keynes presented a bluntly unenthusiastic reaction to Marshall's campaign for an economics tripos. He wrote: 'I should like to see the post-graduate study of Economics developed here, with every encouragement to original work; but I am not so clear that any fundamental change in our undergraduate curriculum is necessary'.[33] Marshall's response was another self-indulgent screed. It began:

> My dear Keynes, In all this weary and oppressive work for the liberation of economics from the incubus by which I believe it to be oppressed, nothing has given me so much pain as the thought that I must necessarily go against your wishes. I have had many pupils whom I have cared for: but only a few whom I have loved. Among those – of the male gender – you and Pigou have a special charm for me.

31. Marshall to JNK, 22 May 1901. Marshall Library, JNK Papers.
32. The final text, dated April 1902, was privately printed by Marshall and widely circulated by him – see Groenewegen (1998), especially pp. 540–9 for a detailed account of the final stages in his personal campaign to create an economic tripos – and summarized in *Journal of Political Economy*, 1902, pp. 429–37. It was reprinted in full in C.W. Guillebaud (ed.), Alfred Marshall's *Principles of Economics* (1961), Vol. 2, pp. 161–78.
33. Printed in Whitaker (1996), Vol. II, p. 349, from a transcript in the Marshall Library.

Marshall went on to insist that he and Keynes were 'almost the only two elderly/middleaged English economists who are perfectly loyal' to scientific and analytical (by which he invariably meant 'theoretical' economics), and he concluded with the fiercely accented wail:

> Economics is drifting under the control of men like Sidney Webb and Arthur Chamberlain. And all the while, through causes for which no one is – in the main – responsible, *the curriculum to wh I am officially attached has not provided me with one single high class man devoting himself to economics during the sixteen years of my Professorship.*[34]

Apart from the brief note of 29 January (quoted above) none of Neville's letters responding to successive drafts of Marshall's *Plea* and his schemes for an economic and political tripos, have survived. Nor – not surprisingly – did he waste time recording in his Diary views and arguments he had already relayed fully and frankly to Marshall, either verbally or on paper. Paucity of evidence, however, has not always discouraged imaginative speculations on the reasons either for Keynes's dislike of the new tripos proposals, or for Marshall's persistence in justifying his personal aims to a stubbornly critical colleague and in seeking the latter's observations on all stages in the drafting process. Maloney, for example, concludes that the lack of references in the Diary to the substantive issues raised by Marshall's campaign reflects Keynes's comprehensive indifference, and that 'by 1900 Keynes' indifference extended to intellectual activity, in general, to economics, to the future of Cambridge economics and above all to the professor of economics'.[35] At the same time he explains Marshall's insistence that Keynes was his principal ally 'as the wishful thinking of an isolated and disappointed man'.[36] It is impossible, however, to reconcile Maloney's interpretation of Keynes's total indifference to these matters with the character traits that emerge unambiguously from the Diary (as well as from the assessments of friends and colleagues) – for example, his solid integrity, persistent concern to maintain high educational standards on all occasions and obsessive preoccupation with smooth and orderly administration. It is equally hard – even allowing for Marshall's devious propensity for flattery – to interpret his stream of affectionately pleading letters to Keynes (in the last crucial stages of his extraordinarily successful campaign to establish the Cambridge economic and political sciences tripos), as the outpourings of a self-deluded individual.

34. Marshall Library, JNK Papers. The letter, dated 30 January, is reproduced in full in Whitaker (1996), Vol. II, pp. 350–3. The passage in italics carries Marshall's emphasis.
35. John Maloney, *Marshall, Orthodoxy and the Professionalisation of Economics* (Cambridge: Cambridge University Press, 1985), p. 63.
36. Ibid., p. 63.

As his colleagues all knew, Keynes was an unreconstructed product of the pre-1883 moral sciences tripos. He held that, at the undergraduate level, economics should be taught alongside logic, psychology and ethics: and that specialized study of it was best reserved for mature students – a view that Marshall himself had once favoured. He dreaded the establishment of a separate economics tripos because he rightly foresaw that it would lead to political economy being excluded from the moral sciences tripos altogether. For his part, Marshall understood the academic principles underlying Keynes's objections and knew that they involved no hidden agenda threatening his own plans for reform. On the contrary, there was no one who could offer him better-informed advice on how to present to the university an acceptable case for a new tripos as well as on devising a curriculum that was feasible in terms of both the teaching resources then available and of undergraduates' needs. Keynes had a wider direct experience than either Marshall or Foxwell, of examining and teaching (not simply pontificating to) a variety of students. As an elected member of the Council of the Senate he sat on the supreme governing body of the university. As secretary to the Council he had been an indispensable personal adviser to a succession of college heads serving their two-year stints as university vice-chancellor. Finally, as an experienced member of the General Board of Studies he was personally well-acquainted with (and trusted by) the university's leading educational reformers as well as with the conservative majority in other boards of studies who could be expected to react instinctively against any new development which might draw on severely limited university resources, in order to promote an ill-understood discipline with potentially dubious political implications.

Above all, Marshall knew that Keynes had no personal axe to grind and that, even if the latter's objections were not accommodated, he could still rely on him as an ally in making it workable. A postscript to Marshall's letter of 14 February to Foxwell said sadly: 'Keynes wrote a letter wh I have not been able to answer. This partly answers it. Would you be so kind as to show him this. And Oh Keynes! please forgive!'[37] This does not sound like a message to an old friend who was then so detached that 'formal duty was all that remained of the relationship'.[38] Marshall's last personal letter to Keynes on the crucial petition to the Council (enclosing the latest version) began:

> Of course you cant sign the Memorial to the Council. But you may like to see the last draft. The words in the M.S.S. near the end are inserted to prevent the

37. The letter to Foxwell is printed in Whitaker (1996), Vol. II, pp. 357–9. According to Whitaker (footnote p. 359) it was returned by JNK to Foxwell with a covering note saying: 'I dont think there is anything more to be said at present; but we must talk the matter over together soon'.
38. See Groenewegen (1998) for this phrase, contained in the concluding paragraph of a section entitled 'John Neville Keynes: From Faithful to Gradually Disillusioned Lieutenant'.

> sentence from being taken to imply a wish that Economics shd be taken out of the Mo.Sc.Tripos. I am telling Ward that I should support a proposal for retaining it in Part I, if made by others.[39]

The Memorial signed by 131 distinguished resident and non-resident Cambridge MAs reached the Council on 26 April 1902; and in May a suitably weighty Syndicate was appointed 'to enquire into the best means of enlarging the opportunities for study in Cambridge of Economics and associated branches of Political Sciences'. It included the vice-chancellor as chairman; four university professors – Marshall, Maitland, J.E. Sorley and Westlake; two university lecturers – Cunningham and Keynes; five college lecturers – Foxwell, G. Lowes Dickinson, W.S. Leathes, J.R. Tanner and McTaggart; and one non-moralist resident MA – Edmund Parker (Cambridge Borough treasurer).

There was time for just one meeting of the Economic Syndicate during 1902/03. That was on 29 May when Keynes reported: 'Marshall said a great many things and I am afraid he had in consequence a rather bad time. Even Maitland was hostile to him'.[40] Three days later the Diary quoted Marshall's letter blaming his poor performance on the weather: '"I am filled with joy at this thunderstorm. It explains why I could not explain myself to some of my co-syndics or understand them yesterday"'. He was no more successful when the Syndicate assembled again at the beginning of the October term. On 15 October Keynes wrote: 'We are to meet every week. Marshall was ridiculous as usual'. At the following meeting the Syndicate set up a smaller, sub-syndicate (which Keynes managed to evade) consisting of Marshall, Foxwell, Westlake, Maitland, Tanner, Leathes and Dickinson. Presumably this more compact working party was able to override Marshall's time-wasting propensities, for it soon drafted a useful basis for systematic discussion. On 12 November, when the full Syndicate was again in session Keynes reported: 'Battle royal between Marshall and Maitland: the latter victorious. I am feeling rather tired'. Four months later, after another ten gruelling sessions, the Syndicate presented a report to the university, signed by all its members except Cunningham (still opposed to treating economics as an independent discipline) and McTaggart (a first class graduate from the 1888 moral sciences tripos who had already established a sound reputation as a philosopher). The report was discussed at a Senate congregation on 7 May, reconsidered by

39. Marshall Library, JNK Papers. Printed in Whitaker (1996) Vol. II, p. 367.
40. According to Whitaker (1996), Vol. II, p. 406, n.1, Marshall took the opportunity to read out to the Syndicate selected extracts from the letters he had received from distinguished outsiders to whom he had circulated his *Plea*. Groenewegen's (1998) biography of Marshall refers to this entry in JNK's Diary as 'gleeful'. It is, however, hard to credit that JNK would have derived any pleasure from Marshall's propensity for wasting time at a meeting with serious matters to discuss.

the Syndicate on 14 May – when Keynes commented in the Diary: 'I am getting to be too garrulous at meetings' – and passed by the Senate on 6 June 1903 by a majority of 28. Marshall had finally achieved his ambition and Cambridge had an economics tripos.

It was not long before Keynes's fears were realized and the philosophers took their revenge. At the first meeting of the Moral Sciences Board in October, McTaggart announced his intention to move the exclusion of political economy from the tripos. His motion (seconded by James Ward) was carried on 26 October after the defeat of Keynes's amendment (seconded by Foxwell) which would have retained political economy as an option for moralists. In spite of Marshall's protestation to Keynes that 'my wishes go against McTaggart's resolution and within the spirit of your Amendment', he offered typically equivocal support at the Board meeting and it is highly likely that he abstained both on the substantive motion and on the amendment.[41] The timing of the vote may have been crucial. On the day that the Moral Sciences Board finally threw out political economy, Keynes had steered the Council of the Senate through a three-hour meeting (which dealt with barely half the items of an unusually long agenda) and had himself been voted on to a new broadly-based Syndicate 'set up to consider what changes if any are desirable in the studies, teaching and examinations of the University, to confer with any persons or bodies and to submit a Report or Reports before the end of the Easter Term 1904'. Had the moralists acted less precipitately, Keynes might have been able to put to this new body the case for preserving a tripos link between political economy and the moral sciences with which it had traditionally been associated. After the door had been so recently (and so emphatically) slammed, however, the university's central authorities (Council and General Board) could have had little interest in re-opening such a contentious issue.

Groenewegen's authoritative biography of Marshall presents a detailed account of the early development of the new tripos.[42] Predictably, there was a considerable timelag before it generated a Cambridge School of Economics on the scale and with the impact envisaged by its creator. To begin with it was underfunded and inadequately staffed. There was no college or university lecturer in economics (as distinct from moral sciences or history), although Marshall had persuaded a London Livery Company, the Girdlers, to finance a lectureship (which went first to Pigou) and himself paid a stipend to D.H. Macgregor (an Edinburgh University graduate who had taken firsts in both parts of the moral sciences tripos). In the first year he recruited W.E. Johnson

41. See, for example, Marshall's letter of 10 October 1903, in Marshall Library, JNK Papers. The Keynes/Foxwell amendment was defeated by four votes to three with one abstention. It seems likely that Marshall was the abstainer.
42. Groenewegen (1998) pp. 531–69.

(eleventh wrangler in the 1882 maths tripos who took a first in the 1883 moral sciences tripos) to lecture on 'Diagrammatic Treatment of Pure Economic Theory'. He also persuaded J.E. Green, a Caius history lecturer, to teach (and assess papers on) elementary economic theory. Meanwhile Foxwell continued to deliver economics courses on his own choice of subjects. So did Cunningham, who instantly and provocatively announced his intention to offer (in addition to his lectures for the History Board on political economy bereft of economic theory) a course on 'The Rise and Decline of the Free Trade Movement', during the 1903 Michaelmas term in the Divinity School. By 1906/07 Foxwell had been persuaded to lecture on 'General Economics' in the first term of the academic year, instead of on his carefully researched 'English Classical Economists'; though he left Macgregor to continue the general theme in the following two terms. Nevertheless it is doubtful whether Marshall found the students who attended his thrice-weekly course on advanced economic theory (listed as 'not generally suitable for students in their first year') satisfactorily prepared for what he defined as 'scientific and analytical economics'. In short, during the three years which elapsed between its first examination (in 1905) and Marshall's retirement (in 1908), the new tripos offered an inadequately structured teaching programme and attracted an unimpressive stream of candidates. True the numbers sitting its examinations had risen from ten to 17; but only one male student (W.T. Layton) passed out with a first, although two Newnhamites made the grade – to the satisfaction of Mary Marshall and the disgust of her husband.[43]

The problem exercising Marshall was that the trickle of 'first class' young men who had come under his tutelage in the ten to 15 years before his economics tripos was launched, and who should have been equipped to teach his kind of scientific economics, had left Cambridge because there was no opening for them there. For example, there was A.L. Bowley (tenth wrangler in 1891) who was snatched up by the newly founded London School of Economics in 1895; and there was S.J. Chapman who obtained a first in both parts of the 1897–98 moral sciences tripos and departed to Manchester's chair of political economy in 1901. Pigou, on the other hand, was caught for Cambridge because, having taken a first in the 1899 history tripos, he attended Marshall's advanced economic theory lectures in 1899/1900 – which was the year when St John's College raised the stipend of its professorial fellows by £200 a year. On 4 March 1900, Marshall wrote confidentially to Keynes (the Moral Sciences Board's secretary as well as a member of the General Board) to say that he no longer proposed to pressure the university

43. Groenewegen (1998) p. 258, quotes Fay's report on the Marshalls' reception of the news that Lynda Grier and Eve Spielman had won the only first-class results in Part II of the 1908 economics tripos.

authorities to appoint another economics lecturer (in addition to Foxwell). He now intended to take matters into his own hands and to use his additional income to fill the teaching gap as soon as the right man presented himself. The letter went on:

> I am now inclined to think that the ideal man is at hand:– Pigou. But he would hardly be ripe for lecturing in 1900–1: & I have not said anything to him about it yet. I have some thoughts of asking Bowley to give a course of about ten lectures on Statistics and statistical method, with special reference to his own subject U.K. Wages. ... I had Pigou in mind at the last Board meeting [24 February]: but I had not then seen much of his papers. I have seen a good deal since then; & I think he is thoroughly satisfactory.[44]

The rift with Foxwell, caused by Marshall's decision to hire his own man to give the lectures that the former had refused to deliver remained. At that stage neither Foxwell, nor Keynes (the uneasy wailing wall for both parties to the conflict), seems to have considered the possible implications for the professorial succession, of Pigou's appearance as a core lecturer on the Moral Sciences Board's list of recommendations. Marshall was not yet 60 and could reasonably be expected to remain in post for some years at least. True, he made no secret of the fact that he longed to retire in order to make faster progress with the projected second volume of his *Principles*. On the other hand, he was plainly unlikely to do so before he had managed to establish an economics tripos. It is not certain when the character of his successor first began to dominate Marshall's own career plans. For example, before the Board formally decided to put Pigou on its list, Marshall wrote a cryptic (confidential) letter to Keynes dated 8 January 1901. In it he raised the question of the future of the Cambridge chair in oblique relation to Foxwell's current financial problems.[45] The University College chair was poorly remunerated, and when Foxwell married in 1898, he lost his Cambridge college lectureship, plus the associated stipend and living accommodation. It was then that he took a house at 1 Harvey Road. Marshall's letter to Keynes reported a recent conversation with Foxwell about the latter's immediate options to relieve his straitened circumstances. One painful, and essentially temporary, stop-gap was for Foxwell to sell his valuable library of economic literature, lovingly collected over more than a quarter of a century. Another option was to apply for the Birmingham chair in political economy, on which Marshall commented significantly: 'even if that post were open to him – & of course there are hitches by the way – it *would not be well that he should leave*

44. Marshall Library, JNK Letters. The letter is reprinted in Whitaker (1996), Vol. II, p. 269.
45. Foxwell lost his fellowship held under the old statutes but was subsequently (1905) re-elected.

Cambridge' (italics added). An alternative option – to which (according to Marshall's version of the conversation) neither of them had alluded – was the possibility of a university post being created for Foxwell in Cambridge. The letter to Keynes went on: 'As to the future of the Professorship here I should retire if I could afford it. But I cannot. If I did I should have an income of only about £150 a year exclusive of the rental equivalent of my house & sundry checks from MacMillan'. This could imply that when he did retire Foxwell would become his natural successor. On the other hand, Marshall's excuse for not launching a private subscription to fund a Cambridge post for Foxwell was that he had already committed himself to lay out £100 a year 'to the right man as Pigou seems to be for the present in order that there may be one general course of lectures suitable for high-class beginners, and treated from the Scientific as distinguished from the historical and the Literary point of view'. Moreover – whilst acknowledging in effect that the only thing Foxwell's colleagues could do for him was to persuade the university to offer him a readership – the rest of the letter was designed to discourage Keynes from taking any steps to achieve that end.[46] With hindsight, it seems plausible to deduce from this equivocal screed that although Marshall did not want to lose Foxwell's lectures, he certainly did not regard him as his heir-apparent.

On 4 October 1907, Marshall wrote to the vice-chancellor formally resigning his chair from the middle of the following Easter term.[47] It is not clear when Keynes first learned of the impending vacancy, though it was certainly known to all members of the Economics Board at their Lent term meeting, for it was then that Marshall drew attention to the fact that he would have ceased to be a Board member by its June meeting, at which the 1908/09 lecture list was to be agreed. The first explicit reference in the Diary to Marshall's retirement appeared when its implications for Maynard's career surfaced. Marshall, who had been deeply impressed by the economics essays Maynard had written for him, in the Michaelmas term of 1905, had been disappointed by the latter's determination to enter the Civil Service. But by March 1908, Maynard, now bored by the India Office, had set his sights on a King's fellowship and wrote to Pigou (then one of the King's fellowship electors) telling him that, if elected, he would at once leave the India Office and come into residence. A little over two weeks later, when Neville and Florence were enjoying a Riviera holiday, Marshall (having been alerted by Pigou of Maynard's interest in returning to Cambridge) seized the opportunity to attract a high-flyer to the economics faculty. His letter dated 3 April 1908 began:

46. Marshall's confidential letter of 8 January is in the JNK Papers, Marshall Library. It is reproduced in full in Whitaker (1996), Vol. II, p. 291.
47. The letter of resignation is in the Cambridge University Archives and is reproduced in Whitaker (1996), Vol. III, p. 168.

> Quite recently, since your father left England, I have heard in a roundabout way that it is just possible you might be willing to return to Cambridge if you had work to do here. I have also heard that your chance of an election to a fellowship at King's next year is good.

After claiming that – had he not been about to vacate his chair – he would have offered Maynard an annual fee of £100 to fill the gap in the 1908/09 lecture list (created by Macgregor's elevation to the Leeds chair of political economy), Marshall made it 'mysteriously' clear that, if Pigou were elected to the Cambridge chair, the Economics Board would invite Maynard to lecture for it and went on to promise that 'the sum of £100 will be forthcoming for you just to make you feel that you really are a lecturer. I do not think that the £100 will be paid by me: but I can guarantee that it will be paid either from some other source or by me'.[48] On this occasion Marshall did not mark his letter 'confidential' – no doubt hoping that its message would be passed on to Keynes (one of the electors to the chair). Of course it was, and on 23 April the Diary reported that Maynard planned to accept this offer 'and give up the India Office without waiting for the Fellowship'. A week later, on 30 April, Marshall followed up his advantage with the son by directly lobbying the father, who wrote:

> Interview with Marshall on the subject of the Election to the Pol.Econ. Professorship. He speaks in the highest possible terms of Pigou and is clearly most anxious that he should be elected. He very distinctly does not want Foxwell to be elected. I very much wish that I were not an Elector.'

The vacancy in the Cambridge chair of political economy was announced in the *University Reporter* of 21 April 1908, the date from which Marshall's resignation took effect, and the election was subsequently set for 30 May. The electors apart from Keynes and the vice-chancellor (then E.S. Roberts, Master of Caius), were: A.J. Balfour, Leonard Courtney, F.Y. Edgeworth (the Oxford Drummond Professor), J.S. Nicholson, R.H. Inglis Palgrave, V.H. Stanton and W.R. Sorley. Excluding Edgeworth, who was nominated (probably on Marshall's initiative) at the January 1908 meeting of the Economics Board, all of them had been appointed a number of years before Marshall resigned. The candidates were two Oxford graduates in their late forties – W.J. Ashley who had held chairs in economic history and/or economics at Toronto and Harvard and was currently in a Birmingham chair; Edwin Cannan who had taught at the London School of Economics since 1897 and was currently its professor and leading economic theorist; and two Cambridge

48. The letter to Maynard is in the King's College JMK Papers and is reproduced in Whitaker (1996), Vol. III, p. 187.

graduates – Foxwell, aged 60, who had held the University College chair since 1881, and lectured successfully in Cambridge for over 30 years; and Pigou aged 31. On the face of it, given Pigou's youth and the propensity of Cambridge electors to prefer Cambridge men, Foxwell could reasonably hope to succeed. He certainly expected to do so. After the election, in a letter to Clara Collet, his colleague at University College, he insisted that it was 'a moral certainty in Cambridge that I should be elected' and attributed his failure to the fact that Marshall deliberately set out to turn the electors against him. The available evidence seems to confirm Foxwell's assessment.[49]

On the 30 May, only eight of the nine members of the electoral board assembled in Cambridge for their meeting. Balfour, a Cambridge graduate and brother-in-law to Henry Sidgwick, had absented himself because he was sensitive to faculty divisions on the tariff reform issue.[50] When he wrote to W.A.S. Hewins asking for advice which he could pass on to the vice-chancellor, he said that he was too involved in 'the economic controversy in its party aspect to make it altogether fitting' that he should actually participate in the election. Hewins's advice – duly passed on by Balfour to the vice-chancellor – described Foxwell as 'a very safe appointment' that would be likely to 'meet with widespread approval'.[51] Two of the electors – Inglis Palgrave and Nicholson – stayed at 6 Harvey Road, as they had often done in the past. Edgeworth stayed with Marshall, of whom he was a great admirer. On the eve of the election, Neville and Florence gave a dinner party in honour of their guests and at 9.30 p.m. Edgeworth gate-crashed it to discuss the election. 'We gathered he had been sent by Marshall', the Diary noted tersely, adding 'Nicholson is intensely annoyed at what he thinks is Marshall's unfairness to Foxwell'. About the election itself, the Diary was extremely brief. After listing the electors, candidates and result, Keynes wrote poignantly: 'I was extremely sorry for Foxwell. The whole thing has worried me very much', and added 'We dined with the Marshalls. Nicholson tells me that Marshall did not speak to him the whole evening'.

Palgrave left on the following day and after remarking that he and Florence had greatly enjoyed the company of their two guests, Keynes commented ruefully: 'I think Palgrave [who seems to have attracted the admiration of 22-year-old Margaret Keynes] thoroughly enjoyed his visit and even enjoyed the election, which I certainly did not'. Nicholson left on the Monday having

49. Foxwell's letter to Clara Collet is quoted in A.W. Coats, 'The Appointment of Pigou', *Journal of Law and Economics*, Vol. 15, 1972, pp. 487–95.

50. See Coats, 'Political Economy and the Tariff Reform Campaign of 1903', *Journal of Law and Economics*, Vol. 11, 1968, pp. 181–229, which quotes the relevant Balfour–Hewins correspondence. W.A.S. Hewins then held the chair of modern economic history in the newly reorganized University of London and had been the first director of the London School of Economics.

51. Ibid., pp. 227–8.

taken the opportunity on Sunday to visit and commiserate with Foxwell. Keynes wrote: 'N. is very severe on Marshall's manoeuvering and I certainly do not think that Marshall has come out of the whole thing well'. He did not refer in the Diary to the way the votes went at the election and one subsequent commentator has speculated that Keynes might have been sufficiently moved to vote against his old friend and colleague by Pigou's readiness to provide £100 a year to finance Maynard's lectures.[52] This is difficult to believe. Had Maynard decided to give up the India Office in the interests of 'returning to Cambridge and a student's life' his father was rich enough and generous enough to support him until he won his fellowship. Moreover, the whole tenor of the Diary references to the recurrent battles between Marshall and Foxwell – whether on the contents of the latter's lectures or on the notorious 1903 manifesto to *The Times* deploring tariffs[53] – suggests that Keynes's sympathies were generally with the latter. Foxwell was a contemporary with whom he had enjoyed a companionable personal relationship for over 30 years – first as a sympathetic teacher, then as an obliging and entertaining colleague, and lately as a near neighbour and family friend. In any case, there is no reason to doubt Foxwell's account of the pattern of votes – obtained, presumably, from Nicholson, his most indignant and independent sympathizer in whom honesty was always a more potent quality than discretion. It was evidently a close-run election. The letter to Clara Collet, referred to above, listed Nicholson, Palgrave and Keynes as voting for Foxwell. Had Balfour attended, taken Hewins's advice and voted for the 'safe' appointment, the vice-chancellor would have been able to settle the issue with his casting vote – and Foxwell was convinced that the vice-chancellor would have given it to him rather than to Pigou.[54]

Not surprisingly, Foxwell, who had devoted many hours and a great deal of research effort to providing economic lectures for Cambridge's male undergraduates, over the past three decades, and whose scholarship in political economy had never been questioned, withdrew his underpaid services at once. He also resigned from the Economics Board. According to Keynes's Diary for Monday 1 June:

> Foxwell has declared his intention of no longer lecturing in Cambridge. At the request of Dickinson and Pigou I went in to see him and to try to persuade him to

52. See T.W. Jones, 'The Appointment of Pigou as Marshall's Successor', *Journal of Law and Economics*, Vol. 21, 1978, pp. 235–43.
53. In 1903, Marshall and twelve other economists signed a manifesto to *The Times* in opposition to Chamberlain's tariff reform proposals. Neither JNK nor Foxwell were signatories but Foxwell responded with a critical letter to *The Times*.
54. It is not obvious why Foxwell should have been so convinced of this. The vice-chancellor at the time of Pigou's election was E.S. Roberts, the Master of Caius, a classicist – not the Master of St John's as Groenewegen (1998), pp. 622–3, has asserted.

> reconsider the question. But I knew of course that he would not. It was one of the most painful interviews I have ever had. He had felt so confident of being elected that he had even begun to write his introductory lecture. He was quite cordial to me personally, but he was very excited and at one time I thought he wd break down. I felt and still feel, exceedingly grieved on his account. He is very bitter against Marshall, and at this I do not wonder.

Meanwhile Florence had 'one or two interviews with Mrs Foxwell' and reported that: 'She and her husband are still dreadfully upset over last Saturday's election'. Ten days later, on 14 June, Neville had 'still not recovered from the Political Economy Professorship election and all that it brought in its train. It has been like a black cloud throwing its shadow over the whole of the term'.

With Marshall in retirement and Foxwell on strike, the tensions among the dons diminished. Keynes allowed himself to be elected chairman of the Economics Board, whilst grumbling to the Diary that it was much against his inclination. Pigou followed Marshall's example by making £200 available to finance two economics lecturers during the following academic year and offered one of them to Maynard, who gladly escaped from the India Office. Keynes continued to worry needlessly over his son's career prospects in Cambridge, but Maynard's lectures were an instant success, and before long he was earning more from freelance lecturing and coaching than from Pigou's fee. By March 1909 he had won his King's fellowship and at the end of 1910 he was appointed Girdlers' lecturer. The black cloud of faculty feuds no longer hung over the Diary. The bitterness left by the Pigou election had not completely dispersed, however, and was still capable of generating unhappy episodes for Keynes. When Henry Higgs, then secretary to the Royal Economic Society, began his campaign to gather support for a personal chair for Foxwell, he naturally, if somewhat naively perhaps, wrote to Marshall. A flurry of letters from Marshall to Keynes in December 1908 made it irritably clear that he was totally opposed to the scheme.[55] In the third of these letters he announced:

> I have decided to urge him to enter into direct communication with you, on the grounds that:– 'Keynes had perhaps a higher opinion of the importance of Foxwell's specialty to Cambridge than I have: he has not committed himself as I have for the last forty years, to the opinion that Professors ought as a rule to resign at the age of sixty: partly for that reason, he does not rate as highly as I do the evils which might arise from the precedent that wd be set by founding a temporary Professorship on the understanding that Foxwell should be elected to it.' I add other reasons connected with your personal qualities and your access to the Council by means informal as well as formal.[56]

55. The letters, dated 5, 6 and 13 December 1908, are all in the Marshall Library JNK Papers. They are reproduced in Whitaker (1996), Vol. III, pp. 212–15.
56. Marshall Library, JNK Papers, reproduced in Whitaker (1996), Vol. III, pp. 214–15.

Marshall then went on to question Foxwell's judgement and to press Clapham's superior claim to a second professorship. He concluded loftily:

> For the sake of auld lang syne, I will stretch my academic conscience as far as it will go. But it has a stiff neck. It may be well that you should have learnt at an early stage how far my benevolent neutrality to Higgs' proposal is likely to reach. I am clear that I cannot *actively* support it in its present form.

Keynes did not comment on this correspondence in his Diary but he did report his interview with Higgs at the Treasury on 6 January 1909 – at which he was presumably obliged to explain that Marshall's implacable opposition to the scheme would effectively kill it in Cambridge.

3 PRESERVING THE ECONOMICS TRIPOS, 1908–18

After his retirement, Marshall ceased to be an active source of dissension among Cambridge moral scientists, and the younger men who took over the task of creating a modern Cambridge school of economics were immune to the resentment aroused in some quarters by the tactics he used to get his favourite pupils appointed. On 10 June 1908 he wrote to Maynard Keynes expressing pleasure that the latter was joining the 'brilliant compact group of earnest men full of promise for the future' which then taught for the economics tripos and artfully disclaiming any substantive role for himself in the matter.[57] A few weeks later he offered a similar welcome to the second lecturer to whom Pigou had committed (out of his own pocket) an annual stipend of £100 – Walter Layton, the only man who had so far graduated with a first in the new tripos. In 1908/09 Marshall's 'brilliant compact group' included four economists (Pigou, W.E. Johnson, J.M. Keynes and W.E. Layton), Lowes Dickinson (a popular political scientist), and three economic historians – J.H. Clapham (who had recently vacated the Leeds chair of political economy), C.R. Fay and H.O. Meredith (Pigou's successor as Girdlers' Lecturer in Economics). The result was that Neville Keynes – initially the reluctant new chairman of the Board – found himself heading a faculty which was more strongly motivated and mutually supportive than any in which he had served since Marshall returned to the Moral Sciences Board in 1885. For the next few years, Board meetings were blessedly brief events and the new tripos had recovered from the long agonizing labour that had preceded its birth.

Meanwhile Maynard won his fellowship at King's in March 1909, took the Adam Smith prize and launched into a successful teaching career.

57. Marshall Papers, reproduced in JMK, *Collected Writings* (London: Macmillan, 1971), Vol. 15, p. 14.

According to his father's Diary for 7 November 1909: 'Maynard says that he is rolling in wealth and that including the £100 1 give him has an income of £700 a year. But he proposes next academical year to do less coaching'. A few days later Maynard Keynes was elected to the Economics Board and to the Indian Civil Service Board. Maynard's success as a lecturer seems to have been instant – and legendary to judge from the running commentary in the Diary. By the Lent term of 1910 (again according to his proud father) attendance at the second lecture in his course on the modern Stock Exchange exceeded 50; on 30 July, the Diary records a rumour that 'the men like his lectures even better than Pigou's'; and on 8 October, after one of many Sundays when Maynard shared family lunch and tea at 6 Harvey Road, Neville wrote: 'In many ways he seems to be taking Pigou's place as Professor of Political Economy'. The 26-year-old had evidently become a popular teacher – as well as Marshall's most responsive contact in the new economics faculty, then developing in stature and confidence. Maynard's letter to Marshall, for example (dated 9 November 1910 just after he had been elected secretary to the Economics Board), confessed: 'in rooting through the archives I read the fly sheets issued by the opponents of the new Tripos – it is wonderful how thoroughly their predictions have been falsified' and added gleefully:

> I have just noted with interest that of the Committee and chief speakers at the Union *more than half* are doing Economics (*six* members of the Com^{ee} and three candidates). I should not be surprised if a year hence the President, Vice-President and Secretary of the Union are all doing the Economics Tripos.[58]

The rise in its popularity certainly confounded the predictions of those who had argued that a separate economics tripos would divert scarce teaching resources to an unpopular subject. In 1910 the number passing with honours in Parts I and II was 29; and by 1914 the number was 44. Meanwhile the moral sciences tripos still stagnated with only 15 successful honours candidates.

Tempers were so relaxed on the Economics Board of which Neville was now chairman and Maynard secretary, that Foxwell was persuaded to rejoin it at the beginning of 1912. Marshall's letter to Neville, rejoicing at the news, persuaded the latter to act as go-between, for the last time. Foxwell responded acidly:

> I return Marshall's note. It has an unpleasantly false ring about it, and he was right not to address it to me. I have no doubt he is glad now as he has always been that others should help in work which he despises and neglects. I mean in providing

58. Marshall Papers, Letter reprinted in Whitaker (1996), Vol. III, p. 272

> for the pol man, for examinations & on correspondence with the outside world. … However, his opinion does not affect me one way or the other.[59]

Nevertheless, Foxwell did not resume his lectures to Cambridge men. They were no longer needed. By 1912/13 the Cambridge School of Economics had access to a relatively rich source of first-class graduates who were willing and able to teach the realistically based analytical skills that its founder had envisaged as the essential equipment of a modern professional economist. The core lectures on economics were delivered by keen Marshallians, most under the age of 40, who personally set and assessed question papers written by their auditors. Maynard Keynes, then in his thirtieth year, carried the heaviest load. Apart from his twice-weekly lectures on principles of economics throughout the year he offered three or four lectures a week on money matters – ranging over theory, institutions and policy problems. Pigou gave twice-weekly lectures on distribution and labour, plus a class on selected current policy problems and was available in his rooms for two hours weekly (as Marshall had been) to be consulted informally by any student seeking guidance on economic questions. Walter Layton, the other lecturer teaching full-time for the economics tripos, gave twice-weekly lectures on the structure and problems of modern industry as well as a class on the use of diagrams in elementary economics. In addition to this substantial foundation layer of analytical economics, various supporting courses were provided by other academics whose interests and expertise synchronized with Marshall's vision of economic science. They included, for example, W.E. Johnson lecturing on mathematical economics, J.H. Clapham on modern economic history, G. Udny Yule on elementary statistical method, and C.R. Fay on elementary economics for beginners. Finally, two recent tripos firsts were listed among the Board's recommended lectures: Gerald Shove who offered a course on the economic functions of government; and F. Lavington (a mature student with eleven years practical experience in banking before matriculating at Cambridge) applied Marshallian techniques of analysis to the market for capital.

With this relatively youthful and energetic talent at its disposal, it is not surprising that the Economics Board did not invite Foxwell to contribute to its unprecedently full lecture list. By then Cambridge was at least as effective as any British university in providing a training ground for modern professional economists and was attracting an increasing number of employable candidates. The effect of the 1914–18 war, however, was drastically to reduce the Board's teaching resources. Neville Keynes, its chairman, then found that

59. Foxwell's letter dated 6 February 1912 is in JNK Papers, Marshall Library. It is reprinted in Whitaker (1996), Vol. III, p. 292.

the bitterness aroused by the election of Pigou still festered in certain college common rooms, and was capable of unleashing another disagreeable bout of academic in-fighting. At the beginning of the academic year 1914/15, the young men who staffed the Cambridge School of Economics moved rapidly into war work – most of them in the civil service or the armed forces. By the Lent term Pigou was the only man left of those who had provided the core teaching for the 1914 tripos. True, the number of male undergraduates reading for the tripos had also already dropped sharply, and one well-qualified woman – Lynda Grier[60] – was available to fill the gap left by C.R. Fay. On the other hand, teachers of the calibre of Maynard Keynes, Walter Layton or Udny Yule were irreplaceable. Since Pigou's vacations were largely absorbed by his front-line Red Cross work in France or Italy, Neville was increasingly worried by the prospect of losing the professor himself, which would render insoluble the problem of providing a minimum basis of teaching for the tripos. On 10 December 1915, he grumbled to the Diary: 'Discussion with Pigou. I have decided that he is necessary for the Economics work at Cambridge. It seems to me a clear case. He would of course like to be back in Italy'. The situation reached crisis proportions when the government decided to introduce compulsory service for single men under the age of 40. It was at its meeting on 28 January 1916, that the Economics Board formally charged its chairman with the task of persuading the vice-chancellor that the university should seek exemption from conscription for its 39-year-old professor of political economy.

The Tribunal that was to hear the case for exempting Pigou was scheduled for 10 May 1916. During the preceding two weeks the dons who shared Archdeacon William Cunningham's views on economics set out to publicize their contempt for Cambridge economists and to get rid of Marshall's successor. The opening salvo in their campaign of denigration took the form of a letter to the editor of the *Cambridge Daily News*, which was printed on 26 April, under the heading 'The Teaching of Economics in Cambridge'. It was signed R.H. Macleod[61] and began:

> Sir: Professor Pigou's case is to be heard by the Borough Tribunal early in May. It will come up as based on a representation by the Special Board for Economics

60. After her first class tripos result in 1908, Lynda Grier had taught Newnhamites economics for several years. Significantly – to the indignation of Maynard Keynes – the secretary to the General Board of Studies had refused to allow her to be listed in the *CUR* when she began lecturing to the male undergraduates.
61. Macleod was a Londoner in his early sixties who joined Caius College, Cambridge in 1913 and began lecturing in Indian Law to ICS candidates in 1915. His interest in Cambridge economics can be attributed to the fact that he was the son of H.D. Macleod – a lawyer and highly unconventional writer on economic matters who had applied unsuccessfully for the Cambridge chair of political economy in 1863, and again in 1884, and lectured in the subject for the Moral Sciences Board in the 1870s.

> and Politics that his services are indispensable. It would be presumption on my part to raise any question as regards Professor Pigou personally, the matter being one entirely for the Board and the Tribunal to settle between themselves. But there is a larger question of public interest, behind and underlying the individual case and opinion is by no means divided on it. That underlying question is: 'Is the teaching of economics, at least of the particular brand in favour in Cambridge indispensable in wartime?'

Macleod then went on to paraphrase and quote from a paper which Cunningham had read to the last meeting of the British Association for the Advancement of Science, and which provided ammunition for an attack on the 'doctrines of the Cambridge School'. The main point of the argument he took over from Cunningham was that the school's exaggerated emphasis on consumption was inappropriate in wartime when economists should be focusing on production. It was laced, however, with observations that were more directly concerned with private malice than public interest. There was a covert dig, for example, at Marshall in the passage which began: 'Those who are anxious to insist on their intellectual kinship with Germany seem to take little heed of national security in the long run', and came to the conclusion:

> Short-sighted opinion as to British interests seems to have played into the hands of the militants in Germany and to have helped to bring about the outbreak of war. There is also some reason for believing that the leading school of economists in England has, by its exaggerations, exerted an influence in preventing the war from being prosecuted effectively.

This spiteful accusation was followed by a sneer at Pigou's monograph *Wealth and Welfare* (1912):

> Professor Pigou and the school of economists who look primarily at individual comfort in the present, and seem to think the welfare of the public in the long run may be trusted to take care of itself are as one-sided and mistaken as the classical economists of a hundred years ago.

Macleod concluded triumphantly: 'If Cunningham is right and there seems to have been no reply to him, how is the continuance of such teaching desirable, let alone indispensable, during the war?'

Macleod's letter also appeared in the *Morning Post*. On 29 April Neville responded with a letter to the *Cambridge Daily News* and Pigou wrote to the *Morning Post*. Pigou's rejoinder appeared on 30 April, under the heading 'The Teaching of Economics in Cambridge', and was an indignant defence of the Cambridge School:

> [Macleod's] letter, while purporting to discuss the general question whether the teaching of economics in war time is indispensable is really an attack on 'the

> particular brand of economics in favour at Cambridge' and therefore indirectly on the competence of our teaching staff. I naturally shall not discuss with the gentleman my own qualifications for the position I hold, but his letter though designed exclusively for my benefit, in fact contains imputations on a number of other people. Of the gentlemen other than myself currently engaged in teaching economics for the Cambridge Honours School, *all* are at present in war service either of Departments of Government or of the Army and the suggestion that the 'brand of economics' favoured by them is of a kind to breed carelessness of the public interest is as stupid as it is gratuitous.

Pigou then went on to suggest that Macleod's critique should be aimed directly at himself instead of 'endeavouring by vague and ignorant innuendos to throw discredit on an important department of the University'.

Neville Keynes's coldly incisive castigation of Macleod's impertinent letter was published in the *Cambridge Daily News* on 1 May and written in his capacity as chairman of the Economics Board:

> The writer disclaims any intention to prejudice the case of Professor Pigou when the appeal for his exemption comes before the Borough Tribunal, although it is difficult to understand what other immediate object he can have in view. His professed object is, by means of quotation from a paper read by Dr Cunningham, to launch an attack against the Cambridge School of Economists. With Dr Cunningham's charges I am not now concerned to deal and of Mr Macleod's qualifications to act as a critic of economic teaching I know nothing.
>
> I should like, however, to point out that with the exception of Professor Pigou, all the full lecturers for the Tripos – five in number – are now engaged on war work in the Army, the Treasury or the Ministry of Munitions; and it may be added that the most recent VC took the Economics Tripos in 1913. As regards these old pupils, there can be no question of their devotion to Professor Pigou; nor can there be any doubt, on the part of those who best know the work he has done, of the utility of his work to the State.
>
> To characterise as detrimental to national interests the teaching of a school which has bred up a body of men, who were among the first to offer their services to their country, and whose services have been accepted by the Government in important capacities is as unique as it is ungenerous.

That letter should have ended the matter, but the pot had been stirred and Cunningham could not resist keeping it on the boil by accepting Pigou's invitation to challenge his competence directly. Cunningham's rambling letter beginning: 'Professor Pigou … shows once more that he is concerned to evade criticism rather than to reply to it', appeared in the *Morning Post* on 2 May. It recalled, imprecisely, an earlier controversy on the incidence of taxation in which Pigou had participated and which 'readers of the *Morning Post* may remember'. It then suggested that Pigou had not bothered to read the British Association paper which Macleod had quoted so faithfully – otherwise he must have known that, far from being a collection of wholesale 'insinuations' its critique was openly 'discriminating'. Cunningham went on to assert patronizingly:

> While recognising the excellent work which the analytic school have done in the investigation of particular economic problems ... [my paper] points out that this is not necessarily a qualification for dealing with the broad issues on which Professor Pigou himself writes. Had the Professor taken this criticism into account he would not have been so ready to discourse airily on the cost of the war.

In a letter published the following day in the *Morning Post*, Pigou – reluctantly provoked by what he described as Cunningham's 'catalogue of past sins and inconsistencies which I am alleged to have committed' – tried to close the correspondence by briefly reiterating his protest against 'a wholesale and singularly ungenerous attack upon a University department ... all the members of which besides myself are now serving the State', and by announcing that he had no more to say on the subject. His letter began, however, with a slighting reference to 'a certain R.H. Macleod, who has recently become attached to the University and who as far as I know, has no acquaintance with economic science'. This gave Cunningham his opening to list Macleod's claims to question 'whether it is essential that the academic study of Economics should be continued in Cambridge during the war'. In a letter printed in the *Morning Post* on 4 May, Cunningham insisted first that 'as the son of my old friend H.D. Macleod he was brought up in an atmosphere of Economics'; second that he had made 'some study' of the subject whilst preparing for the Indian Civil Service examination; and third that 'during the administration of an Indian Province he obtained considerable insight in dealing with practical economic problems'. Two days later, encouraged by this testimonial, Macleod wrote a second letter to the *Morning Post* – beginning triumphantly 'May I call the next witness' – in which he quoted at length from G.C. Coulton's book, *Illusions of Pacifism* (1915) – and attacked Pigou's 'irresponsible idealism'. By then the readers of the *Morning Post* must have had more than enough of this obscure academic controversy. Keynes's impatient reference in his Diary for 6 May described Cunningham's and Macleod's final letters as 'beneath contempt'.

There were many members of the Senate who did not share his view, however, and he found that getting the agreement of the General Board of Studies to the case for exempting Pigou from military service was not at all easy. The Diary for 8 May reports a 'very trying meeting' of the General Board which ended in a vote in which eight members raised their hands in favour, five were against and four abstained; since another five were absent this left Keynes with a good deal of lobbying to bring the absentees in line. He also did his best to persuade Foxwell to rally to the assistance of the Cambridge economics faculty at this time of crisis. After a meeting of the

Economics Board on 19 May, he reported: 'Pigou, Clapham and I decided that it wd be well to ask Foxwell if he wd if necessary lecture in Pigou's place. I called on Foxwell and he said he wd not do so, notwithstanding all the pressure I put on him to decide otherwise'.

Three days later, on 22 May 1916, Keynes presented to the Borough Tribunal the university's case for exempting Pigou. He was watched by an audience which included Florence and Margaret. According to the report of its proceedings which appeared in the *Cambridge Daily News* that evening:

> He [JNK] stated that normally they had 6 lecturers and that Prof. Pigou was the only one left. ... He had been with the Red Cross in France twice during the vacations ... and was a member of the 1st British Ambulance Unit for which he had provided 2 cars at his own expense. ... At the Professor's own request he had seen Professor Foxwell who was at the University of London, but who lived at Cambridge and he had declared that he was willing to do part of Prof. Pigou's work and give some lectures in Cambridge although it would be difficult for him to do this before Christmas. He would not have time to look through papers and give individual attention to students. Even if Professor Pigou continued to lecture they would be glad of his help in Cambridge. The duty of a professor was not only to lecture but also to carry on research work and he (the speaker) attached great importance to the work Prof. Pigou was doing.

All seemed to go well on this occasion and the Diary noted with relief that the Tribunal had let Pigou off very easily.

It was by no means the last battle, however. On 23 May, Keynes was astonished to get a letter from Foxwell complaining that he had been misrepresented at the Tribunal. On 24 May, Foxwell publicized his own somewhat ingenuous version of events in a letter to the *Cambridge Daily News*. He referred to the newspaper's report of the Appeal Tribunal's proceedings 'in which, I am sure by inadvertence, a statement made by me to Dr Keynes is entirely misrepresented'. He then elaborated:

> Dr Keynes asked me on May 19th if I should be willing to act, if necessary, as a substitute for the Professor of Political Economy. The same question had already been put to me by other members of the University. My answer in each case was the same. I said that I should be able to give not less than the average amount of instruction which had been given by the Professor. The offer was otherwise unconditional, either as to time of commencement, or as to the nature of the work. I do not think anyone would gather this from the terms of the report. It is there dressed up in such an embroidery of exceptions as to make it equivalent to a refusal.

Alfred Marshall's feelings on reading this exchange must have been coloured by a wry sense of *déjà vu*. Keynes's instant response appeared in the *Cambridge Daily News* on 25 May and stated the salient facts in characteristically succinct terms:

> I understood from my interview with Prof. Foxwell that he was exceedingly busy and likely to continue so until Christmas, but that he was willing if necessary to give up part of his work and deliver lectures in Cambridge. I understood further that he did not feel sure that he could look over papers or give personal attention to individual students. This was what I stated before the Tribunal. Since it appears, however, that Professor Foxwell does not accept this description of his attitude I can only express my regret that my recollections of the conversation do not correspond with his.

Given the well-orchestrated opposition to Pigou's exemption by the hawkish members of Cambridge's Senate,[62] it is hardly surprising that the military authorities appealed against the Tribunal's decision of 22 May. As a result, Keynes spent another miserable week in mid-June worrying about the outcome. This time John Clapham volunteered to present the case and on 21 June the Tribunal rejected the appeal and unanimously exempted Pigou. Less than a year later, Keynes was plunged back into gloom when the university was again called upon to defend Pigou's exemption; for, since Clapham was not free at the appointed date, the responsibility would fall on himself as the Board's Chairman. 'We wonder how far Macleod & Co. have been at work', he wrote on 29 April 1917, 'The other University men whose cases originally came up with Pigou have apparently not been called upon to appear any more'. In the event, a letter from S.J. Chapman (then Manchester's professor of political economy) seems to have satisfied the Tribunal. Pigou's exemption was confirmed without further formal representations and a skeletonic Cambridge School of Economics survived the war years.

62. The 'hawks' had identified themselves in early 1914 by requesting the Council of the Senate to nominate a Syndicate to consider how best to carry into effect (in cooperation with other universities) certain proposals ventilated in the *Nineteenth Century* for compulsory military training of undergraduates. Their Memorial, signed by 1714 mostly non-resident members of the university, attracted a counter declaration signed by a smaller (and younger) group of relatively active members of the university who claimed that it would be highly undesirable for the university to exert its authority to enforce any form of military service. In the event, the Council did not publish its report in the *CUR* until the start of the October term – by which time the outbreak of war had made it redundant and in December 1914 the vice-chancellor announced that the Council had decided not to bring it to congregation for discussion then.

Florence Keynes (c. 1905)

IX Post-Victorian academic family

1 THE NEW CENTURY

When Queen Victoria died in the first month of the first year of the twentieth century, seven sat down to dinner in the dining room of 6 Harvey Road. In addition to Florence and Neville, there were his mother Anna (with a widowed old friend currently visiting her in Bateman Street) and three teenagers in the last week of their school holidays – Maynard and Margaret from Eton and Wycombe Abbey, respectively, and Geoffrey still a Cambridge day-boy at St Faith's. The Diary for Sunday 22 January 1901 recorded:

> The Queen died at 6.30 pm. The first information we had was the tolling (at intervals of one minute) of the bell of the Roman Catholic Church – begun just after we sat down to dinner (at 7.30). After dinner Maynard and Geoffrey went out and bought a copy of the *Daily News* containing particulars. The German Emperor came over on Sunday to be with his Grandmother at the end.

Less than nine months later all three of the Keynes children were happily settled in boarding schools and the eldest had already won the scholarship to King's College, which he was to enter in October 1902.

For the family in residence at no. 6, life had never been fuller or happier than it was in the first decade of the new century. A growing investment income ensured that there were no money problems constraining their expenditures on holidays or hobbies or on offering hospitality to friends and family members. Neville, as secretary to the Council of the Senate, as well as chief secretary to the Local Examinations Syndicate, normally worked a weekly average in full term, of between 50 and 60 hours on administrative tasks, whilst still carrying the main responsibility for teaching logic to men and women reading for the moral sciences tripos. At the same time, Florence was increasingly occupied by her voluntary activities on behalf of the Charity Organisation Society together with a multitude of women's committees and discussion groups arising out of its welfare functions. As wife to one of the university's leading administrators, she also participated regularly in the ceremonial social occasions of a relatively elevated academic circle. True, her gender excluded her from the customary sequence of college Feasts which sometimes succeeded each other so closely as to play havoc with Neville's digestion. On the other hand she invariably partnered him at the more exclusive lunch or dinner parties where heads of houses, professors, and members of the university's governing bodies privately entertained each other's families as well as distinguished foreign visitors.

Meanwhile, of course, Florence remained the lynchpin in each of the domestic reorganizations called for by changes in the way of life of her husband and children. When Maynard took up residence in King's in the late summer of 1902, for example, it was his mother who arranged the furnishing of his college rooms – just as she was to do for Geoffrey when he entered Pembroke four years later. Similarly, when it was decided that Margaret's education should be 'finished' by sending her to spend six months with a German family, Florence made all the necessary arrangements and herself travelled to Wittenberg in September 1903 – to make sure that her daughter was welcomed into a suitably caring household. She fetched her back home six months later, this time with 20-year-old Maynard as their companion. When Neville wanted to expand his working space by annexing a room from the semi-detached house at no. 5, it was Florence who planned and supervised the day-to-day building, decorating and furnishing operations, so that her husband could move smoothly into the new study which so delighted him late in 1905. 'Florence has of course been taking the thing in hand and she is working tremendously hard at it', he wrote gratefully on 14 December. Two days later, Geoffrey's mother was the parent who accompanied him to his last House Supper at Rugby school, leaving her husband to spend most of that weekend working in the comfortable privacy of his spacious new study. Back in Cambridge, two weeks later, she took over one of his time-consuming tasks (as editor of the *University Reporter*), by carefully revising for the Press the annual Index he had compiled during the Christmas vacation. More significant, however, than her dependable assistance with the minutiae of Neville's multiple workload, was Florence's firm loving support through certain emotionally stressful episodes of a personal nature. It was her sympathetically steadying influence, for example, which rescued her distraught husband from a persistent deep depression that followed the death of his beloved mother in 1907.

2 WOMEN'S WORK

The overriding objective Florence had in view, when she accepted the Newnham College Exhibition that she won at the December 1877 Senior Local examination, had been to acquire higher education qualifications that were relevant to the teaching requirements of her mother's school at the Bedford Manse. Roughly 70 years later she was to write:

> As there was a gap to be filled before going to Newnham I was sent to the family of a Pastor at Bonn where a few girls were received for the finishing touches to be given to the rather elementary education then provided for girls of good family in Germany. Fortunately I was the only English girl there and as I had had a grounding in German grammar from an excellent modern languages tutor … I was able to pick up the spoken language fairly quickly.[1]

Given her mother's urgent perennial need for aid in the Manse school, Florence did not expect to stay at Newnham long enough to face a tripos examination. She therefore concentrated on preparing for the Higher Local examination – where she got the results she needed, in English, German and mathematics, at the end of her second Cambridge academic year. For most girls maturing in the Victorian era, becoming a schoolmistress (or a governess) was virtually the only career opened up by a university education. However, by the time Florence left Newnham, and began full-time teaching at her mother's school, she was already engaged to an established academic with a modest investment income, to whom within a year of their marriage, she had borne the first of their three children. Consequently, until the turn of the century, Florence had been primarily occupied by her domestic responsibilities for home-making, child-rearing and organization of a continuously hospitable household. It was not until early in the first decade of the twentieth century – when her three children were at boarding school or university – that she was free to allow her interest in the work of the Charity Organisation Society to swallow a substantial and increasing proportion of her time and energy.

The Charity Organisation Society (COS) – founded in 1869 under the forbidding title of the 'Society for Organising Charitable Relief and Reforming Mendicity' – originally flaunted a fiercely moralistic set of principles, reflecting sentiments and attitudes that were largely outdated for the thousands of women voluntarily labouring under its auspices a generation later.[2] By the first decade of the twentieth century – when Florence was one of three honorary secretaries administering the Society's Cambridge office at 92 Regent Street – it had developed a more positive, practical and investigative approach to the problems of relieving poverty. In the detailed list of Cambridge charities, the compilation of which Florence herself initiated, she described COS objectives and procedures as follows:

> The object of the Society is to improve the condition of the poor and for this purpose: (1) to effect cooperation between all available agencies; (2) to increase,

1. Florence Ada Keynes, *Gathering Up the Threads* (Cambridge: Heffer & Sons, 1950), p. 35. Bedford was a reputable educational centre for boys and Mrs Brown could hire visiting tutors from a pool of experienced masters, to prepare her pupils at the Manse school for the Cambridge Local examinations.
2. See Michael Rose, *The Relief of Poverty, 1834–1914* (London: Macmillan, 1972), pp. 25–8.

> focus and disseminate scientific knowledge as to the causes of distress and the most efficient remedial methods; (3) to deal with cases coming under the notice of the Society in such a manner as to render them independent of future charitable help.

She went on to emphasize that the condition and history of every applicant (or case referred to the office by interested persons or organizations), was carefully investigated before any decisions were taken on the matter. The Cambridge Executive Committee, she explained, met weekly

> to ascertain the causes of distress and to arrange for such treatment as will permanently benefit the applicant and restore him and his family to independence. The applications are referred, as far as possible to the existing local charities, but failing these are dealt with by the Executive itself. Interim help is given, if necessary, pending enquiries, and aid to obtaining employment, loans, medical assistance, pensions, or other help is granted, or any other means adopted as may seem most conducive to the end in view.[3]

The Cambridge office, which maintained a small social services library, also displayed a 'charity organisation worklist of charwomen, needlewomen, window cleaners, and others wanting employment', and was open each weekday afternoon to members of the public wishing to consult such information or seek general advice from its voluntary staff.

Given her position as wife to the secretary of the university's prime governing body – the Council of the Senate – Florence was particularly well placed to organize the 1901 national Conference of the Charity Organisation Society in Cambridge. She had, moreover, direct personal access to a relatively rich resource of academic wives and daughters with the requisite time, education and intelligence to assist in the advisory or investigative activities of the Society's Cambridge office. After Mrs Jebb (Sir Richard Jebb's sister) moved to set up home near her brother's family in Cambridge, she was joined by her daughter Eglantyne – disenchanted by the schoolmistress's career for which she had been trained and now chasing a new outlet for her energies.[4] It was actually Mary Marshall who sent her to the Cambridge COS office where Mrs Keynes could be relied upon to point a lively well-educated young woman towards useful and worthwhile voluntary work.[5] So, in 1903, Eglantyne involved herself in Florence's project to draw up a complete register of

3. Charity Organisation Society, *The Cambridge Register of Social and Philanthropic Agencies* (Cambridge: Bowes & Bowes, 1911), p. 8.
4. Sir Richard Jebb (1841–1905) was Cambridge Regius Professor of Greek from 1889 and also served as the university's Member of Parliament from 1891 to 1905.
5. Eglantyne Jebb read history at Lady Margaret Hall, Oxford, before going to Stockwell Teachers' Training College and then teaching at elementary school. See Francesca M. Wilson, *Rebel Daughter of a Country House* (London: Allen & Unwin, 1967).

Cambridge charities and went on to write a book entitled *Cambridge, a Brief Study of Social Questions*, which was published locally in 1906. In the following year, she spearheaded another of Florence's COS initiatives by launching, for the first time in Cambridge, a Boys' Employment Registry. The objective was to reduce teenage unemployment by bringing to the notice of suitable employers those elementary school leavers who seemed ready and able to acquire skills that could improve their prospects of permanent employment. Eglantyne had the self-confidence, drive and organizing ability to get this enterprise launched. Operating it, however, called for personal qualities of a different kind. These she was able to generate by inspiring Florence's 22-year-old daughter Margaret to undertake the patient day-to-day legwork (and face-to-face interviews) involved in selecting promising boys, identifying suitable employers and monitoring the success of the resultant employment experience in each case.

Margaret's association with Eglantyne (a charismatic personality nine years her senior) combined with her own clearheaded, unsentimental concern for the immature unemployed youngsters on the Boys' Employment Registry to generate a lasting personal interest in hands-on social work. Since leaving school she had shown no inclination to commit herself to a regular occupation – paid or unpaid. Neville gave his daughter a regular allowance and encouraged her to keep accounts of her annual income, expenditure and saving, but it does not appear that he ever seriously contemplated the possibility of her earning a living. She was active in various hobbies of a practical or artistic nature; she gardened an allotment, for example, and even defrayed part of the expense by selling its produce; and she took lessons in bookbinding – a skill which occasionally earned her a few shillings. The year after leaving Wycombe Abbey school, she got a letter from its headmistress, offering her a position of teacher in bookbinding at a stipend of £10 a term plus full board and lodging. Her indulgent father reported the letter in his May 1905 Diary, with the comment: 'We feel, however, that we could not spare her and her own view is that she is not yet sufficiently proficient in the art'. No doubt her mother took a more positive view, for by the end of September Margaret (then aged 20) was cheerfully in post at Wycombe Abbey. She wrote home: 'I dont find schoolmarming very dreadful after all my qualms but I shouldn't like to spend my life at it'. Evidently Margaret was a welcome member of the school teaching staff and was soon invited to teach German as well as bookbinding. In another of many letters home she claimed that she was enjoying the experience, but it seems merely to have confirmed her view that she did not want to make a career of 'schoolmarming' and she declined the invitation to return for another stint.

Characteristically, Florence responded to her daughter's buoyant enthusiasm for Eglantyne Jebb's newly created Boys' Registry by sending her to

London COS centres in Stepney, Southwark and Whitechapel, where similar schemes were already in operation. There Margaret saw at first hand how experienced volunteers dealt with the practical problems of matching boys to employers and was allowed to conduct some of the crucial interviews unsupervised. The London experience increased her confidence to such an extent that – when the restless, ambitious Eglantyne decided to leave Cambridge in pursuit of more exotic and challenging activities – Margaret was persuaded to take over as organizing secretary for the Boys' Employment Registry. That was in 1908. Finding jobs for 14-year-old boys from deprived, often feckless, sometimes dishonest, families proved an exacting, frequently disappointing, but highly educative, form of social work. She had hoped, for example, that one of her unusually imaginative clients, who had declared a bold ambition to 'go to sea', would 'open out another road for the rougher boys of Cambridge' – only to find that, as soon as he saw the fishing boat on which he was to embark, his courage drained out of him. 'I telegraphed that I would come to Grimsby next day if they would keep him until then but he had started home before they received it', she wrote despairingly in her diary.[6] Despite such setbacks Margaret was to describe 1908 as 'a peculiarly happy year' and at the end of it her father commented with satisfaction: 'Margaret has written a very interesting report on the work of her Boys' Registry during the past year'. A couple of years later she went further, producing a thoughtful and informative pamphlet on *The Problem of Boy Labour in Cambridge*, published in 1911. It concluded with the optimistic observation: 'Already a few employers are realising that it is to their profit as well as of the boys to allow the better boys off an hour earlier on certain days of week to attend classes; but probably legislation will be required before this becomes universal'. She went on to argue: 'no more costly system can be conceived than that which now throws on the community a stream of unemployables, if not of criminals and paupers'.[7]

Before the end of the first decade of the twentieth century then, both Florence and her daughter were cheerfully involved in useful voluntary social work. Florence herself, having at last consented to be nominated in the 1907 election to the Cambridge Board of Guardians, was duly elected and regularly thereafter returned unopposed. In 1914 she was elected the first woman member of Cambridge Town Council of which she remained an active member over most of three decades – becoming the town's first woman mayor in 1932/33. Margaret's public service work in Cambridge was interrupted by

6. I am grateful to Polly Hill, her daughter, for allowing me to read the 1908 diary in which Margaret Keynes recorded some of her early experiences with the Boys' Employment Registry.
7. M.N. Keynes, *The Problem of Boy Labour in Cambridge* (Cambridge: Bowes & Bowes, 1911), p. 23.

her marriage to A.V. Hill (a Trinity fellow who was destined to become a Nobel prizewinner) to whom she bore the first of four children in 1914 and the last in 1919. In the 1920s when this family was living in London (Highgate), Margaret again followed in her mother's footsteps by first going on to the Board of Guardians and then standing for the Hornsey Borough Council to which she was elected in 1929 and served until 1948. Meanwhile, she had founded the Hornsey Housing Trust to provide cheap housing for elderly people and underprivileged large families and continued to pioneer subsidized housing and special-care facilities for the frail and aged poor of London.[8] In 1957 her achievements in the field of voluntary public service won her the award of a CBE.

3 MAYNARD ON THE FINAL EXAMINATION TREADMILL

Neville and Florence had high expectations for their two sons – each of whom took decisive charge of his own career. Maynard, however, having excelled in every competitive examination that he found challenging enough to enter, was to become the natural repository of his father's unfulfilled academic ambitions. Having left school on a cloud of glory with an Open Scholarship to King's College he donned cap and gown, on 2 October 1902, to call on W.H. Macaulay – the tutor who was to direct his undergraduate studies for the next three years. Neville had already arranged that E.W. Hobson (then university lecturer in mathematics, later professor), should coach him for the mathematical tripos and from then on the Diary reflected a nagging anxiety that Maynard would not work hard enough to gain the high first-class result that his schoolmasters were convinced he merited. On 15 October, for example, it reported: 'Tea with Maynard … he finds it quite impossible to do more than 6 hours a day. … [W.M.] Page [his main rival at King's] does 8'. Neville continually quizzed the 19-year-old's teachers. A month later, he wrote: 'Hobson says that Maynard is doing very little work just now … he will have to work much harder … to get a good place in the Tripos'. The fact was that Neville was miserably aware that Maynard found tripos mathematics an uninspiring chore (as he himself had done a generation before) and was absolutely determined not to devote more than six hours a day to routine cramming when there were so many more intellectually and socially pleasurable pursuits open to an Etonian Kingsman in the Edwardian

8. Margaret Neville Keynes, *An Approach to Old Age and Its Problems* (Edinburgh: Oliver & Boyd, 1961) is an instructive record of personal experience of caring for the elderly poor over roughly a quarter of a century including the period of the Second World War.

era. Early in his second term, Maynard was invited into the most prestigious of Cambridge societies – the Apostles or Conversazione Society, a self-perpetuating elite group of (largely) senior academics – in whose discussions he was to participate with active enthusiasm. Meanwhile, Neville had himself made his son a life member of the Union (the leading undergraduate society) in October of his first year. In that popular forum the freshman acquired a reputation as an articulate and intelligent debater and was elected successively secretary and president in his second and final years.[9]

Neville's anxieties about Maynard's tripos prospects rose to an agonized crescendo during the latter's final undergraduate year, 1904/05. In spite of his first-class result in the preliminary examination – the 'May', taken a few days after his 21st birthday – his father's Diary worried that it had been a close thing.[10] Nor did Neville's pleasure in recording the congratulations of colleagues and friends on the speeches, essay prizes, learned papers, journalistic writings and innumerable other evidences of his son's distractions from the straight and narrow path to distinction in the maths tripos overshadow the fears they engendered. He constantly interrogated the King's teaching fellows, as well as Maynard himself, on the boy's preparation for the tripos. On 6 December, for example, the Diary notes wrily: '[Arthur] Berry says he believes that Maynard is honestly giving his "spare time" to Mathematics. In the circumstances he is surprised at how much he gets done'. And according to the entry for 23 February: 'Berry complains that he is not doing enough work; but he says his average is between 5 and 6 hours a day'. The imperturbable good humour with which Maynard tolerated this relentless parental inquisition is a testament to the genuine quality of their relationship. In April 1905, while on holiday in Truro, Maynard (never an early riser) wrote reassuringly to his anxious father: 'This is the most industrious week I have had this year. ... My morning hours would surprise you!' A week later after reporting on a conversation with Maynard (now back at Harvey Road), Neville acknowledged hopefully 'Maynard has planned out his work very methodically', but calculated gloomily that a great amount of work still remained to be covered.

On the morning that the tripos examination began in May 1905, Neville went early to Maynard's rooms in King's to ensure that the candidate was awake and rising. While he was there his tutor, Macaulay, 'looked in for the same purpose'. Thereafter Macaulay, gratefully no doubt, abandoned his tutorial watch in the knowledge that the pupil's father could be relied upon to

9. These were only two of the debating or discussion societies in which Maynard participated as an undergraduate. See D.E. Moggridge, *Maynard Keynes: An Economist's Biography* (London: Routledge, 1992), pp. 68–74 for details of his varied activities.
10. Diary 11 June 1904. Neville persuaded one of the examiners to show him the marksheet before the results were officially announced.

do the wake-up duty each morning and faithfully monitor his son's mental or physical state. In the event the ordeal by examination took the form of two concentrated four-day sessions spent writing answers to questions, separated by twelve days hard cramming. By the end of the first four days the father was much more tired and stressed than the candidate and the Diary reported sadly: 'I think he is going to do badly and I am oppressed by the fact that I ought not to have encouraged him to read Mathematics at all. He has throughout found the subject irksome'. As for Maynard, he merely complained of cramp in his hand while the writing sessions were in progress, but he found the twelve-day spell of revision intolerably tedious and enervating. When Neville walked from morning service at Emmanuel Chapel into his son's rooms on Sunday 28 May, the latter grumbled that he had just done 'the hardest week's work of his life – an average of 7 hours a day'. That was far from arduous by Neville's standards and he commented: 'What he finds difficult is not the intellectual effort, but the moral effort necessary to due concentration of attention'.

After the examination finished, on Saturday 3 June, Neville managed to focus on the article he was writing on butterflies and moths the family had captured during their 1904 summer holiday in Switzerland. But he continued to worry. When Maynard predicted (accurately as it turned out) that he could be as high as the twelfth wrangler, Neville groaned to the Diary: 'I am afraid he is too sanguine', and confessed to repetitive nightmares in which he waited in vain for the name Keynes to feature among the wranglers during the ritual reading of the class list at the Senate House. The results were scheduled to be announced on 13 June but, after the previous morning's Council meeting, Neville managed to wheedle advance information from one of the examiners: 'I called on [J.M.] Dodds, he wrote, 'and he relieved my mind of its worst fears concerning Maynard'. The following day Neville and Florence went together to the Senate House to hear their son bracketed twelfth wrangler and agreed, according to the Diary, that they were satisfied with the result, although 'the boy might have done better had he devoted himself exclusively to Maths'. On 20 June when Maynard marched up for his degree – proudly watched by both parents, grandmother and Aunt Fanny – the Diary recorded Neville's regret that the boy had 'not been very well or wisely taught for Tripos purposes', alongside Maynard's cheerful admission that he was glad not to have given more time to maths even though it would have meant a better place in the class list.

The whole family could and did relax when their golden boy had cleared the tripos hurdle in the first class. For Maynard's scholarship at King's had another year to run and he could take his time weighing up and choosing between different career options. Always risk-averse, Neville instantly introduced an outside possibility by arranging for them to lunch with Arthur

Spokes – his University College contemporary, now a well-established barrister – who could sponsor Maynard's entry to the Inner Temple. However unenthusiastic the latter may have felt about the examination-ridden route to the Bar, he embarked cheerfully on the traditional programme of 'eating dinners' with members of the legal fraternity. Within a week of his graduation, the Diary reported with satisfaction that he had 'now eaten two dinners at the Inner Temple'. Henceforth, although Neville conscientiously avoided pressuring his son's choice of a career he never missed an opportunity of reviewing his options with him. It was open to Maynard to spend the academic year 1905/06 reading for either the moral sciences tripos or the economics tripos, or in preparing for the Civil Service examination in August. Either tripos would involve working on subjects relevant to the Civil Service exam. He would not be eligible to apply for a King's fellowship for another two years and that would hinge on a scholarly dissertation (preferably in a mathematical area) as well as on the strength of the competing field of candidates. Not surprisingly perhaps, Maynard focused first on the economics tripos. The Diary for 28 June described him 'now working assiduously at Marshall's Principles of Economics', and by 3 September 'working at Cournot'. By the time he applied for entry to Marshall's advanced course in economic theory, Maynard had read his way through a formidable list of texts in modern economic analysis.[11] On 26 November, Neville noted with a mixture of irritation and satisfaction that Maynard

> does a good deal of work for Marshall who describes some of his answers as brilliant. I am afraid Marshall is trying to persuade him to give up everything for economics. Maynard himself broached this afternoon that he should give up reading for the Civil Service.

On 18 December, however, when Maynard came home from King's for the Christmas vacation, he put his father's mind at rest by announcing that he was now working on psychology. 'His last idea', Neville wrote with relief, 'is to give up the Economics Tripos so as to concentrate on preparations for the C.S. exam^{n}'. This involved reading for the moral science papers – logic, metaphysics, psychology and ethics – until the end of May when he would begin revising for the Civil Service mathematical papers. Thereafter, the stream of agitated references to Maynard's examination plans and prospects – which had dominated the Diary for roughly a decade – virtually dried up. The 23-year-old was clearly deemed to have taken effective control of his own studies. True, his mother rented a flat in South Kensington to provide her son with a homely family base from which to sit the Civil Service examination. But Neville himself (now content to get his news from Florence's daily

11. Moggridge (1992) lists them in a footnote on p. 95.

letters about their son's state of mind and health) did not join them there until 24 August when he celebrated the end of the examination by taking the family to Bernard Shaw's latest play 'You Never Can Tell'. 'We are very much relieved that the ordeal is over', he wrote, 'I suppose he will never again take an exam'.

Maynard came second of 104 candidates in his last exam and the only vacancy in the Treasury was taken by Otto Niemeyer, an Oxford classical scholar, who came first. Disappointed at having to settle for the India Office, Maynard was enraged by what he interpreted as the incompetence of his examiners. 'Really knowledge seems an absolute bar to success', he exploded in a much-quoted letter to Lytton Strachey, pointing out that his worst results were in mathematics and economics.[12] As it happened, however, being posted to the India Office in October 1906 had its advantages. The hours of work were short, the work was undemanding and his superiors were indulgent,[13] leaving him ample space to concentrate on the thesis he intended to submit for a King's College fellowship. On the other hand, by the time he had submitted his dissertation, in December 1907, he was seriously bored with the India Office. On Sunday 1 March 1908, Neville reported in the Diary:

> Maynard wishes to throw up the India Office if he gets a Fellowship at King's. I have argued with him in vain. I think he would give up the idea if I said definitely that I desired him to do so. But I do not think I ought to take so decided a position as that. He will be throwing up a certainty and taking risks. That fits in with his scheme of life but not with mine.

Hoping no doubt to influence the result, Maynard wrote to A.C. Pigou (one of the electors) to say that, if elected, he would certainly come back into residence at once. A fortnight later Neville reported himself reconciled to the fact that Maynard 'seems so thoroughly to have set his heart on returning to Cambridge and a student's life', and the whole family were to be disappointed and depressed to learn that the King's electors had voted Page and A.E. Dobbs into the two vacancies then available.

Maynard's letter to Pigou may actually have hindered rather than improved his chances at the 1908 election, for the Diary quoted a letter from W.R. Sorley (another elector) to the effect that the deciding factor in a 'remarkably close' election had been 'the fact of Maynard's having another chance' if he submit-

12. See, for example, Moggridge (1992), pp. 108–9 and R. Skidelsky, *John Maynard Keynes*, Vol. I (London: Macmillan, 1983), p. 175, among others.
13. In February 1907, the current head of the India Office, Sir A. Godley did his best to persuade Maynard to take up a resident clerkship, but accepted his refusal on the grounds that the evening work would interfere with his work on the King's fellowship dissertation.

ted a revised dissertation the following year.[14] Maynard himself had a letter from Pigou with a similar explanation and was again furious. In a letter to his father, quoted in the Diary on 19 March 1908 he wrote: '"I am very disappointed for the decision affects not honour and reward as these things usually go, but one's whole manner of life. And I am enraged that they should give as a reason the possession of another chance another year."' Nevertheless, when he got Marshall's offer 'subject to proviso and reserve' of a lectureship in economics with a salary of £100 he told his father that he would like to accept it and to leave the India Office without waiting for the next King's fellowship election. Accordingly, on his 25th birthday he sent in his resignation and left the Civil Service on 18 July 1908. When he won his King's fellowship at the 1909 election he had been lecturing for the economics tripos for two terms. By the time war broke out in 1914 he had been editor of the *Economic Journal* for nearly three years, was Cambridge's Girdlers' Lecturer in Economics, had published a monograph on *Indian Currency and Finance* (1913) as well as a series of articles in learned journals, served as a full member of the Royal Commission on Indian Finance and Currency and established an enviable reputation as a professional economist. In January 1915 he took up an official Treasury appointment for the duration of the war.

4 YOUNGER SON'S ROUTE TO A CAREER

Geoffrey, the youngest of the three Keynes siblings, left Rugby at the end of 1905, having won a £40 Exhibition to Pembroke, his father's old college. His parents had already arranged for him to spend most of the gap (between leaving school and entering university) learning German at the home of a respectable family in Germany, as they had done for his sister the previous year. So Geoffrey left Cambridge on 31 January 1906 and spent his 19th birthday at Lahr-in-Baden, a town on the edge of the Black Forest. Their belief in the professional value of access to the German language belonged to a Victorian tradition, and for Geoffrey the experience does not appear to have been either mind-broadening or useful – although he certainly enjoyed cycling in the German countryside and collecting local butterflies.[15] There he stayed until June 23, when his parents and sister gathered him up at Freiburg

14. A.N. Whitehead, one of the two examiners for his dissertation had been more critical than the other (W.E. Johnson, a close friend of the Keynes family). Since most of the fellowship electors were far from competent in the esoteric field of probability it is not surprising that they should prefer to reserve judgement until the candidate had satisfied Whitehead's criticisms.
15. Geoffrey L. Keynes, *The Gates of Memory* (Oxford: Oxford University Press, 1981), pp. 49–50.

for a family holiday in the Swiss Engadine – leaving Maynard in peace at Harvey Road preparing for the Civil Service examination.

Neville, who still worried neurotically to his Diary about Maynard's career prospects, commented on Geoffrey's educational progress with a placid mixture of pride and sympathy. Perhaps because his younger son was closer to himself in temperament, personality and intellectual potential he felt that he understood him better. A revealing entry in the Diary for 25 February 1900, for example, illustrates their special rapport. On that Sunday afternoon when the two older children were away at their boarding schools, Neville was enjoying a companionable afternoon in the study with his younger son – each absorbed by his own self-appointed tasks. He referred to the occasion with amused sympathy: 'Geoffrey is tidying up Margaret's stamps and putting some in for her. He is himself as tidy as she is untidy and is much shocked at the condition in which he finds things'. This was the earnest schoolboy his Rugby contemporaries used to tease by nicknaming him 'studious Keynes'.[16] Although (unlike Maynard), he rarely topped the list in competitive examinations he could be relied upon to satisfy the toughest examiners – even if it meant a second attempt. His strengths included a capacity for sustained hard work and a realistic view of the kind of professional activity in which he wanted to earn his living plus the determination, modesty and personal charm which enabled him to seek out (often with his father's help) the experts who could share their practical skills and specialized knowledge with him.

As we have seen, Geoffrey's interest in entomology was aroused before he was ten years old. Eight decades later he was to write:

> My childish enthusiasm soon attracted my father's attention and led him to extend his natural instinct for 'collecting', hitherto focused on postage stamps, to include butterflies. This was greatly to my advantage, since he did not grudge adding some of his pocket-money to mine so that we could acquire all the apparatus necessary for the hobby.[17]

Neville soon became as addicted to the hobby as his son and – by the time the latter was 13, his father had recorded proudly that Geoffrey was more skilled than himself at setting the butterflies and moths they caught in the wild or bred in the garden of 6 Harvey Road. Together (as well as separately) father and son consulted and learned from experts in the field, spent many companionable hours sugaring trees; breeding from pupae and caterpillars and naming new specimens; setting, preserving, arranging (and rearranging their collections in the drawer-filled cabinets steadily extending along a dining-room wall; and collaborating in articles for the *Entomological Record* and other

16. Ibid., p. 101.
17. Ibid., p. 28.

relevant learned journals. They searched for new varieties not only in different areas of Britain, but also on a sequence of family continental holidays in Switzerland, Germany, the Pyrenees and Austria. Looking back later on his youthful experience of handling butterflies and moths, Geoffrey was to insist: 'there can be no doubt of the value it had in training my hands for the delicate manipulations needed for success in my later career as a surgeon'.[18]

Natural science was not a prestigious area of study in English public schools when Geoffrey – with his sights already set on a medical career – chose to specialize in it during his final year at Rugby. However, when he sat for the Pembroke scholarship examination, his formal instruction in science was limited to elementary chemistry and physics. On the other hand his youthful enthusiasm for scientific investigations reached well beyond entomology while his family circle gave him access, during school holidays, to a broad Cambridge community of professional (and amateur) naturalists, geologists or archaeologists and their associated laboratory or museum assistants, who were happy to encourage and advise intelligent boys showing interest in scientific fieldwork. There was a site at Barrington, about seven miles outside Cambridge, for example, which was a treasure trove of antediluvian bones that could be carefully pieced together with carpenter's glue 'to form museum objects of worship' and which 'enterprising boys were allowed to dig for themselves and take away what they could find'. According to his autobiography: 'I was the proud donor of a rhinoceros skull to the Woodwardian Museum at Cambridge where for many years it could be seen in a glass case until it was replaced by a better specimen'.[19] Similarly, when the Cambridge market place was being dug up for the construction of underground lavatories, Geoffrey scrambled eagerly over the site to gather fragments of ancient pottery which he could learn to assemble into a pair of almost complete Roman jugs. As a result of such schoolboy experiments and the incidental tuition that Geoffrey's zeal charmed out of local experts, he was able to embark as a freshman on a wide study programme – involving chemistry, zoology, anatomy, physiology and pathology, all of which were required for the natural sciences tripos – fortified by a useful background in rudimentary practical science and an inquisitive zest for serious laboratory work.

Fortunately Geoffrey's untiring enthusiasm was not confined to scientific pursuits. His passions for poetry, art and rock-climbing, for example, leavened three undergraduate years of much heavier reading and course work than Maynard had ever faced for the maths tripos. More important still, these passions were shared with companions whose friendship greatly embellished his quality of life. Like his father, Geoffrey cared deeply and selflessly for his

18. Ibid., p. 31.
19. Ibid., p. 32.

friends and drew strength from the knowledge that his respect and affection for contemporaries such as Sir John Fryer, Rupert Brooke, Maurice Perrin and George Mallory was reciprocated.[20] His instinct for orderliness (also inherited from his father) further enlarged his enjoyment of his artistic interests by opening a lifetime of bibliographical and literary endeavour.[21] In 1909, having graduated with a first-class honours degree, and having identified surgery as his medical specialism, Geoffrey settled down to prepare for entry into St Bartholomew's Hospital (where his mother's eldest brother was senior physician), and to pursue some of his many literary interests in the Cambridge University Library. After what he was later to describe as 'an enjoyable year of work and play, if that is the right word for close study of the lives and works of William Blake, Dr John Donne and Sir Thomas Browne', Geoffrey won a surgical scholarship to Bart's training school and in September 1910 went with his mother to London to seek suitable lodgings. Sensitive as ever to his architectural surroundings he took her first to 'a particularly choice enclave between the House of Parliament and Westminster Abbey', where they found delightful lodgings for him at 14 Cowley Street – within comfortable walking distance of Bart's for a physically active 23-year-old.

20. In an Epilogue written in his 94th year and appended to his autobiography he was to write: 'At every stage of my life friendship has been the main source of my quite outrageously enjoyable existence'.
21. Geoffrey Keynes was to publish a stream of distinguished and scholarly bibliographies and biographies and to become a president of the Bibliographical Society of London. He retired from Bart's in 1951, but later wrote: 'When the severance from professional surgery was complete the centre of my life could still be the College of Surgeons whose Honorary Librarian I remained'.

X The impact of war

1 THE PRELUDE

When war broke out on 4 August 1914, Neville Keynes had reached the peak of his personal ambitions. His election in November 1910 to the post of registrary had elevated him to the top of the university's small paid bureaucracy. For over a century the registrary had been a fellow of Trinity – the largest and academically most eminent of Cambridge colleges. To be returned unopposed to this office was striking evidence of the high esteem in which Dr Keynes – not then a fellow of any college – was held by senior members of the university. It is therefore not surprising that Pembroke hastily elected its ex-fellow into an honorary fellowship. Neville was genuinely gratified by this unexpected honour. More important to his future, however, was the fact that he could retain his unpaid secretaryship on the Council of the Senate, a role which had, within the previous twenty years, become politically far more weighty and challenging than the formalized office of registrary. By holding both posts, Neville Keynes became the most pivotal individual member of the university bureaucracy in a period of radical, difficult and painfully contentious reform. That the two offices could most conveniently and efficiently be held by one individual was later formalized by adding the Council secretary's duties to the statutory obligations of the registrary.

Inevitably Neville was obliged to vacate his administrative post as chief secretary for Local examinations at the end of 1910 (when he was in his 59th year), and his university lectureship in moral sciences at the end of the 1910/11 academic year.[1] He continued to sit on the Local Examinations and Lectures Syndicate, and to examine for some years on its behalf, but he gave up its time-consuming secretaryship with relief. On 1 January 1911, he entered the following calculation in his Diary: 'Last year's work 2068. Omitting Sundays and allowing 5 weeks holiday this is a full 8 hour day for the rest of the year. Henceforward I shall be content if I do a 6 hour day'. This admission was the first indication in the Diary that Neville was no longer a

1. His university lectureship was in logic, although he continued to examine in political economy for the Moral Sciences and Economics Boards and for the Local Examinations Syndicate.

workaholic. Most of the numerous earlier entries referring to his (or even Maynard's) work pattern implied that he envisaged an average of eight hours per working day as the appropriate norm for a serious academic. In January 1907, for example, after noting that he had worked a total of 2199 hours in 1906, he calculated that this amounted to a daily average of well over eight hours and was a heavier stint than he had carried in any previous year except 1895 and 1896. In practice, of course, the workload of an academic tended to be heavily concentrated in university terms. Given his spread of teaching, examining and administrative responsibilities, Neville had often felt obliged to work eleven or twelve hours in a single day as well as up to three or four hours on some Sundays in term and at times daily during a family or golfing holiday. By becoming registrary, however, he could focus primarily on the kind of high-level administrative tasks where his long experience in analysing controversial policy issues, together with his established reputation for total integrity and informed common sense, provided him with a special authority. He now had access to sufficient clerical assistance to meet unpredictable surges in demands on his time and was himself no longer inclined to spend more hours in the office or at routine meetings than seemed actually necessary. In vacations, and even in term, he found time for frequent visits to London to bid at stamp auctions, enjoy the latest theatre shows and art exhibitions, and entertain friends and relatives at West End restaurants. Similarly, when the sun shone in Cambridge, he felt free to spend at least one afternoon each week on the Royston golf course with one or more of his colleagues. By 2 July he had actually managed to whittle his handicap down to 20.

In effect, for most of the four years preceding the outbreak of war, Neville's working responsibilities were concentrated in areas which he found most rewarding and where his skills were most valued. Moreover, leaving clerical trivia to experienced Registry staff gained him time for his family and his hobbies (bridge, stamps, butterflies and golf). During these years the members of his immediate family were flourishing. Maynard, who was in his early thirties when war broke out, had acquired a reputation as a professional academic economist that fully justified Neville's soaring ambitions for his firstborn. He had been an editor of the *Economic Journal* for nearly three years, had written a scholarly original monograph on *Indian Currency and Finance* as well as contributed substantial articles to learned periodicals, and had been appointed a full member of the Royal Commission on Indian Finance and Currency. Geoffrey, too, was successfully pursuing his own surgical career at London's St Bartholomew's Hospital.

Meanwhile, Florence and, for a while, Margaret were both actively involved in local public service. In June 1912 when the Diary reported Neville's visit to his daughter's office in the Cambridge Guildhall, where she was in paid employment as an 'organising secretary', the name of A. Vivian Hill (a physiologist fellow of Trinity) had already figured in various earlier entries – either as a guest at the Harvey Road Sunday lunches or as one of Neville's many golfing partners. By January 1913, Vivian was helping Florence and Margaret to open up and cultivate a new area of garden, and the fact that he proposed to Margaret a couple of weeks later was noted so baldly in the Diary that it can hardly have been a surprise to her father. At any rate, on 6 February, after the prospective new member of the family had been put through the obligatory parental interviews – first by Florence and then by Neville – the latter reported that Morley Fletcher (a senior Trinity fellow), had spoken 'enthusiastically of A.V.H. intellectually, morally and physically', and that 'Maynard thoroughly approves of the engagement'. The pair were married four months later, at the end of the 1913 summer term, by Dr John Brown, the bride's grandfather. After a honeymoon tour to Skye – travelling everywhere by Vivian's motorbike and sidecar – they set up home (with Florence's help, of course) in Cambridge, a short walk from Harvey Road, where their first child, Mary Eglantyne (later known as Polly), was born in June 1914.

Evidently these were among the happiest years of Neville's life. He was fully committed to the central role he now played in the university, as one of a team of academics and assistant staff with whom he enjoyed one-to-one relationships sustained by mutual respect and shared objectives. He had the time and energy to follow hobbies, entertain friends and share the pleasures and successes of the close family which still treated 6 Harvey Road as home. Although the Diary fretted constantly about Florence's bicycle accidents (a common hazard for Cambridge cyclists) and about the dangers of her overworking, these were recurrent rather than persistent worries.[2] There was only one major anxiety to mar the generally cheerful tone of the Diary in this period. That arose in January 1914 when Maynard – on holiday in the south of France – fell seriously ill and was rushed into a nursing home. As ever in a crisis, Florence responded decisively by travelling at once to his bedside at Mentone whence she could reassure her family with daily bulletins until the patient was well enough to accompany her back to England three weeks later.

Among the events that spiced Diary entries during the halcyon years preceding the First World War were picturesque social occasions such as the coronation of George V (where Neville, in court dress and academic robes, occupied one of the three places reserved for representatives of the University

2. All members of the family except Neville had joined in the bicycling craze that swept Cambridge in the 1890s. Though still a vigorous walker and a keen tennis player, Neville proved oddly inept when mounting or dismounting a bicycle. Florence and Margaret did their best to encourage him to master his balance problem but he continued to regard the whole exercise with suspicion and dislike.

of Cambridge), and the regular college feasts or May week garden parties at which the registrary was invariably an honoured guest. In addition, the Diary reported such annual events as London shopping and theatre-going in January; golfing in Norfolk or Surrey (with his sister's family) during spring or late summer; and a month in high summer on the continent with Florence (and sometimes Geoffrey) catching butterflies and sightseeing. By 1913, Neville's daily stint (averaged over the year after excluding five weeks' holiday and Sundays) had reached the six hours he now regarded as a respectable norm, and 1914 seemed likely to conform to the same comfortable pattern. Florence chose to stay at home during her husband's spring golfing holiday at Hunstanton – 'toiling and moiling over the spring cleaning', he grumbled to the Diary, adding 'I do wish Hunstanton suited her'. The fact was that she had more important matters in mind, for Margaret and Vivian were expecting their first child in June and Florence was disinclined to absent herself from Cambridge until the infant was safely delivered and obviously thriving in the young parents' Parkside home. Polly, who was born on 10 June, soon convinced her grandparents that she was 'a model of behaviour in every respect'. Neville and Florence were then free to finalize the arrangements for their annual continental holiday. At that point, the fuse that had been lit in Sarajevo on 28 June, when a Serbian nationalist assassinated the Austrian heir-apparent, was quietly smouldering in the Balkans. There was as yet no obvious reason for seasoned travellers to consider its possible implications for their own holiday plans. Not until ultimata began to fly between nations in Eastern Europe, beginning with Austria's ultimatum to Serbia on 23 July, did this distant Balkan fracas begin to seem at all threatening to Alpine tourists, and by then Neville and Florence were already rambling contentedly through peaceful mountain scenery in southeastern France.

They had set off on 17 July, stopping briefly in Paris, Grenoble and Digne, before riding the electric railway up the Alpes Maritimes to their destination in the remote village of St Martin Vesubie close to the Franco-Italian border. Their plan was to spend about ten days there before moving on to continue walking around the Italian lakes and in Switzerland. They expected to return home in mid-August. It was on 28 July that Austria declared war on Serbia, following this up by bombarding Belgrade on 29 July, thus provoking Russian troops to mobilize along their Austrian borders. On 30 July both Austria and Russia ordered general mobilization and on 31 July Germany entered the conflict with an ultimatum to Russia to demobilize within twelve hours. So, when Neville and Florence returned to their small hotel from that day's walk in the hills they found the group of French, Russian and English guests there assembled for dinner discussing the onrush of events with the gravest concern. It was then that they seriously contemplated cutting short their holiday. Not until the following day when they arrived at the electric train station, to catch the afternoon service to Nice, did they realize how far the preparations for a European war had then gone. According to Florence's article (published later, in the *Cambridge Daily News*):

> The reserves were called out, the summer visitors were hurrying away and we were told that it was impossible to get seats in either of the couple of cars that formed the little train. However, seats seemed of slight importance and we were glad to find standing room on the platform of one of the two cars, and so began a journey through France which extended over 5 days during the whole of which we never knew whether we should be able to accomplish the next stage.[3]

It proved a fearful homeward flight.

At Nice which they reached in the evening of 1 August 1914, the posters announcing a general mobilization were everywhere. During the excellent dinner served to them at the station hotel they were told that their dress-suited waiters were to change into army uniform overnight and proceed to their units in the morning. After a disturbed sleep in an uncommonly noisy hotel, the pair walked into Nice station, now under military occupation, and hastened aboard the only train with seats for civilians. Fortunately it was a train bound for Toulon to connect with another for Marseilles, which they reached in time to occupy the station hotel's last available room. According to Florence's later account: 'The great station at Marseilles was a strange sight on Monday morning. ... Inside the booking halls and waiting rooms, crowds came and went, but all the booking offices were closed, and the entrance to the platform was guarded by soldiers with fixed bayonets'. The only Paris train still taking civilians was scheduled to leave at midday but they failed to fight their way on to it. In desperation they sought help from the British consulate where, after their agitated dash through congested city streets, they were relieved to meet a lively group of English officers on their way home from India. Armed with the Consul's letter of introduction to the Commissaire Militaire they could pass between the men with fixed bayonets and acquire a permit to travel with the English officers on the fast train to Lyons and (they hoped) to Paris. Having left their heavy luggage at the Thomas Cook agency (with instructions for forwarding it to Cambridge as soon as possible), they accompanied the group of Britain-bound officers on to a train, crammed with French soldiers of all ranks. It left Marseilles at 4 that afternoon and arrived in Paris at 10 the following (Tuesday) morning. With the help of their resourceful compatriots, Florence and Neville then found a taxi which carried them across Paris to the heavily barricaded Gare du Nord. There they queued for yet another permit from the military authorities that would enable them to board a late afternoon train for

3. Florence's article on their journey was published in two parts in the *Cambridge Daily News* for 7 and 11 August 1914.

Boulogne. Now wilting, they welcomed the long wait before their train moved off, for it opened the necessary interval for a much-needed breakfast at the station buffet. Dropped, in the small hours of Wednesday morning, at a deserted station they hurried to the Boulogne quay to find that a boat had departed about an hour before. By then, however, they felt themselves almost in sight of home. So they gratefully snatched a sleep in comfortable beds at a nearby hotel, before hastening to the dockside now crowded with English refugees. 'We all sat on the quay for hours on our bags', wrote Florence later, 'looking like a party of emigrants, until at last we were allowed to go on board, every passenger having to produce a passport or some paper of identification'. It was on Wednesday 5 August, that they first learned of the British declaration of war on Germany. Their ship eventually left Boulogne for Folkestone at 1.30 that afternoon, 'to the strains of the Marseillaise piped in high voices by some small boys on the quai'. According to the Diary they reached Cambridge just before 8 the same day – to find that Vivian was already with the Territorials and that Maynard was in London working at the Treasury – having dissuaded an over-eager Geoffrey from enlisting in the Royal Naval Medical Service.

2 THE NIGHTMARE

The impact of the First World War on the Cambridge academic community was sudden and unprecedented. For Neville it was the disruption in family life that hit him first. By Saturday 8 August Vivian had departed with the Territorials leaving Margaret and infant Polly bereft in their new Parkside home. Geoffrey, who had left his post as Senior House Surgeon at Bart's to enrol in the Royal Army Medical Corps, arrived in Harvey Road during the night of 10 August with the news that he had three days leave before presenting himself at a Woolwich Base Hospital with the rank of lieutenant. There, he expected to be put through two or three weeks of training before proceeding to a secret destination. Florence was 'bearing up bravely' according to the Diary, 'but she rather broke down after seeing Geoffrey to bed' the evening before he left home on Sunday 13 August. 'I am constantly thinking of Geoffrey', wrote his father a couple of days later, 'and I am sure Florence is too but we dont talk about him'. Twenty-seven-year-old Geoffrey, on the other hand, was eagerly embarking upon a new learning curve. Looking back on it in his mid-nineties, he recalled that war 'did not suggest unnamed horrors, but to a young surgeon meant useful employment in his own profession while doing his duty for his country'.[4] For Maynard too, the outbreak of

4. Geoffrey L. Keynes, *The Gates of Memory* (Oxford: Oxford University Press, 1981), p. 124.

war opened up new and exciting professional challenges. After a brief flurry of riveting advisory work at the Treasury, in the first few days, he was in principle free to return to expanding his successful fellowship thesis into a monograph on probability theory. Instead, however, he was encouraged by the current emergency to write a series of articles on the financial crisis that coincided with the outbreak of war.[5] Neville, by contrast, was virtually a bystander of events as they unfolded in the Cambridge long vacation of 1914. The Registry was closed, as usual, until the end of August leaving him his annual routine task of revising the university ordinances. Only the fact that he was then reading and correcting proofs of Maynard's new book kept him intellectually alive. By contrast, Florence was rapidly being drawn into a continuous succession of war-related committees to which her local knowledge and organizing experience enabled her to make a useful contribution. Meanwhile, until the university vacation was over, her husband had far too much time on hand to read newspapers and to imagine the dangers that could confront his younger son on the field of battle. 'The war is a constant nightmare night and day; but especially in the early morning', he groaned to his Diary on 23 August. His spirits lifted, however, when Margaret and baby Polly moved in with them at Harvey Road, and on 31 August (his 62nd birthday) he dared to hope that 'this terrible war' would end before his next birthday.

Florence – who had seven years ago broken through a local government gender barrier by being elected to the Cambridge Board of Guardians – now became the first woman member of the Cambridge Borough Council, following an uncontested election in October. Neville's feelings about his wife's 'immersion' in Council work were mixed. On the one hand he was proud of the distinctive part Florence was able to play in forwarding the war effort at the local political level. He gladly joined her in the numerous church services which she attended as a member of the Town Council and accompanied her with interest on various other war-related public appearances. On the other hand, he worried incessantly about the danger of her 'overdoing it', and continued to nag about her cycling through busy Cambridge streets on Council business. At times, Florence's patience seems to have reached saintly levels. In May 1916, for example, he wrote: 'Florence says she cannot get through her work unless she bicycles a little but she promises to do so as little as possible'. More than once, after complaining about her being overworked, he acknowledged how much she enjoyed all her work. Later that year he wrote: 'Florence is doing far too much. But it all seems such useful and reliable work that I do not feel I can do much to restrain her'. By then

5. See D.E. Moggridge, *Maynard Keynes: An Economist's Biography* (London: Routledge, 1991), pp. 235–41, for Maynard's role in the financial crisis.

according to the Diary, she was hard at work 'emptying Cambridge of servants' in order to recruit young women for a munitions factory at Woolwich, where they could earn 50 shillings a week instead of the 15 shillings which they might get in domestic service. Later still, in March 1917, he observed affectionately: 'It is wonderful what a lot Florence is doing. She is always ready for something fresh. I feel constantly that I love her more and more. What an extraordinarily fortunate man I have been'. There was even an occasion in April 1917 when he grumbled irritably to the Diary because, for once, her responsibilities were not increased. On returning from a spring golfing holiday at Hunstanton he reported:

> Florence has been defeated for the Chairmanship of the Board of Guardians by A.R. Hill. The Liberals with one abstention support her; but the Conservatives (some of them probably ashamed of themselves) voted the other way. It was disgraceful as it was the Liberal turn.

The truth was that Florence – in her early fifties at the outbreak of war – was sufficiently free and vigorous to relish the new opportunities for public service then opening up for women in the national emergency. In spite of an increasing and widening workload, however, she never failed to respond decisively to family crises, On the evening of 9 June 1915, for example, she boarded a London train – primarily to spend a couple of nights with her aged parents in Hampstead, but also to see Maynard, recently returned from a hectic official visit to France with the Chancellor of the Exchequer.[6] His cheerful letter home (duly quoted in the Diary) had described '"a most enjoyable trip. We crossed the Channel both ways on a destroyer at the rate of 35 miles an hour"'. When his mother called at the Gower Street house into which he had moved a couple of months previously, she was shocked to find him in bed and in pain. No hospital beds were available, so Florence summoned consultants and nurses to Gower Street. The following day, George Gask – a surgeon who was to be Geoffrey's chief first at a 1916 Casualty Clearing Station and later at Bart's – operated on Maynard's kitchen table to remove a perforated appendix. Neville arrived anxiously from Cambridge at 1.30 p.m.: 'I did not see much of him', he reported in the Diary, 'but I was the first person he recognised when he came to after the anaesthetics. We have two nurses in attendance'. Although the operation itself was apparently successful, the patient developed pneumonia a week later, so Florence remained at Gower Street, organizing and supervising the medical assistance, until he was well enough to be driven to Harvey Road in Dennis Robertson's motor car on 9 July. It was another three weeks before young Mr Keynes was in full working order again at the Treasury.

6. Maynard had been to Nice to act as Treasury back-up for the Chancellor's meeting with the Italian finance minister.

At the same time, Florence had other family concerns on her agenda. Margaret (who had resided at 6 Harvey Road with baby Polly since the end of August 1914) was again pregnant. For Neville, the presence of his daughter and grandchild in house was 'a joy' that enormously mitigated his depressive inclinations during the first five months of the war. Polly was responsible for most of the cheerful Diary entries during that uncertain period. 'Baby leaves us today', he wrote sadly on 1 June 1915, when Margaret returned to her Parkside home to have her second child. On 23 July – with Vivian at home on leave – she gave birth to 'a fine boy', who looked (according to his delighted grandfather) like 'a very wise old gentleman'. Two infants were at least twice as entertaining as one and whenever he could find the time, Neville walked to Parkside to enjoy his grandchildren. That summer Florence took the initiative in organizing a family retreat for themselves, Margaret plus the two babies and Vivian (whenever he could get leave from Windsor where he was currently teaching musketry to infantrymen). In a small village near Woburn, she found a rectory which they could rent for their summer holiday month, in delightfully walkable wooded countryside – less than a couple of hours journey from Cambridge.[7]

The first year of war turned out to be much less devastating than Neville had anticipated at the outset. True, the miserable stream of casualties among ex-students and young dons, who had enlisted so promptly in the armed forces, began to come close to home early in 1915. They included friends of his sons as well as sons of his own friends (such as Rupert Brooke or Erasmus Darwin), who typified the Cambridge social scene in the Edwardian years and had often been welcomed to Sunday lunches or teas at Harvey Road. Nevertheless, not even as relentless a pessimist as Neville then expected such painfully intimate tragedies to recur for another four years. As it happened, the only member of his immediate family to be put at serious risk during the early months of war was Geoffrey, who had been shipped to France as a lieutenant in the Royal Army Medical Corps (RAMC) within three weeks of the outbreak of war. In mid-September, Geoffrey's unit took responsibility for establishing a military hospital at the Hotel Trianon Palace in Versailles. There he was to spend the next four months learning, by grim process of trial and error, how to treat the frightful wounds of modern war. The young doctor rose to the challenge with his usual verve and, at that stage, his vivid weekly letters home – often described in the Diary as 'extremely interesting' or 'v. satisfactory' – generally fascinated rather than worried his parents.[8] In December 1914 Maynard was able to arrange a visit to Paris for a few days, and after calling at his brother's Versailles hospital, he brought home the reassuring information that Geoffrey was 'very well but rather bored'. A month later Geoffrey himself returned to

7. The rectory was in the village of Bow Brickhill near Woburn Sands.
8. G.L. Keynes (1981), contains Geoffrey's own account of his war service.

Cambridge – on a short leave before abandoning the relatively luxurious ambiance of Versailles. In mid-February 1915 he was to join an ambulance train that picked up badly wounded men from field ambulances or clearing stations, sometimes from the battle front itself, and treated them as comfortably as possible en route to a Boulogne hospital. For six months thereafter, he endured peculiarly arduous and fragmented 'conditions of life, with two other officers on a constantly moving hospital'.[9] It was not until 5 August 1915 – after two weeks with a field ambulance – that Geoffrey joined the Ypres headquarters of a Royal Artillery Brigade. Now promoted to captain he was in action for most of the next twelve months 'in one of the hottest sectors of the trench war' as the Brigade's sole medical officer. A letter quoted in the Diary on 9 August, reported that he now lived with another officer in a dugout, about 10 feet square, with a bank of earth as a bed, under a deafening barrage of gunfire that exploded at 2.30 a.m. and lasted for two hours nightly.

It was in the summer of 1915 – actually during the family holiday at the Bow Brickhill rectory – that the war began to assume nightmare dimensions for Neville. Till then, Geoffrey's deliberately cheerful (as well as normally censored) letters home had been reassuringly regular for the most part. The fact that, whilst serving with the RAMC unit, he worked alongside his old school friend Maurice Perrin, gave both their families an additional point of contact when a letter was unaccountably delayed, as well as the detailed information derivable from a regular exchange of letters. By the summer of 1915, however, the horrors of war were dominating national news bulletins and Maynard at the Treasury was too fully occupied to escape each weekend and to put his parents' fears into informed perspective over Sunday lunch. Indeed his own letter home (on 9 September) described an alarming experience of a Zeppelin air raid in London. When Geoffrey came to Harvey Road on leave, in late September – 'looking well' according to the Diary – his uncensored accounts of trench warfare and of friends lost in action plunged his father into a prolonged depression. On the day his younger son left Cambridge to return to the trenches, Neville noted with bitter brevity: 'We have today stopped the Times. I have always taken it and we also took it at Salisbury'. Henceforth the Diary entries shrivelled – rarely containing more than brief notes, usually devoid of detail or comment, and often blank. It seems to have been about this time that Neville began to detach himself from Emmanuel Chapel, of which he had been a loyal member for over forty years.[10] For example, two Sundays after Geoffrey's

9. Ibid., p. 129.
10. The shrunken Diary does not reveal whether he did give up regular attendance at Emmanuel then; but he was there over a year later (24 December 1916) when he wrote with miserable finality: 'I really cannot stand Carter [the preacher] any more and I must I think give up going. Like the American President he appears to see no difference between the Germans and ourselves'.

return to the front in October 1915 Neville complained to the Diary (not for the first time) of his annoyance at the minister's sermon 'although I like the man so much'; this time he added: 'I should like to give up Emmanuel and occasionally go to Church'.

After a Christmas which 'did not seem at all like Christmas', 1916 began gloomily in the shadow of the government's decision to introduce compulsory military service for all single men aged from 18 to 40. Maynard, according to his father took 'an extreme view on the subject of conscription' and spoke, in a letter home, of resigning his Treasury post as a matter of principle. This threat – at a time when the Treasury work 'with occasional excursions into high life' was keeping Maynard so busy that he could no longer visit Cambridge each weekend – deepened Neville's depression. It was also a time when Geoffrey's letters from the battle front had become erratic, often gruesome in content and increasingly pessimistic about the prospects of an early end to the war. Florence, however, perhaps because her visits to London to see her parents enabled her to call on Maynard relatively frequently, was more sanguine about the likelihood of his actually abandoning work that he found so absorbing. In mid-January, for example, still raging at compulsory military service, he wrote home: 'Things drift on and I shall stay on I expect till they begin to torture one of my friends'. In the event, it was Neville, as chairman of the Economics Board, who was more directly harassed by the implications of conscription. His problem was that Pigou, who kept the economics tripos alive, was at risk of being called up and it fell to the chairman of the Board to organize a campaign to exempt its professor.[11]

Neville's depression lifted briefly on 27 July 1916 on reading a letter from Geoffrey with the 'delightful news' that he had been withdrawn from the battle zone and was now at a casualty clearing station working alongside Maurice Perrin again, and under Sir George Gask, the surgeon from Bart's, for whom he had a solid respect. From then on his letters became more frequent, informative and full of enthusiasm for 'serious surgical work'. After his promotion to 'second surgeon' at another casualty station – this time near enough to the front to hear the shells whistling to their targets, if not the full blast of each hit – his parents were again alarmed, on 2 November, by Perrin's letter, saying that Geoffrey's hospital had been bombed. Florence instantly telegraphed Maynard 'who made enquiries and sent a satisfactory reply'. Two weeks later Geoffrey was home again on leave looking surprisingly well and cheerful. This was the ten-day leave on which he proposed to, and was accepted by Margaret Darwin (his junior by three years) whom he had known since boyhood.[12] Her father Sir George Darwin, had been a

11. See above, Ch. VIII, for the battle to exempt Pigou.
12. See G.L. Keynes (1981), and M.E. Darwin, *House by the River* (Cambridge: Darwin College, 1978) for autobiographical accounts of the event.

Trinity fellow since 1868 and the university's professor of astronomy until his death in 1912. The link between two of Cambridge's senior academic families was welcomed by both and the pair decided to marry at the earliest feasible moment. Margaret, who was then working in London as a temporary civil servant at the Admiralty, obtained the special war licence necessary to expedite the wedding and got permission to absent herself from work as soon as Geoffrey's application for marriage leave was granted. The flood of casualties needing specialist surgery was then so great that it took over three months for permission to come through. According to Margaret's own account of events – 'on the afternoon of Thursday 10 May as I was sitting at my table at the office drearily trying to concentrate on my deciphering, an Admiralty messenger brought me a telegram. ... The message was "Meet me at 3.35 Victoria today. Geoffrey"'.[13] They were married on the morning of 12 May 1917 at the Darwins' Cambridge parish church (St Botolph's), and late that afternoon they reached the house in Ashdown Forest which Leonard and Mildred Darwin, the bride's uncle and aunt, had lent them for their eight-day honeymoon. Before then the rapprochement between the two families, had already opened up pleasing opportunities for Neville to share his passion for chess with another keen competitor – his son's future mother-in-law. The war dragged on for a further eighteen months, but it was almost two years before Geoffrey (now a major in the RAMC) was able to return to his civilian career as chief assistant to Sir George Gask who headed (at St Bart's) the first professional surgical unit to be established at a London teaching hospital.

Maynard, at the Treasury, was also stretched to his limits as the war continued and spread.[14] From early 1916 onwards he was increasingly preoccupied by problems of external finance arising out of cooperation between the United Kingdom and its allies. When this involved him in accompanying high-level delegations abroad, as it did from time to time, it added another dimension to his father's special propensity for alarm and despondency. Maynard, for example, was originally selected as a member of the group to go with Lord Kitchener to Russia on 4 June 1916 for meetings on military and supply problems. It so happened that at the last moment he was summoned to other urgent duties in London. Consequently, he was not aboard the cruiser bound for Russia when it was sunk by a mine, with devastating loss of life among the delegates. The disaster occurred on 5 June 1916, Maynard's 33rd birthday. Hence the tersely poignant note in his father's Diary for 6 June: 'News of the death of Lord Kitchener and his party off the Orkneys on their way from London. It is only a chance that Maynard was not with him and we have felt it very much'. Later, in early September 1917, Maynard

13. Darwin (1978), p. 207.
14. On Maynard's war work, see Moggridge (1981), Chs 10–11.

raised still more anxiety in Harvey Road when crossing the submarine-threatened Atlantic on his way to (and from) the United States. The tension at home did not relax until a telegram arrived on 18 October, announcing his return: 'I had been worrying about him for the last day or two', Neville noted wearily in the Diary '7 cruisers came back together with 2 destroyers and 8 destroyers went to meet them'. Like Geoffrey, Maynard continued his war work for another six months after the end of hostilities. He served as a junior official of the Treasury at the Paris Peace Conference which began in January 1919 and ended with the treaty that was signed at Versailles on 28 June. Paris was Maynard's nightmare. Having failed to persuade the conference hawks of the need to keep the reparations imposed on Germany down to levels which he believed passionately were rational and just, he resigned from the Treasury – exhausted, disgusted and disappointed – in early June. He then spent the rest of the summer and early autumn writing his *Economic Consequences of the Peace*, a powerful polemic which brought him international recognition as an outstanding political economist. To Maynard himself, writing twelve years later, it represented the first of his 'croakings of a Cassandra who could never influence the course of events in time'.[15] By the Michaelmas term of 1919/20 he was back in Cambridge, lecturing to undergraduates on the economic aspects of the peace and taking his seat on the Economics Board.

For Neville the persistently dispiriting feature of the war was not the stress imposed on family and friends by the tragic casualties, privations, physical dangers and sheer overwork. There were compensations for largely temporary burdens. His sons and his wife, for example – however fraught they might be from time to time – were obviously willing and admirable contributors to the nation's war effort. In any case, they were learning lessons and gaining practical experience that should enlarge their horizons and raise their skills when the oppressive conditions had passed and they were free to design their own way of life. His daughter was equally valuably occupied in maintaining a family home and rearing the children of her soldier-husband who had a promising career awaiting him when he returned to academia. It was totally different for Neville himself. As registrary he had become the central administrative agent in an ongoing, intellectually challenging and fiercely controversial process of academic and institutional reform. All progress on this front was abruptly halted by the outbreak of war. Instead, the governing bodies of the university were faced with an unprecedented upheaval in its normal operations.

15. *The Economic Consequences of the Peace* was first published in November 1919. Parts were reprinted in his *Essays in Persuasion* (1931) with an editorial preface including the passage quoted.

The immediate effect of the outbreak was to more than halve the population of male undergraduates which the colleges were expecting to accommodate in the academic year 1914/15. The previous decade had been one of continuous expansion in numbers, to a peak of 3263 men resident in Michaelmas term 1913. Just a year later, in 1914, the numbers had dropped to 1658, and down again, in October 1915, to 825. The numbers of those entering for the first time fell from 1112 at the beginning of 1913/14 to 665 at the start of 1914/15 and 296 one year later.[16] In his annual address to the Senate in congregation, Dr M.R. James, Provost of King's – resigning on 1 October 1915 from his two-year stint as vice-chancellor – sketched the transformation that had overtaken the University over the academic year 1914/15:

> The University has shrunk to less than one third of its former numbers. Its buildings – laboratories, lecture rooms, examination halls – have been filled with soldiers. Colleges have been converted into schools of instruction for officers, into headquarters for the military staff, into lodgings for nurses and into billets for men. A great military hospital, which, when I last [October 1914] addressed you was located in Nevile's Court, Trinity College, now covers one of the largest college fields. Many Professors, Readers and Lecturers have gone out of residence to take up scientific work, or commissions as officers; others, still with us, are devoting themselves to tasks not less useful to the common welfare. Yet again, others have engaged in work in government offices, and have placed their attainments, linguistic, economic, administrative, historical, at the service of the country.

He then explicated the policy issues and decisions that had confronted the Council over the past year:

> The policy of the University in this crisis had been to render all employment of its resources, material and intellectual, as easy as it can be made. It is not indeed conceivable that we should do otherwise than grant leave of absence in every possible case and keep open all temporarily vacated posts. Whatever measures bearing on the services of University officers and teachers have passed the Senate have had this objective in view.[17]

The other policy objective that assumed high priority in the university in its first year of war was providing special dispensations to undergraduates who had interrupted their education to volunteer their services in defence of their country, with a view to enabling them to proceed to their degrees as soon as possible after resuming their studies. According to the vice-chancellor's retiring address, in October 1915 at least 10,000 Cambridge men were currently fighting, or training to fight in defence of their country. Of

16. Figures cited by the vice-chancellor in his address to the Senate on 1 October 1915, *CUR*, 2 October 1915, p. 38.
17. Ibid., p. 37.

these he estimated that 'between 2000 and 3000 would in the ordinary course of events still be living and studying among us'. To protect their interests it was necessary to draft, to pass through the Senate and to coordinate with the colleges, a multiplicity of changes in statutes and regulations covering the special circumstances of those whose studies had been disrupted.

> The aim has been to secure on the one hand for those who have completed part of their residence, an easy passage to a degree, mainly by the allowance of as much as 4 terms and by permitting them to count the time spent on active service as the equivalent of a Special Examination in Military Service. For those who have not yet begun residence the object of legislation by the University and Colleges has been that, when they come here they should be able to enter forthwith upon the study that they have selected and upon the enjoyment of such awards as they may have gathered before joining the forces of the Crown. That the provisions applicable to the former class are effective was seen in June and July; more than a hundred degrees were conferred by proxy at the last Congregation upon men at the front.[18]

Nor were these the only procedural changes occasioned by the current emergency. In the early months of the war the university had taken the initiative in arranging for a number of professors and students from Belgium – refugees from the German invasion of their country – to come into residence in Cambridge and organize lecture courses from which students could qualify for properly sanctioned certificates awarded on the recommendation of their professors. This enterprise involved resident senior members in a successful appeal for funds and committed them to participate in its management. In all the practical problems raised by such unprecedented situations, Neville Keynes was the ultimate oracle.

By the time the tempest of the First World War hit Cambridge University, Neville was not only the head of its administrative system, he was also a widely experienced senior officer. He was experienced in teaching and examining at all levels, in mediating academic conflicts (within and between faculties), in identifying feasible options for policy makers constrained by traditional democratic procedures and in drafting explanatory reports that dealt sensitively with the dogmatic obstacles to mutual understanding that afflict most professional (as well as religious) communities. An elected member of the Council of the Senate – nominated consistently on both the conservative and the liberal 'tickets' – he had been its secretary since 1893. For over three decades he had steered each of a dozen college heads through their two-year stints as the university vice-chancellor, personally written the Council minutes and drafted the Graces or reports reflecting its proposed decisions. He had reported and digested the relevant discussions in congrega-

18. From the vice-chancellor's retiring address to the Senate, *CUR*, 2 October 1915, pp. 41–2.

tion, and expedited the resultant amendments necessary to implement feasible changes. He was responsible, as registrary, for incorporating all agreed changes in the university statutes and ordinances. Clearly, no one knew better than Neville Keynes where its procedures were problematic and where the sharks or rocks were located that could halt or hinder any attempt to alter academic or constitutional practice – whether in the interests of educational progress or to deal with the abnormal conditions imposed by total war. He became the beacon in that tempest as he had been in earlier, more localized storms, provoked by academic conflicts between and within disciplines. Each senior member (of a greatly depleted Senate) needing advice on how to facilitate the changes in customary practice precipitated by war had to climb the steps to the top of the Cambridge University Press's Pitt Tower, where the registrary had his private office. In October 1914, the Provost of King's, the first of the wartime vice-chancellors declared himself 'most particularly and constantly beholden' to Keynes, 'to whom the gratitude of successive Vice-Chancellors must be cloying'. In October 1917, the President of Queen's (the Provost's successor as vice-chancellor), expressed the customary gratitude by describing the registrary as 'the most helpful of men'.[19]

Neville started the 1914 October term with a violent migraine – so severe that Florence called in their GP, who examined the patient's ears and eyes and recommended that he wear his spectacles all the time. The migraine lasted for over a week, aggravated no doubt by stressful war news. This was the week when the seige of Antwerp ended and the German army covered the European shore opposite to East Anglia. Shortly afterwards the even tenor of life at 6 Harvey Road was disrupted when both Florence and her daughter wore themselves out in dealing with the influx of Belgian refugees to Cambridge. In general, of course, Florence was adept at minimizing the consequences of the national emergency for family life at home. Neville, at work, however, was most troubled and discouraged by the fact that the normal business of the university's governing bodies (Council, General and Financial Boards) must be hastily shelved to make way for a drastic redeployment of staff and resources necessitated by the novel and unavoidable combination of events and circumstances into which they were suddenly plunged. Not surprisingly he felt tired, flustered and uncharacteristically bad-tempered; so much so that Florence invited her brother Walter Langdon-Brown (then a physician at a London Territorial hospital attached to St Bartholomew's)[20] to come for the

19. *CUR*, 2 October 1914, p. 43 and *CUR*, 1 October 1917, p. 41.
20. Walter Brown, later Sir Walter Langdon-Brown, was a frequent visitor to 6 Harvey Road before and after coming to Cambridge to read natural sciences in 1889 at St John's College. He entered St Bartholomew's Hospital in 1896. In 1932 he was to become Cambridge's Regius Professor of Physic. See Neville Brown, *Dissenting Forbears* (Chichester: Phillimore, 1988), pp. 123–8, for a brief biography.

weekend of 14 November 1914 – 'to give me an examination', according to the Diary. Walter diagnosed overwork. 'It seems to me quite unnecessary', wrote Neville, 'but I think I shall have to give up the Financial Board'. This he did, at the end of December, but with some regret – perhaps because the Financial Board's problems of juggling funds between sources and uses then seemed more challenging and important than those currently agitating the Council or General Board.

The fact was that Neville was less pressured by work in the academic year 1914/15 than he had been for over a quarter of a century. The long-term policy problems that dominated his Council work during the previous decade and a half had dropped off its agenda. He no longer had to draft lengthy reports on contentious and difficult issues destined to be discussed and voted upon by the verbosely dogmatic ancients of the Senate in congregation, before generating the slightest improvements in conditions of administration, teaching or research. Instead he had to invent, or assist other senior members to invent, coherent new procedures and rules for operating a university in desperate, if temporary, decline and for protecting the prospects of staff and students absent on national service. As its administrative head and the ultimate authority on its statutes and ordinances he was the man to whom all responsible senior members went for advice on the appropriate shifts in their own operational regulations. The Financial Board's juggling of funds, for example – largely a matter of depleting reserves, anticipating revenue and postponing expenditure – necessitated a programme of emergency legislation designed to open up a variety of special trust funds to serve the general purposes of the university for the duration of the emergency. Each of the complex series of emergency statutes involved in this process had to be cleared by, if not personally drafted by the registrary. Its success can be gauged by the fact that at the end of 1915 (according to the vice-chancellor's 1916 annual report to the Senate): 'The audited accounts for the year 1915 shew a substantial balance though the income of the Chest was reduced by 37% from that of the year 1913'. The V.C. Fitzpatrick went on to elaborate:

> The expenditure for 1915 and the present civil year has been reduced (1) by the suspension of vacant offices for the period of the war, (2) by the suspension of stipends of posts of which the holders are absent in various forms of service, (3) by the returning of stipends and fees by members of the University, also (4) by the loyal cooperation of Heads of Departments and by the postponement of liabilities in respect of loans and pensions.[21]

The consequence was that although wartime Council meetings (and their preludes and aftermaths) took a diminishing share of Neville's time, he spent

21. *CUR*, 2 October 1916, p. 37.

many hours of that first war year, offering direct advice and support to the miscellaneous stream of puzzled enquirers who came to him for help. The Provost of Queen's (who had succeeded the Provost of King's as vice-chancellor in October 1915), groaned wearily to the Senate in congregation a year later: 'I have been in almost daily contact with the Registrary and can only hope that the time is not far distant when there will be a Registry more easy of access'.[22] As each year of war further depleted the university's reserves and postponed more of its expenditures, however, the prospects of finding funds for urgently needed extensions in its central buildings receded into an increasingly distant future. In addition, as chairman of the Economics Board, Neville played the leading role in organizing the most suitable available replacements for lecturers whose war work took them away from their posts. In 1916, as chairman of the Economics Board, he had led a difficult campaign to exempt Pigou, 'the youngest professor in the youngest Tripos', from being conscripted into some form of war work.[23] Neville had not lectured to students himself since 1911, but he continued to examine and he chaired the economics tripos examiners in June of each of the war years – punctiliously returning his fees for all his invigilating or chairing, or marking examinations.[24]

The war lasted over four years and was roughly halfway through its uncertain course when the Council and the General Board began to give serious consideration to the problems of postwar reconstruction facing an increasingly impoverished university. Till then, the only substantial reform issue still actively lingering on their agenda after 1914 was modernizing the Previous examination, which had provoked miserably inconclusive debates ever since the early 1900s. By October 1916, when T.C. Fitzpatrick the President of Queen's (1914/17), was beginning his second year as a wartime vice-chancellor, he had been persuaded by the secretaries of the Council and the General and Financial Boards that the university would require massive external financial support if it were to be even in a position to resume its prewar scale of operations, still more if it were to expand and progress. Its governing bodies therefore needed to develop and coordinate plans for postwar reconstruction if they were not to face major changes dictated by external paymasters. 'We need no hasty legislation', he warned in his annual address to the Senate on 30 September 1916, 'but we shall not be doing our part for the future reconstruction if we can present nothing but individual opinion when the war is over and when pressure from outside may lead to hasty decisions'. The initial response

22. Ibid., p. 39.
23. See above, Ch. VIII. Pigou was already spending his vacations in ambulance work and would have preferred to continue in that activity for the rest of the war.
24. By June 1916 the number of candidates for Part I of the tripos had fallen to 15 (of whom five were women and most of the rest Asians or Africans); for Part II there were twelve candidates (including nine women).

to his plea came in a memorandum entitled 'The University After the War' and signed by 135 resident members of the Senate – including most of those then actively managing the university and colleges. As published in the *University Reporter* in December 1916, it offered a starting-point for debate in the form of a list of proposals and observations on selected avenues of reform – excluding the Previous examination which was already under contentious review. According to the preamble to the memorandum:

> [Its signatories] have in view both general and special demands which may be expected to be made open to the University as a consequence of the conditions prevailing after the war. While it is impossible to anticipate what those conditions will be, we believe that the demands will make desirable longer terms, a simplification of the arrangement of examinations, provision for short courses of study and the possibility of a more economical standard of living.[25]

The memorandum was on the agenda of the Council and General Board in the following Lent term and a Special Syndicate was then set up to consider and report on suitable reforms in the university's teaching and examination procedures. The Syndicate met regularly in the Easter term but had not reported when the President of Queen's made his retiring address as vice-chancellor in October 1917. He drew the Senate's attention to the fact that there had been no fewer than six reports in the *University Reporter* over the past year, two of them dealing with the thorny issue of compulsory Greek. 'I hope', he commented wearily, 'that one way in which the University will mark the conclusion of the war will be by asking candidates for admission only whether they have had a sufficient education and not as to whether they can qualify in particular subjects'. Having delivered his address, Fitzpatrick gave way gratefully to the third of the wartime vice-chancellors – Dr A.E. Shipley, Master of Christ's, who was to spend much of 1917/18 travelling in search of alumni benefactors for the university, at home and abroad. He was abroad in October 1918 so that it was Fitzpatrick (now serving as acting vice-chancellor) who read his successor's annual address to the Senate on 1 October warning them:

> [T]he estimates for 1918 forecast a further diminution in receipts [into the Chest] while the expenditure remains the same. It is not easy to see how the University will be able to meet the claims upon its resources after the War without substantial assistance from outside.[26]

At this point, the task of precisely identifying the dimensions and relative importance of the problems that must emerge for the university, at an unpredictable date in a world already transformed by total war, was outside the

25. *CUR*, 12 December 1916, p. 316.
26. *CUR*, 2 October 1918, p. 39.

experience of any of the elderly academics then diligently discussing reconstruction issues – including Neville Keynes. Whether or not grappling with these largely indeterminate problems caught his imagination sufficiently to dispel some of the depressive boredom characterizing his Diary entries in 1916 and 1917 it is impossible to judge, for the available record stops altogether at the end of 1917.

In the event, of course, the Armistice was signed a few weeks later and the war ended during the Michaelmas term – so that university expenditures for 1918 soared. When Dr Shipley addressed the Senate before resigning as vice-chancellor on 1 October 1919, he reported that 1835 students had actually matriculated over the past year, of whom 1552 had arrived in the Lent and Easter terms. This included 'some 400 Naval Officers who were with us for the first half of the year', as well as 'some 200 American soldier-students who were with us till the end of the Easter term'.[27] During the last peacetime year the number of matriculations was only 1178.

3 THE AFTERMATH

The speed of the postwar recovery in Cambridge (and Oxford) universities called for a rapid redeployment of human, physical and financial resources and a correspondingly sharp increase in administrative effort needed at both university and college levels. If Neville Keynes had become too dispirited to maintain the Diary into 1918, he was almost certainly too fully occupied to resume it in 1919 or 1920. He remained the beacon to which the elderly academics who had steered the university through four and a half years of war, were accustomed to look first when refocusing on peacetime goals. For recently demobilized men, struggling to orientate themselves to practical problems of teaching examining and researching within the framework of a desperately impoverished university, he was still the familiar, highly accessible adviser at the top of the Registry. No doubt Neville himself shared in the brief euphoria that characterized the end of the long nightmare. He must have felt enlivened at being on a full daily working schedule – although the evidence of the Diary suggests that he had ceased to be a workaholic well before the war broke out. In any case, by 1920 (at the age of 68) he had reason to feel cheered by the knowledge that some of the traditional obstacles to modernization of Cambridge University were beginning to crumble. For him the long-term outlook had positively brightened.

Before the war, every scheme to improve teaching and research in any branch of learning had been tightly constrained by the shortage of funds at

27. *CUR*, 2 October 1919, pp. 40–41.

the disposal of the central governing bodies and the boards of studies. Attempts to ease the situation by revising the financial arrangements between the university and its richer colleges, or by appealing for funds from wealthy or influential alumni, could offer only limited possibilities for progressive improvement. The obvious way forward was to apply for substantial government aid. For many senior dons in the two ancient English universities, however, this solution seemed to threaten their operational independence and was stubbornly resisted. Cambridge had in the past received small grants from government departments to support particular courses of instruction – for example from the Indian Civil Service to service its candidates in training, or from the Board of Education to promote courses in engineering, teacher training, or agriculture and forestry. Yet in the last prewar academic year (1913/14), when Sir Clifford Allbutt, Cambridge's Regius Professor of Physic, proposed to apply to the Board of Education for a grant in aid of medical education, J.J. Thomson then the Cavendish professor, was among the intellectual heavyweights who opposed the application at the relevant Senate Discussion. By 1919, however, Cambridge University was not simply short of funds, it was confronting virtual bankruptcy. When the last wartime vice-chancellor, Dr Shipley, finally addressed the Senate on 1 October, he announced grimly that – in spite of 'many costly endowments', promised during his last year in office:

> The financial outlook is serious. Some members of the Senate when faced with the position during the last two terms were of the opinion that help might be got from private savers, others doubted if this was possible. I was willing to make an attempt and informed those most responsible for the financial state of the University that I was prepared to devote the Long Vacation to a campaign for funds which if successful would free us from all external control. This proposal met with so little support, however, that it was resolved to appeal for Government Aid. An interim grant has been promised, but this does not amount to 50% of the minimum stated by the various Departments as necessary to reopen the University in October on a pre-war basis. With a view to a more permanent grant the Government proposes to set up a Commission to enquire into the whole Resources of the University and its Colleges and into the use which is being made of them. Owing to the inadequacy of the emergency grant it may be found necessary to increase the fees charged to the students. At the present time in some Departments the fees do not meet the expenses incurred by the students, so that the increase in numbers is really a source of financial embarrassment.[28]

28. Ibid., p. 43. The benefactions listed included: a substantial sum raised by R. Waley Cohen in a scheme to endow a Chemical School at Cambridge (which brought in £200,000 from British Oil Companies topped up by a personal contribution of £10,000); £5500 from the Goldsmith's Company to equip and extend the Department of Metallurgy; and annual grants from the Drapers' Company to endow professorial chairs in agriculture and in French over ten years.

In November an emergency government grant of £30,000 was promised to each of the two ancient universities on the understanding that it would recur annually (without strings) until the Royal Commission had published its report and recommendations for reform.

Nor was the financial crisis the university's only crippling legacy of the war identified by Shipley. Postponing the constitutional and educational reforms, which had been under active discussion until the war swept them aside, had meant that subsequent, inevitably piecemeal, changes had simply added to the frictions inherent in the untidy system of relations that had developed over the past quarter of a century between the university and its colleges. Accordingly, when Shipley, Master of Christ's, retired as vice-chancellor, he took the opportunity to remind the Senate:

> We are in a period of reconstruction, in the process of which I earnestly hope simplifications will not be overlooked. The multiplicity of Examinations and the complexity of their Regulations, which increase yearly is a very heavy tax on College Tutors and on the staff of the Registry. To mention but one instance, the present form of the Previous Examination is the despair of College Tutors.

He went on to lament the proliferation of syndicates and boards appointed to advise on the reconstruction process: 'I venture to think we have too many of them; I feel certain that they are usually too large, and I know that in a great majority of cases they lack the inspiration and effectiveness of youth'. He pointed out: 'when our young men were fighting and middle aged men were at War work, the management of the University passed almost exclusively into elderly hands'. On the other hand, he acknowledged gloomily that the failure to rejuvenate the bodies *currently* planning reconstruction was

> not entirely the fault of those who are responsible for nominating members of the Syndicates and Boards and above all Electors to Professorships. Many of the younger men have looked upon our methods of Government of the University and have turned away feeling that their time and energies can be more profitably employed in other directions.[29]

The Royal Commission for Oxford and Cambridge was appointed in November 1919 and reported in April 1922.[30] It contained a broad, largely high-profile, membership of 23 persons under the chairmanship of Lord Asquith. There were two women – the Vice-Principal of Newnham and the Principal of Somerville. Among the Cambridge members with whom Neville

29. Ibid., p. 43.
30. *Royal Commission on Oxford and Cambridge Universities*, Cmd 1588 (1922) X. See Christopher Brooke, *History of the University of Cambridge, 1870–1990* (1993), pp. 341–69, on the Royal and statutory commissioners in the Cambridge context.

Keynes had enjoyed an agreeable working relationship in times past were Miss B.A. Clough (later to be Principal of Newnham); M.R. James, who – as Provost of King's from 1905–18 – was the first of the wartime vice-chancellors and currently headmaster of Eton; Sir Hugh Anderson, who had been a member of the Council of the Senate since 1910 and Master of Caius since 1912; and Sir Horace Darwin (his daughter-in-law's uncle and his own contemporary). Neville had probably made the acquaintance of Albert Mansbridge of the Workers' Educational Association during his years as chief secretary to the Local Examinations and Lectures Syndicate. That the commissioners were generally sympathetic to the spirit of independence prevailing in the two ancient English universities, was demonstrated by their insistence that: 'if there were any danger that grants of public money would lead to state interference with opinion in the universities, it might be the less of two evils that they should decline in efficiency rather than lose their independence in order to obtain adequate means'.[31] Nevertheless their recommendations broke the log jam that had persistently obstructed all radical proposals for constitutional reform offered by the Council for the approval of a hidebound Senate during the prewar decade. The crucial breakthrough lay in restricting the vote on university legislation, or central elections, to resident members of the Senate directly involved in teaching or administration. This effectively excluded the army of non-resident MAs who had invariably proved ready and willing to swamp with their votes any proposal to alter traditional educational or administrative rules and procedures. Once the electoral roll had been rationalized by limiting it to the House of Residents (now called the Regent House), all that was necessary to give effect to the Commission's recommendations was for them to be embodied in statutes and regulations that were acceptable to the university and college officers who would be responsible for implementing them.

As had happened with the preceding Royal Commission on Oxford and Cambridge (set up by William Gladstone in 1872), the Royal Commission that reported half a century later was followed by the appointment, for each of the two universities, of a statutory commission whose task was to negotiate with the relevant college or central governing bodies each change in statutes or ordinances needed to bring its recommendations into effect. This process was complete by 1926 – after which each institution operated under its new set of statutes and regulations. Since it was the university rather than the colleges that were urgently in need of state aid, it was the central university bodies which were subject to the most radical changes. The constitutions of the Council and the Financial Board were streamlined and an office of treasurer was established. The Registry was strengthened and enlarged and the

31. Quoted by T.E. Howarth, *Cambridge between Two Wars* (London: Collins, 1978), p. 84.

registrary's role as secretary to the Council was formalized – though he was no longer to be an elected member of Council. An assistant registrary was designated as secretary to a reorganized General Board which coordinated (and was elected by) a system of faculty boards that managed the teaching and examinations in their own areas of interest and allocated duties to an enlarged staff of university lecturers. At the same time, revisions in college statutes were introduced with a view to ensuring that stipendiary college fellowships were given only to individuals engaged in teaching, research or college administration and that at least half of each college's fellows were lecturers appointed by the university. Women became eligible for university lectureships and titular degrees, but the Royal Commission carefully avoided recommending that Cambridge should follow Oxford's example (in 1921) by giving women full membership of the University.[32] So, although it paid lip service to the principle of giving women equality of status with men, and even went so far as to recommend 'an annual grant from Public Funds for the benefit of the women's Colleges at both Universities',[33] it approved limiting the number of women in residence to 500 and expressed a strong desire 'that Cambridge should remain mainly and predominantly a "man's University" though of a mixed type as it is already'.[34]

Cambridge's second revolution by Royal Commission was completed by 1926. The statutory commissioners of 1923 had taken not much more than three years to organize the radical revision in university and college statutes and ordinances. Their predecessors, the commissioners appointed in 1877 during Neville's first year as a college fellow, took five years to get their revolutionary changes finally accepted. They, of course, had not had their path cleared by the bonfire of customs and prejudices lit during the First World War. It was not thus until 1882 – the year when Neville resigned his Pembroke fellowship in order to marry Florence – that he could centre his career on a modern University of Cambridge, dedicated to education, learning and research. When he retired as registrary at the end of 1925, the statutes and ordinances of the university embodied most of the administrative improvements which he had spent a large part of his working life striving to promote. The only serious shortfall of the 1922 Royal Commission lay in its failure to reach the final solution to the problem of what the 1920/22 vice-chancellor, Dr E.C. Pearce, referred to wearily as 'the vexed question of the admission of women'.[35] It is impossible to judge how great a disappointment

32. See Rita McWilliams-Tullberg, *Women at Cambridge* (London: Gollancz, 1975), for a full account of the long battle to gain admission to the university for Cambridge women students.
33. *Royal Commission*, Cmd 1585 (1922), p. 56.
34. Ibid., p. 173.
35. *CUR*, 2 October 1922, p. 41.

this was for Neville, who had (for over 30 years already) loyally served on Newnham College Council when he reported with pride to his Diary (in November 1915) that he had now been elected as a life member of the college's new governing body. Never a visionary, he may have felt, pragmatically, that once women had become eligible to participate fully at all levels of the university's teaching, examination and research functions, the fact that they did not yet play an equal role in its central government was a minor disability, and that while the limit imposed on the number of women students in Cambridge fell below the numbers Girton and Newnham wanted to admit, it was not necessary to press for the quota to be adjusted. In any case, it must surely have seemed to a nonconformist logician in the mid-1920s that if the other ancient university had – even before the Royal Commission had actually reported – safely admitted women students to full membership, sensible Cambridge men would soon prod their colleagues in the all-male Regent House into removing an embarrassing anomaly. As it happened, however, a paralysing inertia prevailed until, at the end of a second world war, the traditionally slow motion of legislative change in Cambridge was initiated by a Memorial to Council in September 1946, followed by a Council proposal for a Syndicate to explore the issue, a Senate Discussion, an unopposed Grace to admit women to full membership, ending with the Royal Assent in May 1948.[36]

36. See McWilliams-Tullberg (1975) for the full story.

Florence and J.N. Keynes in the garden of their home on the occasion of their Golden Wedding (1932)

XI Beacon in retirement

John Neville Keynes was aged 73 when he retired at the end of 1925, after having kept Cambridge University terms continuously since 1872. He could look back on a satisfyingly full working life. Best of all, he knew that most of the administrative, constitutional and educational reforms that he had striven to promote were in process of being systematically embodied in the statutes and ordinances of the university and colleges. His three children were then happily married and steadily achieving laudable personal goals; while his wife was an active, respected, long-term member of Cambridge Town Council of which she was to become the first woman mayor in 1930. More light-hearted than he had been since his 25th birthday,[1] Neville was able to indulge freely in a variety of familiar hobbies – acquiring and exchanging stamps among other enthusiasts, playing golf, bridge or chess with old friends and taking holidays abroad with Florence to revisit cities and favourite landscapes or to extend his already remarkable collection of continental butterflies. As Honorary Fellow of Pembroke College and a sociable ex-registrary he could continue to participate in the customary stream of college feasts and other institutional occasions – without any of the oracular responsibilities that might have limited his earlier enjoyment of High Table conversations. Meanwhile, he still drew recurrent pleasure in the company of his extended family, who, with his (and their) friends, enriched the frequent informal mealtime gatherings at Harvey Road. By the time he retired the family had been enlarged by the addition of Lydia Lopokova – the enchanting ballet dancer with whom Maynard had fallen deeply in love in the early 1920s and married in August 1925.[2] By then also he and Florence had rejoiced over seven grandchildren and their eighth was born shortly afterwards; before the end of his long life there were eight great-grandchildren. These direct family descendants were, of course, out-

1. See above, Ch. IV, p. 65 for the extract from the 1877 Diary, announcing: 'If the rest of my life is as happy as my first 25 years have been I shall have very much to be thankful for'.
2. See R. Skidelsky, *John Maynard Keynes, 1920–37* (London: Macmillan 1992), for references to Lydia's affectionate relationship with Maynard's parents. Milo Keynes, their seventh grandchild, recalls that for him and other family members the presence of Lydia and Maynard at Harvey Road Sunday lunches was *the* event of the week in Term – whenever Maynard (as bursar of King's) was able to escape his wartime duties in London for a couple of days in Cambridge.

numbered by those of Florence's five siblings, and of his half-sister Fanny's seven children. Fanny Purchase, who lived into her 100th year, died a year before the Second World War cast its shadow over family and friends and blocked continental holidays.

On 8 March 1927, Neville accepted an invitation to personalize his own story during an uncharacteristically relaxed speech delivered in Pembroke College Hall.[3] The occasion was the ceremonial presentation to the university of the portrait that the Pembroke fellowship (of which he had been an official fellow for six years ending in 1882) had commissioned Sir Gerald Kelly to paint of the ex-registrary (now their Honorary Fellow). The portrait still hangs in the Registry. He spoke, as ever, briefly and to the point, but for once with transparent pleasure – before an appreciative audience of old and new friends. He began:

> I have always thought myself fortunate in being able to spend my life in University work. I cannot imagine any other surroundings that would have been so congenial to me. … Nowhere outside this University could I have enjoyed the companionship of such colleagues as have been mine in constant succession for almost half a century.

When reviewing the successive stages in his career, he peopled them with selected personalities who had evoked his affectionate gratitude. Among the mentors, for example, who had encouraged the academic ambitions of the unpretentious nonconformist undergraduate from London's University College, he identified Dr Searle (then Pembroke's senior tutor) as well as Professors Fawcett, Marshall and Sidgwick – each of whom was to became a valued colleague and friend. He reminisced with amusement about his first year as a graduate bachelor when he regularly trudged the two miles to Girton (and back) to instruct in logic a student destined to become a future Mistress of the college – whilst the click of the obligatory chaperon's knitting needles reminded both coach and pupil that they were in the presence of the reigning Mistress. After illustrating a rapid survey of his administrative career with brief character impressions for each of the vice-chancellors whom he served as Council secretary, he reminded his audience:

> [My] administrative work for the University covered the period between the Statutes which came in force in 1882 and those adopted by Parliament on the recommendation of the recent Commission. It was a period of activity and expansion in all directions. Numbers increased steadily, one subject after another was added to the curriculum, and buildings sprang up on on every side to house the new departments.

3. The speech is reprinted in full in F.A. Keynes, *Gathering Up the Threads* (Cambridge: Heffer & Sons, 1950), pp. 109–14.

At that point of the story he sidelined his own share in all this as 'a modest one. It was my duty to help to keep the administrative machine free from grit, to help it function smoothly and to secure continuity and – so far as possible – accuracy in the official records'. Finally, whilst acknowledging his indebtedness to named members of the Registry assistant staff, he teased them with the thought that he looked forward to remaining in effigy among them – before thanking the artist and the college for having 'honoured me too much'.

A decade and a half later, another speech at another celebration offered a more revealing personal perspective on the life of Neville Keynes. In August 1942, Maynard Keynes withdrew briefly from his duties as economic adviser to a government at war, to organize a family lunch party at King's College in celebration of his parents' diamond wedding and his father's ninetieth birthday. In proposing the toast, he described his father as 'a perfect lovable, dependable parent, generous, reserved and shy, leaving you always to your own will but not concealing his own counsel'. Maynard – already famous for his perceptive essays in biography – then took the opportunity to envisage his father:

> as he was *before* I knew him. For this is the only way in which I can see him really different from what he is now – and even so perhaps it is not really different, one never changes – elegant, mid-Victorian high-brow, reading Swinburne, Meredith, Ibsen, buying William Morris wall-paper, whiskered, modest, and industrious, but rather rich, rather pleasure-loving, rather extravagant within carefully set limits, most generous, very sociable; loved entertaining, wine, games, novels, theatre, travel; but the shadow of work gradually growing, as migraine headaches set a readiness to look on the more gloomy or depressing side of any prospect. And then his withdrawal, gradual, very gradual, to his dear wife and the bosom of his family, but just the same as before in his firm habits and buttoned shoes.

Maynard then drew on his own long experience as a Cambridge academic to assess his father's administrative contribution to their shared *alma mater*:

> For thirty-three years he was one of the best administrators there ever was, and during those years this University was a better place in my judgment than it has ever been before or since. Perfect order and accuracy without a shadow of pedantry or red tape, the machine existing for the sake of the University, and not the other way round as it sometimes seems to be now. He helped to create a framework within which learning and science and education could live and flourish without feeling restraint or a hampering hand. And he combined this with himself pursuing learning and science and education at the highest level – which no-one now seems to be able to do.[4]

At the time of the diamond wedding celebration, Maynard – then riding the crest of an extraordinary career – was dealing with problems of war finance at

4. I am grateful to Polly Hill for letting me have a copy of the speech.

domestic and international levels. Over the next three years he was to become increasingly involved in planning postwar reconstruction and international currency agreements. Then suddenly, eight months after the Second World War ended, Maynard collapsed and died from a heart attack in April 1946. With hindsight, given the terrific pace at which he had been working throughout the previous five years, this is not surprising. Just a week before his collapse he had returned from the inaugural meetings, in the United States, of the International Monetary Fund and the International Bank for Reconstruction and Development – for each of which he was the British governor. It must, of course, have been a devastating shock for his parents who had seen him survive many earlier health crises. On the other hand, it does not appear that Neville, in his 94th year, was as shattered by Maynard's sudden demise as he had been in 1878 by the death of his father, in 1895 that of his Aunt Mary, or in 1907 by that of his mother. The nonagenarian may by then have been resigned to the inevitability of mortality – even in respect of his beloved firstborn. No doubt frequent contact with Lydia and with his other two children (and their families) but especially the support of Florence – the ideal partner and unfailing source of emotional strength – continued to brighten the last three and a half years of his own life. Florence and Margaret had each developed public service roles for themselves in which Neville could take pleasure and pride; while Geoffrey had achieved distinction among medical practitioners for his creative contributions to British surgery in the treatment of breast cancer, and in his operations on the thyroid and thymus glands; during the Second World War, he went on to serve as senior consultant surgeon to the Royal Air Force, with the rank of Acting Air Vice-Marshall. Certainly Neville was strong enough to attend the Westminster Abbey Memorial Service where the nation's statesmen honoured Maynard Lord Keynes in 1947. According to Maynard's biographer, who also attended that service: 'John Neville Keynes, aged ninety-three, walked up the aisle with a firm tread, leading his wife Florence'[5] – as well, of course, as the long procession of their children and grandchildren. In the same year, as Pembroke's Honorary Fellow, he was sufficiently interested to participate proudly in his college's sexcentennial celebrations. When Neville himself died, two years later, on 15 November 1949, he was in the middle of his 232nd term of continuous residence in the University of Cambridge.[6]

The loss of a such a memorably active academic personality drew personal tributes from a broad spectrum of old and new friends and colleagues. At the Memorial Service held for Neville Keynes in Pembroke College Chapel on 18 November 1949, S.C. Roberts, then Master of Pembroke and university

5. R.F. Harrod, *The Life of John Maynard Keynes* (London: Macmillan, 1951), p. 643.
6. An all-time record for continuous residence according to his grandson, Milo Keynes.

vice-chancellor, gave the formal Address. Roberts had been Geoffrey's contemporary when entering Pembroke as an undergraduate and had first met his friend's father, 43 years previously, at the Harvey Road home where (in common with a great many other freshmen and -women) he was to enjoy his earliest experience of domestic hospitality in Cambridge. His first impression, he recalled, was of meeting an individual of 'wide culture, sweetened by simple friendliness'. Later, in the early 1920s, Roberts worked in harness with Neville Keynes, when employed as the registrary's assistant in editing the *University Reporter*:

> It was then that I began to appreciate not only the care and precision of one who was at the helm of University business, but the easy companionship with which he welcomed the co-operation of a younger colleague. There are few better tests of the finer points of character in a high official than his manner of treating his juniors and subordinates. Judged by this test, no University officer ever had finer manners than the Registrary whom we knew in the years 1910 to 1925. There must be many here who remember with gratitude the equanimity, as well as the efficiency with which he conducted the university business of his time.

Another twentieth-century colleague who found his association with Neville Keynes particularly rewarding was A.C. Pigou (Marshall's successor in Cambridge's chair of political economy) who had examined when Keynes was chairman of examiners in the early years of the economics tripos and sat on the Economics Board with him from 1908 to 1919. Pigou, in his early seventies, was sufficiently moved by this experience to add his own personal recollections to the obituary by C.D. Broad in the *Economic Journal* of June 1950. On Keynes as an examiner he wrote: 'Nobody working with him could have failed to be impressed with his carefulness and fairness'. On his role as chairman of the Economics Board he wrote with rare feeling:

> I always think of him as far and away the best chairman I have ever had to do with. Perfectly courteous and always completely unruffled, his mere presence seemed to prevent pointless loquacity; so that everything went through smoothly and all with surprising speed. I personally owe him a great deal for help and guidance in those days when I was the youngest professor in the youngest Tripos.[7]

7. *Economic Journal*, Vol. 60, June 1950, p. 406. The obituary by Broad is referred to above on p. 122.

Index